Also by Kerry A. Trask

In the Pursuit of Shadows: Massachusetts,
Millennialism, and the Seven Years' War

Fire Within: A Civil War Narrative from Wisconsin

BLACK HAWK

BLACK HAWK

THE BATTLE FOR
THE HEART OF AMERICA

KERRY A. TRASK

A John Macrae/Holt Paperback

HENRY HOLT AND COMPANY   ◆   NEW YORK

Holt Paperbacks
Henry Holt and Company, LLC
Publishers since 1866
175 Fifth Avenue
New York, New York 10010
www.henryholt.com

A Holt Paperback® and ⓕ® are registered trademarks
of Henry Holt and Company, LLC.

Library of Congress Cataloging-in-Publication Data

Trask, Kerry A.
   Black Hawk : the battle for the heart of America /
Kerry A. Trask.—1st ed.
      p.   cm.
   "A John Macrae book."
   Includes bibliographical references and index.
   ISBN-13: 978-0-8050-8262-3
   ISBN-10: 0-8050-8262-X
      I. Title.
E83.83.T73 2006
973.5'6—dc22   2005050283

Henry Holt books are available for special promotions and
premiums. For details contact: Director, Special Markets.

Originally published in hardcover in 2006 by John Macrae/Henry Holt and Company

First Holt Paperbacks Edition 2007

Designed by Victoria Hartman

Printed in the United States of America

10   9   8   7   6   5   4   3

To Victor E. Trask

Contents

BLACK HAWK

PROLOGUE

_____

I will tell you something about stories
[he said]
They aren't just entertainment.
Don't be fooled.
They are all we have, you see
All we have to fight off
Illness and death.

You don't have anything
If you don't have the stories.

Leslie Marmon Silko, *Ceremony*

MEN WITH MUSKETS slung over their shoulders and women carrying infants and heavy loads of food and supplies made their way slowly to the broad brown river that lay ahead. It was early April of 1832. Spring had arrived reluctantly that year, with cold rains and scowling skies, following a hard winter in the hunting camps far up the Des Moines and Iowa rivers. But as the light of spring began to warm the frozen earth, a large band of Sauk people, warriors and women, old people and children—more than fifteen hundred of them in all—were moving toward the Mississippi.

Two days before they had gathered near the charred ruins of what had been Fort Madison, on the west side of the Mississippi about fifteen miles above the mouth of the Des Moines River. There were a few Fox and Kickapoo among them, and all headed northward together from the old fort until they were directly across from the long, sandy bluffs known as Yellow Banks, which stretched between the Pope and Henderson rivers on the Illinois side. At that place the great river made a slight bend and narrowed a little, and there the entire band crossed over to the other side.

Throughout the morning of April 9, more than a hundred canoes carried packs and people across, while at least five hundred horses, tethered on long reins, swam behind the boats. And while the people who had already landed ascended the high bluff to the flat and treeless plateau above, the small bark boats returned again and again, without mishap, until everyone and everything had been carried over.

Once everyone had regrouped above the river, their northward journey was resumed. The older members of the band, accompanied by most of the women and children, were sent off across country with nearly a hundred heavily laden packhorses. Most of the warriors—maybe as many as five hundred of them—all well armed and on horseback, made their way up the east bank of the Mississippi in battle formation, having sent flankers on ahead to reconnoiter and fast-moving messengers on to the friendly Winnebago and Potawatomi villages beyond the Rock River. The rest of the warriors and all the young men remained with the canoes and, paddling hard against the powerful, flood-swollen current, moved most of the band's supplies and equipment upstream.

Silently witnessing the crossing was Black Hawk. He was a thin, ascetic-looking man, with a grand roach-cut crest of hair bristling down the middle of his otherwise bald head. His ears were studded with trade-silver rings, and a large round medal, bearing the likeness of the British king, hung on his chest. He was a man of small physical stature—probably no more than five feet, four or five inches tall, and weighing only about 125 pounds—and well past his prime. By his own reckoning he was sixty-five years old. And yet he was the undisputed leader of the band, even though he held no official position of authority within the Sauk tribe, being neither a chief nor a shaman. Indeed, the source of his authority was mysterious, and one of his earliest biographers indicated he was "a remarkable instance of an individual, in no wise gifted with any uncommon physical, moral, or intellectual endowments, obtaining by force of circumstances, the most extraordinary celebrity."[1]

Certainly circumstances contributed to his rise to prominence, but it was mostly what he represented that made him important. As an unyielding traditionalist, he honored the old customs and ways, never wearing white people's clothing or tasting their alcohol in any form, and in upholding the ancient virtues he often engaged in long and punishing periods of fasting and self-purification and experienced powerful dreams believed to contain messages from the supernatural forces that governed the world. And amid the great confusion and vicissitudes unleashed by the white people, he had held steady and was seen to be the very personification of the tribe's authentic collective identity. He was, thought his followers, what a Sauk man ought to be, and for the people who crossed the river that day he represented what they had all once been and hoped to become again.

That was what they wanted, but because they believed the true Sauk way of life was inseparably connected to a particular geographic place, they were returning to Saukenuk, at the very center of their world, to regenerate what had been lost in themselves. Saukenuk was their great community near the confluence of the Rock and Mississippi rivers, in northwestern Illinois, to which all the Sauk had traditionally returned each spring. When they were all there together it had a population of more than six thousand inhabitants, making it the largest settlement of any kind in the upper Mississippi region. It was where the tribe experienced its fullest physical reality, where all the great cycles of its collective life began and ended, where they held their most important feasts and festivals, and where all their dead were laid to rest on the brow of the long ridge that arose just beyond the town. It was also there, they believed, the four cosmic layers above and below the visible world were connected, thus making it a place of extraordinary magical power. That power was manifest in the fertility of their gardens, their horses, and their women, and in the abundance of the fish they caught below the last great rumbling rapids of the Rock River. They had always had plenty there and felt safe and happy together—"as happy as the buffalo on the plains," exclaimed Black Hawk.

But all of that had begun to change after 1822, when white people swarmed into the region looking for lead and the American Fur Company aggressively took tightfisted control of the fur trade. Their arrival set powerful, unwanted changes in motion, upsetting the old rhythms and cycles of life. It was as if some terrible curse had been cast upon the land, fouling the water and air, driving the animals and good spirits away, and corrupting even the character of the Sauk people. In less than a decade, their ancient way of life was in ruinous decline. Hunger and want had become common, as had drunkenness and debt. White people invaded their gardens and hunting grounds, even took possession of their lodges and plowed up the graves of their beloved dead. Dissension and anger divided them, and in the spring of 1831 the soldiers came and expelled them from Saukenuk itself.

It was in defiant reaction to their banishment beyond the Mississippi that Black Hawk and his followers, longing for what they had lost, recrossed the great river and headed homeward to the center of the world.

By doing so they had traversed a Rubicon of sorts from which there was no going back. Soon after they reached the eastern side, in a manner that appeared almost preordained, they were caught in what seemed an inalterable pattern of violence that had been repeated again and again with awful certainty since the very beginning of the English encounter with America. Fear of the "other," and fear of what they themselves might become in the New World wilderness, drove Englishmen to lash out in angry violence against the native people, making Indian war a defining characteristic of the Anglo-American colonial experience, and resulting in King Philip's War becoming, as one historian observed, "the archetype of all the wars which followed."[2] Forever after, the "metaphysics of Indian hating," as Herman Melville called it, persisted in the very identity of white America, perpetuated and made stronger by the frequent shedding of Indian blood and the constant retelling of heroic tales about great battles amid the dark shadows of the continent's wild regions against the monstrous savages.

It was a somewhat simple dualistic worldview of the "us" and the "others"—the good people of the light against the evil wild men of the darkness—until the Revolution greatly complicated the entire matter of identity. As a consequence of the colonists' successful rebellion against their king, not only did they sever their ties with the "home" country, they also renounced their own historical and cultural past, and on that very first Fourth of July ceased forever to be English. With that sudden and complete rejection of the old identity, there was a compelling need to create a new one, and efforts to do so became especially intense during the decades immediately following the War of 1812.

But that was no easy undertaking. It was not a time for clear and cogent visions. The explosive growth and spread of both the economic market system and the national population were rapidly and radically changing the very nature of the society itself. The number of people increased at an astounding rate of more than 30 percent each decade, and many moved in waves of mass migration over the Appalachians and into the West so that the very size and shape and density of the country continually changed. It was a young and restless society in constant motion; by 1820, 58 percent of its inhabitants were under the age of twenty, and ten years later a full one-fourth of them lived in the sprawling territory between the old mountains and the Mississippi River. Old norms and customs were undermined and discarded as new demands and desires asserted themselves. Traditional influences of social restraint became increasingly anemic. Long-accepted roles and relationships of deference and subordination, once so essential for public order, eroded away and the authority of fathers and father figures was everywhere in decline. Public life grew ever more fragmented and chaotic, and people more self-focused and combative.

Territorial expansion, and the way it was accomplished, intensified a painful conflict that lay lodged in the very heart of the young Republic's ideological self-image and pulled and prodded the country in contrary directions. On the one hand there were the humane and life-affirming republican values with their strong emphasis on human rights and personal freedom, all of which had been the primary justification for the Revolution. On the other there were the powerful imperialistic drives and ambitions and a seemingly insatiable appetite for new territory, usually acquired by armed aggression with little regard for the rights and interests of the continent's indigenous people. It was a paradoxical alignment of principles and priorities, and the more Americans emphasized the importance of their own rights and goals, the less they regarded or respected the rights or even the lives of groups of people they considered to be "others." The country was deeply divided and ambivalent about itself, being boastful, arrogant, and stridently self-righteous while, at the same time, harshly self-critical and even repentant about its collective failures to live up to its own ideals. Some preachers and intellectuals delivered scathing jeremiads, bewailing the nation's faults and transgressions, calling the people back to the virtues of the republican covenant, while politicians, businessmen, and land speculators pointed to the promised land across the mountains and advocated the fulfillment of the nation's "manifest destiny" and the westward course of empire.

The regional divisions within the country itself matched those inner conflicts of interest and purpose. Regionalism became quite strong, producing distinctive attitudes and subcultures, which militated against the coalescence of a truly national identity. Easterners, for example, and particularly intellectuals of the urban Northeast, looked down disparagingly upon the people of the Midwest interior, finding them a backward, ignorant, uncouth lot who lived in near barbaric conditions. Not surprisingly, westerners had a very different sense of who they were, and in psychological self-defense returned the insult by dismissing the men of the East as soft, arrogant, effeminate elitists, while regarding themselves to be hardy, courageous, and manly. The contrasting views of East and West produced fundamentally divergent images of the Indian as well. From the 1820s on, people in the East were increasingly inclined to view the native people as victimized "noble savages." Westerners, on the other hand, regarded them as morally depraved, diabolically cruel killers of innocent white women and children, and brutish, subhuman obstacles to the advancement of republican civilization. There, in the early nineteenth century, along the violent edge of the American empire, the metaphysics of Indian hating came into full and ugly bloom.

So much of what the national identity and its regional variations consisted of was imaginary stuff—myths and metaphors and stereotype images—but a great deal of it related to deeply disturbing concerns and insecurities about gender, region, and race, which went to the very heart of America's ambivalence about itself. And when Black Hawk and his band crossed the Mississippi River that early spring day, they were inescapably caught and eventually dragged under by the stress and storm caused by the clash of such powerful symbols. The band's actions quite predictably provoked a hostile response from the Americans. Troops of the federal army were sent. The Illinois militia was raised. And the old pattern, which had occurred so many times before, was played out once again, ending, as it always did, with the brutal blood-sacrifice of the native people. Trapped along the east bank of the mist-covered Mississippi, just a few miles south of the Bad Axe River, the Indian fugitives were descended upon by shouting soldiers and militiamen who emerged into the early morning light from the dimness of the dense forest above. The Indian agent from Prairie du Chien watched and described how horses and Sauk men, along with defenseless women and children and old people—even infants held in the arms of terrified young mothers—"fell like grass before the scythe," and the river changed color, "tainted with the blood of the Indians who were shot on its margin & in the stream."[3] But all of this would recur again many times, like the compulsive playing out of the pathological urges of a serial killer, down to the bloodbath in the snow along Wounded Knee Creek in 1890 and then beyond the seas. The Black Hawk War was a single manifestation of that tragically redundant pattern, but it also had special significance because it happened at the very time national consciousness was emerging and the national identity was being formed. It had direct impact on that and also dramatically revealed the origins and nature of this country's collective character. By looking into this brief but horrific conflict, we may begin to better understand ourselves by discovering in the events of that angry, not so long ago, rain-soaked summer how we came to be who we think we are.

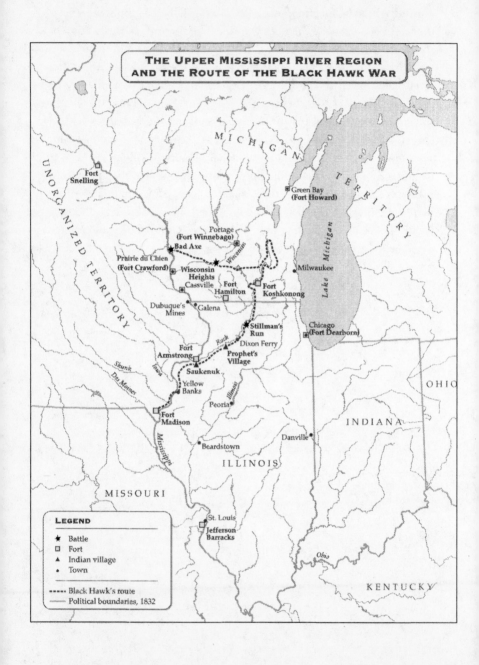

THE UPPER MISSISSIPPI RIVER REGION
AND THE ROUTE OF THE BLACK HAWK WAR

MICHIGAN

TERRITORY

UNORGANIZED

TERRITORY

Fort
Snelling

Green Bay
(Fort Howard)

Portage
(Fort Winnebago)
Bad Axe

Prairie du Chien
(Fort Crawford)

Wisconsin
Heights
Cassville

Milwaukee

Lake Michigan

Wisconsin

Fort
Hamilton

Fort
Koshkonong

Dubuque's
Mines   Galena

Stillman's
Run

Chicago
(Fort Dearborn)

Dixon Ferry

Fort
Armstrong

Rock

Prophet's
Village

Skunk

Des Moines

Iowa

Saukenuk

OHIO

Yellow
Banks

Illinois

Peoria

INDIANA

Mississippi

Fort
Madison

Danville

Beardstown

ILLINOIS

MISSOURI

St. Louis

Jefferson
Barracks

Ohio

KENTUCKY

LEGEND

★ Battle
▫ Fort
▲ Indian village
♦ Town

---- Black Hawk's route
—— Political boundaries, 1832

1

THE BEGINNING OF SORROWS

And ye shall hear of wars and rumours of wars: see that ye be not troubled: for all these things must come to pass, but the end is not yet. For nation shall rise against nation, and kingdom against kingdom: and there shall be famines, and pestilences, and earthquakes, in diverse places. All these are the beginning of sorrows.

Gospel of St. Matthew, chapter 24: 6–8

CONFLICT WAS EVERYWHERE, flaring up and spreading throughout the tribal territories of the upper Mississippi. There had always been intertribal clashes, but violence intensified after the War of 1812—following the departure of the British and the arrival of ever-increasing hordes of Americans. It signaled the collapse of the old balance of power, especially after 1822 when the interests and security of the native people were threatened even further by the arrival of frenzied migrants who swarmed into northwestern Illinois and the adjacent region of what became Wisconsin, hoping to strike it rich in newly discovered lead mines. The invention of the steel trap in 1823, which escalated the slaughter of animals, and the voracious greed of the American Fur Company, eager to swallow up its competitors, soon commenced the downfall of the traditional fur trade. Suddenly an ancient way of life was dying. Old cultures and relationships were subjected to powerful new pressures, not least of which was the increasingly crushing indebtedness of native hunters. Rivalries for land and resources grew more dangerous, setting in motion a chain reaction of Indian attacks and calls for vengeance among white settlers. Soon,

American officials on the scene feared a catastrophic Indian war, one involving all the tribes and engulfing the whole region in a rampage of unimaginable terror.

Eventually those mounting anxieties produced a major effort to halt the deadly attacks and counterattacks. During the summer of 1825 some of the chiefs had suggested a conference at which the conflicting tribes might come to some agreements about boundary lines for their various hunting regions. Secretary of War James Barbour liked the idea and put Lewis Cass and William Clark in charge of arranging and conducting such a conference. Cass was then governor of the Michigan Territory, which included all of what would later become the states of Michigan and Wisconsin, and Clark, the experienced Indian fighter and captain of the Lewis and Clark expedition, was superintendent of Indian affairs for the upper Mississippi and Missouri River regions. Once granted authority, the two men set about planning what would become a grand and important gathering involving thousands of Indians from a wide assortment of tribal nations. It was to take place with appropriate pomp and solemnity at Prairie du Chien during the first week in August. In preparation, Clark ordered 85,000 pounds of fresh beef, 900 barrels of flour, and, surprisingly, 100 gallons of whiskey.

When the appointed time arrived, large numbers of people converged on the site, creating a sprawling camp along the east bank of the Mississippi River, above and below Fort Crawford. Delegations of Sioux, Ottawa, Menominee, Winnebago, Ojibwa, Potawatomi, and Kickapoo were there and settled in by August 3, but it was not until the morning of the next day when the Sauk, Fox, and Iowa arrived. When they did, they made a grand show of it, moving upriver in a large flotilla of war canoes, more than a dozen men in each, beating drums and loudly chanting. They could be heard long before they were seen, and the people encamped around Fort Crawford, aroused by the noise, flocked to the riverbank and stood waiting as the canoes gradually drew into sight. When the Sauk and their allies finally reached the place, rather than coming directly ashore, they remained out upon the river, paddling and drifting back and forth before their enthralled spectators. The men in the large bark boats were naked except for breechcloths and leggings, and all were painted, with heads newly shaved, ready for battle. After passing by a number of times, they stood upright in their canoes, thrusting their paddles high into the air and chanting with an intense ferocity. All were well armed, and when they finally came ashore they did so with sullen and angry looks upon their faces. Hardly what the crowd expected from people coming to a peace conference.

The next morning William Clark, who was known to the tribesmen as the "Red Headed" chief, added his own theatrical flourishes by standing on a raised platform and conducting the opening ceremonies of the council. Martial music and waving flags, soldiers on parade and solemn speeches were followed by animated negotiations and accompanied by much pipe smoking and political posturing, which continued for twelve days. Clark and Cass worked tirelessly among the tribal delegations to "reconcile and adjust their conflicting claims" and "remove all probable cause of future difficulties," as Cass put it. With much hard bargaining and considerable compromise, boundary lines were eventually agreed upon, and Clark felt convinced "all parties were well satisfied" with the results. Both he and Cass were quite sanguine about the prospects for a peaceful future, and although they remained realistic enough to anticipate minor disturbances caused by young warriors eager to win war honors by stealing some horses and taking some scalps, they were confident that the tribal leaders would keep troublemakers under control. They emphatically informed Secretary Barbour: "But we are certain that the feelings of the tribes, heretofore hostile to one another, are entirely changed, and we believe, that if individual aggressions are committed, they will not lead to important results." Both felt certain all the tribes were sincerely "desirous to terminate their wars, apparently satisfied that their hostilities, without any reasonable object, would produce only mutual injuries."[1]

Their high hopes seemed fully justified throughout the next year. But in the spring of 1827 the peace was threatened once more. In early May Sauk hunters discovered some Sioux hunting parties encamped along the Raccoon fork of the Des Moines River, well within Sauk territory and in clear violation of the agreement made at Prairie du Chien. When the Sauk hunters retreated to Saukenuk, their grand tribal community near the confluence of the Rock and Mississippi rivers, people there became quite upset on hearing the news of the latest Sioux aggression. There were soon cries for war, and some of the angriest and most insistent came from Black Hawk.[2]

Little had been heard from him for years. Although a warrior of considerable reputation and accomplishment while a young man, he had spent most of the middle portion of his life attending to the private needs of his family, and because he was neither a chief nor a shaman, he had not participated in the Prairie du Chien conference. In May of 1827 he was sixty years old, and most of his people probably assumed his best days were well behind him. His bellicose demands undoubtedly surprised some of them, while attracting the attention of a number of the community's rowdier youths.

What sparked his hostile outburst against the Sioux is not clear. Perhaps he had simply reached a breaking point where he could no longer tolerate the further insults of enemies or hold back his own accumulated feelings of grievance and outrage. Or maybe the rumors of an impending war between the United States and Great Britain had reawakened within him a zeal for battle that had remained dormant since the War of 1812, in which he had fought on the side of the British "fathers." In any case, at the very same time the Sauk and Fox were sending a delegation off to Fort Malden in Upper Canada (Ontario) "to hear the straight story from the British Indian Agent at that place"[3] concerning the latest dispute with the Americans, Black Hawk raised the battle cry against the Sioux. His call for action had probably been preceded by a vivid dream in which he felt urged on by spirits to take up the tomahawk against the enemies of his people. But whatever provoked him, Black Hawk eagerly set about recruiting a war party and adamantly demanded approval for his efforts from the entire community. While that was occurring, upriver at Dubuque's Mines, Morgan, a métis war chief of the Fox village there, raised another war party to also go against the Sioux.[4] Thomas Forsyth, the Indian agent at Rock Island, was concerned. He worried that Black Hawk and Morgan might very well "find some worthless young men to follow them," and by their rash actions set off a major conflict with the Sioux and their allies.[5]

The chiefs at Saukenuk shared his concerns and strongly opposed Black Hawk's efforts, and Forsyth reassured Clark: "A very great majority of the Sauk and Fox Indians are for peace." In their first attempt to avert trouble, the chiefs tried to buy off Black Hawk and offered him three horses and "other property" if he would give up his attempts to raise a fighting force. He was insulted by the offer and became more enraged than before. The chiefs tried again. All of them went to the old man's lodge and pleaded with him to stop his call for bloodshed. They also increased their offer to seven horses. Once more he spurned their entreaties, declaring that "nothing but death should prevent him from going to war."[6]

Forsyth backed the chiefs by sending his own message to Black Hawk, warning him to give up his reckless intentions or he and his misguided followers would be arrested and "sent down in irons to St. Louis, where they would pass the remainder of their days in prison." The Indian agent also threatened to call upon William Clark to come up to Saukenuk with an armed force of two thousand soldiers to destroy them if they tried to carry out their plans or attempted to resist arrest.[7] That combination of threats and bribes appears to have had some influence. Finally, there were also some mollifying overtures from Wabashaw, an important Sioux chief of a large village on the west side of the Mississippi, above Lake Pepin. He sent pipes and conciliatory messages to both Dubuque's Mines and Saukenuk, and in mid-June Forsyth was relieved to inform Clark that both Black Hawk and Morgan had given up their plans to make war on the Sioux.[8]

Although that crisis passed without bloodshed, it was not the only disturbance of the peace that spring. In fact, in early March a French Canadian resident of Prairie du Chien, a man by the name of Methode along with his Indian wife and their five children were brutally murdered and their bodies viciously mutilated in their sugar camp. This seemed all the more tragic to William Snelling, the youthful literary adventurer and son of the founder of Fort Snelling, who regarded Madame Methode to be "one of the most beautiful women [he] ever saw." When Indian agent Nicholas Boilvin investigated the crime, the Winnebago chief De-kau-ray (Decorah) rather matter-of-factly admitted that some "foolish young men" of his village had gotten drunk and committed the killings. "It was the whiskey and not they, that killed Methode and abused his wife," the chief told Boilvin in a feeble attempt to excuse what had been done.[9]

But matters became even worse in early summer when a large number of Winnebago warriors joined forces with some of the Sioux to make war on the Ojibwa, and Forsyth reported to Clark that in one of their raids they had killed twenty of the Ojibwa's people. He also told the superintendent about the Indian named L'Arc (or Lark), a half-Sioux, half-Winnebago chief of a Sioux village above Prairie du Chien, who, he said, had plans to send an assassin up to Fort St. Anthony to murder Lawrence Taliaferro, the Indian agent there, and to "shortly go up to St. Peter and kill Col.

Snelling's hogs (meaning his soldiers)." Forsyth admitted he was unsure of the origins of those hostile feelings, but informed Clark that "something of an irritated nature" was "brewing" especially among the Winnebago, and that he felt certain they were embroiled in an elaborate plot with the Sioux, saying, "[I] am much mistaken if something very serious is not at the bottom of this affair."[10]

At the very same time Forsyth felt those apprehensions, a small Winnebago war party led by the chief Red Bird attacked the farm of Registre Gagnier, located in McNair's Coulee, about three miles southeast of Prairie du Chien. Gagnier was one of the five sons of an African-American woman affectionately known in the community as Aunt Mary Ann and held in high esteem for her knowledge and skill as a midwife and nurse.[11] According to William Snelling, Registre Gagnier was also well regarded by his fellow settlers particularly "for his humanity to the poor, especially [among] the Indians." On June 24 Gagnier was at home with his young wife and their two children—a boy of ten and an infant daughter of eighteen months—along with their hired man, Solomon Lipcap, a retired soldier from Fort Crawford. None of them were particularly surprised when Red Bird and two companions appeared at their door asking for food. Gagnier, who was well acquainted with Red Bird, invited them in for a meal of fish and milk. They ate their fill, and then Red Bird arose from the table and with cold-blooded deliberateness shot Gagnier dead, while one of his companions killed Lipcap as he sat quietly in a rocking chair near the fireplace. The baby girl was then grabbed from her mother's arms, stabbed, scalped, and thrown to the floor. But in the commotion, Madame Gagnier picked up a musket and pushed the muzzle into Red Bird's chest. Then, while her would-be murderer stood paralyzed in anticipation of his own death, she and her son turned and swiftly dashed from the house into the forest. Almost miraculously they made it safely to town.

As Madame Gagnier and her boy made their escape, Red Bird and his accomplices fled the murder scene northward to a Winnebago camp at the mouth of the Bad Axe River. Thirty-seven warriors and their families awaited them there. Six days later, and following some heavy drinking, they opened fire on the keelboat *Oliver H. Perry*, which was heading downriver after delivering army supplies to Fort St. Anthony. The boat moved slowly, fighting a brisk headwind, and seemed an easy prize for the

Indians, who opened fire on the vessel as it drew near the Mississippi's east bank. A fierce battle ensued in which Winnebago warriors not only fired round upon round of musket shot into the boat but also rushed upon it in their canoes, boarding it briefly and killing some crew members at close range. In the struggle seven Winnebago were killed and fourteen wounded, while four people aboard the keelboat died and two others suffered minor wounds.[12]

News of those attacks caused consternation among the settlers in and around Prairie du Chien. People fled their farms, deserted their homes, and rushed to Fort Crawford for protection. The panic soon became widespread. Madame Adele Gratiot, living inland about sixty miles southeast of Prairie du Chien at Gratiot's Grove, later recalled: "The news spread like wild-fire, and all was terror and confusion; families were flocking to the Grove from the neighboring 'diggings' and preparations were making [sic] for defense."[13] The men hurriedly built a strong stockade, while the women and children were sent off to Galena. Daniel Parkinson was in Galena at the time and reported thousands of people to be rushing into the town. "The roads were lined in all directions with frantic and fleeing men, women, and children, expecting every moment to be overtaken, tomahawked, and scalped by the Indians."[14] At Galena Adele Gratiot observed that "the flat prairie between the bluff and the river was covered with wagons, the families camping in them; block-houses were erected on the hill, companies forming, drums beating, and Gen. [Henry] Dodge was busily engaged in organizing troops, creating order and confidence out of terror and confusion."[15] Another camp of fearful refugees, numbering more than three thousand, gathered near the mouth of the Apple River, a few miles south of Galena.[16] Chicago too was in a panic and sent a messenger to the settlements along the Wabash River pleading for help. An armed force of fifty men eventually arrived from Danville to defend the village from the bloody onslaught of savages, which they all felt certain would soon crash down upon them.[17]

On the Fourth of July Lewis Cass came to the rescue of Prairie du Chien. He and Thomas McKenney, head of the War Department's Indian Office, had been holding another of their large Indian councils at Butte des Morts, near Green Bay, when news of the Winnebago attacks reached them. Cass departed immediately in a large canoe propelled by six strong

French Canadian voyageurs. They traveled up the Fox River, through Lake Winnebago, and crossed over at the portage to the Wisconsin River, which they descended as fast as humanly possible, covering more than four hundred miles in just six days. When he arrived at Prairie du Chien, where no regular troops were any longer stationed, Cass ordered a militia company under Captain Thomas McNair to occupy Fort Crawford and protect the people who had taken refuge there.

Cass was personally well aware of the dangers posed by the hostile Winnebago, for during his trip down from Butte des Morts he had come perilously close to losing his own life at the hands of one of their warriors. While still on the Fox River, he and his crew had encountered a small band of Winnebago hunters and had gone ashore to converse with them. No sooner had they landed when one of their young men boldly approached Cass, cocked the hammer of his musket, pushed the muzzle into the governor's bulging belly, and pulled the trigger. Nothing happened. Cass then abruptly pushed the weapon and his assailant aside, returned to his canoe, and continued the journey.[18]

After attempting to organize the situation at Prairie du Chien, Cass then rushed off to Galena. There he raised a volunteer company of riflemen under the command of Abner Fields. Alexander Hamilton's youngest son, William, was a lieutenant in that company and Daniel Parkinson its sergeant, and they all boarded the keelboat *Maid of the Fever River* and were sent up to reinforce the militiamen already guarding Fort Crawford. Soon after their departure, Henry Dodge, who had recently moved there from Missouri, organized a company of mounted volunteers, which Parkinson said was "constantly in the field . . . keeping [a] lookout for Indians."[19]

Meanwhile, regular troops were sent down to Prairie du Chien from Fort St. Anthony, and on July 15 another force of 580 soldiers moved upriver from Jefferson Barracks, near St. Louis, commanded by Brigadier General Henry Atkinson. Not long after that, Major William Whistler, the officer in charge of Fort Howard at Green Bay, collected one hundred regular soldiers and militia volunteers, along with sixty-two Oneida and Stockbridge warriors, and set off for Portage, between the Fox and Wisconsin rivers, in a small fleet of canoes and Mackinaw boats. They arrived on August 31. Two days later, Red Bird and his principal accomplice, Wekau, surrendered voluntarily to Major Whistler.

Thomas McKenney was there to witness their capitulation, and what he saw, or imagined he saw, seemed more like a scene from James Fenimore Cooper's recently published novel *The Last of the Mohicans,* than any actual event. McKenney was emotionally moved by the drama of the occasion. Flags lazily floating in a gentle early autumn wind, the clank of swords and scabbards, a military band softly playing a solemn hymn, the straight and ridged rows of soldiers, the stoic procession of painted, unarmed Indians, and the eerie echo of the Winnebago death chant from the nearby forest all combined to create for him a near enrapturing experience. Then into the scene entered Red Bird and Wekau, who, like Uncas and Magua of Cooper's woodland romance, seemed to McKenney the very embodiments of what he and many of his countrymen believed were the light and dark sides of the Indian's paradoxical character. He remarked about there being "something heroic" about Red Bird, who was a dignified man about six foot tall, with a well-toned athletic build, and handsomely dressed in newly made, white elk skin garments decorated with blue and white wampum and feathers. "Of all the Indians I ever saw," wrote McKenney, "he is without exception, the most perfect in form, in face, in gesture." Half of his face was painted red, and the other side covered with green and white pigment, but McKenney declared he had "never beheld a face that was so full of all the ennobling, and, at the same time, the most winning expression." Dwelling upon the young chief's countenance, and apparently forgetting the cruel events that occurred at the Gagnier farm, he wrote: "It appears to be a compound of grace and dignity; of firmness and decision, all tempered with mildness and mercy." There, that day in the midst of the Wisconsin wilderness, Thomas McKenney must have felt certain he had come face-to-face with the elusive "noble savage." But, in contrast, he saw in Wekau all that was alleged to be menacing and malevolent in the Indian character. "Never before, were there two human beings so exactly, in all things, so unlike one another," he observed, finding Wekau to be a repulsive, "miserable-looking being," "dirty in his person and dress—crooked in form—like a starved wolf, gaunt, hungry, and blood-thirsty—his entire appearance indicat[ing] the presence of a spirit wary, cruel, and treacherous." While Red Bird seemed "a prince . . . born to command," Wekau was, by comparison, a cruel and coldhearted "man who could scalp a child" and had "been born to be hanged."[20]

Such imagery was common to the era, but Lewis Cass, with his extensive personal experience with the Indians, was not at all inclined to indulge in any such romantic illusions. Cass was appointed governor of the Michigan Territory during the War of 1812, at the young age of thirty-one, and served there until becoming Andrew Jackson's secretary of war in 1831. He was a large, imposing man whose knobby face, sagging jowls, puffy eyes, and portly, bearlike body gave him a physical resemblance to a dour Sir John Falstaff. A New Englander by birth with a well-ordered mind, he took a keen scholarly interest in Indian culture and was considered one of the nation's preeminent experts on such matters. McKenney had great respect for him on that account, declaring, "Few men have so intimate a knowledge of the Indian character as Governor Cass."[21]

For a long time Cass believed it was the duty of the American Republic to "reclaim" the native people from "the savage situation in which they were placed," and to transform them into civilized people who were hardworking, property-owning farmers.[22] By 1827, however, he had changed his mind and come to the conclusion that no matter what was tried, the Indians could not be improved since all their many defects and deficiencies were deeply rooted in an inalterable racial character. "A principle of progressive improvement seems almost inherent in human nature," he observed, "but there is little of all this in the constitution of our savages."[23] In one of his long, elaborate essays, published in the *North American Review* in 1828, he reiterated this view and asserted quite emphatically that the failure to reform the natives was most definitely "not to be attributed to the indifference or neglect of the whites," but rather to "an inherent difficulty, arising from the institutions, character, and condition of the Indians themselves." Because of that, he concluded, it was "utterly impracticable" to even try "to remodel the Indian character, and fashion it after the Civilized form."[24]

Reflecting his own puritanical perspective on the human condition, Cass was convinced the problem had its origins in what he believed to be the Indian's almost total absence of emotional self-control, characterizing him as "a child of impulse" and a person "unrestrained by moral considerations." And of all the passions that stirred the savage soul, Cass declared it was the Indian's lust for violence and his seemingly insatiable appetite for bloodshed that most dominated his life and drove his actions.[25] "The

Indians are impelled to war by passions, which acknowledge no control," and he described them as being every bit as "wild, and fierce, and irreclaimable, as the animals" with which they shared the forests.[26] They made war, he insisted, for the sheer sadistic ecstasy of it, working themselves into a frenzy, killing, scalping, mutilating, wantonly slaughtering even the smallest of children and most innocent female inhabitants of their enemy's camps, and committing atrocities "of which no parallel can be found in other ages or nations."[27]

Because he was a leading expert on Indian affairs, Cass's ponderous writings about the natives carried great weight and received considerable attention. And yet his convictions about the Indian's instinctual propensity for violence reflected surprisingly little accurate understanding of the complex cultural characteristics of woodland warfare.

That was most certainly the case when it came to the Sauk's methods of making war. To his credit, there could be no disputing the importance of war to them. It was central to their notions of manhood and essential to the preservation of their society. But far from being the consequence of the violent venting of undisciplined passions, it was, in fact, a highly structured and organized social activity involving principles of morality and religion, with rules and procedures that had to be adhered to down to the most minor of details. Although Cass seemed unaware of any of that, a great deal was recorded about the Sauk way of warfare by Thomas Forsyth and Major Morrell Marston, both of whom observed Sauk life at very close range.[28] Forsyth was their Indian agent at Rock Island from 1818 to 1830, and Marston the army officer in charge of Fort Armstrong on Rock Island in 1821. Each of them wrote detailed, ethnographic-like reports, which went a long way in correcting the bloodthirsty stereotypical images perpetuated by Lewis Cass.

Forsyth concurred with Cass about the eagerness of young Sauk men to engage in battle. "Young Indians," wrote Forsyth, "are always fond of war . . . and it may be said, that the principle of war is instilled into them from the cradles, [and] they therefore embrace the first opportunity to go to war . . . so that they may be able to proclaim at the dance, 'I have killed such a person.'" In his view, their love of war was clearly attributable to social influences rather than to an inalterable racial predisposition, and, according to Forsyth, their taking to the warpath was never an endeavor of mere hotheaded exuberance, most especially not with the Sauk.[29]

Any Sauk warrior in good standing could initiate the process of going to war. If the man wished to become the leader of a war band, he would begin by blackening his face with charcoal, and then in a state of somber humility, he would neglect his appearance, dressing in rags and allowing the hair on his otherwise clean-shaven head to grow out. He would also fast, refraining from all food and drink from dawn until dusk for a succession of days, and cut himself off from all contact with women. In that state of deprivation he would pray to the Great Spirit, pleading for a visionary dream that would empower him to make war. If he had a dream containing bad omens, he would immediately give up his quest. On the other hand, if the dream was favorable, the warrior would erect a small lodge beyond the village in which he would hang belts of red wampum and strips of scarlet cloth, and there he would sit and wait for volunteers to join him.[30]

To succeed at this, a man needed a reputation for personal courage and an impressive collection of scalps from previous raids. Nevertheless, personal prowess alone was not enough, for like all the central Algonquin people, the Sauk were deeply insecure about their own personal powers and abilities and anxiously sought to supplement them with supernatural assistance. That was most especially the case when it came to warfare, and therefore the spiritual potency assumed to be contained in the would-be war leader's dream was considered of great importance.

But even the most potent dream was insufficient, and only a man who possessed a medicine bag—what the Sauk called a *mi´shâm*—reputed to have extraordinary powers could hope to attract a war band. Medicine bags were usually made from an otter skin and contained some sacred tobacco and relics. They were believed to have been presented to the ancestral founders of each of the tribal clans by the great culture hero Wisaka. Passed down through the generations in an unbroken succession of oldest sons, they were regarded as powerful talismans and mnemonic symbols of the commandments given to the Sauk at the very origins of the tribe. If the people respected his teachings and revered the *mi´shâms* he had given them, then, it was believed, Wisaka would enable them to triumph over their enemies. "Ye shall retain the vigor of youth even to old age, ye shall increase in the land, . . . ye shall be clothed with strength all the days of your lives; your faces shall be a terror to your enemies, and in battle they shall not be able to stand before you," the hero had promised them long ago.[31]

Any young man wishing to become a member of a war party would simply go to the leader's lodge, enter it without saying a word, draw one of the hanging belts of red wampum through his left hand, and then quietly sit down. After a period of unbroken silence, he and the leader would smoke a pipe, and by sharing the sacred smoke enter into a pact with each other. That process would be repeated until a band of twenty or more members had been gathered, and then all would commence their spiritual preparations for the campaign. Each warrior blackened his face and fasted, hoping to experience a personal dream of power.[32] Just before departing for battle, the fast would be broken when the leader held a dog feast in honor of his followers. While they ravenously gorged themselves on huge amounts of steaming dog meat, their leader made a brief speech calling on them to "behave like men and not fear death." When the feasting was finished, and just before setting off, each man was given a last chance to back out of the venture without losing face. If anyone among them was "fearful of anything whatsoever," he was urged to remain at home. (It was rare for anyone to do so.) After that, those who remained departed, loudly singing their war song.[33]

On the trail, their behavior was every bit as prescribed and ritualized as it had been during their preparations. The band made its way toward enemy country with great caution, traveling slowly, hunting and leaving behind food caches for the homeward trek, and Marston reported that rather often, "in consequence of unfavorable dreams or some trifling accident," the whole party would give up the venture "and return without ever meeting the enemy."[34] There was no shame in that. Indeed, extreme care was taken in all matters, and to guard against any bad fortune befalling them, the leader walked in front of the band, carrying the medicine bag upon his chest "between him and the enemy, in order that its power might protect the party" from any mishaps or attacks.[35]

When the war party drew near to the enemy's village, they sent "forward some of their smartest young men as spies," said Forsyth. Once everything had been surreptitiously checked out, the warriors concealed themselves in the forest, patiently waiting throughout the night, softly singing their war song to themselves. Then, just before dawn, they would arise and attack, hoping to catch the enemy by complete surprise, coming like some terrifying nightmare out of the dim light, and striking the village before its inhabitants were fully awake.[36]

Only after the battle had commenced would Sauk warriors cast caution aside and allow their passions free rein. Painted and naked except for moccasins and breechclout, with heads clean-shaven except for a scalp lock, they hurled themselves into the action with great ferocity. All were extremely eager to do brave deeds and to have stirring tales to tell when they returned home. And because the greatest honors went to men who killed the enemy at close quarters in hand-to-hand combat, they entered the fight armed only with knives and war clubs and tomahawks, putting their lives at great risk.[37] It was not enough to simply kill a man. A warrior had to be observed defying death itself, and scalps had to be taken to verify one's bravery to the people back home. But if the raid went badly and worse came to worse, the band would scatter and each man was left to make his escape as best he could. On the other hand, if they were victorious—slaying many enemies, taking numerous scalps, and carrying off captives—they would make their way back preceded by the warrior who had made the very first kill in the raid. During this part of the journey the war leader followed his men, carrying the medicine bag upon his back to protect them all from being overtaken by their enemies.[38]

Once the homeward-bound band came within a few miles of its village, a messenger was sent to inform the people of their victory. That announcement allowed all the women associated with the returning men ample time to prepare themselves by putting on their finest clothes and painting their faces with vermilion before setting out to meet the heroes. Likewise, the warriors applied fresh paint to their faces and stretched the scalps they had taken on small hoops or hung them from poles. Then they headed home "with great pomp and ceremony," beating their drums and boisterously singing their war song, observed Marston.[39] After the warriors entered the village, if the chiefs were satisfied with the success of the raid, they would grant permission for a scalp dance to be held. Such dances were often huge celebrations, in which, according to Marston, "the women joined the successful warriors," so there might be scores of people dancing together "all painted, and clad in their most gaudy attire."[40] And while they danced, the young men showed off their grisly trophies and boastfully told stories about their brave exploits.[41]

But the Sauk's grandest celebration of war was the National Dance, held each year in late spring soon after the planting of the corn. On the morning of the festival everyone would congregate at the large, well-swept square in the midst of Saukenuk. All the community's old and distinguished warriors and hereditary chiefs would seat themselves on mats along the top of the square, flanked on either side by standing rows of men, women, and children. The young unmarried women all gathered near the bottom of the square. Once everyone was in place, drums began to beat and singers commenced wailing out mournful chants. Then, one by one, warriors entered from the open bottom of the square, each elaborately dressed and painted and rhythmically moving to the throbbing music. One at a time they occupied center stage, and with the undivided attention of the entire community, each reenacted a past battle and retold the story of his own heroic part in that violent encounter. All was done in elaborate detail, and when each man had completed his performance the entire assembly applauded, and then another entered the square to take his turn. Having such a role in the National Dance was a very high honor. It was also an occasion on which Sauk fathers felt especially proud of their sons, as well as proud of their own past deeds of valor. "What pleasure it was to an old warrior," remarked Black Hawk, "to see his son come forward and relate his exploits—it makes him feel young, and induces him to enter the square, and fight his [own] battles o're again."[42]

Through such rituals and stories the whole community regularly recalled its own history and did so by focusing upon individuals who had upheld its values and expectations. Indeed, the National Dance was an emotionally charged experience that not only reaffirmed shared values but also inspired in everyone—participants and spectators alike—a heightened sense of group cohesion and solidarity.[43]

The National Dance also provided an especially important lesson for the uninitiated adolescent boys of the community. Concerning that, Black Hawk observed: "Such of our young men as have not been out in war parties, and killed an enemy, stand back ashamed—not being able to enter the square." Those feelings of inadequacy were made even more acute by the reactions of the young unmarried women gathered near the bottom of the square. In recalling this, Black Hawk admitted how worthless he had felt before his first experience with battle. "I was ashamed to look where our young women stood, before I could take my stand in the square

as a warrior," he said.[44] But that uncomfortable sense of personal defi-
ciency merely made those awkward boys all the more heedful when
watching dance before them the very living embodiments of what they
themselves were expected to become.

War was certainly an activity of great significance to the Sauk, and
among them it was always about much more than winning or the control
of territory and resources. Through war their collective identity was clari-
fied and strengthened by the clear-cut distinctions warfare always draws
between the "us" and the "others," while reinforcing male role expectations. Also, the traditional form of warfare, involving small bands, cost few
lives and resources and was especially well designed for the social man-
agement of the highly volatile energies and emotions of the community's
young men. In their raids much of the irritation and aggression unavoid-
ably generated by the rivalries, jealousies, and frictions of their highly
competitive society were vented outward, inflicted on "others" in ways
that allowed testosterone-crazed youths to exuberantly indulge their lust
for destruction, while actually strengthening the social cohesion of their
own community. Ultimately those novice warriors who survived such close
encounters with violent death emerged from the experience with a strong
sense of self-worth and personal confidence. Thus, by slaying and scalping
"others," Sauk warriors contributed to the well-being of their own society
at rather low costs and engaged in an activity that promoted the development of the strong, stoically self-disciplined kind of men necessary for the
preservation of their way of life.[45]

Nevertheless, the old form of warfare, like everything else, underwent
change after 1822. As competition for resources and hunting territory
increased, so too did the magnitude and severity of intertribal conflicts.
Sometimes large armies were assembled consisting of several hundred
warriors who took to the warpath on horseback, armed with muskets and
rifles in what the historian Leroy Eid has called "national wars."[46] For
example, in the summer of 1822 the Sauk and Fox sent out a force of five
hundred warriors against the Sioux in central Iowa, and in 1826 Forsyth
indicated that the Sauk alone could field a force of "twelve hundred warriors, three fourths of which were well armed with good rifles and [the]
remainder with shot guns and some few with bows and arrow."[47] But large
or small, the same ritualistic procedures were followed, and each raid, no
matter what its size, inevitably demanded, in turn, the violent avenging of

the fatalities it had suffered or caused. As a consequence, the attacks and counterattacks of retaliatory vengeance became extremely difficult to stop once they began. Still, they might be interrupted if the killers, or someone acting on their behalf, paid the relatives of those they had slain a proper recompense in goods or money. The practice was much like the ancient Germanic custom of paying a *wergild*—a blood price—in reparation for a death. In the case of the Sauk, only the relatives of the dead could determine how much was required to even the score, "thus covering the blood, and satisfying the relatives of the man murdered," explained Black Hawk.[48] However, once hostilities were renewed after 1827, no amount seemed sufficient to ever "cover the blood" or placate the grief and rage caused by the vindictive attacks that occurred and reoccurred with increasing ferocity throughout the upper Mississippi region.

Unfortunately the U.S. government was unable to do much to stop or even diminish that bloodletting because of the general weakness of its military presence in the region. Indeed, the army was too small, too weak, and simply too inadequate in every way to enforce the treaties the government had made with the tribes or the agreements they had made with one another. Furthermore, Indian agents and military commanders lacked the means of protecting the natives and their vital interests from the self-serving designs of unscrupulous traders and intrusive lead miners. Because of that, the Indians were responsible for whatever policing was taking place in the mining district, and the little peace there was depended on their voluntary restraints.[49]

Part of the problem arose from the fact American society was decidedly ambivalent about its military forces. Although the people of the Republic took excessive pride in past martial virtues and victories, the national government was unwilling to spend the money necessary to maintain a strong military establishment. Old Whig attitudes concerning the threats posed to civilian rule by standing armies persisted and were compounded by republican prejudices against the elitist values inherent in the hierarchical structures of military institutions. In fact, in the eyes of many citizens, any army at all seemed out of place in a society so highly individualistic as their own, in which almost everyone appeared to be in rebellion against all forms of subordination and regimentation.[50] The cost of supporting the military was especially disliked. As a result, immediately after the War of 1812 the size of the army was cut by more than two-thirds, from about 62,000 officers and men down to a mere 10,000. Then again, in 1821, Congress drastically slashed the military budget, reducing the entire army to just 6,183 officers and men and shrinking the size of an army company from eighty-one soldiers to only fifty-four. For the next forty years there were not enough positions in the officer corps to absorb all the graduates coming out of West Point, and for those who managed to get commissions, promotions were agonizingly slow and hard to come by. Matters were made worse by the lack of any pension program and the extremely low pay.[51]

A proposal surfaced in the Congress in 1828 to increase the wages of enlisted men as a positive means of combating the extremely high rates of desertion. But the legislators procrastinated for five years, and when a bill was finally passed it only increased a private's pay from five to six dollars a month in an economy where ordinary laborers were able to earn average wages of $230.64 a year.[52] Paltry compensation and miserable conditions—bad food, slavish labor, harsh discipline, social isolation, and the general absence of respect granted to soldiers by the society as a whole—had a profoundly negative impact upon the quality of men the army was able to recruit. For the most part, the military got what it paid for, and Charles J. Latrobe, an Englishman traveling in the Midwest during the early 1830s, observed that the U.S. Army consisted mainly of "either the scum of the population of the older States, or of worthless German, English, or Irish emigrants."[53] A great many other reporters confirmed Latrobe's scathing assessment.

The weak condition of the army contributed to the instability of the upper Mississippi region. Indeed, out of the entire army never more than 40 percent of the troops were assigned to the frontier areas.[54] At the time of the Winnebago disturbances of 1827, the largest concentration of such soldiers was at Jefferson Barracks, just south of St. Louis, where a total of nine hundred officers and men were stationed. Nevertheless, at all the other forts in the upper Mississippi and Lake Michigan regions garrisons were quite small. In fact, they were of modest size to begin with and then dwindled away to mere skeletons of their former selves through precipitous rates of desertion, and it commonly took more than two years before replacements were sent to fill the gaps left by those who had gone over the hill.[55] Between 1823 and 1830 a total of 6,952 soldiers deserted the army. In fact, during 1830 alone, 21 percent of all men in the ranks simply vanished.[56] Attrition rates were especially high in the western forts, where conditions were the worst and where soldiers who shed the uniform and slipped away were seldom caught and returned to their posts. The problems caused by insufficient and diminishing numbers were made all the worse because the frontier army was also a slow, unwieldy, immobile force consisting exclusively of infantry units, which, whenever in the field, remained dependent on elongated supply lines of cumbersome wagons and carts. It was virtually impossible for such earthbound troops to patrol the vast territories assigned to them, or to control the fast-moving, mounted native warriors intimately acquainted with the terrain.

That combination of inadequate military forces and the increasingly violent and volatile relations among the people living in the upper Mississippi made it a place that seemed doomed to destruction, and Indian agents and military officers alike warned of the impending eruption of a truly horrendous war among the tribes and against the white people if something decisive was not soon done to avert disaster.

2

THE CENTER OF THE WORLD

A person is born through the land in a manner similar to the way one is born of woman. Where a person is born becomes the basis for seeing one's path and one's life. It is to say that our perceptions of the world are filtered through senses fully rooted in the earth. Thus our expressions are, ultimately, all facets of the same dream.

Jim Stephens, *The Journey Home*

AT THE VERY heart of that turbulence lived the Sauk. They had been there since the decade immediately preceding the American Revolution, when they migrated to the junction of the Rock and Mississippi rivers. Before occupying that place, they had made their home in the Wisconsin River valley, just a few miles downstream from the mile-long portage between the lower Fox and Wisconsin rivers. The geographer-explorer Jonathan Carver was somewhat surprised to find them there in October of 1766, when he came upon what he called the "Great Town of the Saukies." He marveled at its immense size and orderly arrangements, saying it was "the largest and best built Indian town" he had ever seen. It contained about ninety multifamily lodges made of planks and covered with bark. Those dwellings were all neatly organized along straight, wide streets, and the whole settlement, he remarked, "appears more like a civilized town than the abode of savages." Carver also observed their expansive, well-tended fields in which they raised large crops of corn, beans, and melons. The people there, he noted, enjoyed a quality of life well above subsistence, and their community, said Carver, was "esteemed the best market for traders to furnish themselves with provisions, of any within eight hundred miles of it." But not only were the Sauk economically prosperous, they were also a formidable military power in their region as demonstrated by the fact they were able to raise a force of about three hundred well-armed warriors.[1]

Some of the Sauk Carver met that October were the survivors of the unusually brutal and prolonged Fox Wars in which they had fought against the French from 1712 to 1738, and which had brought them and their Fox allies perilously close to extinction.[2] Long before those bloody wars, according to Sauk oral tradition, they had lived much farther east, along the St. Lawrence River, close to the place where Montreal would eventually be established. They had been there when the French first arrived, claimed Black Hawk, who said his great-grandfather Na-nà-ma-kee (Thunder) had been forewarned of their coming in a dream.[3] The Sauk were later driven westward into Ontario, and then, in desperate flight from the terror of the Iroquois, they took refuge near Saginaw Bay, in eastern Michigan, in the mid-seventeenth century. Their trials did not end there; once again they were driven westward, this time by marauding Ojibwa raiding parties. Eventually the Sauk people established camps among an assortment of other refugee tribes that congregated near the bottom of Green Bay and along the Fox River of northeast Wisconsin. Father Claude Allouez found them there, among the Fox and Potawatomi in 1667, and remarked that because of their warlike ferocity they "above all others can be called Savages."[4]

It must have been soon after Carver's 1766 visit to their town at Sac Prairie when they moved to the confluence of the Rock and Mississippi. Black Hawk claimed to have been born in the Rock River settlement in 1767. In describing that part of their history Black Hawk indicated that after the Sauk resided at the village on the Wisconsin for "some time," a "party of young men (who had descended Rock river to its mouth) returned and made a favorable report of the country." Immediately after that, he stated, "they all descended Rock river—drove the Kas-kas-kias from the country," erected their grand village, and "determined never to leave it."[5] In Black Hawk's mind they had finally come to rest after centuries of tribulation and westward wandering; they had reached their promised land at last—a land that, he declared, "the Great Spirit had given us to live upon."[6]

According to the Sauk creation myth, that land had originally been made by their great culture hero Wisaka in the days soon after a great flood had covered the world. The flood had been caused by the wicked manitous who had sought to murder Wisaka, who had killed and cooked the flesh and bones of their two great chiefs. Enraged by his bloody deeds, the manitous "howled and wailed, and the tramp of their feet was so heavy that the whole world shook beneath them." They hurled down fire into all the places they suspected Wisaka might be hiding, and then, when that failed to kill him, the manitous caused a hard and heavy rain to fall. It rained and rained, and the deluge rose so that Wisaka was driven from his hiding place and forced to climb the highest hills and mountains to a place where he could climb no more. There, "as the water was about to lay hold of him," a lofty pine tree appeared and gave him the saving gift of a fine canoe.[7]

In time Wisaka found a turtledove and muskrat floating dead upon the calm water. He reached out and pulled them to his canoe, and lifting them up he breathed into their mouths and brought them back to life. On the fourth day after the rains had ceased, Wisaka sent the turtledove in search of a tree. At the same time he asked the muskrat to dive down into the depths to see if it could find and retrieve some earth from the bottom of the great lake that covered the world. Both went forth, but neither returned. Eventually, however, Wisaka found the turtledove dead, clutching a twig tightly between its toes. Later he found the dead muskrat. Once again, Wisaka breathed life into them and while doing so was surprised to discover some mud beneath the claws of the muskrat's forefeet. He took the mud and rolled it in his hand, forming a small ball. Into that ball he stuck the twig the turtledove had held, and then placed this on the water. "And lo, as soon as the ball and twig touched the water, the flood began to fall, till by and by the canoe was resting upon dry land."[8]

Upon leaving the canoe, Wisaka looked with disapproval upon the flat and featureless land and commanded the buzzards to reshape it. Some of the buzzards then pushed their breasts against the soil, forming the river courses. Others dug the ground with their talons and piled up huge mounds of earth. Afterward they soared slowly along the slopes of those mounds and shaped them with the undersides of their wings. Hills and valley were thus formed. "Wisaka then created the people, making the first men and the first women out of the clay that was as red as the reddest blood." He cared for them and "taught them how to hunt and . . . grow food in the fields," as well as how to play games, sing songs, dance, and pray.[9]

The Sauk believed that different regions of the world had been assigned to different peoples and that the land they occupied had been granted to them by the supernatural powers. Black Hawk declared, "The Great Spirit gave it to his children to live upon, and cultivate as far as is necessary for their subsistence; and so long as they occupy and cultivate it, they have the right to settle upon it." He also asserted that "nothing can be sold but such things as can be carried away."[10] Therefore, their land could never be purchased, and he felt certain the Sauk were exactly where they were meant to be, for there they prospered and flourished and enjoyed a great measure of happiness.

Land and a sense of place can exert a powerful spell upon people, affecting their moods, stirring their imaginations, even engendering in them a strong and lasting sense of identification. Who we are has a great deal to do with where we are, or where we are from, as the great Canadian literary critic Northrop Frye suggests,[11] and one's sense of place has profound influence on the shaping of self and culture. The historian Frederick Turner observed that "every environment encourages a special mythology" and worldview.[12] Therefore, it is no wonder that before science dominated our thinking with its mechanical view of nature, we imagined there to be spirits in the natural world, which infused hills and lakes, forests and meadows, and all the land with mysterious magical powers.

When the Indian commissioner Caleb Atwater traveled upriver from St. Louis aboard the steamboat *The Red Rover,* in early July of 1829, to participate in an important intertribal conference at Prairie du Chien, he marveled at the landscape's spectacular beauty. Nearing where the Rock River joins the Mississippi, he exclaimed, "At every turn of the river . . . new bursts of wonder and admiration were poured out by the passengers." He went on to describe the bluffs that rose beyond the western bank of the broad river and a bottomland covered with tall grasses. The woods, he said, stood "thick, lofty, green, and delightful" upon the hills, and then declared the entire country within a thirty-five-mile radius of Rock Island to be "the handsomest and most delightful spot of the same size, on the whole globe, so far as nature can produce any thing called beautiful."[13]

By the middle of August, having completed his business at Fort Crawford, Atwater decided to see even more of that land by riding cross-country to Dodgeville and Galena. He and his small party forded the Wisconsin River at a shallow place of sandbars and small islands where the wild rice was in full bloom, and passed through both dense grass and a "thick forest of timber trees" on the south bank of what he described as "the deep and gloomy basin of the Wisconsin." Ascending from the valley, he gazed upon "the open widespread prairie," over which, he said, "an awful silence reigned." The sky was blue and cloudless, the sun burned hot and bright, yet "not even one breath of air was in motion, nor a spear of grass, nor a dry leaf rustled in the plain." Then suddenly he noticed sunflowers and the blue blossoms of the "mineral plant" growing in clusters, bunches, and rows among the grass. The scene transfixed him, and he "stood in breathless silence several minutes, looking on this diluvial plain, absorbed in deep contemplation."[14]

This was the land where the Sauk and Fox lived and the place that shaped their consciousness and character.

In the summer of 1824 Thomas Forsyth, their Indian agent at Rock Island, wrote a report to Thomas McKenney in Washington, informing him in some detail about the scattered Indian communities within his jurisdiction. The most important Fox village, where the principal chiefs of the tribe lived, he said, was on the east bank of the Mississippi just a little south of the Rock River. There were other Fox villages along the west bank of the Mississippi: one about twenty-five miles north of Rock Island, another about forty-five miles still farther north at a place Forsyth identified as "Sticker's Prairie," and twenty-five more miles beyond that there was "a very small Fox village." Still farther upriver was yet another Fox community of major size at Dubuque's Mines. Altogether he estimated the Fox to have about four hundred warriors and a total population of about sixteen hundred people. There were only three Sauk settlements. A rather small one was located near the rapids of the Des Moines River, just west of the Mississippi, about one hundred and fifty miles south of Rock Island. Another, also of modest size, was found east of the Mississippi, seventy-five miles below Rock Island, on the Henderson River. But most important of all, two miles up from the mouth of the Rock River and about four miles south of Forsyth's own agency was what he called "the great Sauk village where the principal chiefs, braves, and warriors reside." It was there, he told McKenney, that "all the affairs appertaining to the Sauk Nation of Indians are transacted."[15]

In June of 1817, on first seeing Saukenuk, as that great town was called, Forsyth exclaimed, "Indeed I have seen many Indian Villages, but I never saw such a large one or such a populous one." At the time it was the largest human settlement anywhere in Illinois and the entire upper Mississippi valley. It stood upon the north bank of the Rock River, at the foot of its last set of rapids, in between the river and a gradually rising ridge of hills running in a northeastern-southwestern direction. The town was enclosed within a three-sided brush palisade, one side of which extended north and south along the base of the ridge, another west to the Mississippi, and the third along the south bank on the Rock River. Inside those protective barricades the personal dwellings and public buildings were neatly arranged along straight streets. Most of the lodges were substantial structures similar to the longhouses of the Iroquois—"fifty or sixty feet long and capable of lodging fifty or sixty persons," observed Forsyth.[16] And right in the midst of the town was a large public square and council house where the people assembled for ceremonies and important community events. Behind the town, on the side of the ridge, which Black Hawk indicated extended "about two miles up," were their gardens. In total, he said, they had "about eight hundred acres in cultivation."[17] Ringing the settlement was the flat and open uncultivated land that Black Hawk described as being "covered with blue-grass, [and] which made excellent pasture" for their large herds of horses. According to all descriptions, it was an idyllic place, where cold clear springs poured forth from the hillsides, providing the people and their gardens with a constant supply of sweet pure water. There were even more gardens on Rock Island, where the Sauk also gathered plums, strawberries, raspberries, gooseberries, blackberries, chokecherries, and crab apples, all of which grew there in great abundance. It was a rich and fertile place of great beauty. "The land being good, never failed to produce good crops of corn, beans, pumpkins, and squash," remarked Black Hawk. "We always had plenty—our children never cried with hunger, nor our people were never in want."[18]

The Sauk flourished there, and according to Forsyth, Saukenuk probably contained more than one hundred of the large lodges in 1817.[19] Seven years later, in a report to Thomas McKenney, Forsyth indicated that in 1818 "the Sauk nation could number one thousand warriors, without counting old men and stout boys." They were the major regional military power, he claimed, not simply because of their superior numbers but also because "about six hundred of their warriors were then well armed with good rifles and always ready, except when dispersed for hunting, at a minute's warning, to take the field." As impressive as that may have been, Forsyth also told McKenney that by 1824 the Sauk had grown considerably stronger. "The Sauk nation are increasing, and in my opinion rapidly," he asserted. He then estimated they had "twelve hundred warriors, two thirds of whom are well armed," and their total population was about "Four Thousand and Eight hundred souls."[20] Still later, in 1831, he informed Lewis Cass that the combined population of the Sauk and Fox exceeded "some six thousand souls."[21]

The Sauk were clearly not to be counted among the "vanishing Americans." Quite the contrary, and their growing numbers Forsyth thought were due in part to the fact there were very "few women among the Sauk and Fox Indians who are sterile." Indeed, he continued, "the population of sterile women to them who are bearing children, are about one to 500, [and] . . . each married woman on an average have three children." Sauk girls married young. "Fourteen is the usual age of getting married for the young girls," Forsyth indicated. They almost always had a child during their first year of marriage, but, after that, new births were staggered at intervals of about two years. Sometimes the birth intervals were even longer since the Sauk mother usually breast-fed her children "at least twice as long as a white woman," he observed. Typically, that continued to be the pattern for about sixteen years, and then, wrote Forsyth, they "leave off child bearing about the age of thirty."[22]

High fertility rates were a major reason for the increase in population, but other factors also contributed to this growth. As Forsyth pointed out, "The Sauk and Fox Indians encourage polygamy and the adoption of other Indians in[to] their nations, which serves to augment their nation[']s rapidly [expanding population]."[23] Sauk men often married a number of women, especially women who were sisters, as well as their brothers' widows if the need arose. Sisters were preferred since they were "more likely to agree and live together peaceable," observed Major Morrell Marston of the U.S. Army.[24] Both Marston and Forsyth indicated that married couples seldom separated. Therefore, families were quite large, and their crowded lodges overflowed with the noise and commotion of life. The adoption of war captives and the marrying of women from other tribes also added to an expanding demographic mix. That pattern of intercultural assimilation must have been quite extensive, for when W. H. Keating stopped briefly at Saukenuk in 1823, on his way to Lake Winnipeg, he estimated that of the one thousand warriors there, only about two hundred could claim to be of pure Sauk ancestry.[25]

For the Sauk there were the additional healthful consequences resulting from their general abstinence from alcohol. The widespread ruinous effects of whiskey and rum on other native societies are well known, but the Sauk apparently escaped those ravages for a long time. Black Hawk admitted that during the 1820s their old men would get "a few kegs of rum" from the traders in the springtime and enjoyed a brief "frolic," but declared, "at this time our young men never drank."[26] In that regard Forsyth contrasted them to their close cultural cousins the Fox, whom he described as "an improvident people" who were "generally addicted to spirituous liquors," which, in turn, Forsyth claimed accounted for why "their population is at a stand[still], if not decreasing in some measure."[27]

Above all else, a remarkably prosperous economy sustained the Sauk, allowing them to increase their numbers and enrich the quality of their lives. They lived in a region rich in natural resources, which, for many years, lay well beyond the margins of American settlement. There the Sauk developed a highly diversified economy that supported their needs, without either exhausting the resources or severely damaging the ecosystem.

Saukenuk was at the very center of all that and was the place where the annual cycle of communal activities began and ended.

Each April the people returned to Saukenuk after the long winter's hunt far beyond the Mississippi. Upon their homecoming, they dug up the caches of corn and other provisions they had concealed in the ground the previous autumn, and once they had cleaned their lodges and settled in, the women took to the fields to loosen the damp earth with their hoes and plant new crops. All their food crops were planted together, and when they sprouted and grew, the bean vines wrapped themselves around the corn stalks and reached toward the sun, while the tentacles of the pumpkin, squash, and melon plants meandered among the rows, their broad leaves blocking out the weeds. The land was always fertile, and the crops were abundant.

At the same time the women were planting the fields, the men finished trading what remained of the pelts and other commodities produced during the winter. The Sauk, said Forsyth, "always reserve the finest and best furs for the spring trade" and thereby got the very best prices.[28] Indeed, for nearly two decades after the War of 1812, the trade remained a substantial business in the upper Mississippi, and the Sauk and Fox were major participants in that commerce. A clear indication of that was provided by the volume of business done by them at the federal fur-trade factory near Fort Edwards, on the east side of the Mississippi, directly across from the Des Moines River. During the 1819–20 hunting season, for example, they sold a total of 60,082 pelts, which included 13,440 raccoon, 12,900 muskrat, 28,680 deerskins, as well as 5,002 assorted beaver, bear, otter, mink, and lynx pelts. In addition to that, and quite revealing of the diverse nature of their commerce, they sold 286,800 pounds of tallow, 3,000 pounds of feathers, and 1,000 pounds of beeswax.[29] That same season they also traded 2,000 pounds of maple sugar.[30]

Once the spring trading was completed and the gardens sowed, the people of Saukenuk put on their finest clothes to feast and dance the Crane Dance. In sharing food and the rhythmic motions of the dance, the entire community renewed the emotional bonds that held it together after having been fragmented into small bands throughout the winter. Also, during the three days of the Crane Dance festival love-smitten youths played haunting melodies upon their flutes and marriages were arranged. It was the parents who negotiated such unions, but Sauk girls had a great deal of influence on the outcome. Before marriage, girls were permitted to be quite generous with their sexual favors in order to sample various suitors. If disappointed with one or even somewhat unsure, they were encouraged to try again and were even allowed to veto matches made for them by their mothers. On the other hand, if everyone was satisfied, the marriage was consummated without ceremony, and the newlyweds moved in with the bride's parents, where they remained in a condition of ill-treated servitude until their first child was born.[31]

Sauk marriages were usually quite stable and affectionate, even in cases of multiple wives, and Forsyth observed that although there were "many loose girls among them, the married women [were] generally very constant." While there were severe penalties for a woman who committed adultery—hair and ears were cut off and sometime noses bitten off by cuckolded husbands—inflicting such punishments was rarely necessary. Also, although divorces were easily obtained, Forsyth reported, "Women seldom leave their husbands [and] the Sauk and Fox [men] Indians as seldom beat or mistreat their wives."[32]

Just a few weeks after the Crane Dance, the entire community held the National Dance, and then in mid-July most of the young men rode off into the west to conduct the summer hunt. According to John W. Spencer, an early Rock Island settler, this grand hunting expedition required considerable planning and preparation as the participants had to travel great distances and remain in the field for well over a month. Therefore, plenty of equipment and supplies had to be taken along. When they departed, said Spencer, "each man was armed with a gun, bow, and a large bundle of arrows."[33] They traveled on horseback, making their way deep into what must have seemed to be endlessly rolling grassland stretching all the way to the western horizon. Their mission was to find and slaughter as many deer and bison as possible. It was an adventuresome quest, but also hard and dangerous work in open country among the snorting herds; men rode at full gallop, their thighs tightly gripping the ribcages of their horses, dodging among prairie dog holes and charging bulls. The earth shook. The air was filled with sounds: the bawling of bison, the crack of rifles, the screams of horses gored by sharp horns, and of hunters shouting out exaltations following a successful kill. Meat and fat and hides were piled high on the blood-soaked ground, and when it was all over, the men, with their horses weighed down with the bounty of the hunt, headed home again to Saukenuk.

If time permitted and opportunities presented themselves, some of the young men would eagerly slip away to raid Sioux camps and take scalps.

During the time the young men were hunting on the plains, the old men who stayed behind gathered rushes and reeds, basswood and nettle bark, which the women wove into mats. According to Morrell Marston, the women tied the rushes together with twine made of boiled basswood bark, which they twisted and rolled with their hands upon their legs, and they "usually made about three hundred mats every summer." Those mats were handsome and durable, some being up to six feet in length, and were used for flooring and the external covering of their winter wigwams.[34]

But not all the women and older men were employed in mat making. Some caught and dried fish, and others, as Black Hawk pointed out, went "to the lead mines to make lead."[35] The historian Lucy Eldersveld Murphy noted that in the region along the Mississippi, between the Rock and

Wisconsin rivers, lead mining became "an increasingly important part of the Indians' economies during the early decades of the nineteenth century."[36] That was particularly so for the Fox people living near Dubuque's Mines and around the Fever River, as well as for the Winnebago in the Driftless Area of southwestern Wisconsin. But lead mining also played an important part in the Sauk economy as well.

Murphy's observation that "the women continued through this period to be the principal Indian miners"[37] is corroborated by the accounts of Moses Meeker. Meeker, a native of New Jersey and a trained physician, settled in Galena in 1823, where he operated a lead smelter for nine years. He took great interest in the Indians' mining operations and remarked that "their women [were] quite industrious miners." In the summer of 1828 Meeker visited some of their diggings in the area worked by the Sauk and was quite impressed with their methods. "I saw one place where they dug forty-five feet deep," he noted. He went on to explain: "Their manner of doing it was by drawing the mineral dirt and rock in what they called a macock, a kind of basket made of birch bark, or dry hide of buckskin, to which they attached a rope made of rawhide." He was amazed by what they were able to accomplish, for "their tools," he observed, "were a hoe made for the Indian trade, an axe, and a crowbar, made of an old gun barrel flattened at the breach, which they used for removing the rock." To loosen the rock, they employed an ancient but ingenious process originally developed by the people of the Old Copper Culture in the Lake Superior region. Meeker described that process: "Their mode of blasting was rather tedious, to be sure; they got dry wood, kindled a fire along the rock as far as they wished to break it. After getting the rock hot, they poured cold water upon it which so cracked it that they could pry it up."[38]

Once the ore had been extracted from the ground, they smelted it by piling logs in a hole dug in the side of a hill. The ore was placed on top of the logs, which were set ablaze, and when the galena in the rock melted it ran down into a bar-shaped depression cut in the earth or stone beneath the fire. There it eventually cooled and hardened into plats or "pigs."[39] Major Marston gave something of an indication of the magnitude of their enterprise, noting in November of 1820 that "four or five hundred thousand weight of this mineral is dug by them during a season" and sold in St. Louis for about "two dollars pr. hundred."[40] For the Sauk, lead mining had become a big business, which made an important contribution to their increasingly market-oriented economy.

In mid-August, when the women were back from the mines and the young men home from the hunt, there were a few glorious weeks of eating, relaxation, and play. By then crops were ripening. About this interlude Black Hawk remarked, "This is a happy season of the year, having plenty of provisions, such as beans, squashes, and other produce, with our dried meat and fish, we continue to make feasts and visit each other, until the corn is ripe."[41] Some families feasted "to please the Great Spirit," while others "made feasts for the Bad Spirit, to keep him quiet," he said, but whatever the case, they all indulged in a great deal of enjoyable gluttony. They also gambled and played games, holding foot races, horse races, and huge *puc-a-haw-thaw-waw* (lacrosse) contests, often involving between three hundred to five hundred players on a side, including women. Spectators and players alike wagered "horses, guns, blankets, and any other kinds of property" they had.[42] For a few weeks Saukenuk resounded with laughter and singing as the days grew shorter and summer waned.

The corn was harvested at the end of August, and Marston indicated they usually gathered in "from seven to eight thousand bushels of corn, besides beans, pumpkins, melons, etc." Some of that was set aside to be taken to the wintering grounds, but a great deal of the corn, noted Marston, "they put into bags and buried in holes dug in the ground for their use in Spring and Summer."[43] According to John Spencer, the corn, along with beans, dried squash, and crab apples, was placed in bark-lined holes from five to six feet deep and then covered with dirt and sod in a way "to make it look perfectly natural . . . so there was nothing to indicate anything had been buried there."[44]

Traders arrived at Saukenuk in early September. They came to purchase corn, and Marston said the Sauk annually sold them more than a thousand bushels of it.[45] Of equal or even greater importance were the transactions through which the traders gave to the Sauk hunters and their families the goods they needed for the winter on credit. The credit system dated back to early French days, and although indispensable to the trade, it was often inadequately understood by American policy makers. In a letter Thomas Forsyth wrote in September of 1824 to Secretary of War John C. Calhoun, he emphasized how vital it was to the interests of the

Indians. "Indeed," he declared, "if ever the traders refuse to give the Sauk and Fox Indians credit of arms, ammunition, axes, traps, and some Blankets and Strouds, the Indians must literally starve as they cannot commence their hunt and support their families without a credit from the traders every fall."[46]

Once that business was done, the people of Saukenuk set out for their winter hunting grounds in the upper regions of the Iowa and Des Moines rivers. The tribal council carefully prepared for the departure, and when the appointed day arrived, a man with an unusually strong voice walked throughout the community loudly declaring it was time to leave. There was great commotion. "The old men, women, and children embarked in canoes, the young men go by land with their horses," observed Marston.[47] It must have been an impressive sight, as more than six hundred riders and horses and about two hundred canoes were all suddenly set in motion.[48]

Upon reaching their destination, the large group of several thousand people was divided into small bands consisting of only a few related families. "We dispersed, in small parties, to make our hunt," explained Black Hawk.[49] Throughout the winter the Sauk lived in single-family wigwams, constructed by the women by sticking small poles in the ground to form a circle ten to twelve feet across and then bending them over into a dome-shape frame, which they covered with reed mats. The wigwams were easy to heat and were erected in well-wooded river valleys protected from the harsh winds that swept over the prairies. There, throughout the cold months, the men hunted for food and pelts. Once they had settled into their winter routine, "the traders followed them and established themselves at convenient places in order to collect their dues and supply them with such goods as they need," stated Marston.[50] Concerning that, Forsyth explained to Secretary of War Calhoun that the traders "go into the interior . . . to receive their pay in skins for credits given them [the Indians] in goods by the traders in the fall of the year." That was crucial to the Sauk hunters, who often needed to replenish their supplies of gunpowder and procure articles and provisions to meet unanticipated developments. Furthermore, it was important for the traders to take pelts and skins during the winter, since, as Forsyth pointed out, the Sauk had "not a sufficiency of horses . . . [to] bring out of the interior of the country in the spring of the year all . . . [their] packs of skins, tallow, and jerked meat" acquired during the winter.[51]

Throughout the dark, cold season, from the falling of the first snow until the time when the frogs began to croak again in spring, Sauk boys blackened their faces and fasted in the hope their regime of solemn deprivation would bring on powerful dreams. In such dreams, it was believed, they would be visited by supernatural beings who would provide them insights into the ways of the world and magical spiritual power, which would enable them to succeed when they came to manhood. That was thought to be especially so if they dreamed of Shawanu-tasiu, the Spirit of the South Wind, who always appeared in such visions as a great serpent.[52]

Winters on the prairies were always hard and must have seemed interminable, and to help them make it through the long, bitterly cold nights, families often crowded together into a single wigwam to listen to stories of Great Hare, the trickster. These narratives were filled with the crude body humor of flatulence, excrement, and sexual buffoonery, all guaranteed to produce belly laughs intense enough for everyone to forget their hunger and discomfort, as well as their nagging fears of starving to death in the bleak and frozen land.[53] The trickster tales were not just an entertaining means of contending with boredom. More important, they were clever creations of imagination that moved people's minds beyond their own self-sorry concerns, and used language and narrative to enhance their ability to survive the bone-chilling rigors of winter on the open plains.

By March the winter hunt was at an end and the scattered bands began to drift eastward to congregate once more in sugar camps along the Mississippi. There they tapped the maple trees, simmering the clear sweet sap in great iron cauldrons until it was transformed into thick amber syrup and then into rich brown sugar. Among the smoke and steam of those camps, they were reunited with people they had not seen in months, and there they rejoiced together over their survival of another northern winter. Commenting on that part of the annual cycle, Black Hawk said: "We always spent our time pleasantly at the sugar camp. It [also] being the season for wild fowl, we lived well, and we always had plenty."[54]

But when the sap ceased running and the cauldrons finally cooled, they all headed home again to Saukenuk. "In this way," declared Black Hawk, "the year rolled round happily."[55]

The springtime return to Saukenuk not only was the completion of another annual cycle for the living but was also a homecoming for the dead. When the people returned, they carried with them the bodies of relatives who had died in winter, to be laid to rest in the vast cemetery, which the Sauk referred to as Chippionnock (the City of the Dead). It was located above the town, on the ridge, at a place cut by a deep ravine, and there thousands of their dead had been laid to rest in the hallowed ground. Bodies were often transported great distances, wrapped in blankets or buffalo hides and slung from poles, and upon reaching that final destination were "generally carried to the grave by old women, howling at intervals most piteously," said Forsyth.[56] In conjunction with those early April funeral rites, the entire community engaged in what Black Hawk called the "great medicine feast." About that he said, "The relations of those who have died, give all the goods they have purchased [from the traders], as presents to their friends—thereby reducing themselves to poverty, to show the Great Spirit that they are humble, so that he will take pity on them."[57] For those grieving family members, who fasted and blackened their faces with charcoal, mourning the dead continued for several months. For widows, the grieving was even more severe and prolonged. Forsyth described such women as being "all in rags, their hair disheveled, and a spot of black made with charcoal on their cheeks, their countenance dejected, never seen to smile but appear always pensive, seldom giving loose to their tears unless it is alone in the woods, where . . . they retire at intervals and cry very loud for about fifteen minutes, [and then] they return to their lodges quite composed."[58] The Sauk believed the spirits of the dead "hovered above the village or lodge for several days" after burial, before setting off for the land of the dead beyond the setting sun. They were also convinced that "deceased friends appear[ed] occasionally to them in the shape of birds and different kinds of beasts"[59] and that the living were sometimes haunted by the ghosts of the troubled dead.[60] That was always the case with unavenged murders or when the graves of the departed had been desecrated or disturbed.

Such close proximity of the living and the dead must have enabled the people of Saukenuk to feel a strong sense of connection and continuity over generations, as well as an awareness of being a part of a way of life that had persisted for a considerable time. Within the extended community, their relationship with the ancestors was ongoing. People returned to the graves particularly in times of great stress and sorrow, as if to share their concerns with departed friends and kinfolk. "There is no [other] place like that where the bones of our forefathers lie, to go to when in grief," for there, among the dead, observed Black Hawk, "the Great Spirit will take pity on us."[61]

In pondering all that took place at Saukenuk, Black Hawk confessed, "When I call to mind the scenes of my youth, and those of later days—and reflect that the theatre on which these were acted, had been so long the home of my fathers, who now slept on the hills around it, I could not bring my mind to consent to leave this country . . . for any earthly consideration."[62] In saying that, the old man gave voice to a deep and powerful sense of place and belonging he shared with the other members of the tribal community. For it was there—at Saukenuk—where everything in their world and way of life seemed tied together. Not only was it the abode of the living and the dead, it was where the cycles of life began and ended, and then began again in harmony with the unending rhythms of nature. Therefore, Saukenuk was much more than a mere congregation of dwellings and people, infinitely more than a mere matter of land and location. To the Sauk it was a place of powerful spiritual dimensions. The town and surrounding territory—where they hunted, grew corn, grazed horses, and dug galena from the earth—contained all the primal and essential elements of personal and collective identity, which linked them to their past and made the place the sacred center of their world.[63]

It was there that their tribal community experienced its fullest physical reality, where all the people came together to dance and feast, to marry and share stories, to bury their dead and renew their strength after surviving another hard winter apart. There everything and everyone were interconnected and set in motion by the passions and dreams that had been part of their existence since the very beginnings of their nation. And there, as in no other place, their traditions and beliefs and everything that combined to make them Sauk, says the historian John E. Hallwas, "were bound up with the spirit world of their forefathers, and to sever the tie of heritage as embodied in a village like Saukenuk was to cut themselves adrift in a world without meaning."[64]

3

THINGS FALL APART

Turning and turning in the widening gyre
The falcon cannot hear the falconer;
Things fall apart; the center cannot hold;
Mere anarchy is loosed upon the world,
The blood-dimmed tide is loosed, and everywhere
The ceremony of innocence is drowned;
The best lack all conviction, while the worst
Are full of passionate intensity.

William Butler Yeats, "The Second Coming"

THE SAUK LIVED a good life that had purpose and meaning and which was quite affluent by native standards. Yet beneath the surface there surged a powerful current of insecurity. They were a cautious, uneasy people constantly concerned about something going terribly wrong—people who relied on medicine bags to keep themselves from harm, who went to self-punishing ascetic extremes to win the pity and assistance of the supernatural forces, and who lived in dread of the black magic of witches and of being devoured by cannibalistic giants in their isolated winter camps.[1] They anxiously anticipated enemy attacks and worried about the deceit and betrayal of others, and while they faced very real dangers and hardship, the world they inhabited was made all the more ominous by their own fearful imaginings.

But at the very sacred center of their world, Saukenuk was their safe haven, where they felt most protected and in touch with the transcendental powers of the universe through their ancient ceremonies and rituals. They believed that if they strictly adhered to the precise words and movements of those ceremonies, as taught to their ancestors by Wisaka, they would be safe and prosper. As a result of such beliefs, observed the American missionary Cutting Marsh, the Sauk were a very conservative people "strongly attached to their pagan rites and superstitions and guard[ed] with jealous care against any change."[2] Forsyth also remarked about those same tendencies, describing them as being "very religious so far as ceremony is concerned, and even in passing any extraordinary cave, rock, hill, etc., they leave behind them a little tobacco for the manitoo, who they suppose lives there."[3] Such polite, placating gestures were precautionary efforts to avoid disturbing the spirits and thereby increasing the risk of making life even more threatening and unpredictable than it already was.

It had always been that way, they believed, ever since the evil manitous of the underworld had sent great serpents and long-tailed panthers to kill and skin Wisaka's younger brother Yapatao. Upon discovering that awful murder, and in a state of grief-stricken rage, Wisaka fasted for ten days, blackened his face with the soot of his fire, and then descended into the dim chaos of the underworld to kill the killers of his beloved brother. A terrible battle ensued in which the great hero slew them until "the Great Serpents relented and feared him." But, unfortunately for the world, not all the monsters were annihilated, nor did they remain forever subdued. From time to time, without warning or provocation, they crept back into the world to sow all manner of sorrow and evil.[4] Mache-manitoo, "the Great Serpent" and leader of those forces of darkness, was the archfiend—the Grendel and "dragon of chaos" that stalked the gloomy wetland and dismal forests of the Sauk's mythic imaginations—and, according to Thomas Forsyth, the Sauk believed he "revenged himself upon mankind through the agency of bad medicine, poisonous reptiles, killing horses, sinking canoes, etc." Indeed, stated the Indian agent, "every accident that befell them, they imputed to the bad spirit's machinations."[5]

Through such stories, endlessly retold, the Sauk explained the workings of the world and accounted for the presence of evil and suffering within it. With them, as with all oral societies, virtually everything they knew depended upon the telling of stories, and that way of knowing, in turn, had profound influence upon how they interpreted experience. In oral societies, because so much depends upon memory, most important cultural information is communicated in narrative form employing a rhetorical style in which rhyming and rhythmic cadence, repetition and vivid imagery are used to hold the listener's attention and make the message especially memorable. For the same reasons the stories themselves remain essentially unchanged from generation to generation and are firmly grounded in the well-known physical facts of life, with plots involving magic and mystery and larger-than-life characters engaged in dualistic struggles and spectacular deeds of great importance. They are highly emotional and well designed to enhance remembering, but the form and style also create patterns of thought that people, in turn, impose upon the world. To them reality appears to be like the stories, and it is through the stories they make sense of and find meaning in what might otherwise pass for absurd experience. Because narration and memory have such high priority, little attention is given to abstract or analytical reasoning or to the critical evaluation of traditional belief and folkways. Therefore, orality itself fosters a strongly conservative disposition and a worldview that characterizes life as an ongoing, black-and-white conflict of good and evil, waged by heroes and monsters, where sacred order is under constant threat from profane chaos.[6] Among the Sauk it produced a tenacious commitment to the old ways—even to orality itself—which was made evident by Taimah, identified by Forsyth as "the head medicine man of the Sauk and Fox nation,"[7] who told Morrell Marston that "the Great Spirit had put the Indians on the earth to hunt and gain their living in the wilderness; [and] that he always found that when any of their people departed from this mode of life, by attempting to learn to read, write, and live as white people do, the Great Spirit was displeased, and they soon died."[8] For a very long time the Sauk seemed able to hold off the threats posed by the powers of chaos, but then suddenly, in the early summer of 1822, unwanted and unanticipated events occurred from which poured forth a cascade of disruptive developments that changed almost everything and ultimately unraveled the traditional order in which they lived. Their deepest fears were soon realized. The center could not hold, and their way of life rapidly fell apart.

Colonel James Johnson, an enterprising veteran of the War of 1812 from Tennessee, was an army contractor whose small fleet of keelboats supplied the military posts upriver from St. Louis. In the regular course of conducting business, Johnson became aware of how successful the

Indians were at the mining of lead in the valley of the Fever River, located about sixty miles north of Saukenuk. Excited by his discovery and eager to cash in on it, Johnson applied for a federal mining grant. Not only did he get the grant, but he was given exclusive access to the area along the Fever River already being worked by a Fox chief known as Old Buck, who, with his wife, had been mining there for more than fifteen years and had constructed twenty smelting furnaces from which they produced several million pounds of "pig" lead. In early June, when the Indian agent Thomas Forsyth informed Sauk and Fox leaders of the impending arrival of American miners, he said they listened "with silent sullenness, after which some murmuring was observed" and all were "much irritated that any white people should work any mines up the Mississippi." Nor were they placated when Forsyth gave them their treaty annuity payments and reassured them that "Col Johnson & friends would have no objections to any Indians working any of the mines that they did not occupy."[9] Their anger did not cool, and when Johnson and his brother Richard arrived at the mouth of the Fever River about a month later, they were given a hostile reception. But the Johnsons had not come alone. Forsyth was with them, along with a work crew of twenty laborers, including at least four black men, and a substantial contingent of soldiers—about one hundred of them altogether, reported James P. Beckwourth, one of the black members of the group. Beckwourth said they were met there by a large group of Sauk and Fox warriors, who "were all armed to the teeth" and "presented a very formidable appearance."[10] But no violence occurred, and Forsyth attributed that to the "imposing force of the whites," which deterred the Indians from making any attempt to "put it out of the power of the white people to work the mines."[11]

The sudden unwelcome arrival of Johnson and his crew, and the disturbances they immediately caused, were soon compounded by major changes in the fur trade as well. That very summer, the "factory system"— the network of federally owned trading posts managed by government-appointed "factors"—was closed down. Since the War of 1812, the factories had offered native hunters fair treatment and reasonably priced trade goods while eliminating both alcohol and debt-entrapping credit from the trade. Unfortunately, the entire system had proven to be an expensive and perhaps overly idealistic experiment that failed for a long list of reasons, but chief among them was the ruthless, unrelenting opposition of John Jacob Astor's American Fur Company. After years of aggressive lobbying in Washington and cutthroat competition in the field, the company finally won. Following much bitter debate, Congress ended the factory system once and for all on June 3, 1822. After that, both the methods and attitudes of the fur trade became decidedly more businesslike, with most of the paternalism of the old system quickly being forsaken, as Astor's behemoth corporation became, in the words of federal Indian commissioner Thomas McKenney, "one vast engine of monopoly."[12]

Portents of such transforming change first appeared in the Sauk's world soon after the War of 1812. In the summer of 1816 General Thomas A. Smith arrived at Rock Island with a troop of soldiers and commenced the construction of what became Fort Armstrong. They built the fort atop a limestone cliff, thirty-five feet above the Mississippi River. To the Sauk, whose community of Saukenuk was only about four miles away, Rock Island was regarded as a very special place that was under the care of a "Good Spirit," who lived in a cave directly below the site the soldiers had chosen for their fort. Whenever the Indians had gone to the island's cool, green glades in summer to pick berries and fruit, they had always taken great care not to disturb the spirit by making noise. Sometimes, in the quiet peace of the morning or when the whippoorwills called in the early dusk, they would catch a glimpse of the Good Spirit, which they described as being "white, with large wings like a swan's, but ten times larger."[13] They believed that this spirit ensured the opulent natural abundance of the place. Unfortunately, the newly arrived Americans had no such sense of reverence toward the island or its spiritual guardian, and according to John Spencer, an early settler there, the Sauk were convinced "the noise and confusion incident to building and maintaining the fort drove him away."[14] Black Hawk was sure of it and also had "no doubt a bad Spirit had taken his place,"[15] for after that the island was never the same. Indeed, when the Americans arrived they appeared determined to remake the world, to drain it of all its magic and mystery, and drive out all the spirits and reduce the land to something that was no longer really alive.[16]

The Sauk were distressed by such changes. And yet Sauk society had already undergone significant changes since leaving the Wisconsin River valley more than half a century before. Their economy had become more diversified and commercial, and they had adopted a good many of the ways of the French and British traders. But even as major as those changes actually were, they had occurred gradually enough to be integrated and assimilated with the traditional folkways of the tribe, and, as a result, there had remained a strong and reassuring sense of social continuity. However, once the Americans arrived—and most especially after the abrupt and traumatic developments of 1822—the rate and character and magnitude of the changes were so much greater and so unlike anything the Sauk had ever previously experienced, they found they could neither reverse them nor bring them under control. There were far too many changes, coming too fast to ever be integrated into their traditional way of life, and soon they began eroding away the very underpinnings of Sauk society.

After the British had deserted the region and the great intertribal confederacy lead by Tecumseh had been shattered, the same kind of sound and fury that had driven the Good Spirit away from Rock Island also became widespread throughout the interior of the continent. Within five years of the last war with the British, five new states were admitted to the Union, and by 1830 a full one-quarter of the American population lived west of the Appalachian Mountains. Alexis de Tocqueville, the twenty-five-year-old French aristocrat who rode through the country with Gustave de Beaumont from May of 1831 until February of 1832, marveled at that mass migration of people. "Millions of men are marching at once towards the same horizon; their language, their religion, their manners differ; their object is the same. Fortune has been promised to them somewhere in the West, and to the West they go to find it," he declared. It was a momentous development, the likes of which, he remarked, had not been seen since "those irruptions which caused the fall of the Roman Empire."[17]

The participants in that migration had little in common with the Indians, French, or métis people already living in the Great Lakes and upper Mississippi regions. Before the Americans arrived in large numbers, the Indians and French, and even the British who arrived in the late eighteenth century, shared vital interests in the fur trade. They did business together, intermarried, and created a cultural "middle ground" where their values, worldviews, manners, habits, and even physical appearances became more and more like one another's, as could be plainly seen in such fur trade communities as LaBaye and Prairie du Chien.[18] But the westward-moving Americans came with different fantasies and hopes, believing in different stories and myths, and were driven by longings and fears quite unlike those that moved the Sauk and their neighbors. And when they arrived, they immediately set about remaking the new places they found into ones greatly resembling those they had left behind in the East. In the process they drove out the old spirits and replaced the existing network of interdependent relationships with a tumultuous market system of getting and spending. It all happened so fast that by 1824, in Green Bay at least, John Lawe, one of that old community's surviving patriarchs, lamented, "The old times are no more, that pleasant reign is over & never to return any more."[19]

In fact, the "old times" soon passed away throughout most of the trans-Appalachian West, brought to an end by the hordes of restless, rootless people who rushed in looking for fresh starts and fast fortunes. De Tocqueville remarked in one of his notebooks that "everyone here wants to grow rich and rise in the world, and there is no one but believes in his power to succeed in that. . . . From that," he observed, "there springs a wearisome social activity, ever-changing intrigues, continual excitement, and an uncontrollable desire of each to outdo the others."[20] All of that was in jarring contrast with the Sauk's communal way of life and their strong attachment to the land and their ancestors, for the American, said de Tocqueville, had "no memory that attaches him to one place more than another, no inveterate habits, no spirit of routine."[21] Indeed, he declared, the way the Americans lived made "every man forget his ancestors, . . . [and it] hides his descendants and separates his contemporaries from him," and "throws him back forever upon himself alone and threatens in the end to confine him entirely within the solitude of his own heart."[22] And he witnessed all of that to an exaggerated degree in the wild country beyond Lake Michigan, overrun by a new "nomad people which the rivers and lakes do not stop, before which the forests fall and the prairies are covered with shade."[23]

By the time de Tocqueville and Beaumont met up with those new nomads, they had already swarmed into Illinois, arriving there with great noise and confusion. To the Sauk they must have seemed the very incarnation of chaos itself, and every bit as threatening as the wicked serpents of their ancient stories. In fact, Black Hawk actually compared them to snakes that coiled themselves around the Indians and poisoned their lives.[24]

When peace was restored in 1815, people flocked to Illinois looking for land. During the war itself, as a means of inducing men to enlist in the army, Congress had offered land grants of a quarter section of land (160 acres). But when the battle went badly and enlistments fell off, those grants were increased to 320 acres for every man who served in the ranks of the national army. Initially, 2 million acres were set aside in Illinois for that purpose, and then, when the military tracts in Michigan proved unsatisfactory, another 1.5 million acres were reserved in Illinois for the former soldiers. All that land was located in the western part of the state, in the wedge between the Illinois and Mississippi rivers, and it was anticipated that the settlement of those tracts by army veterans would create a military buffer zone between the already settled areas to the east and the Indian tribes still living farther west. Although only about one-third of all the individuals eligible for such land grants ever took advantage of the opportunity, nearly three-fifths of those who did claimed land in the Illinois Military Tracts. However, rather than actually settling there, most of those veterans sold their patents to speculators, receiving an average of about seventy cents an acre. The speculators, in turn, resold the land at greatly marked-up prices to eager settlers. Although the program did not produce the results originally intended, it greatly encouraged settlement in Illinois, which by 1818 was admitted to the Union and in 1830 had a population of 157,000.[25]

A great many of those people moved up from Kentucky and Tennessee, crossing the Ohio River to take possession of the good farmland in southern Illinois. Others, in more modest numbers, migrated west from New England, New York, and Pennsylvania. The year after statehood was granted, Lucius Langworthy came from Ohio and settled on a farm near Jacksonville, in Scott County, a little southwest of Springfield. Most of the people already there, living on modest homesteads, were from the South and subsisted, according to Langworthy, mostly on corn dodgers and hominy, wild game and pork, and raised their own tobacco and cotton. They were a rough, hard-drinking, disorderly lot who often became violent. That was especially the case on election days. On those occasions people would gather in large numbers to cast their votes orally, and "not infrequently," said Langworthy, "different parties met and fought just to show their manhood, gouging out each other's eyes, peeling off noses, pulling out hair, pounding and tramping on one another in the most approved style of the day." Those who triumphed in such brawls, he went on to say, "would jump upon their feet, swing their arms, beat their fists, and swear they are the best men and can whip their weight in wild cats." When not beating up one another, they delighted in picking on people from the East. "A Yankee was looked upon with great aversion as a spy, a sharper, one who would not fight, but kept his skill for buying up the dollar," Langworthy remarked. Because of that, if a man from New England or New York attended a public gathering, "no one must suspect him of coming from further east than the mountain range of the Blue Ridge and Alleghenies. If so, then he must fight some one or leave the ground."[26]

Thomas Ford, who settled in Edwardsville and later became governor of Illinois, described the early inhabitants of that area as "ignorant, illiterate, and vicious" people who were "hostile to any action of the government tending to their improvement and civilization." They usually dressed in hunting shirts, buckskin trousers, raccoon caps, leather moccasins, and "delighted to wear a butcher knife as an appendage of dress," said Ford. Because they were so aggressive and so eagerly disposed to violence, they had a great influence on state and local politics so that "the candidate who had the 'butcher knife boys' on his side was almost certain to be elected."[27]

When the poet William Cullen Bryant visited his brother in Illinois during the summer of 1832, he too was unimpressed with the quality of the people he found living there. One woman he encountered at Cox's Grove, about twenty-five miles east of Jacksonville, seemed to him all too typical of the lot. She was, Bryant informed his sister back East, "a fat dusky looking woman barefoot with six children as dirty as pigs and shaggy as bears. She was lousing one of them and cracking the unfortunate insects between her thumbs." Even in the larger settlements, he found the people and their ways disgustingly crude and primitive. That was certainly his impression of Jacksonville itself, which he called a "horribly ugly little village." He then found Springfield to be even worse. The houses there, he reported, were mostly "miserable log cabins, and the whole town having the appearance of dirt and discomfort."[28]

The English traveler Charles Latrobe had very similar reactions to Peoria and Chicago. The former was one of the state's oldest French communities and was, he asserted, "a wretched and ruinous collection of habitations." In describing Chicago, he said, "The interior of the village was one chaos of mud, rubbish, and confusion." It was also a fast-growing settlement in which "frame and clapboard houses were springing up daily under the active axes and hammers of the speculators." Latrobe was uncomfortable there and described the hotel in which he stayed as a "vile, two-story barracks" in "a state o[f] most appalling confusion, filth, and racket." In taking an "inventory" of the community's human contents, he wrote: "You will find horse-dealers, and horse-stealers—rogues of every description, white, black, brown, and red—half-breeds, quarter breeds, and men of no breeding at all—dealers in pigs, poultry, and potatoes—men pursuing Indian claims; . . . sharpers of every degree, peddlers, grog-sellers, Indian agents and Indian traders of every description," all on the move and hustle in that "little village [that] was in an uproar from morning to night."[29]

Even St. Louis, the great and growing metropolis of the region, with a population of seven thousand by 1830, was little more than a rough and disorderly frontier town. When young Lieutenant Philip St. George Cooke landed there in 1827, he was immediately struck by "the muddiness of the streets—the badness of the hotels—the numbers of Creole-French, speaking the French language—working on the Sabbath—a floating population of trappers, traders, boatmen, and Indians—and finally, an absence of paper currency. . . . Rowdyness was the order of the day," he declared.[30] However, by the time Caleb Atwater arrived two years later, some improvements had been made. For example, the main street had been paved with limestone slabs, some of the buildings were large and made of brick, and Atwater was pleasantly surprised to find a considerable number of well-educated young ladies and enterprising young men residing there.[31] Nevertheless, an incident occurred in 1832 while Bryant was there that revealed something of the inner struggle going on within the community—a struggle between its lingering frontier character and the civilized qualities it so eagerly wished to acquire. It involved one of the community's largest and best-known brothels and a prostitute by the name of "Indian Margaret."

One night Margaret had an altercation with one of her customers, during which she stabbed the man. A few days later he died. For many of the more respectable residents of the community, that must have been the last outrageous straw, and, according to Bryant, "they rose en masse and attacked all the houses of ill fame in the place, tore down two, set fire to a third, and burned the beds and other furniture in all of them." In addition to venting their disapproval on the infrastructure of the trade, they focused some of their rage on one of its most successful and notorious entrepreneurs. Bryant described him as "a black man called Abraham who was the owner of 14 houses of this description having made a fortune in this way," and reported that he "was seized, a barrel of tar was emptied upon him and he was slipped into a feather bed." In the end, "Indian Margaret" went to jail, and Abraham made his escape across the Canadian border. Nevertheless, the whores who remained continued to do a brisk business.[32]

While all that was happening south of the Illinois River, life was also undergoing tumultuous upheaval in the northwest corner of the state.

Right after the closing of the factory system, Ramsey Crooks, John Jacob Astor's top field commander, rushed to St. Louis to begin in earnest the absorption or destruction of what remained of the American Fur Company's competition. Although the company never achieved a complete monopoly, it certainly dominated what soon proved to be the closing chapter of the fur trade era in mid-America. By limiting competition and manipulating prices, credit, and the supply of goods, the company forced both traders and native hunters to work harder for less in return; at the same time, their frantic taking of more and more pelts reduced the animals virtually to extinction. Lewis Cass understood what was going on and in one of his essays, published in the *North American Review* in January of 1830, he pointed out the disastrous consequences all that commercial activity was having: "The exchange was altogether unfavorable to them [the Indians]. The goods they received were dear, and the peltry they furnish was cheap. A great number of animals were necessary for the support of each family, and increased exertion was required to procure them. We need not pursue this subject further. It is easy to see the consequences, both to the Indians and their game."[33]

In the region around Saukenuk it was the Englishman George Davenport who dominated the trade. He had immigrated to the United States in 1804 and soon became a soldier. He served under General James Wilkinson during the War of 1812 and a year after being discharged was at Rock Island in business as an army supplier. It did not take Davenport long to get into trade with the Sauk and Fox. At the time of his arrival in the upper Mississippi, he was married to Margaret Lewis of Cincinnati. But he also had a very close relationship with Margaret's sixteen-year-old daughter Susan, the offspring of her mother's previous marriage. In 1817 Susan gave birth to Davenport's son, whom they named George.

Even after that Margaret, Susan, her brother William Lewis, and little George continued to live with Davenport in the substantial house he had built on Rock Island. Then, in 1823, when Susan reached the age of twenty-two, she and Davenport produced a second son. How all that influenced his reputation among the soldiers and settlers in the area, or affected the emotional climate within his own household, is not known, but there was no question about his success in business.[34] At that he greatly prospered, especially after 1824 when he teamed up with Russell Farnham of the American Fur Company. Between the two of them they had six trading posts in the Mississippi-Rock rivers region, and although the fur trade was by then becoming a tough business, both of them became wealthy men.[35]

Davenport and Farnham even had ambitions of establishing their own regional monopoly. As Davenport wrote his partner in November of 1826, "If whe can onely secure the trade to our Selves for two three years whe will make the winnebagos pay well for the goods we know [sic, now] give them at so low a price."[36] On the other hand, in looking at the trade from the perspective of the Indians' interests, Forsyth did not regard the prices charged for trade goods to be "so low." The Sauk and Fox, he told Cass in October of 1831, were "compelled to take [the] goods of the traders at their very high prices because they cannot do without them." When they received those expensive goods in the fall of the year, just before departing for the winter hunt, they got them on credit. In a successful season, as the result of unusual hard work, Indian hunters might be able to accumulate sufficient pelts to pay off their debts, and when that occurred, said Forsyth, "the trader is a gainer of more than 100 percent." To illustrate and verify what he claimed, he gave Cass some examples of how inflated the prices of trade goods were: Davenport purchased three-point wool blankets at $3.52 a piece and sold them to the Indians for $10.00 each; a rifle that cost Davenport $13.00 was sold for $30.00. Forsyth was well aware of the constant complaining of the traders concerning their alleged inability to collect on all the goods they had allotted out on credit, but he told Cass he had no sympathy for them and explained why: "It appears to me, that as all the above named traders [Farnham, Davenport, and Joseph Rolette of Prairie du Chien] are become wealthy (and are yearly growing more) in trade with the Indians, their claims for bad debts ought not to be listened to at any treaty [conference] or otherwise."[37]

Once traders like Davenport had the Indians deeply indebted, it was far easier to control and deliberately exploit them. Under those circumstances native hunters would simply have to become more productive. But the law of diminishing returns soon went into effect, and then when more Americans moved in, the entire ecological system was severely disrupted. The destruction of animal habitats combined with overhunting to quickly diminish the number of animals that could be taken within a geographic area. When hunters then attempted to move on to new locations, they usually found themselves in violent conflict with other tribal groups. Warfare thereby became more common, and, in reference to that and the disappointing returns from the Sauk and Fox, Russell Farnham wrote to Pierre Chouteau at company headquarters in St. Louis in 1830: "For the last few years, the Indians have been unable to pay by Reason of the constant war which has raged between them & the Sioux, [and] that war while it created necessity for a greater supply of Goods, cut off the means of payment by driving them from their accustomed Hunting grounds."[38]

It became a vicious cycle. During the period from 1824 to 1831 Davenport and Farnham invested between $33,000 and $60,000 a year in trade goods and equipment, and at the same time gave Indian hunters a total of $137,000 worth of goods on credit.[39] In 1829 Davenport and Farnham claimed that $40,000 was still owed them by the Sauk, Fox, and Winnebago, and by 1831 indicated the accumulated debt had grown to $53,500.[40] Forsyth was convinced the traders had actually created that situation quite deliberately, for when native hunters were unable to bring in a sufficient supply of pelts to pay their debts, operators like Davenport were then in the advantageous position of laying claim to the treaty annuity funds paid to the tribes by the federal government for past land concessions. In 1827, for example, when the Sauk and Fox received their $2,000 annuity allotment, Davenport and Farnham immediately took $1,481 of it for debt payments.[41] Two years later, when Forsyth delivered another annuity payment of the same amount, the first thing the Sauk and Fox did was to turn over $1,900 of it to Davenport, while the remaining $100 went to nearby settlers in compensation for property damage they claimed the Indians had caused.[42]

The economic system that had long sustained the Sauk and allowed them to flourish was obviously breaking down from overhunting and the ever-increasing burdens of indebtedness. But there were other serious problems associated with the changing character of the fur trade, and the destructive influence of whiskey was among the very worst.

A primary purpose of the factory system had been to eliminate alcohol from the Indian trade, and even after that system was ended, Congress passed legislation reaffirming that policy. Accordingly, there was to be a total prohibition of all spirituous liquors and alcoholic drink of any kind from all aspects of the fur trade everywhere within Indian country.

No one was more committed to that policy than Thomas McKenney, who had been federal superintendent of Indian trade and chief administrator of the factory system. Shortly after its demise he was made head of the War Department's Indian Office, where he continued his crusade to protect the tribes. A lapsed Quaker of strong humanitarian sentiments, McKenney worried about the ruin of the native people at the hands of unscrupulous traders, especially those who dealt heavily in spirituous liquors. With the strong backing of his boss, Secretary of War James Barbour, he became a zealous adversary of whiskey sellers among the Indians.[43] In September of 1825 he wrote to Cass telling him how it was "the anxious desire of the Secretary of War that the evils so terrible in their consequences, both to the Indians and the whites, and which are consequent upon the introduction of ardent spirits among the Indians, be destroyed." He insisted upon all Indian agents vigorously enforcing the policy enacted by the Congress.[44] In the spring of 1827 he wrote to Cass, once again reiterating the policy and his desire to have it strictly enforced to the letter. He wanted absolutely no exceptions, no matter how minor, and argued that even "one single license to exercise *a discretion* . . . is equivalent to a universal grant." McKenney then declared in no uncertain terms, "Th[ere] is no controlling the evils of the practice short of an *unqualified prohibition*."[45]

From deep within the interior, Colonel Josiah Snelling, commander of Fort St. Anthony at the confluence of the Minnesota and Mississippi rivers, proclaimed his total agreement with McKenney's position. In a letter to Secretary of War Barbour, written in the late summer of 1825, Snelling asserted that the trading of whiskey to the Indians resulted in "the introduction of every species of vice and debauchery by the traders and their engages" and was the "source of . . . nearly all of the murders committed in the Indian country. . . . If permitted *at all*," he declared, "no limit can be set to it." He also informed the secretary about what he had witnessed during a visit to Detroit, where he had been shocked at "seeing the road literally strewed with the bodies of [Indian] men, women, and children, in the last stages of brutal intoxication."[46]

Right from the start, however, the American Fur Company worked aggressively to subvert the policy. It began by seeking minor exemptions, but its ultimate aim was the complete repeal of all regulations restricting the use and sale of alcohol in any aspect of the Indian trade. In June of 1827 Robert Stuart, Astor's chief lieutenant in the upper Great Lakes, wrote to Cass complaining about the hardships caused for his business by the prohibition policy. He argued that if the company and its traders were not permitted to sell whiskey to the Indians, the company would surely be ruined due to its inability to compete with British traders and their newly enlarged and very assertive Hudson's Bay Company. Working on Cass's well-known Anglophobia, Stuart asserted, "Unless a small quantity [of whiskey] be allowed to the traders of the region, the whole trade must be abandoned to the British, . . . who will then, not only enjoy all of the advantages which belong exclusively to our citizens but [will] also acquire unbounded influence over the Indians." He further informed Cass of his deep concern for the welfare of the voyageurs employed by the company, declaring that "some liquor is absolutely necessary for the health and comfort of the voyageurs." Stuart then ended his letter by arguing that the whole policy was far too extreme, and too harshly enforced by the Indian agents, complaining, "We are by most of the agents, prohibited from giving any Liquor whatsoever for our men, and some go so far as to prevent the Traders taking even a little wine etc. for their own use. . . . This cannot be the intention of the Gov[ernmen]t, or the Law!" he concluded.[47]

Although Cass was a strong temperance advocate who remained unconvinced by Stuart's arguments, the company's unrelenting lobbying in Washington eventually paid off. In early 1828 McKenney, with great reluctance, informed Indian superintendent William Clark that the secretary of war had granted permission to the "traders to take whiskey *for their boatmen.*" But McKenney wished to keep tight control over that, fearing even such a modest concession was a dangerous loophole through which disaster could soon pour into the upper Mississippi region. Therefore, he insisted that the quantity of whiskey taken into that territory be limited to one gill a day—just four fluid ounces—for each voyageur for the duration of time they would be traveling. He also demanded that all traders post bond equal to the value of their cargoes when setting forth, and that those funds be forfeited if any of their whiskey whatsoever was "used in trade, or barter, or *given* to the Indians."[48]

The policy had considerable success at Rock Island, at least for a time. Forsyth informed Clark in July of 1826 that he had made inquiries among the Indians to see if any traders were packing whiskey into the region, and had been pleased to discover none were doing so. Then in a statement that must have referred to Davenport, Farnham, and Anthone Gauthier, who traded with the Sauk, Fox, and Winnebago on the Rock River, Forsyth reported to Clark: "Generally speaking the present traders in the country are a moral and a good people and are not wanting in giving good advice (occasionally!) to the Indians." Furthermore, he pointed out how the threats of the chiefs had been so adamant that even the most despicable "whiskey peddlers" from downriver had stayed away.[49]

Unfortunately, success was all too fleeting. The territory was simply too vast, the profits were too tempting and easily acquired, the traders too devious, and neither the Indian agents nor the army had enough staff, time, or power to plug all the holes that developed in the enforcement system. As early as 1824, for example, Forsyth was informed by the subagent John Connolly, who was stationed among the Fox near the Fever River, that great quantities of whiskey were being sold to the Indians in his area, and it was "impossible to prosecute those venders of whiskey for want of proper testimony." Connolly also pointed out how those unscrupulous merchants were taking the Indians' horses in payment for whiskey.[50] The next year Forsyth was upset over the "great quantities of whiskey brought up to the Indian villages from the settlements by every Indian canoe which arrives."[51] And that autumn Clark informed Secretary of War Barbour that, even though the soldiers were searching all the boats, they were unable to control everyone or intercept all the illegal spirits being smuggled into the territory. The task was made even more difficult, he said, because the Indians "soon become acquainted with the various little distilleries and Grocery establishments on the frontiers." In no time it seemed whiskey was available everywhere. "It is an evil most sincerely felt, and the more to be dreaded from the increase of the evil," Clark told Barbour.[52]

Whiskey did great damage especially to the Fox. As early as 1824 Forsyth told McKenney they were "generally addicted to spirituous liquors [and] that very many of them sell their canoes, guns, and any personal possessions they may have for the support of their families for a little whiskey."[53] The Sauk, on the other hand, remained determined to resist the temptation. They did so for some time, but eventually their self-discipline also broke down and some of them began to drink as well. "I used all my influence to prevent drunkenness, but without effect," Black Hawk confessed. By the late 1820s the situation took on tragic dimensions. Men stopped going west for the winter hunt, but instead loafed around the settlements, killing whatever they could find and selling the skins for whiskey. As a consequence, they were unable to pay the traders for goods taken on credit, and, even worse, they "returned in the spring [to Saukenuk] with their families, almost naked, and without the means of getting anything for them."[54] Even among those men who continued to go to the western hunting grounds, their almost unquenchable cravings for whiskey took a bitter toll. Concerning the winter of 1830–31, Black Hawk recalled: "The winter passed off in gloom. We made a bad hunt, for want of guns, traps, etc. that the whites had taken from our people for whiskey! The prospect before us was a bad one."[55]

Those changes in the fur trade brought increasing misery and chaos into the lives of the Sauk people, but the men who rushed into the region looking for lead made the situation even worse. It was not long after Johnson and his crew commenced their operations along the Fever River that others began arriving in large numbers. By 1826, according to Lucius Langworthy of Scott County, Illinois, people in his area began to "hear the wild murmuring of the lead mines away to the north. . . . Accounts come sweeping down by each traveler," he said, "of the great lead mines just opened up at Galena," and in no time farms were being sold and "young men and maidens, old folks and all, start for the lead mines."[56] The next summer Langworthy himself set off with high hopes of striking it rich in the Fever River valley. He was merely one among thousands, all with the same idea, who altogether began transforming the life of northwestern Illinois. John Marsh, the Harvard-educated subagent of Indian affairs at Prairie du Chien, was astounded by what was happening and wrote home to Massachusetts in January of 1827 to tell his father about it. "Five years ago," he said, "some Americans discovered lead mines at Fever River about eighty miles below this place, and now there are four or five thousand men employed in working the mines in that place and the adjacent country. Some thousands of tons of lead have been mined, and many poor men have suddenly become rich."[57] Concerning that inundation of people, John Reynolds, who became governor of Illinois in 1830, wrote, "It seemed the people were literally crazy, and rushed to the mines with the same blind energy and speed that a people would in a panic flee from death."[58]

Moses M. Strong, a young attorney who was among the earliest settlers in the Wisconsin mining region, claimed it was all "stimulated by the greed for suddenly acquired wealth, and the irrepressible love of adventure." As a consequence, the population of the mining district exploded from about two hundred in 1825 to around four thousand in 1827, and then shot up to at least ten thousand a year later.[59] Most came from southern Illinois, Missouri, Kentucky, and Tennessee, and between 1825 and 1828, according to Strong, they increased lead production from 439,473 to 12,957,100 pounds a year.[60] Precise population figures were difficult to ascertain since so many of the miners were seasonal migrants, moving north in spring and then departing again before the rivers froze in late fall. That was particularly so for the people from southern Illinois, who, because of those migratory habits, became known by the nickname "Suckers," after the fish that also seasonally ascended and descended the rivers of the region. Indeed, much of the population was transient, constantly coming and going, and settling nowhere for very long. Morgan L. Martin was in the region in 1829 and observed of the miners that "few of them thought of permanently settling in the lead country; their object being to get what they could from the diggings . . . and be prepared to leave for the Illinois settlements again, on short notice."[61]

Although few people planned to stay for long, a great many of them congregated in places where it was known, or at least rumored, the lead was plentiful and easy to dig. That first happened at Galena, the community established by Colonel Johnson in the summer of 1822. When Caleb Atwater stopped there in 1829, he noted it had become "the largest town in Illinois," and contained "several taverns, a considerable number of stores [and] . . . perhaps one thousand inhabitants."[62] People converged there from far and wide, and when John Reynolds paid his first visit to Galena in 1829, he found a "mysterious medley of people" residing there. "People from all quarters of the earth had flocked there on account of the celebrity of the lead mines," he reported.[63]

Galena was at the eye of the storm, and from there the uproar of the lead rush swirled out and into the surrounding territory. Theodore Rodolf, a Swiss immigrant to the area, observed that "the country around Galena for a distance of forty miles east and north was dotted with crude log furnaces for smeltering the mineral."[64] And John Reynolds declared, "The whole earth north, east, and south of Galena was covered with people, prospecting, digging, and looking for lead ore."[65]

When it all reached its full force and fury, the lead rush surged northward into the Driftless Area of Wisconsin. New mining and smelting settlements quickly materialized, the most significant of which were at Gratiot's Grove, Shullsburg, Blue Mounds, Hardscrabble, Cassville, Coon Branch, Fair Play, New Diggings, Dodgeville, Platteville, and Mineral Point. The most important of those was Mineral Point. Daniel Parkinson settled there in 1829 and opened a tavern. "Mineral Point," he later recalled, "was then the great center of attraction to all miners; some of the largest leads were there struck and extensively worked, and quite a number of mining and smeltering establishments erected there and in the vicinity." As a result, he pointed out: "Business was of a most animated character. The town grew up with great rapidity, and every thing wore the most pleasing and encouraging aspect."[66]

But the prosperity did not last. In fact, the fortunes of the entire region ebbed and flowed with the rising and falling of lead prices, and people came and went in restless reaction to their own fluctuating hopes and disappointments. They were a tough lot with few refinements. One resident of Galena described the people there as "thievish, poor, dirty, low-lived, rough scruffs."[67] And when Juliette Kinzie visited Hamilton's Diggings, a mining settlement owned and operated by Alexander Hamilton's son William, in March of 1831, she said of the workers there, "They were the roughest-looking set of men I ever beheld, and their language was as uncouth as their persons." This was a candid assessment coming from a woman who had spent most of her adult life in the close company of voyageurs and fur traders, who were themselves a notoriously rough tribe.[68]

From the very beginning, the mining boom caused trouble for the Indians, who were soon driven from their own diggings along the Fever River and then throughout much of the region.

In November of 1827 Joseph Street, then the newly appointed Indian agent at Prairie du Chien, wrote his friend Ninian Edwards, then governor of Illinois. Street had traveled through the mining region on his way north to assume his post and had been disturbed by much of what he saw and heard. He informed Edwards: "The Indians had been soured by the conduct of the vast number of adventurers flocking to and working the lead mines of Fever River. Those who went by land, by far the greatest part, passed through the Winnebago country. Many of them had great contempt for 'naked Indians,' and behaved low, gross, and like blackguards amongst them."[69] That same month Street described to the secretary of war a troubling incident he had witnessed while in Galena. It involved an Indian woman—"a Menominee, well known . . . and reputed [to be] a good Indian"—he said. One night, while she was engaged in "drinking much whiskey," reported Street, "a white man knocked her down and stamped on her head." When Street saw her the next morning, he was shocked because she "appeared to be dying from the effects of some severe contusions on the head, by which her face was much lacerated, and one eye [was] apparently put out. . . . She was senseless, [and] her remaining eye turned up untill the dark part of the ball was just visible," he wrote. The poor woman soon died, and Street warned the secretary, "The Indians are not so stupid, or astounded by late events, as to let these things pass unnoticed . . . and I am not without serious apprehensions, that, if a more vigilant eye is not kept upon the heterogeneous mass of population, which *Europe* and the United States have furnished at the Mines," the general peace would soon break down and the entire region plunge into violent chaos.[70]

The trouble quickly spread northward, and in January of 1828 a Winnebago chief named Carumna went to Street's agency house and angrily protested: "*Now a large camp* [of white people] *has gone far into our country,* and they are taking our Lead where it is easy to be got, and where Indians have made Lead many years. We did not expect this, and we want to know where they will stop. The hills are covered with them & more & more are coming, and shoving us off our lands and taking them to make Lead."[71]

That summer Thomas Forsyth was visited by Wabokieshiek, well known in the region as the Winnebago Prophet, who presided over a tribally mixed village of followers located about thirty-five miles up from the mouth of the Rock River. Forsyth called him a man "of very great influence among the Indians" and informed Clark that the Prophet was extremely upset about the lies white people were spreading about the Indians stealing their horses, as well as very indignant about miners trespassing upon the Winnebago lands east of the Pecatonica River. Even more, the Prophet told him he was infuriated because "sometimes some of the white people are insulting to the Indians and take liberties with their women which the Indians do not like."[72]

Some of the Indians contributed to their own worsening situation but may have also ironically gotten even with a few of their white tormentors. Moses Meeker, himself a mine and smelter operator, reported: "The Indians were very fond of whiskey, and as fruitful of their resources to procure it as the white man. One of their modes was to promise to show, for a given number of bottles of whiskey, where the mineral could be found. By this plan they procured a great deal. Another mode was to offer lewd women to the whites for whiskey, which too many of the young men accepted to their sorrow."[73]

During his travels, Alexis de Tocqueville had discovered the United States to be a society filled with people "without roots, without memories, . . . without routines, without common ideas, without a [sense of] national character."[74] That was certainly the case to an alarming degree in the region between the Wisconsin and Illinois rivers after 1822. In the following ten years it became a place of noise and commotion overrun by people who were as radically unlike the Sauk as could be imagined. De Tocqueville had also observed: "In the midst of this American society, . . . a cold selfishness and complete insensibility prevails when it is a question of the natives of the country."[75] Indeed, few Americans felt greater contempt toward the Indians than those who migrated up from Kentucky, Tennessee, and southern Illinois in search of better land and rich veins of lead. From the perspective of the Sauk, those unwanted intruders let loose a torrent of havoc and hardship upon their tribal homeland. Like the vicious serpents of the underworld—the spreaders of chaos and the enemies of all that was good—they came in ever-increasing numbers, creeping closer and closer to the sacred center of the world. Then, in the winter of 1828–29, while the Sauk were away on their winter hunt, the white people invaded Saukenuk itself.

John Spencer was one of those "Suckers" who had gone to Galena in the spring of 1827 hoping to make a lucky strike. But like so many others, he went home again in the fall no better off than when he had come. After a winter back on the farm in Morgan County, he returned once more for a second season of wishful searching. On his journey north he passed by Saukenuk. He was astonished by what he saw. That fall, when heading home empty-handed once more, he was informed by Rinnah Wells, another would-be miner from southern Illinois, that the Sauk had abandoned their great town on the Rock River with no intention of ever returning. After two disappointing summers looking for lead, both Spencer and Wells decided to try their hand at farming again, but this time in the expansive, well-worked fields around Saukenuk. On March 1, 1829, young Spencer moved in and took up residence in one of the deserted lodges. Another twenty families of squatters either were already there or moved in soon after. Among them was Judge John Pence from Indiana, who, with his wife and children, took possession of Black Hawk's own lodge.[76] With that, the Sauk's place in the world, and all they were and ever had been, was in the gravest of danger.

4

A TANGLED WEB

Oh, what a tangled web we weave,
When first we practice to deceive!

Sir Walter Scott, "Marmion"

THE SAUK WERE not alone in facing the prospects of their own ruin. All native societies throughout the trans-Appalachian West were under increasing assault. Many were weak and impoverished, their people debilitated by alcohol and malnutrition, and they were losing their land, exhausting their resources, and declining in numbers. Unwilling or unable to fully assimilate into the expanding American market system, and incapable of sustaining their traditional ways of life, the Indians, it seemed certain to most Americans, were fast becoming a vanishing race, "melting away each day like snow in the rays of the sun, and . . . visibly disappearing from the face of the earth," as Alexis de Tocqueville so poetically put it while traveling through the wilds of Michigan.[1]

The plight of the native people provoked a contentious national debate over what should be done about their sorry predicament. People took sides and vociferously disagreed. Most of those who had moved into the West showed little sympathy and advocated no support for the Indians, and the more contact they had with them the harsher and more hostile became their attitudes. On the other hand, a significantly large number of citizens living in the urban Northeast, especially intellectuals and artists moved by strong feelings of moral rectitude and romantic sentimentalism, expressed outrage over what was happening to the natives. Some of them, wanting to know firsthand just how tragic the situation really was, traveled to the tribal zone to see for themselves. In the summer of 1830, for example, the artist George Catlin left Philadelphia for the West. He traveled with a sense of urgency, hoping to find and paint authentic native Americans before it was too late—before they were all gone forever. That same summer, Calvin Colton also went west to the wild country of northeast Wisconsin.

Colton was a Yale-educated Presbyterian minister, originally from Long-meadow, Massachusetts, who, because of problems with a failing voice, had left his parish in Batavia, New York, to make his way in the world as a writer. In July of 1830, at the age of forty-one, he departed Buffalo, New York, aboard the steamship *Superior*. He was exhilarated by the journey and eagerly anticipated seeing real Indians in an unspoiled state of nature when he attended an important intertribal conference at Green Bay in late August.

His anticipation increased as the time for the great event drew near, and then on the day before the conference commenced he became quite enthralled by the scene that took shape along the banks of the Fox River. The surface of the water "swarmed with canoes," and an immense multitude of people came ashore and erected temporary lodges for a considerable distance beyond Fort Howard. Men dressed in feathers and fur came with wives and children, dogs and pet bears, and Colton estimated there to be three thousand of them in all, "thrown together without any order" and raising a loud tumult. "Many acres of the plain were completely covered, and exhibited a rare spectacle to the eye," he wrote in a burst of elation. It was exactly what he had hoped to find amid the "wild and romantic regions of the American lakes."[2]

Colton was fascinated by the noise and commotion of the boisterous throng, but in looking upon it he suddenly caught sight of a single individual—"a beautiful young woman, richly dressed, full of smiles, and really charming." Like a sublime vision, she emerged from the chaos, and there before him "she shone in all her maiden pride and loveliness." But then, as quickly as she had appeared, she was soon again gone, a fleeting but unforgettable glimpse for him of someone and something fine and noble and of unspoiled natural beauty.[3]

The next morning she reappeared. Colton spotted her while he was walking near the river with a companion. To his amazement, in the course of a single night she had been greatly changed. Her hair was disheveled, her slender and attractive figure concealed beneath a soiled and dirty blanket, and her "countenance [was] dejected and disconsolate." She made her way with downcast eyes and "moaned piteously" as she walked along the margin of the stream. When Colton asked his companion what might account for her sudden transformation, he was told, "She has doubtless been tempted by drink and then dishonored, and . . . deserted by a white man." During the night, the beautiful, bronze-skinned maiden had become a poor, fallen creature whose wretched appearance, remarked Colton, was the outward sign of "her irretrievable ruin."[4]

For Calvin Colton that fallen "child of nature" became a poignant and pathetic symbol of what he was convinced was happening to the entire Indian race. In their innocence, and with virtually no natural resistance to the temptations thrust into their world by American society, they were, he declared, easy prey for the "vicious and unprincipled white men," who were "corrupting their morals and manners, and fast plunging them into deep degradation, and to final ruin." By the time he departed Green Bay, Colton was convinced that the fate of the American Indians hung precariously in the balance, and the question before the nation—indeed, before the entire civilized world—was "whether they should exist or be annihilated."[5]

Throughout the upper Mississippi region the situation was becoming more and more as Colton imagined it to be. There, too, deceit and distrust were on the rise, and everyone—both Indians and white people alike—grew increasingly apprehensive. But it was not just a matter of a few unscrupulous individuals taking advantage of some gullible natives. Rather, by the late 1820s there were far too many people and interest groups, with too many different and conflicting needs and ambitions, generating too much suspicion, and spreading too many rumors and lies. All of that, in turn, produced an environment in which it had become extremely difficult to know whom to trust or what to believe.

That state of affairs for the Sauk became particularly disturbing in the winter of 1828–29. Rumors reached them in their hunting camps about white people occupying some of their lodges back in Saukenuk. The news so distressed Black Hawk, he decided to set out to see for himself if it was true. Although sixty-two years old, he traveled alone, making his way into the cold, snow-drifted countryside on what turned out to be a ten-day journey. Upon reaching the old village, he was deeply troubled by what he found. White people were indeed occupying the village, and one family had taken up residence in his very own lodge. He attempted to explain to them why they had to leave, but soon became frustrated with their indifference and his own inability to make himself understood. Getting no satisfaction from the squatters, he backed off and went up to Fort Armstrong, where he asked Antoine LeClaire, the government interpreter, to compose for him a note instructing the trespassers to vacate the village. Well aware of the great power written words had among white people, the old man naively assumed the note would immediately bring about their departure. "I expected . . . that they would remove, as I had requested them," he indicated.[6]

Nevertheless, neither LeClaire's letter nor his own exhortations had the desired results, and, in time, Black Hawk departed feeling deeply discouraged, intending to rejoin the hunting bands in the West. But he did not get far before he decided to seek advice about what to do about the occupation of the village from individuals he still trusted. He first made his way to Rock Island, where he spent a night with George Davenport. In their discussions the trader urged him to give up all notions of ever returning to Saukenuk again. The wisest course of action, he told Black Hawk, would be for the entire tribe to establish a new summertime settlement for itself, west of the Mississippi, near the mouth of the Iowa River, as some of the chiefs had already proposed. Dissatisfied with that advice, Black Hawk then traveled north to Prairie du Chien and there conferred with John Marsh, the well-educated Indian affairs subagent, whose marriage to a métis-Sioux woman gave him an especially good understanding of the Indians and their concerns. But Black Hawk was surprised and disappointed when Marsh made the same recommendation as Davenport had. Unwilling, or perhaps even unable, to accept that advice, he retraced his route back to the Rock River, which he ascended until he reached the village of Wabokieshiek, the Winnebago Prophet, whom he regarded as "a man of great knowledge."[7]

Wabokieshiek was described as "a very tall big man," over six feet in height, and quite "stout and athletic" in physical build. He had "a large broad face, short blunt nose, large full eyes, broad mouth, thick lips, with a full suit of hair." A man in his early forties of mixed parentage—half Winnebago and half Sauk—he presided over a village that was "a mixture of different nations of Indians," located about thirty-five miles up the Rock River.[8] The white people in the region were suspicious of him, and Joseph

Street, who was sometimes too glib for his own good, snidely commented about his village being a despicable collection of "renegadoes" who had "attached themselves to a man who passed for a prophet."[9] Contrary to that opinion, Forsyth regarded Wabokieshiek as a highly intelligent individual, who, he said, used his considerable influence "to keep peace and quietness among all the Indians who reside in the surrounding country."[10]

It was precisely because of his "very great influence" that Black Hawk sought him out with hopes of getting wiser council than what he had already received from Davenport and Marsh. Wabokieshiek clearly understood Black Hawk's attachment to the old village and empathized with his desire to see the squatters depart, and in responding to the old man's entreaties urged him not to abandon the village or surrender the gardens and graves to the white people. Instead, he recommended the Sauk return again to Saukenuk in the spring, and assured Black Hawk there would be no trouble between his people and the settlers if they did.[11]

Wabokieshiek's advice was in conflict with what Forsyth had advocated they do the previous spring. In mid-May of 1828 he had told them that the upcoming summer ought to be the very last one they spent at Saukenuk. At the same time he had reminded them that they no longer owned the land on which the village was located, but had sold it to the U.S. government some years before; the time had finally come for them to give it up and resettle elsewhere. That, however, was an assertion most tribal members refused to accept, and some of their leaders angrily claimed that none of their land above the Rock River had ever been sold. In a heated exchange with Forsyth a succession of Sauk spokesmen had adamantly declared "they would not move from the place where the bones of their ancestors lay, and that they would defend themselves against any power that might be sent to drive them away."[12] Mess-con-de-bay (Red Head), an important hereditary chief, had spoken out for the group on that occasion and had been "somewhat insolent," said Forsyth, in his categorical rejection of any suggestion of abandoning Saukenuk and removing west of the Mississippi. Mess-con-de-bay was a man in his midfifties whom Forsyth characterized as "a vile unprincipled fellow"[13] and later dismissed as "a poor trifling, mean, insignificant old man."[14] Nevertheless, he was a man of considerable standing with the tribe and articulated views shared by a great many of his people.

In replying to Mess-con-de-bay's objections, Forsyth had indicated he had no interest in quibbling and quarreling, but only in what was in the tribe's best interests. At the same time he warned that more and more white people would soon be moving into the area and many others passing through on their way to the mining country to the north. As a consequence, he asserted, "misunderstandings and accidents must happen between the white people and the Indians." If they foolishly refused to listen to reason, and returned to the village ever again, then they should not "be surprised at any thing that in the future may happen to them."[15]

Some of the Sauk did not remain resolute for long. By early July a considerable number of inhabitants of the Sauk and Fox villages along the Rock River came around to Forsyth's way of thinking and resolved not to ever again return to their villages after departing in the autumn. Forsyth was delighted, and by the time the Sauk and Fox had departed for the winter he was convinced the matter had been settled once and for all.[16]

The white people who moved into the abandoned village accepted the news of the Sauk's intentions not to return again to Saukenuk at face value and simply sought to take advantage of a good opportunity. That was certainly the case with John Spencer. On learning that the Indians had left their old village, he inquired among the soldiers at Fort Armstrong about their future plans and was told "they would not return."[17] That was in December, and by then there were already seven white families living in and around Saukenuk. They were the same people Black Hawk discovered when he returned prematurely from the winter hunt to check on the rumors about white people being there. Spencer later recalled the old man's unexpected visit and described him as having been highly agitated, scolding them "in a loud voice in the Indian language," which none of them understood.[18]

Later, when Forsyth returned to Rock Island in May of 1829, after spending the winter with his family in St. Louis, trouble was already brewing. By then a large party of Sauk had come back from the West and were extremely upset to find fences erected around their cornfields and garden plots. They were disturbed even more by discovering many of their lodges had been destroyed. Although Forsyth felt some sympathy for them, he sternly told them they had no other alternative but to resettle themselves west of the Mississippi. But not only did that admonishment fail to quell their discontent; it set off another vociferous argument about who really owned the land and had the right to reside in Saukenuk.[19]

The dispute over land ownership had its origins in a conference held in November of 1804 by William Henry Harrison, in St. Louis. Harrison was then the territorial governor of Indiana and the newly acquired Louisiana Territory, and he had called the meeting in reaction to a murderous raid by a small party of Sauk warriors on an American settlement on the Cuivre River, just north of St. Louis. A delegation of five Sauk and Fox chiefs attended. They were Layowvois, Pashipaho (the Stabber), Quashquame (Jumping Fish), Outchequaha (Sun Fish), and Hashequarhiqua (the Bear), and once discussions got under way, attention soon turned to issues of land. Harrison, eager to make a big land grab, engaged in some fast talk and was overly generous with promises, presents, and whiskey (depending on who recalled the meeting), and almost before they knew it the chiefs had agreed to a treaty. According to that agreement, the Sauk and Fox (referred to as the "united Sac and Fox tribes") put themselves under the "protection" of the United States and "relinquished forever" all their land east of the Mississippi between the Illinois and Wisconsin rivers, as far east as the Fox River of Illinois. They also gave up a small hunting region in eastern Missouri.[20] For all that territory they received an immediate payment in goods worth $2,234.50 and were promised thereafter an annual payment of $600 worth of goods for the Sauk and $400 for the Fox. Also, according to article 6 of the document, the Sauk and Fox were granted the "privilege of living and hunting" on the ceded land as long as it remained the property of the U.S. government—in other words, they could inhabit and use the land until the federal government sold it to private parties.[21] In making that compact, both Harrison and the chiefs probably exceeded their authority by transferring the ownership of land neither the Sauk nor Fox had any right to sell or give away. Nevertheless, the U.S. Senate ratified the treaty in January of 1805, and in May of 1816 the leaders of the Sauk and Fox tribes signed another treaty in which they "unconditionally recognize[d], reestablish[ed], and confirm[ed]" all that had been agreed to in 1804. Black Hawk himself put his mark on that document.[22]

There seemed no room for debate about any of that. The treaties were perfectly clear. But in May of 1829, when many of the Sauk returned to Saukenuk, they believed the land was still theirs. In response to Forsyth's urging them to depart and never return, Quashquame, the last surviving signer of the Treaty of 1804, protested and declared they had every right to be where they were, adamantly denying "he ever sold any land above the Rock River."[23] Black Hawk jumped to his support, saying Quashquame had assured him many times over that he "never had consented to the sale of the village."[24] And when Forsyth challenged the old chief's veracity, Black Hawk defended him by claiming that the Indians were always honest while "the white people were in the habit of saying one thing to the Indians, and putting on paper another." Then confronting Black Hawk directly, Forsyth bluntly asked him about his own consent to the Treaty of 1816. Black Hawk sternly "denied that any mention was made to him about lands in making the treaty," and claimed the "commissioners must have inserted in the treaty what was not explained to him and [his] friends [in the speeches]."[25]

In all likelihood, Black Hawk and Quashquame believed their assertions to be true. The Presbyterian missionary Cutting Marsh said the Sauk were a people who generally regarded "lying as very bad, and many of them [were] very honest and trusty especially when anything is committed to their charge."[26] Therefore, rather than telling deliberate lies, their statements most likely reflected their honest understanding of the situation as comprehended through the epistemological processes of oral culture. In all oral societies knowledge is transmitted and retained by spoken repetition usually in narrative form. Regular repetition not only perpetuates information but also seems to validate it, while information not repeated with some frequency is quite naturally regarded as unimportant and may often be soon forgotten. Furthermore, because oral societies live essentially in the present, information that lacks present relevance loses validity. One scholar of orality referred to that tendency as a form of "structural amnesia" through which "the integrity of the past" is "subordinate to the integrity of the present" and people reject information they no longer need or wish to know.[27] Therefore, because Quashquame repeated over and over again his claim about the chiefs not selling the land above the Rock River, the Sauk undoubtedly thought that information to be true. Why would he say otherwise? After all, he had been present at St. Louis when the treaty had been made and was therefore thought to have much more credibility than any of the white men who only knew what they read on pieces of paper. Also, because the Sauk had continued to live on the land long after the conferences of 1804 and 1816, and had freely returned to

Saukenuk each spring without any objections from white officials, that certainly must have reinforced their sense of ownership. The land was theirs in every practical and observable way, much more so than was the case with the squatters, who had only recently arrived and occupied what the Sauk had created and cared for through generations of hard work. When the intruders laid claim to that land and government officials, like Forsyth, ordered the Sauk to leave, it must have seemed apparent to the Indians that the white people were trying to fool them with their written words into believing what had always been true had suddenly become false. None of them could be trusted, for, as Black Hawk claimed, he had "not discovered one good trait in the character of the Americans."[28]

In reporting this acrimonious debate to Clark, Forsyth said there had also been three other Sauk chiefs who "spoke very fiercely on the subject and said the land was theirs [and] that they never sold the land." They declared that most vehemently because the land at Saukenuk contained the bones of their ancestors, and for that reason alone they "would defend it as long as they lived." The same speakers also warned Forsyth that the Sauk had alliances with other tribes in the region, who, they claimed, "were ready to assist them at any time in defending their country against any forces whatever." Forsyth was convinced they were not bluffing, and informed Clark that "a number of Chippeways, Ottawas, and Pottawatamies, with some Kickapoos were present [at the talks] and assented to what the Sauk Indians had said."[29] The existence of such a large coalition of tribes caused him deep concern.

Clark immediately apprised Secretary of War John Eaton of those developments, telling him the Sauk who had returned to the old village "were strongly impressed with the belief that they had been defrauded of an immensely valuable country." He also predicted there would be trouble between those Indians and the settlers during the coming summer.[30] A few days later Clark wrote to Eaton again, complaining about being virtually powerless to prevent any such problems, and of possessing no other means but "persuasion" to induce the Indians to remove themselves to the west side of the Mississippi. So far, he said, mere talking had been ineffective. Besides being upset with the Indians and his own lack of power, Clark was irritated with the squatters, whose intrusion made a difficult situation all the more troublesome at a time when discontent was on the rise throughout the upper Mississippi region.[31]

But he and Forsyth were fortunate in that they only had to deal with a disgruntled minority of the tribe. At the time it was only "Black Hawk and a few others" who were causing trouble, and Forsyth gladly informed Clark, "Most of the principal chiefs and braves had gone to live at a place a few miles from the mouth of the Iowa River." There they were establishing a new summertime settlement to replace Saukenuk. Furthermore, the Indian agent was also relieved to report "more than one-half of those . . . at Rocky [sic] river would also go shortly to the same place." There was also encouraging news about the Fox living along the Rock River. Forsyth had learned that they too had decided to move west and establish a new village at the Grand Mascatin.[32] Therefore, by mid-May the problem seemed to be solving itself, and all that remained to be done was to persuade Black Hawk and his faction to give up their futile protest and accept the inescapable necessity of permanently moving west.

Even the Sauk who stubbornly remained at Saukenuk were not all of the same mind. Keokuk, a war chief of considerable influence and importance, had been asked by the principal chiefs of the Iowa River village to accompany the people returning to the old Rock River settlement "to keep things in order if possible." Upon reaching the old village, he had admitted to Forsyth how foolish he thought it was to be returning there. Keokuk also informed Antoine LeClaire, the government interpreter, that he very much disagreed with Quashquame and Black Hawk and all the others who denounced the treaties, saying "that the Sauks who spoke did not know what they were saying, which was the reason he would not have anything to do with their talk."[33]

Forsyth liked Keokuk, who, in 1829, was a handsome man in his early forties with a well-deserved reputation for being a gifted orator. Forsyth described him as "a smart and active Indian," who was a courageous warrior, excellent hunter, and one of the tribe's most important medicine men. His métis mother was the daughter of a Frenchman and was "much attached to the white people," and those attitudes had apparently been passed on to her son, for Forsyth described Keokuk as being "naturally fond of white people." All the same, the Indian agent was quick to point out that Keokuk was also "a good man" who had "the good of his nation at heart and . . . would willingly and unhesitatingly lay down his life for the good of his people if he thought it would avert any great calamity to his nation."[34]

Clark also liked Keokuk and found him useful. Although he recognized and appreciated the man's talents, he also understood his weaknesses and skillfully played upon them. Even Keokuk admitted to some of his own flaws, observing on one occasion that he thought he had been "born to be a great man, but was now too avaricious to be great."[35] Narcissistic about his appearance, he loved to make a grand display of himself, and the well-known western writer Judge James Hall noted that he spared no expense on his dress and elaborate regalia. Keokuk wanted the best and had acquired a large collection of superb horses and very expensive weapons, as well as six wives.[36] Clark pandered to his appetites, giving him expensive gifts and making him feel important, and then used his considerable influence with his tribe to advance American interests and maintain peaceful relations between the Sauk and the other people of the region. Keokuk became Clark's political ally and perhaps even Forsyth's friend, and provided both men with important information they most likely would not have otherwise known. Their relationship worked well for all three of them, and even as early as 1821 Forsyth was confidently predicting to Clark, "If things are well managed[,] in two or three years more his [Keokuk's] word among the Sauks and foxes will be their law."[37]

Not everyone liked Keokuk. Even though James Hall called him "a magnificent savage," Black Hawk despised him and regarded him as a conniving, self-serving, ostentatious dandy who betrayed his own people to gain personal favor with the Americans. In the late spring of 1829, when Keokuk attempted to persuade the people to leave Saukenuk and join the new community on the Iowa River, Black Hawk remarked, "I looked upon him as a coward, and not brave, to abandon his village to be occupied by strangers."[38]

John Spencer, who was one of those strangers, later credited Keokuk's calm and conciliatory actions for making the potentially disastrous summer of 1829 into a rather uneventful season. Indulging in some selective remembering, he claimed Keokuk had persuaded the settlers to fence in their cattle during the nights in order to prevent them from getting into the Indians' gardens and cornfields. That removed the greatest source of potential conflict, suggested Spencer. Only Rinnah Wells refused to cooperate, and his cows continued to get into the Indians' crops until the Sauk turned the tables on him by driving those cattle into Wells's own cornfield. After that, there were no further problems with any wayward critters.

Indeed, recalled Spencer, there was no more trouble of any kind that summer except for when Black Hawk and several young braves smashed the whiskey kegs of a settler who persistently ignored all their reasonable requests to stop selling their rotgut swill to the Indians. Spencer painted a rosy picture of a mostly pleasant season in which the white people tried to help the Indians and everyone lived in a state of near-perfect concord.[39]

Forsyth's account of the same summer was quite different. By June, after many of the Sauk men had left for the summer hunt, Forsyth informed Clark that for those who remained in the village, there were "almost daily quarrels between them and the whites." Also, the whiskey problem got quite out of hand until the Sauk confronted the sellers and threatened to smash their barrels. In the same report he recounted an incident in which a young Indian had confronted a settler after the white man had badly beaten the young man's mother while she had been planting corn. Resenting the young brave's challenge, "the white man presented his rifle to the Indian's breast and shoat him," stated Forsyth. He also described how the whites were fighting among themselves over land and property lines.[40] It was a quarrelsome time and later, when looking back on that season of discontent, Forsyth wrote, "The squatters tried every method to annoy and trouble the Indians, by shooting their dogs, claiming horses not their own, complaining that the Indian horses broke into their cornfields, selling Indians whiskey for the most trifling articles against the wishes and requests of the Indian Chiefs and particularly the Black Hawk who solicited and threatened the Squatters not to sell any whiskey to Indians, but all to no purpose."[41]

Late that spring, the squatters attempted to enlarge the conflict by drawing Illinois governor Ninian Edwards into the squabble. Thirty-two of them, including Spencer, sent off a letter to Edwards in early May, informing him of their "alarming situation" and pleading with him to protect them from "the cruelties and depredations" of the "blood thirsty Savages." They also claimed to have every right to be where they were since they knew the Indians had been "ordered off successively for three years." But alas, they said, the savages had defiantly returned, thrown down their fences, and threatened to kill them and their families, while the military commander at Fort Armstrong, insisting he had no authority to remove the Indians by force, did nothing to protect them. The petitioners pleaded with the governor for help, describing themselves as poor and defenseless folks living in constant fear of meeting the same fate as those unfortunate settlers viciously massacred by the Winnebago two years before near Prairie du Chien. They also told Edwards they suspected some self-serving white people living on Rock Island were encouraging the Indians to commit violent acts against them.[42]

What was the truth? That was becoming increasingly difficult for anyone in the region to ascertain. But it plainly appears that the Americans at Saukenuk were quite deliberately stirring up trouble with the Sauk and then exaggerating the results, playing upon anti-Indian prejudices with the willful intent of getting support from a governor who made no effort to conceal his own contempt for the natives. They wanted the land and had no desire to share it with the original occupants or pay anyone for it.

Black Hawk found the situation intolerable. He complained to Forsyth that the squatters burned down lodges and "ill-treated" Sauk women. But most of all it was the whiskey that infuriated him, and on one occasion he took decisive action against the most offensive of the whiskey sellers who was getting the Sauk men drunk and "cheat[ing] them out of their horses, guns, and traps."[43]

The disturbances at Saukenuk were nevertheless not the only sources of anxiety for white officials that season. In early spring Joseph Street became quite alarmed over the likelihood of a major Indian war erupting throughout the region, and described to Clark the conditions in his own district as being like "a Pandora Box, filled to the brim and ready to fly open at the least mishandling and deluge our frontiers in blood."[44] Then, in late March, an article appeared in the Galena newspaper, the *Miner's Journal,* reporting the Sioux were planning to descend the Mississippi River with a force of four thousand warriors and lay waste to the entire Fever River region. That article produced a sudden panic among the white population, and fears mounted until John Marsh responded in the April 11, 1829, edition assuring people the Sioux had no such intentions.[45]

But Forsyth was not reassured. He continued to hear rumors, which led him to believe a major uprising instigated by the Sioux was imminent, and for that reason he became extremely irritated with the Sauk when their war parties carried out some vicious raids on some Sioux hunting bands. Such reckless action, he feared, could provoke a devastating bloodbath. He therefore worked earnestly with the chiefs who were eager to maintain the peace, and they, in turn, confiscated medicine bags in an effort to discourage their young men from going off on war parties.[46] Nevertheless, determined young braves, passionately eager to gain personal honors, continued to slip away at night to rendezvous with like-minded warriors from the Fox village at Dubuque's Mines, and then to go off together seeking Sioux scalps.[47] Forsyth denounced them, calling them "a most worthless set of fellows."[48] Then, in September, one such war party attacked a Sioux camp near the mouth of the Calumet River, south of the Missouri, and savagely slaughtered sixteen men, women, and children. When asked about the incident, one chief told Forsyth he deeply regretted what had happened but admitted it was "impossible to keep their young men within bounds as they are all so eager for war."[49]

The tribal members who had remained at Saukenuk finally made ready to leave for the winter in late September. Before they departed, Forsyth called them together once again to chide them about the need to cease their dangerous blood feud with the Sioux, and to sternly admonish them not to return to Saukenuk ever again. In a private conversation Keokuk assured him most definitely that he and his relatives would not be coming back in the spring. When all had at last departed, Forsyth must have breathed a deep sigh of relief when informing Clark, "They were gone . . . and I hope never to return again."[50]

No sooner had the Sauk vacated their village than all their land in the lower Rock River valley was put up for sale at the federal land office in Springfield. George Davenport immediately purchased nearly three thousand acres of it. In the end, however, only a few of the squatters purchased small portions of the land they had so acrimoniously squabbled about during the summer.

The winter of 1829–30 proved another harsh ordeal of deep snows, bitter cold, and poor hunting for the Sauk, who, once again, endured considerable hunger in their camps. In the midst of all that, Black Hawk learned of Davenport's purchase of their land at Saukenuk. Looking back and recalling the advice the trader had given him the previous winter about abandoning the old village, he declared, "The reason was now plain to me why he urged us to remove!" He had trusted Davenport and felt betrayed, and in reaction to that treachery became more determined than ever before to hold on to the village. He resolved to return to Saukenuk with his followers in the coming spring, and decided that if there was any attempt to prevent them from reoccupying their village, he would have Davenport,

Forsyth, LeClaire, William Clark, Keokuk, and the commander of Fort Armstrong all killed—"these being the principal persons to blame for endeavoring to remove us," asserted Black Hawk.[51]

In the meantime, as all that was transpiring, vicious intertribal attacks continued to occur. In late October a Sioux man and his Winnebago wife were killed at the American Fur Company post on the Cedar River in central Iowa. The Fox were suspected.[52] Even before then, Street had complained about the Fox and Sauk having killed a Menominee, a Winnebago, and several Sioux, and predicted that if "some forcible interference" in this ongoing bloodletting was not undertaken "on the part of the U.S.," there would be a "dreadful retaliation before next June. . . . Our present course of mediation by words," he declared, "is worse than useless, and only tends to lessen the consequence and influence of the officers of the government with the Indians."[53] He wanted military force employed to impose peace and order on the region in a manner that would restore the government's credibility.

Street was not alone in favoring a get-tough approach to dealing with the Indians. With the coming of spring and the unanticipated return once more of Black Hawk and his band to the Rock River valley, a completely exasperated Thomas Forsyth wrote to Clark, "It would appear to me that nothing but a shew of a few troops will make them move as I have told them that I am done speaking to them on that subject, and in my opinion you would turn this affair over to the American Braves Commanded by the White Beaver (General Atkinson) who all the Indians in the country know very well." Forsyth also strongly recommended a sizable militia force of three or four hundred mounted volunteers, "under the command of judicious officers," be brought in to supplement the pressure applied by Atkinson's regulars in a final concerted effort to force the "mutinous Indians" to abandon Saukenuk once and for all.[54]

Forsyth worried about what might happen if the government did not forcefully take control of the situation, and his anxieties seemed all the more justified when Taimah, the chief of the Fox village at Flint Hill, came to visit during the first week of May. Taimah had been to Prairie du Chien, where, he said, the air was filled with rumors and tension, and where John Marsh had told him the Sioux, Winnebago, and Menominee had all "joined together in confederacy to make war against the Sauks and Foxes."[55] Forsyth found his report credible but suspected white people to be behind the trouble, trying their best, as he said, to "blow the coal of discord among the Indians," in order to provoke a "cruel and barbarous war among the Indians." He told Clark he hoped the Sioux and their allies would back off, for if they attacked, the Sauk and Fox would not be timid in their response. Besides, they too had a powerful alliance with the Kickapoo, Chippewa, Ottawa, and Potawatomi. Therefore, if trouble came, every major tribe in the region would be embroiled in the conflict. It would be catastrophic, he said. "God knows when such a war would end," declared the gravely concerned Thomas Forsyth.[56]

Soon after Taimah's visit to Rock Island, a combined Sauk and Fox war party attacked a Sioux camp on the Blue Earth River, in what was later southern Minnesota, killing ten women and two boys. Almost immediately, Lawrence Taliaferro, the Indian agent to the Sioux at Fort St. Anthony, fired off a letter to Clark, telling him that a war party of five hundred enraged Sioux warriors had come to his agency all "painted [and] prepared for war."[57]

Not long after that, Wyncoop Warner, the Indian affairs subagent residing at Galena, traveled to Prairie du Chien by steamboat to confer with Street about how best to prevent the volatile situation from blowing sky-high. When he arrived, Street was already holding a council with some Winnebago leaders. He asked Warner to join in the discussions. Joseph Rolette, the local American Fur Company agent, was serving as interpreter, and because of his well-known reputation for being a conniver of dishonest deals, Warner suspected him of using his role to further his own interests. Nevertheless, the Winnebago seemed genuinely interested in keeping the peace, and Warner extended to them amicable greetings from the Fox village at Dubuque's Mines.[58] The Winnebago chiefs then asked Warner to return to the Fox and invite them to send a delegation up to Prairie du Chien so they might confer together about averting further bloodshed between them. They especially wanted the subagent to reassure the Fox that the Winnebago "were willing to become friendly, [and] that they need not be afraid to come to the Prairie [du Chien]."[59]

Warner did what he was asked. He returned directly to Dubuque's Mines. When he arrived there, however, he found virtually everyone drunk. He waited. Eventually some of the Fox leaders sobered up enough to talk with him and expressed a willingness to meet with the Winnebago at Prairie du Chien. They said they would leave for there on April 24.

Having accomplished his mission, Warner returned home to Galena, arriving back on April 15. As soon as he got home he wrote to Street, excited by the possibilities and telling him the "Foxes seem[ed] very anxious to be at peace," and indicated they would arrive at Prairie du Chien on April 28.[60] Warner also urged Street to encourage the Menominee to become participants in those impending peace talks.

Street replied to Warner on April 22, telling him how delighted he was about the Fox's good intentions, but some of his message was peculiarly ambivalent. He began by reassuring Warner there would be no trouble between the Winnebago and Fox when they came up, and indicated the Menominee would "perhaps" join the discussions. Also, with an unmistakable tone of optimism, Street told Warner, "I have strong hope of entirely drawing off the Winnebagoes from the war." Nevertheless, he admitted some of their young men were still likely to join the Sioux, who continued to feel a deep hostility toward the Fox. Therefore, he advised Warner to tell the Fox going to Prairie du Chien to "be on their guard against the Sioux." Then, in a strangely equivocating pronouncement, Street said: "Whether it will be better for the Foxes to come up, I cannot say—the Winnebagoes and Menominees would not molest them. The Winnebagoes say . . . let the Foxes come up and see us and we will speak with them as brothers and not hurt them." Street ended by leaving the final decision completely up to Warner, saying, "Do as you deem best." [61]

Warner never received that letter. He had already departed for Dubuque's Mines when it arrived in Galena.[62] Street later lied about its contents, asserting in a written deposition that he had considered Warner's plan to bring the Fox up to Prairie du Chien to be "imprudent, and that it would be extremely impolitic to bring the Indians together under the existing high state of excitement amongst them." He also claimed to have clearly informed Warner that he "did not think it advisable to bring the Foxes up—but he must act as he saw fit."[63]

Warner returned to Dubuque's Mines on April 24, only to have the Fox inform him that they were not prepared to leave for Prairie du Chien just then. (Street later claimed the Fox were all drunk once again, but Warner made no mention of that.) After Warner conferred with Kettle Chief, it was decided that the subagent should go on ahead by himself in order to arrive by the start of the meeting, so the Winnebago and Menominee would not misinterpret the Foxes' tardiness as a sign of indifference toward peace. Warner arrived at Prairie du Chien on the designated date of April 28. As soon as he landed, Street asked if he had received his letter of April 22. Warner told him he had not. Street then informed him that some of the Menominee villages had refused to accept the wampum sent to them by the Fox. He suspected trouble was brewing, and advised Warner to hurry back and tell the Fox it would be unwise for them to come to Prairie du Chien at that time.[64]

Street later testified that Warner had come up by steamboat and then waited two or three days at Prairie du Chien to catch a return voyage on the same vessel. Warner himself indicated he had arrived by canoe but had in fact waited three or four days for a steamboat to take him back downriver. On the journey south Warner stopped briefly at Cassville. There he spoke with two men, Wayman and Holly by name, and asked them if they had seen a group of Fox Indians paddling north. They had not, they said. He then requested they be on the lookout, and if they saw the Fox, they should tell them not to go on to Prairie du Chien. Warner then resumed his southward journey. Sometime later the Fox stopped at Cassville, where Wayman and Holly gave them the message to turn back, but, the two men said, "they paid no attention and proceeded on."[65]

Street blamed Warner for not warning the Fox, asserting that the sub-agent had never even stopped at Dubuque's Mines on his return trip, as he should have, but rather passed right by the community on his way to Galena. Street also claimed he knew on good authority that Wyncoop Warner had been so drunk he had not even been conscious enough to notice when the steamboat passed by the Fox village. Indeed, Street blamed Warner for mishandling the entire situation.[66]

The Fox delegation, suspecting nothing, pushed on upriver toward Prairie du Chien. There were eighteen members of the party in all, traveling in three or four canoes, and they included three chiefs—Piemosky and his brothers Kettle Chief and Cut Head—as well as one woman and a fourteen-year-old boy. All the others were warriors. On May 5, about noon, they stopped and went ashore on the east side of the Mississippi, a few miles below the mouth of the Wisconsin River. They planned to rest and eat a meal before completing the journey, but as they were unloading their canoes they were brutally attacked by a large war party of Sioux and Menominee warriors. The strike came as a complete surprise. None of the Fox were armed, and all of them, except for the boy, were killed in a matter of minutes. He alone was spared, theorized Forsyth, because he was half Winnebago. All the same, the attackers broke one of the boy's arms and pushed him out into the river in a canoe and told him to go home and tell his village what the Sioux and Menominee had done.[67]

Following the massacre, the Sioux and Menominee returned to Prairie du Chien. There they "presented a horrid appearance," remarked John Fonda, a settler from New York who had moved to Prairie du Chien two years before. Fonda described how the returning Indians "were painted for war, and had smeared themselves with blood, and carried fresh scalps on poles." But it was more than scalps they brought back. They had not simply killed the Fox. They had also savagely mutilated their bodies. "Some had cut off a head and thrust a stick in the throttle, and held it on high—some carried a hand, arm, leg or *some other portion of a body,* as trophies of their success," reported Fonda. After parading through the settlement, they began to dance and celebrated their victory with considerable noise until the commander at Fort Crawford ordered them to move to an island in the Mississippi. They did so and continued their macabre revelry there long into the night.[68] They roasted Kettle Chief's heart and cut it into pieces, which, as if in some dark and primal sacrament, they devoured in order to give themselves greater courage.[69] Elizabeth Baird, the métis daughter of a Scottish trader and Winnebago mother, and the wife of Green Bay attorney Henry Baird, was there at the time visiting her old hometown and said she "saw sights too terrible to be told" that day.[70]

Soon after the bloody, surprise attack, some of the Fox from Dubuque's Mines rushed off to Saukenuk, to tell their old allies they had seen Sioux warriors skulking about their village preparing to attack. In mid-May Forsyth informed Clark that a Sauk war party of eighty to one hundred warriors had gone north "for the purpose of assisting the Fox Indians to defend themselves, or [to] bring them all away, as necessity required."[71] At the same time, news of the Sioux attack on the Fox peace delegation provoked a state of crisis among all the Sauk and Fox villages as far south as the Iowa River. Soon there was a gathering of the principal chiefs at Rock Island, where a well-armed force of at least three hundred Sauk warriors joined them. They came thundering in on horseback, extremely agitated and eager for vengeance. Loud and insistent demands were made for ruthless retaliation. But Forsyth, using all his well-honed diplomatic skills, was eventually able to quiet them down and restrain them from madly rushing off to war.

Then, on the morning of May 15, the crisis abruptly ended. All the chiefs went to Forsyth and informed him they had decided to return home in peace.[72] No explanation was given. As that was occurring, the Fox people at Dubuque's Mines evacuated their village and resettled down-river, at a site directly across from Fort Armstrong on the west side of the Mississippi. They felt more secure there close to the Sauk, while the Sioux were on the prowl, hunting for scalps and more Fox hearts to eat.

Immediately, however, the situation became even more complicated and potentially dangerous. When the Fox abandoned their village at Dubuque's Mines, the vacuum they left behind was quickly filled by a mob of white miners who rushed over the river to take possession of the Indians' mines. Clark reported what was happening to the Indian Office in Washington. "I am just informed," he told McKenney, "that a large party of white men from the country above Galena crossed over and took posses-sion of the Fox mines called debuck [sic] Mines, immediately after they (the Foxes) had moved from that place."[73]

That rash, greed-driven trespass upon Fox land disturbed Forsyth most deeply. By the first of June he observed that the Sauk and Fox had reached their boiling point and "were disposed to do almost any thing for revenge."[74] Also, Forsyth did not hesitate to admit he "trembled" when contemplating what the consequences of the white invasion of Dubuque's Mines might be, and ruminated about how all things seemed to be con-spiring against the peace. Resentments toward the whites, and fear of sur-prise attacks from tribal enemies, as well as widespread distrust among all the groups within the region, had been accumulating for some time, build-ing into a great emotional thunderhead, which Forsyth felt certain would soon bring on a terrible storm of violence to the entire upper Mississippi valley.[75] But in an effort to stave that off, he told Clark, "I shall by all means keep the Fox Indians now near this place in ignorance of the white people having taken possession of their mines, for it appears to me, if they knew it, blood would be shed."[76] Deliberate deception had become a nec-essary part of his strategy to maintain some control over the increasingly volatile situation.

Behind all those developments Forsyth detected a foul smell of con-spiracy. He was certain the Sioux and Menominee had been tipped off about the plans of the Fox peace delegation. "A lot of people at Prairie du Chien must have known about the Fox coming up and also about the

Sioux, Winnebago, and Menomonee plot to attack them," he informed Clark. Then he cynically observed how no one had ever bothered to warn the Fox of the dangers awaiting them on the river.[77] A little later, he wrote to Clark again, describing the paranoid mood of the Sauk and Fox, and how they were convinced an evil plot, involving both whites and Indians, had been devised against them. Forsyth admitted he found their claims quite credible, as they had presented to him considerable evidence and even the names of individuals engaged in such intrigues. Nevertheless, he told Clark he thought it would be imprudent of him to mention in a letter anything of "what the Indians say about the conduct of some white people . . . whom they blame for the loss of their chiefs and others of their people by their Indian enemies." But before signing off, the old Indian agent predicted that the "day may come when that nefarious affair may be known to the world."[78]

Much later—in fact, more than two years after the actual events of that spring—Forsyth wrote a long letter to William H. Ashley, an old fur trade acquaintance then serving in the U.S. Senate, revealing to him his suspicions about the killing of the Fox peace delegation. "General Street furnished the trap," he asserted, and "Mr. [Joseph] Rolette set it and completely caught them." Furthermore, he pointed out that Lawrence Taliaferro, the agent at Fort St. Anthony, had met with the very same Sioux war party that would carry out the massacre just before it set off downriver, and gave them ammunition and provisions. The Sioux had told Taliaferro where they were going and what they intended to do, but Forsyth claimed the Indian agent had made no effort to dissuade them from their bloody mission, nor did he make any attempt to warn the unsuspecting, unarmed Fox. Accordingly, Forsyth declared to Ashley, he felt "both Street and Taliaferro ought to have been made to account for the evil doings in . . . fomenting the murdering of inoffensive Indians unarmed and going on the invitation from a Government agent to make peace." But no such accountability was ever demanded, because, he charged, William Clark had suppressed what Forsyth called the entire "truth of that shameful affair."[79] Once again, the truth had been a victim of self-interest and political intrigue.

Wyncoop Warner reinforced those suspicions about plots and conspiracies. He wrote Forsyth in early June of 1830 and told him about the white miners who had moved into the Fox village at Dubuque's Mines and were "determined to remain there." He also said he had heard rumors that "Mr. [Henry] Gratiot had gone over with forty men to take possession" of the mines and that he was a participant in "a concerted plan to dispossess the Indians for that purpose."[80]

Lies and plots and violent deeds had come to dominate the affairs of the upper Mississippi region by the summer of 1830, and everyone there was caught in a thickening web of duplicity and distrust. Disaster seemed all too certain.

5

BANISHED

———————

Exiled I make a vow to be what I don't know
to a land I haven't inherited, while the old homeland,
the one that becomes extinct in the distance, survives
only in my mouth, in the flavors I long for,
in the mother tongue I teach to my children.

Ana Doina, "The Extinct Homeland—
a Conversation with Czeslaw Milosz"

ALL THE STORM and stress, brought on by intertribal conflicts and increasing friction between the native people and white intruders, threatened terrible consequences for everyone in the region. And following the ugly massacre of the Fox peace delegation on its way to Prairie du Chien, it was evident that talk alone would not be sufficient to prevent the complete disintegration of what fragile order still remained. Trust was gone. Military force seemed the only means left to avert catastrophe.

The intrigues and backbiting politics of the situation certainly took their toll on the personnel of the Indian service. John Marsh, who had personally disliked Joseph Street from the start, and whom Street considered far too biased toward the Sioux due to the influence of his Sioux-métis wife, was fired as the subagent at Prairie du Chien in the spring of 1829. After that, it was Wyncoop Warner's turn to fall. His ambiguous involvement in the Fox massacre incident sealed his fate. In May of 1830 Clark wrote to Secretary of War James Eaton, pointing out that Warner had "lost the confidence of the Fox and needed to be removed." In June Warner was discharged and William S. Williamson appointed to take his place as sub-agent in the Fever River area. Then, that same summer, Thomas Forsyth was dismissed. Forsyth had grown increasingly critical of Clark, and his letters sometimes bristled with the irritation and distrust he felt toward his supervisor, whom he regarded as lazy, self-serving, and dishonest. Clark, on the other hand, had become ever more frustrated with Forsyth's insubordinate attitude and his refusal to remain at his Rock River post throughout the year. Each fall, when the Sauk departed for their winter hunting grounds, Forsyth flagrantly defied Clark's wishes and went home to his family in St. Louis, and usually did not return to his post until late April. Therefore, when the springtime troubles of 1830 began, Forsyth had not been on the job. Clark complained to officials in Washington, and in early June McKenney wrote back, telling him Secretary Eaton would soon send Forsyth a letter of dismissal. Later on, when checking with a friend in the War Department about the reasons for his firing, Forsyth was told there was nothing in his file at the Indian Office critical of his job performance other than a letter from Clark, written in April of 1830, complaining about his "continued absence from his post."[1]

After eighteen years of service, fifty-nine-year-old Thomas Forsyth was unceremoniously cashiered, and Felix St. Vrain, a thirty-one-year-old sawmill operator from Kaskaskia, was appointed to take his place. Although St. Vrain had almost no experience in dealing with Indians, he was a member of a politically important St. Louis French family and a good friend of U.S. senator Elias Kent Kane. Kane, in turn, was a close acquaintance of William Clark's, and it was Kane who recommended St. Vrain to Clark for the position.

Felix St. Vrain traveled up to his Rock Island agency that October in order to acquaint himself with the lay of the land. After looking around and talking with people, he sent Clark a message—telling him exactly what he had no desire to hear. He informed Clark he had reliable information that Black Hawk and his followers, whom Forsyth had persistently tried to persuade to abandon Saukenuk, were once again "determined to return to it [Saukenuk] in the spring for the purpose of keeping possession" of the fields, lodges, and graves.[2] Indeed, St. Vrain talked directly with Black Hawk himself, and from what he heard, he, like Forsyth before him, strongly advised that armed force be used to put a halt to the Sauk returning to their old village ever again. Felix St. Vrain was convinced that strong and unambiguous action was long overdue. "As those Indians have been threatened several times to be driven away and those threats not put into effect, it would be useless for me to say anything to them on the subject, unless a sufficient number of Troops should be ordered to prevent them from taking possession in the spring," he declared to Clark.[3]

Just a few months before that, Forsyth had complained about the same lack of forceful government action, saying it was most unfortunate that nothing had been done to remove the "mutinous Indians" from the old village, and pointing out that "to use threats to the Indians and not put them into execution" was, in his view, "doing worse than nothing."[4] In a later analysis Forsyth noted that even the Sauk chiefs from the Iowa River village had also urged the use of military force to remove the Black Hawk band, and although Clark had been well aware of those recommendations, he had done nothing to implement them. As a consequence, observed Forsyth, "Black Hawk and party thought the whole matter of removing [them] from his old village had blown over . . . and in the spring of 1831 the Black Hawk and party were augmented by many Indians from Iowa River." That additional support from within the tribe, Forsyth continued, "made the Black Hawk proud and [he] supposed nothing more would be done about removing him and his party."[5]

Many people in Illinois agreed with the old Indian agent on that score, and they too advocated the use of force to remove the Sauk from the state as soon as possible. In January of 1831 Judge R. M. Young of the northern Illinois circuit court, along with three lawyers from Galena, informed Governor John Reynolds about how the Indians from the old village on the Rock River had committed all manner of insults and injuries against the settlers in that same area the previous autumn. Those offenses, they claimed, included an attempt to murder two of Rinnah Wells's sons, as well as the killing and stealing of a considerable number of the settlers' horses, hogs, and cattle. Grievances pertaining to such malicious actions were "almost universal" in their part of the state, they claimed. But what concerned them most, pointed out the petitioners, was the angry declaration made by one of the Indian leaders, who announced as the Sauk were departing for their western hunting grounds that "they should return in the spring and raise corn in the White Peoples fields."[6]

Similar complaints about Indians—presumably the Sauk—shooting hogs and cattle, stealing horses, and cutting down much-valued maple trees were also sent to Reynolds by residents of Knox and Hancock counties. In one account the writer indicated that "women and children have been greatly alarmed in consequence of the insolent demeanor of the Indians." In one particular case the threat to women had allegedly become quite serious. Parnack Owen, a settler in Knox County, told the governor that an Indian had gone to the house of a Mr. Morris and there had "laid hands on his wife, and committed violence upon her person," so that the much frightened Mrs. Morris "believed he intended to violate her chastity."[7]

Reynolds reacted swiftly to those complaints and immediately referred them to the General Assembly, wherein a special committee was formed to deal with the Indian problems. Then, without conducting any investigation to determine the facts, the committee sent a resolution to the state legislature in mid-January, expressing utter outrage about the many assaults and the "constant state of alarm" caused by the Indians throughout the northern section of the state. They also identified "the well known War Chief called the 'Black Hawk'" as the leading villain and claimed that he had clearly declared his intentions of retaining possession of land north of the Rock River "by force of arms, if necessary." In their resolution, which was resoundingly passed and sent on to the secretary of war, they called upon the president and federal government to provide military protection for the people of the frontier region, and to employ whatever means might be necessary for the removal of all the Indians from Illinois as expeditiously as possible.[8]

President James Monroe had introduced the idea of Indian removal to the Congress in December of 1825, asking it to develop a "well-digested plan" for the resettlement of the tribes still living east of the Mississippi into the unsettled territory west of the great river. Because he thought such a policy was urgently needed for the survival and future well-being of the native people, he insisted it be carried out in a humane manner without the use of force. Coercive methods, he insisted, would be "revolting to humanity and utterly unjustifiable." Therefore, the Indians would have to be persuaded to move.[9] Thomas McKenney was soon convinced, as he said, that the "removal of the Indians west of the Mississippi [was] the only measure" still left, which could "preserve them" from extinction.[10] In time, however, both he and Lewis Cass concluded that the humanitarian goals of the policy could not be achieved "without some species of compulsion." Indeed, because the Indians had not voluntarily

participated in their own salvation and seemed incapable of even understanding what was in their own best interest, Cass claimed that the government had a moral duty to assume a paternalistic responsibility for them.
"We must judge for them, and act for them," he said, and "nothing but the
display of a respectable force, and the vigorous execution of the system"
could deliver them from complete ruin and death.[11]

But ruin and death were precisely what the Sauk seemed to be facing
in their hunting camps west of the Mississippi during the harsh winter of
1830–31. The hunting itself was unusually poor due to the severe cold and
heavy snows, and also because so many of the Sauk hunters had traded
away their guns and traps for whiskey. At a brief conference held by a few
of the Sauk and Fox at the Iowa River subagency in February, Matosee,
identified as a "principal chief," complained about their wretched conditions. "We are poor and distressed, our people are imposed upon by our
Traders," he asserted. Plumb Chief also indignantly repeated those accusations and protested about being tricked and manipulated by traders,
demanding of Andrew Hughes, the subagent there: "Why do you allow us
to be made poor—our Traders cheat and impose upon us?"[12]

For Black Hawk himself, it was also a hard season of soul-searching and
discontent. He fasted with unusual severity and called upon the Great
Spirit for guidance because he felt a great many people were turning
against him. Keokuk opposed him at every turn, it seemed, doing anything
he could to discredit him. All the white people who had once been his
friends adamantly urged him to give up any further thought of ever returning to Saukenuk again and grew exasperated whenever he voiced his desire
to retain the tribal lands in the Rock River valley. "I was in deep sorrow" and
"began to doubt whether I had a friend among them," he confessed.[13]

But he was not completely forsaken. In his gloom there was one ray of
light, for he observed, "All the women were on my side, on account of the
corn-fields."[14] The land at the new village on the Iowa River had been
almost impossible to break and cultivate with their hoes. Even with plows
it would have been an arduous task. And the tough, unyielding soil had
produced only a meager crop of corn that previous summer, which, in
turn, resulted in hunger in their winter camps. They had never before
experienced such want in all the years the women had cultivated their
fields at Saukenuk, and therefore, many of those women sided with Black

Hawk and demanded a return to the old village with the coming of spring. They were convinced their survival depended on it.

Perhaps due mostly to those harsh conditions and the sense of desperation they produced, Black Hawk and his band, against all advice and pressure to the contrary, returned to Saukenuk in April of 1831. Clark informed the secretary of war that the band contained between 300 and 400 warriors, thus making the size of the whole group somewhere between 1,200 to 1,600 people, and considerably larger than the year before.[15] St. Vrain, LeClaire, and Davenport were all there to meet them when they arrived, and immediately urged Black Hawk to turn around and leave right then and there for the Iowa River village. In fact, in his initial encounter with LeClaire, Black Hawk admitted, "The interpreter . . . gave me so many good reasons [for leaving again], that I almost wished I had not undertaken the difficult task that I had pledged myself to my brave band to perform."[16] St. Vrain warned him that troops would surely be sent to drive them out, and Davenport scolded him for causing such great distress to the women and children. Davenport also asked him what it would take for him to give up the land and leave. In response, Black Hawk stated he "could honorably give up, by being paid for it," according to their customs.[17] Apparently even a righteous traditionalist like Black Hawk had his price, but he ironically explained to Davenport that he could not propose a cash settlement for to do so would not be "honorable." Therefore, he asked Davenport to do it for him. Davenport agreed to make an offer to William Clark, and when he suggested a sum of six thousand dollars, saying the money could be used to purchase badly needed provisions for the band, Black Hawk agreed. The proposal was sent to Clark on the very next steamboat heading to St. Louis. The whole scheme was carried out quite surreptitiously and Black Hawk admitted: "I did not let my people know what had taken place, for fear they would be displeased. I did not like what had been done myself, and tried to banish it from my mind." In the end, however, nothing came of the proposal. Clark's reply arrived on the next steamboat that docked at Rock Island, and the answer was an emphatic "NO." He would make no deals nor pay any price for land that was no longer the Sauk's to sell, and he warned Black Hawk to leave the old village quickly and with no further fuss, or he and his followers would be driven out at gunpoint.[18]

But even with that stern rebuke from Clark, Black Hawk remained stubbornly determined to hold fast and not be moved. "I now resolved to remain in my village, and make no resistance, if the military came, but submit to my fate," he declared. He said he planned no violent resistance, and, in fact, instructed his followers to remain passive if the soldiers came and "not to raise an arm against them."[19]

It did not take long for the settlers to let out their howls of protest. On April 30, thirty-seven men sent an angry petition to Reynolds. They said the Indians were threatening their lives and demanded protection. In fact, the petitioners informed the governor that the Indians were behaving in an "outrageous and menacing manner" and were "determined to extermi-nate" all the white people who were occupying their land. Furthermore, they complained that neither the Indian agent nor Major John Bliss, the commander of Fort Armstrong, would come to their defense. Because of that, they claimed to be in desperate need of the armed protection of the state.[20]

That message was sent off with expectations of fast results. But to their disappointment they anxiously waited for nearly three weeks—until May 19—without receiving any response whatsoever. By then, having become extremely annoyed with Reynolds's inaction, twenty-one of them, includ-ing eight who had not signed the first petition, sent Benjamin F. Pike off as their personal emissary to carry a new statement of grievances to the governor.[21]

While that was happening, St. Vrain told Clark he remained hopeful the Sauk could be persuaded to leave voluntarily so that military force would be unnecessary.[22] Toward the end of May he wrote to Clark again, concerning the complaints the settlers had sent to Reynolds. Most of their charges, he asserted, were either false or gross exaggerations, and he sug-gested their petitions had created a highly distorted picture of what was really happening. Without denying there were some problems, St. Vrain nevertheless pointed out that most of the troubles were "occasioned in a great measure by whisky being given to the Indians in exchange for their guns, traps, etc."[23] Also, while the settlers accused the Indians of burning down their fences, St. Vrain informed Clark that only one fence had been burned and it had "caught fire by accident." As for the accusations that the Indians were destroying their wheat, the Indian agent made it clear that the only destruction of wheat had occurred when the settlers themselves had forgotten to put a fence back up after pulling it down to haul a load of timber through, and their own horses had gone into the field, where they trampled and devoured the crop. The situation was not nearly as bad as the settlers wanted the outside world to believe, St. Vrain told Clark.[24]

Regardless of what the truth may have been, Reynolds took action. On May 26 he informed Clark he had called up a force of seven hundred militia volunteers to protect the citizens of the state from the "invasion and depredations" of the hostile Sauk, and the men of that force would summarily remove those renegades from Illinois—"peaceably, if they can, but forcibly if they must," either "dead or a live," declared the governor. The militia would be assembled at Beardstown, on the Illinois River, and made ready to march within about fifteen days, he predicted, suggesting to Clark that would be sufficient time for him and his agents to persuade the Indians to remove themselves before it was too late. If they failed to do so, the armed might of Reynolds's frontier army would make short work of the problem, he informed the Indian superintendent.[25]

John Reynolds, who had become governor of Illinois just the year before and seemed caught up in a perpetual quest for personal attention, thought of himself, and was eager to be thought of by others, as a tough-minded man of action. He was good-looking, in his early forties, tall, in fine physical shape, with a long, narrow, weather-creased face, and had a reputation for being a self-made success who had come up the hard way in life. Born in Pennsylvania in 1788, he had spent his early years in Tennessee, where Indians had menaced his family, and perhaps because of that had grown up to be an inveterate Indian hater. But politics was his strongest passion, and in Illinois, where everyone was a Jacksonian Democrat, Reynolds convincingly played the role of the outspoken advocate of the common man. He was amiable enough and had the ability to mingle and glad-hand his way among the voters, and liked being called the "Old Ranger," a nickname he had picked up while in the militia during the War of 1812. But even with all those skills and assets, he had fought a hard election campaign in 1830 in order to win, and once in office had exploited the Indian issue to broaden his popularity and enhance his own rugged, machismo image.

Two days after informing Clark of his intention to mobilize the militia, Reynolds wrote to Major General Edmund P. Gaines, commander of the army's entire Western Department, informing him that the northwestern part of Illinois had been "invaded by a hostile band of the Sacks Indians, headed by the Black hawk." He also let the general know he had called up the militia to protect the people and repel that invasion. Reynolds simply asked Gaines to cooperate with those efforts.[26]

Suddenly there was a fast flurry of letters. Clark wrote to Reynolds on May 28, telling him he had made every effort, many times over, to persuade the Sauk to vacate their old village, but to no avail, implying that any further efforts to reason with them would be a waste of time. The same day both Clark and Reynolds wrote to General Gaines, and the next day— May 29—Gaines sent a short note back to Reynolds, informing him he had ordered six companies of regular army troops stationed at Jefferson Barracks to make preparations to move out for the Rock River valley on the morning of May 30. Gaines was clearly making his move to take control of the situation, and was trying to do so swiftly, before Reynolds and the Illinois militia could get involved. He told Reynolds he would handle the Indians on his own and that as the situation then stood he did not "deem it necessary or proper to require militia, or any other description of force, other than that of the regular army."[27] At the same time, Gaines wrote to Roger Jones, the adjutant general of the army, telling him he would not call on the militia unless there was an outbreak of major hostilities involving numerous tribes. The less the amateur soldiers of the militia were involved, the better it would be for everyone, he suggested.[28]

Gaines was a man with a stern look about him, with high cheekbones, a thin-lipped mouth, heavy brows, almond-shaped eyes, and a great tawny, lionlike mane of hair. He was fifty-four years old and had plenty of experience with Indians as a result of his service in the War of 1812, and even more so from his time with Andrew Jackson in the campaigns against the Creeks and Seminoles. Although not personally in favor of the removal policy, he was a professional soldier fully prepared to do his duty. However, in assembling his forces at Jefferson Barracks in late May, he seemed more intent on preventing Reynolds and his Illinois volunteers from heavy-handedly provoking a major Indian war than on coercing the Sauk into a westward retreat from their old village.

The general and his small army set off from St. Louis around midnight on May 30, aboard the steamboat *Winnebago*. He had six infantry companies, two light cannons, enough salt pork for fifteen days, and a month's supply of hard tack. If a need arose for additional troops, Gaines was prepared to get them from among the regulars stationed at Fort Crawford.[29]

Lieutenant George McCall, a graduate of West Point, had been appointed General Gaines's aide-de-camp just a few months before. He was twenty-nine years old and maintained a close relationship with his father. As a result, a great deal of what happened on the expedition was captured in his richly detailed correspondence home. Their first night on the Mississippi was, for Lieutenant McCall, like a passage into an enchanted land. The river was bathed in the soft, silvery light of the full moon, treeless prairie on one side and "dark and flowing woodland" on the other, and the warm late-spring air was filled with the fragrance of thousands and thousands of wildflowers.[30] They arrived at Fort Armstrong on June 4, and once the troops had landed, all the settlers were moved into the stockade and all their horses and cattle driven over onto Rock Island for safekeeping. The next day Gaines held a general council with the Sauk leaders. By then both Keokuk and Wapello had arrived from the Iowa River village.

Before any of that happened, but fully aware that troops were on the way, Black Hawk once again consulted with Wabokieshiek, the Winnebago Prophet. When he did so, the Prophet told him of another of his visionary dreams and assured Black Hawk nothing bad would happen and that none of his people would be harmed as a consequence of the coming of General Gaines, whom he referred to as the "great war chief." According to Black Hawk, Wabokieshiek's dream had revealed the general's primary purpose was simply to frighten the Sauk into leaving their old village so that the white people might get the land for nothing.[31] All Black Hawk and his followers needed to do, the Prophet advised him, was to stay calm and peaceful, remaining where they were and offering no resistance to the soldiers, who, in the end, would not force them to abandon their land if they did not put up a fight.[32]

Black Hawk's response to the Prophet's advice was oddly ambivalent. When the council called by Gaines first convened on the morning of June 5, there was an almost palpable feeling of tension in the air, and Black Hawk was nowhere to be seen. Then, just as people were settling in for the opening session, there came a dramatic outburst of noise. Approaching the council house were Black Hawk and a large group of his followers, all painted and armed "as if going to battle," loudly and defiantly singing war songs. Black Hawk himself described how they came with "lances, spears, war clubs, and bows and arrows" and entered the council house with "a war-like appearance."[33] It was a sight that struck fear into everyone in the hall. Spencer said there were between seventy-five and a hundred painted and chanting warriors and "those who understood the Indians best, thought from the singing and the manner of the Indians, that there would be a general massacre."[34] Their appearance made McCall decidedly uneasy. "They approached the council house, bounding from the earth and whooping, in all the extravagance of the war dance. We observed too that they were much more completely armed than is usual on such occasions," he told his father. He also said he noticed how even the "old traders" were quite fearful, and that some of them later told him "never before at a similar scene did they see so strong a demonstration of hostility as on this occasion."[35]

But it was all for show. Black Hawk said later he had intended no violence but only wished to demonstrate that they "were not afraid." Nevertheless, once again the message was confusing and the truth of the matter far from clear.[36]

Whatever his intentions may have been, a mood of undisguised hostility carried over into the conference itself. There was no mistaking it, for as soon as the proceedings got under way one of Black Hawk's principal braves, Kinnekonnesaut (He-who-strikes-first), jumped to his feet and challenged Gaines just as the general was shuffling his notes and preparing to make his opening remarks. "When white men talk, they talk from paper; but when Red men have any thing to say, they speak from the heart," chided Kinnekonnesaut. Once again the deep gulf existing between the people of the oral tradition and those who were literate and white was revealed with the unambiguous implication that written words were filled with trickery and lies.[37] Gaines became visibly irritated and made a clumsy, unconvincing response, and then proceeded to read his written address, appearing to the Sauk unwilling, or perhaps even unable, to speak to them man-to-man from the heart. To the audience it seemed a contrived performance, insincere and full of hollow words that were not really his own. They distrusted Gaines's intentions. "How smooth must be the language of the whites, when they can make right look like wrong, and wrong like right," Black Hawk cynically observed.[38] In the end, Gaines's fumbling attempt to address them using prepared written remarks made it all too obvious he understood none of the issues implicit in Kinnekonnesaut's challenge. Indeed, he showed little understanding of the Indians themselves.

Gaines began by scolding the audience. Then, in a condescending tone, he proclaimed his "fatherly" displeasure with what he called their "improper conduct," and pedantically instructed them on the treaties, which, he said, they had knowingly agreed to and through which they had freely relinquished their claims to the land on which Saukenuk was located. He also told them that due to the troubles they had caused for the settlers, he could no longer permit them to remain anywhere east of the Mississippi. When his tirade was finished, Quashquame again protested, repeating his well-worn arguments, but to no avail. Then, before being impolitely dismissed, to add further emphasis to the Indians' suspicions of the white man's written words, the old chief acerbically added, "I am a red skin & do not use paper at a talk, but my words are in my heart, & I do not forget what has been said."[39]

On the second day of the meeting, Keokuk spoke. He complained about the Sioux making life exceedingly difficult and dangerous for them west of the Mississippi, and also mentioned that it was already far too late in the season to plant and raise another corn crop in a new location, suggesting the people be allowed to remain at Saukenuk to harvest the corn they had already planted in their old fields. But Gaines held firm. He told them in no uncertain terms "that if the Band did not move in a few days, they would be visited by the troops & driven off."[40]

During the third and final day, Black Hawk also raised the issue of the cornfields. He told the general that the Sauk women, "having worked their fields till they had become easy to cultivate, were now unwilling to leave them; & that they had decided not to move."[41] Immediately after Black Hawk made those remarks, an "ill-looking woman" arose to speak, said Lieutenant McCall.[42] She was the daughter of Mat-ta-tas, one of the old village chiefs, and had been selected by the women of the band to speak on their behalf. The Prophet had recommended they do so after claiming to have received another message from the spiritual powers in a dream. In her short speech she declared the land—especially the cornfields and gardens— actually belonged to the women rather than the whole tribe, and let it be known that the women had never sold any of the land nor consented to the transfer of it to the United States. She also said she hoped they would be allowed to remain at Saukenuk long enough to gather in the crops they had planted. Much hard work had already been done to grow food for their families, she explained, and then asserted, "If we are driven from our village without being allowed to save our corn, many of our little children must perish with hunger."[43]

Gaines remained unmoved. He gave the Sauk three days to vacate the village. He did agree, however, to provide them with corn enough in October to replace the harvest they might have otherwise gathered from their old fields.[44]

According to George McCall, Gaines felt confident about having enough soldiers to drive the Sauk from their village if the need arose, but knew he could not secure the entire frontier region against any widespread Indian reprisals without the assistance of a large number of mounted troops.[45] The general had tried to get reinforcements from Fort Crawford, but the four infantry companies there refused to leave until replaced by soldiers from Fort Winnebago. That would take far too long.[46] Gaines also knew full well the Sauk could be a most formidable enemy if forced to fight. In fact, McCall said they were "perhaps the most warlike, and the fiercest as well as most determined Indians" in the whole country.[47] On top of all that, there was concern about the possibility of the Prophet's people, along with some of the Potawatomi and Kickapoo, rising up in support of Black Hawk's band. For all those reasons, Gaines finally broke down and asked John Reynolds for help. He wrote to Reynolds on June 5, even while the conference with the Sauk was still in session, and requested a battalion of mounted volunteers be sent to Rock Island as soon as possible.[48]

The governor and his men were eager for action. Always the politician, Reynolds had stirred up anti-Indian feelings among the citizens of the state by printing and distributing carefully selected portions of the petitions sent to him by the agitated settlers of the northwestern counties. When that information predictably provoked hostile public reactions, Reynolds somewhat disingenuously said he found the intensity of the "war-spirit" among the people quite "astonishing."[49] Maybe he was also astonished when three times as many men volunteered for militia service as he had called for, despite the fact it was a particularly busy time on the farms.

The volunteers came flocking into Beardstown from all direction and kept coming until June 10. Many showed up without firearms of any kind.[50] The federal government quickly sent weapons from Jefferson Barracks, and others were purchased by the state from a Mr. Earnst, a Beardstown merchant who just happened to have a large supply of muskets on hand.[51] The frontier army, once armed and assembled, contained about fifteen hundred mounted militiamen under the command of Joseph Duncan, a congressman Reynolds had transformed into a brigadier general. But because provisions and wagons took time to procure, it was not until June 15 that all were prepared and ready to move out. When the marching commenced, the column extended for more than a mile.

Most of the men, remarked Reynolds, "hated Indians" and eagerly "wanted fun," which meant they were keenly anticipating the opportunity to hunt, kill, and scalp some of the native people. In fact, so many of them had such an "excess of the Indian ill-will, so that it required much gentle persuasion to restrain them from killing, indiscriminately, all the Indians they met," observed the governor.[52] All the same, they made a "grand display," and when they passed through Rushville one man living there declared, "A more cheerful and ardent little army was never marched against an enemy."[53]

At Rock Island Gaines waited impatiently for them to arrive, and Lieutenant McCall grew bored with "the sameness of the scene."[54] The militia did not get there until June 25, an entire fortnight having elapsed since first being sent for. When the mounted column finally came into sight, McCall was sent out to meet it. At first he had difficulty locating the governor, but with persistence and some information from the troops, he eventually found Reynolds about halfway down the line, in an enclosed wagon, which McCall said could have been mistaken for a "Jersey fish-cart." There, behind leather curtains, "lay his linsey-woolsey Excellency, coiled upon a truss of tarnished straw," declared McCall in another of his letters home. At the sight of him, the young lieutenant confessed he nearly burst into convulsive laughter, but, instead, like a good soldier, retained his self-control and bowed deeply before the governor, who remarked to his well-mannered greeter that he had been suffering from "chills and fever" for three days. Then, apparently oblivious to how ridiculous he must have appeared, Reynolds told McCall he had "accompanied the militia of his State, merely with the view of inspiring them with his presence."[55]

The "Old Ranger's" health did not improve in time for him to participate in any of the actions taken against the Indians the next day. He remained confined to a stateroom on the steamboat *Winnebago*.

Regardless of Reynolds's personal condition, the arrival of so large a mounted force had a decisive impact upon the Indians. Some of the Sauk, knowing the Illinois volunteers were on their way, abandoned the old village well before the troops ever arrived. Among those who remained, said Gaines, it was "their women [who] urge[d] their hostile husbands to fight rather than move."[56] On Sunday morning, June 26, General Gaines made his move. He sent his own soldiers south, across the narrow channel between Rock Island and the mainland, and on to Saukenuk, which was about four miles from Fort Armstrong. At the same time, the militia, covered by the guns on the *Winnebago,* forded the Rock River just below Vandruff's Island, a little upstream from the village. As they did so, artillery blasted through the brushwood down upon Saukenuk from the heights north of the river. McCall knew the Indian position was a strong one, and he and Gaines were prepared for a tough battle. But upon reaching Saukenuk itself, they were all shocked to discover the settlement to be completely deserted.[57] Fires were still burning, and fresh moccasin tracks were visible in the dirt, indicating that some of the Sauk had remained in the village until just before the onslaught of the soldiers. In the end, Saukenuk fell without bloodshed, and soon after the soldiers took possession of the town it began to rain. It poured down in torrents until nightfall.[58]

The militia camped in Saukenuk for the night and burned down many of its deserted bark lodges. Then, before departing, perhaps as a substitute for not getting the opportunity to kill and mutilate live Indians, the militiamen attacked the Sauk dead. They vandalized the great cemetery. The Indians had frequently expressed their reverence for the bones of their ancestors and repeatedly declared their reluctance to abandon those sacred remains to the white people. The men in the militia undoubtedly knew that—certainly their leaders did—and in what appears to have been a deliberate attempt to inflict the most insulting affront they could imagine on the Sauk, the Illinois volunteers desecrated the graves, digging up and mutilating some of the most recently buried bodies. Once the volunteers had left for home, Felix St. Vrain and Antoine LeClaire went over to the village, and there, St. Vrain later reported to Clark, he was astonished to find "about fifteen or twenty graves had been uncovered, and one entire corps taken out from the grave, and put into the fire and burned."[59]

But the damage done by the militia was not confined to the Sauk settlement alone. The amateur soldiers also tore down the settlers' fences and burned the rails for firewood, and turned their horses loose to graze in their grain fields. There were 1,459 horses belonging to the militia, along with the horses they had stolen from the Sauk, and the morning after the "battle," the sound of the steamboat startled them.[60] They broke into a stampede, running "altogether in a confused mass away from the river for miles,"[61] and by the time they were rounded up they had destroyed most of the crops planted by both the settlers and the Sauk. Spencer said he had twenty acres of corn and potatoes, and all were lost; "the soldiers doing me ten times as much damage as the Indians had ever done," he complained.[62]

The militia volunteers were a rough bunch of undisciplined men, and that was precisely why they had such a decisive impact on the situation with the Sauk. Originally, Black Hawk had said he intended to resist passively, and that his people would also remain peacefully in their lodges until physically removed by the soldiers, who, the Prophet had assured him, would do them no harm. But later, when asked why he had not carried through on that plan, he replied, according to Spencer, "If General Gaines had come with only the regular troops at the Island, he should have remained in his wigwam, but to have done so with men [of the militia] that the officers had no control over would have been sure death to him."[63] Black Hawk confirmed all of this, saying he was "afraid of the multitude of pale faces, who were on horse back, as they were under no restraint of their chiefs."[64]

However, there were a great many indications he really wanted to put up a fight and perhaps even set in motion a far-flung major conflict. Throughout the winter he had been at the very center of massive efforts to put together a grand alliance of tribes. Clark informed Secretary of War Eaton of those intrigues, reporting that the Sauk were "using great exertions to induce other Tribes and Bands to unite in opposition to the Government."[65] And Felix St. Vrain revealed how extensive those efforts were in a report he sent to General Gaines in mid-June. In it he said he had reliable information from Antoine LeClaire that Kinnekonnesaut, the very man who had confronted the general about his written speech at the beginning of the council, had traveled all the way to the southwestern part of the United States in search of allies. He had made that journey the previous fall and winter, accompanied by a group that included two other important Sauk leaders—Ioway and Namowet—and they had held discussions with twelve different tribes. The group had ventured as far away as Nacogdoches in Texas, reported

St. Vrain. In 1828, before going south, Kinnekonnesaut had wintered in Upper Canada, near Niagara Falls, and there too had tried to persuade the tribes to support the Sauk cause. Since his trip to the Southwest, said St. Vrain, Kinnekonnesaut had also worked tirelessly to form a strong anti-American confederacy with the Potawatomi, Ottawa, Chippewa, Winnebago, and Kickapoo in Illinois and the Michigan Territory.[66] St. Vrain shared the same information with the secretary of war and said Black Hawk's band of "Sac Indians had been indeavouring to unite all the Indians they could to defend their village."[67]

Henry Gratiot, who had a large mining and smeltering operation at Gratiot's Grove, just north of the Illinois border, was appointed a subagent to the Winnebago for the region south of Prairie du Chien in March of 1831. He too informed Gaines in early June of the intertribal nature of the problem they faced. Gratiot indicated he had indisputable evidence that Wabokieshiek, the Winnebago Prophet, was right then attempting to "get as many of his band and of the other Bands of Winnebagoes . . . as he can for the purpose of joining the Sacks and of Supporting them in their present pretensions."[68] A group of Winnebago chiefs had told Gratiot that the "half breeds Socks" from the Prophet's village had offered them "black wampum to assist them in holding their ground against the Whites."[69] Soon after Gaines received Gratiot's report, Paul Chouteau, the Indian agent to the Osage, informed Clark about a delegation of perhaps as many as a dozen Sauk leaders, "having a considerable quantity of wampum," visiting the Osage in the spring near the Arkansas River and attempting to persuade them to join the Sauk in making war on the Americans. That same delegation had already been to see the Creeks and Cherokee and "other nations of Indians," he said.[70]

Sauk efforts to enlarge the scope of the conflict were quite extensive, and the arguments they made to their potential allies were "well calculated to rouse the savage disposition," said Chouteau. They emphasized the "avaricious disposition of the whites in depriving the Indians of the lands of their forefathers" and pointed out how the U.S. government did not uphold the promises made in treaties. Furthermore, they described the Indian agents as a "set of unprincipled men who aided the Government in depriving them of their lands, and defrauding them of money which they were entitled to." The Sauk spokesmen also characterized all the Indian agents as the authors of deceit and the tellers of great lies, saying none of them could be trusted.[71]

Those accusations must have rung resoundingly true in the ears of many of the native listeners. Nevertheless, the sharp words failed to produce the hoped-for results. No grand alliance emerged. No widespread uprising occurred. And General Gaines undoubtedly breathed a deep sigh of relief when Gratiot informed him that although the Winnebago "had been invited to join the Sacks[,] they . . . [had] refused to do So."[72] Soon after hearing from Henry Gratiot, Thomas Burnett, the subagent replacing John Marsh at Prairie du Chien, told Clark all the Winnebago in his district remained peaceful and were most likely "waiting to see the first result of the movement below" before deciding on any course of action.[73] Even Wabokieshiek himself was persuaded to stay clear of the conflict involving the Black Hawk band. Gratiot took credit for that.[74] Then, with the arrival of the militia at the Rock River, all remaining hope Black Hawk may have had for a pan-tribal uprising simply collapsed. In a triumphal tone, Gaines reported to Acting Secretary of War Hugh White on July 6: "Deserted by their allies, this disorderly Band was left alone to seek security in a precipitate flight to the right Bank of the Mississippi, where they were found the next day under the protection of a white flag."[75]

Five days later, twenty-eight chiefs and warriors were forced to sign the Articles of Agreement and Capitulation drawn up and dictated to them by General Gaines and Governor Reynolds. The Sauk band, which had followed Black Hawk, was required to agree not to recross the Mississippi or return to Saukenuk ever again. Gaines gave them some corn to compensate for their lost crops, but that was the only concession he made. For the Sauk it appeared to be the end of a long and important era of their history. Henceforth and forever more, they were to be banished from the center of their world, cast out and cut off from the fields of their mothers and the graves of their fathers. And when it finally came time for the chiefs to affix their marks to the document, McCall clearly recognized some of the tragic dimensions of what was taking place. That was most apparent in the appearance of Black Hawk himself, especially when it came his turn to mark the paper. "He arose slowly, and with great dignity, while in the expression of his fine face there was a deep-seated grief and humiliation that no one could witness unmoved," McCall wrote to his father. When the old leader reached the table where the paper lay, it was McCall who handed him the pen. Black Hawk then made "a large, bold cross with a force which rendered *that* pen forever unfit for further use," said the young soldier.[76] It was then finished. The written words had triumphed in the end, or so it seemed.

Clark was very pleased with the results. The cool and determined show of force had finally accomplished what years of talking had failed to do.[77] On learning of the outcome, Forsyth wrote an I-told-you-so letter to George Davenport, saying that if Clark had only listened to his advice the previous year and used some military muscle then, all the expense and effort of the current operations would have been unnecessary. Nevertheless, he assured Davenport that all their fears of a major Indian war were finally behind them.[78] However, one unidentified militia officer encamped at Saukenuk was not so sure of that. He indicated the volunteer troops were quite dissatisfied about the outcome of the campaign and that he, for one, had "little faith in the duration of the peace." Neither he nor his comrades trusted the Sauk, and they assumed the savages would arise again whenever the opportunity presented itself.[79]

They proved to be right, for not long after matters had been settled at Saukenuk, a war party of eighty to one hundred Sauk and Fox warriors struck an encampment of Menominee in the predawn darkness of July 31, just above Fort Crawford, "butchering them in the most shocking manner."[80] John Marsh was first on the scene, and he immediately rushed over to the Indian agency to inform Street of what had happened.[81] Street then went to see for himself, arriving shortly before seven o'clock in the morning. He was sickened by what he found. Later in the day he reported to Clark that the attackers had killed twenty-five Menominee and wounded many others.[82] The unusually brutal blow had been struck almost silently, observed Captain Gustavus Loomis, the recently arrived commander at Fort Crawford, who indicated the weapons used in the gruesome attack had been mostly tomahawks, spears, and scalping knives. As a result, even though the fort was just a few hundred paces away, no one in it—not even the sentries—had heard anything or been aroused by the sounds of the slaughter.[83] Lieutenant Joseph Lamott said he had noticed a party of Indians in canoes ascending the river around nine o'clock the night before but had no idea who they were or what they were up to. Seeing them had caused him no concern since a great many Indians were coming and going at the time.[84] When the attack came, most of the Menominee were drunk and unarmed. In fact, when they had commenced their drinking binge in the early evening, the Menominee women had hidden their weapons to prevent them from harming one another. The Sauk and Fox struck by complete surprise and carried out their bloody work in about ten minutes.[85] In taking count, Street reported that eight men—including one war chief and three headmen—six women, and eleven Menominee children had been killed and their bodies "mangled wantonly in the most shocking manner."[86]

The attack was clearly in retaliation for the Sioux and Menominee massacre of the Fox peace delegation the year before. Clark immediately suspected the killings had been carried out by the Black Hawk band.[87] But Marsh informed Atkinson, on good authority, that the war party had been made up mostly of Fox warriors from Dubuque's Mines, who afterward had fled with all the other inhabitants of that community downriver to a place a few miles below Rock Island. Etienne Dubois, a trader who lived across the Mississippi from Dubuque's Mines who personally knew most of the members of the war party, confirmed all of what Marsh had said. In fact, Dubois thought there might have been only five or six Sauk warriors among the attackers.[88]

In the meantime, Lewis Cass was appointed secretary of war. Soon after reaching Washington, he wrote to Clark, telling him President Jackson was adamantly insisting that the perpetrators of the brutal assault upon the Menominee camp be brought in and surrendered to federal authorities at Prairie du Chien. Cass instructed Clark to confer with General Atkinson as to the best means of apprehending those responsible for the savage actions. They must be brought to justice, insisted Cass. Otherwise, he feared, the entire frontier would be violently undone in a new outburst of attacks and counterattacks. The consequences of inaction would be too terrible to contemplate, he warned.[89]

6

SPIRITS OF THE FATHERS

———

Things were growing worse. There were no deer in the forest. The opossum and beaver were fled; the springs were drying up, and our squaws and papooses without victuals to keep them from starving; we called a great council, and built a large fire. The spirits of the fathers arose and spoke to us to avenge our wrongs or die.

Black Hawk's speech to Joseph Street,
at Prairie du Chien, August 27, 1832

UNABLE TO STIFLE his anger, Black Hawk jumped to his feet during the conference held at Fort Armstrong in early June of 1831 to object to General Gaines's stern insistence that the Sauk had to abandon Saukenuk forever. "Our braves are unanimous in their desire to remain in the old fields," announced Black Hawk, claiming that the Great Spirit had given the land to their forefathers as a home and they were therefore "unwilling to leave it." Visibly irritated, Gaines lashed back, demanding to know: "Who is the Black Hawk that he should assume the right of dictating to his tribe? . . . I know him not—he is no chief—who is he?" Watching it all was Lieutenant George McCall, who said Black Hawk "was very much cut down by this, and took his seat quite mortified." But then, after a few minutes, and upon regaining his composure, he arose again, advanced to the front of the hall, where, with "infinite dignity and energy of manner," he responded to the general's rebuke by declaring: "I am a Sac! My forefather was a Sac! And All the nations call me a Sac!"[1]

The issue of identity was at the very core of this confrontation. It always is in such conflicts in which the participants almost instinctively draw boundaries along which the "self" and "other" confront each other, and see themselves and the enemy in sharp focus and clear definition.[2]

By the time of Black Hawk's verbal clash with Edmund Gaines, it was already quite clear, to those who knew him, who and what he was not. He was not, for example, a physically attractive, charismatic leader who inspired people with the power and majesty of his words as had Tecumseh or as was the case for his rival Keokuk. By 1831 Black Hawk was a man in his midsixties, a physically unimposing individual well beyond his prime, who possessed only the most modest of oratorical skills and who held no official position of leadership whatsoever within his tribe.

Early in his life he had gained an impressive reputation as a warrior, which had been enhanced in middle age by his participation in the War of 1812 on the British side. At that time, Robert Dickson, the legendary red-haired, larger-than-life Scottish trader, who was married to the Sioux woman To-to-win and who recruited widespread Indian support for the British throughout the up-country, called him "General Black Hawk." Dickson had placed a medal around his neck, given him a silk Union Jack flag, and put him in command of the Indians who had gathered at Green Bay in May of 1813. Black Hawk fought in lower Michigan and western Ohio in the battles of Frenchtown, Fort Meigs, and Fort Stephenson, but quit the war in midcourse, disappointed with the lack of loot to be plundered and the British decision to retreat into Upper Canada. "I determined on leaving them and returning to Rock river, to see what had become of my wife and children," he said.[3] Nevertheless, the war followed him home, where he was soon again engaged in new battles, including one that successfully defended Saukenuk against a 430-man American force that came upriver from St. Louis in keelboats under the command of twenty-nine-year-old Major Zachary Taylor. That was in September of 1814, at which time the British and their Indian allies were in control of all the territory in the upper Mississippi, as well as the waterway of the Wisconsin and Fox rivers, Michilimackinac, and Sault Sainte Marie. But soon after returning from the winter hunt the following spring, the Sauk were disappointed to learn the British and Americans had made peace.

On first hearing of the British king's decision to give up the struggle,

Black Hawk said he thought it must be a lie. "At this news I many times rubbed my Eyes and cleared my ears before I could believe what I saw and what I heard," he later said.[4] He traveled to Prairie du Chien in April to learn the truth, and during a council there he told the British commander, "I have fought the Big Knives, and will continue to fight them till they are off our lands. Till then, my Father, your Red children cannot be happy."[5] But when it became apparent the British would no longer support him in that fight, Thomas Anderson, the British Indian agent there, reported that "the whole-hearted man and unflinching warrior, Black Hawk, cried like a child, saying our Great Mother, Great Britain, has thus concluded, and further talk is useless." Anderson gave him some ammunition, a hardy handshake, and Black Hawk departed for Saukenuk in a downcast mood.[6]

After the war Black Hawk retreated more and more deeply into private life. That withdrawal was intensified by personal grief. Not long after the war, his oldest son, who "had grown to manhood," took sick and died, and then soon after that tragic loss, his youngest daughter, whom he described as an "interesting and affectionate child," was also struck down by illness. The losses were devastating. He clearly loved his children, and his emotional suffering was deep and prolonged. He withdrew from the community and into himself, reducing himself to poverty by giving away all his possessions, taking up residence in a hut encircled by a fence within a cornfield, and going naked both summer and winter except for a piece of buffalo robe. He blackened his face with soot and fasted for two whole years, drinking only a little water in the middle of the day and eating just a small amount of boiled corn at the going down of the sun.[7] Even after breaking his fast, Black Hawk continued to live a somewhat ascetic existence, abstaining completely from the consumption of alcohol in any form, and before 1833, said John Spencer, he never "knew him to wear any part of a white man's garb."[8] Like a good "puritan," he abhorred the contaminating influence American culture was having upon the traditional Sauk way of life and lamented the growing moral depravity of his own people caused mostly by the whiskey trade, and criticized them for becoming hypocrites, liars, and adulterers just like the whites.[9]

For a long time, however, his struggle against the forces of cultural destruction was a personal battle, for he remained essentially a private person concerned mainly with family matters. He "was always a good man to his family," noted William Carroll Reed, an American settler who lived near Black Hawk after 1832. Unlike most Sauk men, he had only one wife and by all accounts had an unusually affectionate marriage. Reed described his wife, Asshewequa (Singing Bird), as "a very fine looking woman much lighter in color than most Indians," and surmised from that she must have been part French.[10] She was, said Black Hawk, "the only wife I ever had, or will ever have." While explaining that it was not their custom to say much about their women, he nevertheless made his admiration for her apparent, complimenting her by saying, "She is a good woman, and teaches my boys to be brave."[11] At the time Reed knew the family, there were two sons: Nasheweskaska, "as fine a specimen of manhood as I ever saw," he said, and a younger one, Wathametha, known among the settlers as Tom Black Hawk, or sometimes just Jack, who was also handsome but "was a bad Indian and hated the whites bitterly," reported Reed. An earlier report had great praise for Nasheweskaska's appearance, calling him "the living personification of our *beau ideal* of manly beauty." There was also a daughter, Nauasia, described by Reed as the "prettiest Indian girl" he had ever seen, and "as spry and agile as a fawn." She was, he said, a young woman "of such striking beauty that she would attract attention anywhere."[12]

As with most people, Black Hawk's experiences while growing up had a profound influence on his character and worldview. There is conclusive evidence indicating that Black Hawk was the firstborn child of his parents, and probably their only child.[13] Although he never so much as makes mention of his mother, Summer Rain, his strong attachment to his father, Pyesa, was made very apparent in his autobiography. In his account of his life, he also described the great veneration he felt toward his great-grandfather Na-nà-ma-kee, who had been one of the great war chiefs of the Sauk. Lineage was of great importance in Sauk culture, but it was only the males who counted, and it was through war that their worth was measured and their status established. In fact, Black Hawk recounts virtually nothing of his own early life before he goes off to war for the first time at about age fifteen, and because he succeeded in wounding an enemy, and afterward was allowed to wear paint and feathers, he was then counted among the ranks of the braves. It was as if before then he had not existed as a person.

Soon after that first encounter with battle he went off with another war party against the Osage. He and his father went together, and when they joined battle, Black Hawk watched with admiration as Pyesa slew an enemy warrior and then ripped the scalp from the man's bleeding head. On seeing this, young Black Hawk went off in a state of emotional excitement, boldly intending to emulate his father's example. Indeed, he most eagerly sought his father's approbation, and once he had engaged one of the Osage opponents, striking him down with his tomahawk and then running him through with his lance, he proudly returned to his father with the scalp, "hoping to prove to him" he was "not an unworthy son." It was the first time he had killed a man and therefore a momentous event in his young life, but his father's response was all too understated. "He said nothing, but looked pleased," said Black Hawk. Pyesa's reaction appears not to have been nearly reassuring enough for the young warrior overly eager for validation.

Later (probably in 1786), when Black Hawk was about nineteen years old, he became a member of another war party led by his father. In that raid against the Cherokee Pyesa was killed, and Black Hawk, who was near at hand, saw him go down. Although still quite young, he assumed command of the attack force, ferociously carried on the fight, and personally killed three of the enemy and wounded several others, perhaps frantically trying to prove himself to his father before it was too late. Nevertheless, the much venerated Pyesa expired soon after the victory had been won and may have departed this life before Black Hawk felt certain of his father's approval.[14] Much later, in August of 1832, after Black Hawk had led his uprising against the Americans, he declared, with much satisfaction, that he could then finally "go to the world of spirits contented" and "his father" would "meet him there, and commend him." Maybe he had been striving for that validation most of his life.[15]

The sudden loss of his father was for him a traumatic development, which provoked in him exaggerated and contrary emotional reactions. On the one hand, he said, "The loss of my father, by the Cherokee, made me anxious to avenge his death, by the annihilation, if possible, of all their race." On the other hand, rather than remaining bellicose, upon returning home he blackened his face, withdrew completely from the community, and fasted and prayed for a period of five years, during which time he abstained entirely from warfare.[16]

As an only child with a strong affinity for his father, Black Hawk undoubtedly internalized the values of his parents quite fully and saw himself as a perpetuator of those values. For Black Hawk, those traditional values were embodied in his *mi´shâm,* or medicine bag. When describing his own genealogical lineage, he gave special attention to the passing on of the medicine bag from Muk-a-ta-quet, his great-great-grandfather, to Na-nà-ma-kee, his much revered great-grandfather. In his account of that important event, he said, "He presented the great medicine bag to Na-nà-ma-kee, and told him 'that he cheerfully resigned it to him—it is the soul of our nation—it has never yet been disgraced—and I will expect you to keep it unsullied!'"[17] That medicine bag was for Black Hawk a magical object containing or symbolizing the very essence of the Sauk identity— the very "soul" of the nation, as he put it—and upon the death of his own father it was passed on to him. "I now fell heir to the great medicine bag of my forefathers, which had belonged to my father," he stated with a strong sense of responsibility and pride. From that time on he saw himself as the preserver of the true Sauk identity. Although he was not a hereditary chief, it was probably the responsibility he inherited through the medicine bag that gave him special significance within Sauk society. In 1832, while in flight from American forces, he turned his attention once more to the sacred medicine bag, telling his followers that since being passed down from Na-nà-ma-kee it had never been disgraced and that he expected them to protect it with their lives if necessary so it would not fall into degradation in the hands of the white people.[18] Then, following the final confrontation with the Americans near the mouth of the Bad Axe River in August of that year, Black Hawk fled into the wilderness, taking the medicine bag with him. He eventually took refuge among the Winnebago at Prairie LaCrosse and there gave the bag to the chief of the village for safe-keeping. In doing so, he once more referred to it as "the soul of the Sac nation," which "never had been dishonored in any battle," and told his host, "It is my life—dearer than life."[19]

The medicine bag not only symbolized the traditional values of the tribe, but also gave Black Hawk a special personal relationship with the fathers—with his own father, Pyesa, and with Na-nà-ma-kee, and the long succession of fathers before them all the way back to Muk-a-ta-quet, whom he referred to as "the father of the Sac nation."[20] That was a bond much more powerful and significant than even the usual tendency of first-born children to identify with their parents. It reflected a deeply rooted reverence for cultural continuity and a powerful sense of the historical connectedness with the succeeding generations of Sauk patriarchs. The same sense of connection and continuity was also made apparent in his very strong attachment to the land and community of Saukenuk. There, once again, the emphasis was upon the link with the "fathers."

Saukenuk was the place where the bones of the ancestors rested beneath the ground on the high ridge above the community. Being there, in such close proximity to the dead, the living members of the tribe must have been quite conscious of their membership in a society that had persisted over considerable time from generation to generation. While the physical death of the individual is of course unavoidable, and although most societies have a negative attitude toward death itself, their special treatment of the dead often reflects the deep needs of the living to retain a sense of connection with the people who have gone before and to feel as if they belong to something greater and grander than themselves, which will endure for ages to come.[21]

Remembering the dead helps the living feel less forlorn when anxiously contemplating the hour of their own death, and certainly such thoughts of impending personal extinction must have occurred to Black Hawk as he moved ever farther into the final stage of his own life cycle. Where he was to be buried was a question of increasing concern to him. It tormented him, in fact. It came up in a conversation he had in 1832 with the Potawatomi chief, Shaubena, as he described his deep sense of loss at having been driven from his old village. "Here," he told Shaubena, "is the grave of my father, and some of my children; here I expected to live and die and lay my bones by the side of those near and dear unto me."[22] The thought of eternal exile from Saukenuk was virtually unbearable to him. At the time when he learned that Saukenuk had been sold, Antoine LeClair, the Indian interpreter at Fort Armstrong, reported that "he cried like a child, blackening his face," and became unusually "melancholy and morose."[23] Later, after reluctantly scratching his mark on the Articles of Agreement and Capitulation dictated by General Gaines in June of 1831, and then declaring his intentions to still have his bones buried among his ancestors, he went off to see George Davenport, who owned the land where the old cemetery was located. "I then went to the trader," said Black Hawk, "and asked for permission to be buried in the grave-yard at our village, among my old friends and warriors; which he gave me cheerfully."[24] That must have given him at least some measure of relief.

Black Hawk had reached the stage in life where he had to come to terms with his own mortality; he was also at the age when most men feel compelled to look back and take stock of their lives. By 1832 his eyesight was failing and his other physical powers were in noticeable decline. The time for undertaking new quests was clearly running out. Perhaps he was like many older men, especially those who for whatever reasons may feel they have not accomplished enough or lived up to their own or other people's expectations. For such as these, this final stage of life may bring on a sense of crisis and even a desperate desire to do something grand and bold and reaffirming—something to be remembered by—before it is too late.

Such concerns may have been on his mind when members of the tribal faction opposed to leaving Saukenuk called upon him for his advice. He listened to them attentively and then talked with Keokuk, who favored the abandoning of the old village. Then Black Hawk took a firm stand: "I now promised this party to be their leader, and raised the standard of opposition to Keokuck, with a full determination not to leave my village."[25] He chose to act as he thought a good man ought to act.

Surely the issue of manliness was of importance to him when taking that step. Perhaps that too had been brought into question by his advancing years, years in which, for many men, masculine powers begin to wane. Perhaps in opposing Keokuk, whom he "looked upon . . . as a coward,"[26] and thereby unmanly, he fought against the characteristics within himself that were making him more womanlike. But whatever complexities their personal rivalry entailed, questions of gender identification were at the center of Black Hawk's considerations concerning his defense of Saukenuk and the way of life associated with that place. In April of 1833, upon meeting President Jackson in the executive mansion in Washington, D.C., the very first utterance Black Hawk felt compelled to make was the declaration "I am a man!" Maybe in saying that he wished to emphasize that he was not a "beast," or to point out that he and the president were equals in that very basic way. But in what proved to be more a soliloquy than a conversation, it was clear Black Hawk had masculinity on his mind. He told Jackson that he had taken up the tomahawk against a storm of injuries and injustices brought upon the Sauk by the white people, and then he made a self-revealing statement: "Had I borne them longer without striking [back], my people, would have said, 'Black Hawk is a *woman*; he is too old to be a chief; he is no Sac!'"[27] Even earlier, soon after being captured and

taken to Prairie du Chien in August of 1832, he told Joseph Street, referring to himself in the third person, "Black Hawk is a true Indian, and dis-
dains to cry like a *woman*."[28] There was some unintentional irony in this,
since he was reputed to be a man who often wept profusely. Perhaps that
in itself intensified his need to assert his masculinity.

It was the women who were most supportive of Black Hawk's intentions to return to Saukenuk. Later, on the third day of the humiliating conference with General Gaines at Fort Armstrong, Black Hawk came to the
meeting accompanied by several women of his tribe, which McCall said
was "a circumstance of rare occurrence" on such occasions.[29] Together
Black Hawk and the women confronted the general. The daughter of the
deceased chief Mat-ta-tas scolded the general, saying the land actually
belonged to the women and they had never agreed to sell it.[30] Gaines
rudely dismissed her comments, saying that the president had not sent him
to "make treaties with the women, nor to hold council with them."[31] But it
was the women—not the men—who challenged him. A few days later,
when it had come to the issue of making a stand in defense of the village,
Gaines observed an "uncommon" situation had developed among the Sauk
in which it was "their women [who] urge their hostile husbands to fight
rather than to move."[32] By taking such assertive actions, the women had
implied, and perhaps even declared, that the men had become weak and
unmanly and needed the women to stiffen their wills and prod them on.

Fears of an emasculating loss of power are common among men
caught in circumstances of disorienting social change in which culturally
defined gender roles are undermined and men experience a diminished
sense of control—even a loss of self-control—and feel increasingly helpless to reverse their own downward slide toward chaos and ruin.[33] Such
feeling must have been strong among Sauk men who were failing at most
of their traditional responsibilities, particularly by their apparent inability
to prevent the abuse of their own women by intruding American men.
They "ill-treat our women," protested Black Hawk,[34] and make the poor
Indian man drunk "to deceive him, to ruin his wife."[35] Wabokieshiek, the
Winnebago Prophet, also complained to Forsyth that white men were too
often "insulting to the Indians and take liberties with their women,"[36] and
the historian Lucy Eldersveld Murphy observed that white "male miners'
relations with Indian women during the 1820s were increasingly exploitive
and violent."[37] The Americans also deliberately shamed the men with

beatings and tricked and made laughingstocks of them in front of their own people. But one incident occurred at a large intertribal treaty conference at Le Petit Butte des Morts, west of Green Bay, in August of 1827, the news of which must have spread swiftly throughout the woodlands and intensified the gender anxieties of a great many Indian men.

Lewis Cass had called the conference, and hundreds of Chippewa, Menominee, and Winnebago had gathered with their families in a huge camp. When the business had been concluded, presents were distributed. Soon after that, as they were breaking camp and loading their canoes, an agonized scream arose from amid the commotion. It came from a woman—"a fine looking squaw," said Thomas McKenney—who was being attacked by a knife-wielding man who had slashed open a great bleeding gash in the woman's arm, just below her shoulder, when she had raised it to protect her face and chest. Fortunately for her, a military officer hastily intervened and knocked her assailant to the ground. Upon investigation, it was discovered that the woman's attacker was her own son-in-law, who had gone berserk when she had tried to prevent him from taking their presents and trading them off to the whiskey peddlers who lurked like vultures along the fringe of the encampment. She had pleaded with him not to take their blankets and newly acquired provisions to be squandered on a drunken spree; when she had persisted, he had drawn his knife and assaulted her.

The man was taken prisoner. His hands were bound, and he was brought to the top of large mound by two husky voyageurs. A great assembly of nearly a thousand people gathered as the prisoner stood quietly, appearing almost indifferent about what his fate might be, and McKenney asked what was to be done with him. Cass promptly replied, "Make a woman of him."[38] Through an interpreter, Cass, a large man with a thunderous voice, announced that the man would no longer be considered a brave, and that through his attack upon the woman he had "forfeited his character as a man." *"From henceforth let him be a woman!"* declared Cass.[39] As soon as the sentence had been pronounced, McKenney took the man's knife and broke off the blade, returning only the handle to him. That symbolic emasculation was probably not missed by anyone in the crowd. Then McKenney preached to the assembly. "Woman, whoever she is, should be protected by man. . . . She is man's best friend," he proclaimed, perhaps unintentionally suggesting the female of the species ought to share equal status with the dog.[40] While he spoke, the two voyageurs stripped off the man's leggings, took away his ornaments, and put upon him a filthy, grease-stained petticoat they had procured from an elderly Indian woman. He was then pushed down the mound into the jeering crowd. The man lost his balance and fell on his face. As he sprawled upon the ground he was heard to utter: "I wish they had killed me. . . . I'd rather be dead. I am no longer a brave; I'm a woman!"[41]

That incident surely appeared to many Indian men a sign of what the Americans had in store for them all. Fear of being emasculated by the Long Knives must have haunted their anxious imaginations.

In the summer of 1832 William Clark acquired some information that indicated such fears were especially acute among the men of Black Hawk's band. In late July Taimah, the chief of the Fox village at Flint Hill, and his son, Apanosokeman, wrote to Clark through an interpreter, telling him Black Hawk and his band had visited them during the spring on their journey northward toward Saukenuk. Forsyth had described Taimah as "a very shrewd and sensible man," and a "good man" who was always in favor of peace,[42] and when Black Hawk had invited him to join his campaign against the Americans, he turned him down. But he did listen to the explanation Black Hawk's followers gave for their aggressive intention to return to the east side of the river and fight the Long Knives. In those conversations Taimah had found out "that their minds were greatly corrupted with various foreign fables," which had been brought back from Canada by the members of the band who had recently visited the British fort at Amherstburg, he told Clark. There were many men among Black Hawk's band, he said, who were terrified by the warnings given to them during that visit. They were convinced, asserted Taimah, "the Americans were determined shortly to lay hands on all [their] males, both old and young, and deprive them of those parts which are said to be essential to courage." Perhaps the "fable" had credibility with them because it reinforced and even appeared to confirm fearful suspicions they already had. They also told Taimah the Americans not only would come to castrate all the Sauk and Fox men but would also bring with them, they insisted, "a horde of negro men . . . from the South, to whom our wives, sisters, and daughters were to be given, for the purpose of raising a stock of *slaves* to supply the demand in this country where negroes are scarce." That, of course, would result in the physical extinction of the Sauk and Fox as a people.

Taimah and Apanosokeman told Clark how that story and "many other similar stories" had great influence on the "minds of all, or at least of most, of that unfortunate band." The proof of that, they said, could be seen in the "enthusiastic madness with which our women urge their husbands to this desperate resort." Furthermore, it was those fears, said Taimah, that explained why the Indians engaged in the uprising of that summer "uniformly treated the dead bodies of the unfortunate white men . . . with the same indignities which they themselves so much dreaded."[43]

In the violent conflicts of that fearful summer there was plenty of evidence the Sauk warriors and their allies did, in fact, grotesquely mutilate the bodies and genitals of many of the white people they killed. The occurrence of such acts was vividly described in a report written by Reuben Holmes, a West Point graduate from Connecticut who was then a colonel with the Illinois volunteers. In his communication with Benjamin McCary, probably of Beardstown, written in late May, Holmes described the conditions of the dead after a battle on Sycamore Creek, generally known as Stillman's Run. He said the bodies "were cut and mangled in the most shocking manner; their hearts were cut out, their hands and limbs severed from their bodies, besides having other acts of indignity perpetrated on them too outrageous and indecent to be named." In another violent raid, this one on the small settlement at the William Davis farm on Big Indian Creek, west of Chicago, similar atrocities were committed. Holmes commented on those as well, telling McCary that fifteen of the men, women, and children there had been the "victims of the most inhuman butchery." He elaborated some by telling how the "men were mutilated beyond the reach of a modest description; the women hung up by their feet, and the most revolting acts of outrage and indecency practiced upon their bodies."[44]

Sexual insecurity would appear to have contributed to the mounting sense of terror that drove Black Hawk and his followers to engage in such vicious deeds that summer. But vengeance—the need to "cover the dead"— was also a powerful driving force behind their actions. That had been the reason why some Sauk men had murdered and mutilated more than a score of Menominee near Fort Crawford the summer before. Officials in Washington, including President Jackson, were outraged by that attack and demanded the immediate surrender and punishment of all those who had participated in it. They were convinced a strong, unambiguous response was necessary to forestall the outbreak of a major intertribal conflict. To them it was simply clear-cut, but General Atkinson had a better appreciation for what had happened and why. He understood the brutal attack upon the Menominee in cultural terms and knew full well it had been a predictable act of retaliation and revenge, as sure and certain as the rain following the sound of thunder, in response to the Sioux and Menominee slaughter of the Fox peace delegation in 1830. Atkinson attempted to explain to General Gaines that, for the Sauk and Fox men, it was a question of "honor" involving a deep sense of moral obligation "to retaliate in Blood for similar wrongs." "If they failed to do so," he asserted, "they fall under the ridicule of their neighbors and even their own women."[45] Once again, the Sauk men must have been anxious not to lose face in the eyes of their women and thereby be seen as womanly themselves in failing to fulfill their duty as men.

Nevertheless, the government was determined to apprehend and punish the Sauk men who had engaged in the raid, and that, in turn, surely must have seemed to the Sauk to be yet another attack upon their manhood and code of honor. Their anger about the government's stance was made unmistakably clear at a conference held at Fort Armstrong in the early autumn of 1831. Major John Bliss, the fort commander, began by demanding that the chiefs immediately turn over to him everyone who had participated in the raid. Quashquame, the feisty old chief associated with Black Hawk's faction, simply explained that vengeance was the only acceptable morally correct response to the Menominee's killing of their own people, and that they had done nothing wrong in taking retributive action. But it was Keokuk who cut to the very heart of the matter and forcefully expressed views with which all the other tribal leaders vehemently agreed. He commenced by asserting that the Americans were treating them unfairly by discriminating against them and in favor of the Menominee and Sioux. "I expect it is because our names are Sauks & Foxes that you make a noise about it, when we do the least thing, you make a great noise about it," he declared, and then asserted that other tribes literally got away with murder without there being even so much as a disapproving word from the government. "Why do you not let us fight?" he demanded. Then Keokuk angrily pointed out: "You Whites are constantly fighting! . . . Why, [therefore], do you not let us be as the great Spirit made us, and let us settle our own difficulties?" For him, it all boiled down to the issue of being allowed to be themselves, and his protestation was greeted by the strong applause and approbation of all the other chiefs at the conference. In the end, he told Bliss and St. Vrain that the Sauk could not comply with the government's demands. They would not turn over to the Americans any of their tribal members who had taken revenge upon the Menominee. Those men would have to voluntarily give themselves up, said the chiefs, and on that there was complete agreement.[46] The next spring, when a military force was dispatched from Jefferson Barracks to hunt down the fugitives, they sought refuge among Black Hawk's band.

Refuge was granted to them because no one could stand alone, or was meant to. In the Sauk worldview, the solitary individual was a frail and vulnerable being with little strength or ability to withstand the great perils and powers of the world. The protection of strong fathers and the support of the whole community were seen as essential for personal survival. And beyond that, there was also the need for supernatural assistance given through dreams and visions and rituals. Life was sustained by an intricate network of interdependent relationships, constantly reinforced by the power of the ceremonies and the retelling of the old stories. Only by standing together could the people ever hope to contend with the threats that stalked them on the prairies and in the woodlands, and which lurked beneath the waters and haunted the dark places of their anxious imaginations.

The welfare of the group depended, in turn, on strong alliances, like the one that had long bound the Sauk and Fox together and made them virtually inseparable in facing the outside world. But in addition to such intertribal connections, during the eighteenth century, as the power alignments of the heartland became increasingly complicated by the imperial rivalries of the Europeans, the Sauk engaged in the politics of what the historian Richard White calls the *middle ground*. Rather than a place, the middle ground was a network of agreements, understandings, and alliances worked out over time among the tribal peoples of the Great Lakes and upper Mississippi regions with the French and British. The European powers of course wished to undo one another and became quite Machiavellian in their methods. But because no one could control the entire continental interior alone, both sides found it necessary to engage with native groups in an ongoing search for mutual interests, shared aspirations, and reciprocal support in order to build alliances. In doing this, it was mediation and compromise, rather than force and domination, which brought order and stability to the middle ground. However, after the War of 1812 and the retreat of the British from the Old Northwest Territories, the Americans, with no power left on Earth to restrain their will, were in a position to impose their hegemonic control upon the entire Midwest region. Then the middle ground simply disintegrated, greatly to the disadvantage of tribal groups like the Sauk.[47]

But even while the balance of power shifted radically within the region, some of the old loyalties and mutual interests lingered on. That was due to some extent to the kinshiplike qualities of the associations formed in the middle ground. The natives, whose own societies were structured and held together mostly by kinship relations, had simply expanded those relationships during the colonial era to include the French and British. It was common, indeed almost necessary, for the white men of the fur trade and even the Indian service to marry tribal women. As a consequence, the early history of the Great Lakes region was characterized more by intercultural cooperation than by conflict. Intermarriage substantially reduced the identity gap between the "us" and "others" of the region and promoted the pursuit of shared interests.

Beyond the purely personal level, kinship concepts were also extended to include the highly paternalistic relationships that developed between the European political elites and the native people, particularly among the Algonquin-speaking tribal groups. The Indians in such relationships almost invariably referred to European men of power as "fathers" and to themselves as "children," not so much out of a sense of submissive inferiority, but rather from their strong inclinations to define and understand interpersonal relationships in kinship terms. Moreover, for both the Algonquin-speaking peoples and the Europeans, all political authority was seen as essentially patriarchal in nature. That was most emphatically the case with the Sauk. Yet on neither side was this paternalism understood to be a relationship of dominance and subordination. Rather, the language reflected deeply held sentiments of mutual affection and loyalty, and expectations, certainly on the part of the natives, of generosity, fair treatment, and protection from their white "fathers."[48]

Thomas Forsyth understood the nuances and implications of such terminology quite well and had great respect for the manner in which both the French and British conducted their Indian affairs. He was especially impressed with the French who were "married to Indian women and followed a life similar to that of the Indians." He observed that each autumn the "frenchman and his family and the Indian and his family would paddle their canoes off together and chuse out a proper place to hunt the ensuing winter, they would hunt together, eat and drink together as much so as if they were one & the same family." Furthermore, the French learned the Indian languages and thereby better understood how the natives thought and expressed their ideas, and as a consequence, said Forsyth, "the Indians become attached to the frenchmen and the frenchmen to the Indians and the french always had . . . more influence over the Indians than any other nation of white people." The British, he also pointed out, continued to use most of the concepts and methods that had proven so successful during the French period, and although not as physically intimate with the natives as the French, they maintained the kinship qualities of the relationships formed between themselves and the tribal people. The British, like the French, learned the Indian languages. "No man is eligible for the place of agent but one who can talk some one of the Indian languages, from which it is supposed that he must be acquainted with the Indian customs and manners," pointed out Forsyth. Also, the British were unusually generous in their distribution of presents to the tribal people, and in doing so, he asserted, "the agent pays particular attention to particular leading men among the different nations." Such practices reinforced the prestige of those men among their own people and thereby strengthened their paternalistic role within their societies. Above all else, declared Forsyth, "the British Indian agents take very great care not to deceive the Indians in any of their promises. . . . Indeed," he concluded, "they [the British] have brought their treatment of Indians to a perfect system."[49]

Black Hawk also observed that one of the primary differences between the British and Americans was their strikingly different attitudes toward truthfulness. "The Americans," he said, "made fair promises, but never fulfilled them: Whilst the British made but few—but we could always rely upon their word!"[50] Words, and the keeping of one's word, were at the heart of the matter, and Forsyth complained that the U.S. government almost always appointed men to the Indian service who knew nothing of the natives' words or their subtle meanings, and who seldom followed through on their promises. Most of them were "young men," he said, "who in all probability ha[d] never seen more than three or four Indians together in the course of their lives, and those Indians [were] perhaps civilized."[51] In light of the problems caused by such cultural ignorance, Forsyth strongly recommended to Secretary of War John C. Calhoun that no one should be considered eligible for the office of Indian agent "unless he can speak some one of the Indian languages." On that account he was especially critical of the political appointees who became territorial governors—men who knew nothing of the natives' customs and cultures, and who had no idea how to treat the Indians or how to communicate with them. Such men soon acquired bad reputations among the tribal people, who came to believe, asserted Forsyth, that "their new Father [was] a man of no sense and [was] not fond of his Indian children[,] by which means all the Indians became prejudiced against the Gov[ernment]."[52]

Those anti-American feelings were made even more intense, argued Forsyth, by the government's stinginess when it came to the distribution of presents and supplies. Good fathers were expected to be generous to their children, and gift giving was not only a sign of paternal affection but also the mark of a truly great man. Indeed, great men demonstrated their greatness through elaborate and exaggerated displays of self-impoverishing generosity. But the Americans were not generous. They were takers not givers, and Forsyth pointed out the practical political advantages that could be gained by changing such practices and impressions through a much more substantial gift-giving program. Besides the goodwill it would generate, "it would make them [the Indians] totally dependant on us for their supplies and keep them from traveling 4 or 500 miles more or less to the British," asserted Forsyth.[53] But in spite of all his urging of the federal government to emulate the examples of the French and British more fully, his recommendations fell on deaf ears. Forsyth must have shuddered and even cursed as Congress continued to cut the budget of the Indian service and the executive branch persisted in its appointment of men to that service who had little knowledge of and even less respect for the Indians. They were individuals who could never become true "fathers."

That must have been especially irritating for Black Hawk, whose life was full of fathers he greatly admired and respected—and not only those who were blood relatives but also the British "fathers" with whom he had formed a powerful bond during the War of 1812. While many tribes were enraged, feeling the British had betrayed them in the Treaty of Ghent,[54] that was most definitely not the case with Black Hawk and a substantial portion of the Sauk people, who continued to regard the British as their "true fathers."

After the War of 1812, even though the Americans immediately began asserting their dominance over the Old Northwest, British officials in Upper Canada (Ontario) continued their efforts to court and maintain their connections with some of the midwestern tribes, and the Sauk were certainly among them. Regardless of the Treaty of Ghent, the British government and most especially the people and officials living in Upper Canada anxiously assumed the Americans would sooner or later make another attempt to conquer Canada. Indeed, Lord Bathurst, secretary of state for the colonies, lamented in February of 1816 that the people of Canada were "unfortunately doomed to a constant, anxious speculation about the probable loss, or preservation of everything they possessed," depending on the ambitions and actions of the Americans. He compared their situation to living on the slope of a powerful volcano, where life was made uneasy by every rumble and shudder from the south.[55] Such anxieties were not simply symptoms of unwarranted political paranoia, for some of the public statements made by U.S. officials long after the war gave the British good reasons for concern. For example, Secretary of State John Quincy Adams considered the Treaty of Ghent more of "a truce rather than a peace"[56] and subscribed to a doctrine of geopolitical predestination by which he regarded the "proper dominion" of the United States "to be the [entire] continent of North America." "From the time when we became an independent people it was as much a law of nature that this should become our pretension as that the Mississippi should flow to the sea," he said during a cabinet meeting in November of 1819, adding that it was a "physical, moral, and political absurdity" that it should remain otherwise.[57] Because of such statements, the fear of invasion from the south remained quite strong in Upper Canada, and leaders there, such as John Strachan and John Beverley Robinson, were convinced the province was in constant danger from its "powerful and unprincipled neighbor" who would "seize the first opportunity to repeat the attack."[58]

Besides the fear of outright military invasion, there were growing concerns about the influences of the American political system spilling over the border to confuse and corrupt the life of British Canada. Conservatives in Upper Canada were convinced that American republicanism was based upon unsound and dangerous ideas[59] and amounted to little more than a free-for-all of "galloping factionalism" and unbridled self-interest, which stoked the "inner fires of social jealousies" and "awakened in the breast of the

American citizen a spirit of personal ambition, unknown to any Englishman."
Such a system, they believed, would inevitably degenerate into a state of
"terrific anarchy," which, in turn, would beat upon the Canadian border
and then overrun their society if permitted into the colony.[60] Furthermore,
the disorders and unruly passions of the American political system, it was
thought, were exacerbated by the extreme emotionalism of its explosive
and chaotic religious life.[61] Men like Robinson and Strachan were firmly
committed to keeping all such dangerous and disorderly influences out of
Upper Canada.

Concerns about American attacks and annexation increased during
the 1820s when the United States wanted secure access and free naviga-
tion of the St. Lawrence River, which offered the easiest and least expensive transportation route to and from the growing settlements in Ohio,
Indiana, Illinois, and Michigan. British insistence on a policy restricting
access to the waterway frustrated and angered officials in Washington,
and sabers were rattled. Even after those tensions diminished with the
opening of the Erie Canal in 1825, new friction immediately occurred the
very next year when the British closed down all their West Indian ports to
American shipping. Renewed threats and fears of invasion flared up once
more in Upper Canada.

The security of the British provinces in America became the concern of
the Duke of Wellington when he entered the British administration in 1819
and undertook a thorough evaluation of Canadian defenses. The duke and
his War Office proceeded with the assumption that the Americans retained
ambitions about the acquisition of Canada, and he was convinced that any
serious dispute between Great Britain and the United States would very
likely provoke renewed American aggression against the Canadian
provinces. Wellington therefore developed a very elaborate and ambitious
plan to strengthen the defenses of British North America. He proposed
the rebuilding of the citadel at Quebec City and the construction of new
fortifications at various places along an eight-hundred-mile-long frontier.
His plan would also require a military force of 13,500 British regulars, as
well as an extensive canal system for the rapid movement of troops and
supplies.[62] Greater detail was added in 1825 when Colonel James
Carmichael Smyth was sent out to Canada with a contingent of engineers
to study defense needs right on the scene.

However, at the very time the Iron Duke was devising those expensive plans, there was heavy pressure on the British government to cut costs. In order to retrench without abandoning the defense of the Canadian provinces, the government tried a number of alternative measures to those proposed by Wellington. One of those was a renewed effort to substantially increase the population of Upper Canada. At the end of the War of 1812 the population of the province had been about 150,000. Then, beginning in the mid-1820s, with British government encouragement, the number of people emigrating from the British Isles to Canada soon surpassed those going to the United States.[63] By 1838 there were more than 400,000 people living in Upper Canada.[64] At the same time, policies there were changed in an attempt to discourage further American immigration because of concern about the threat those people might pose to the security and social stability within the provinces.

Part of the British migration also involved a very deliberate effort to enhance the size, quality, and leadership of the colonial militia. That was fostered by policies at home, which reduced the size of the military forces, and then encouraged, with pension and land grants, the resettlement of discharged officers and soldiers on the Canadian frontier.[65] The policy worked to some degree, and large numbers of retired, half-pay officers accepted land grants and eagerly set forth to become the "advanced guard of civilization" and the nascent landed aristocracy of the new society arising in the wilderness of British America.[66] There was also a program for the settlement and support of Anglican clergy and the establishment of the Church of England as a bulwark in Upper Canada against the disturbing influences of "itinerant fanatics" heading north from the United States.[67] As a consequence of those efforts, the American traveler Chandler Robins Gilman observed in the summer of 1835 that the people of Upper Canada were "more English than the English," and because there were so many retired army and navy officers among them, there was, he remarked, "a sort of military tone to the feeling of the people."[68]

During that same period, the British shrewdly continued to cultivate close relations with the Indian tribes that could be useful in the defense of Upper Canada against future American aggression. In the 1790s, John Graves Simcoe, the founding leader of Upper Canada, had regarded the Indians as indispensable to the protection of the province,[69] and then, even after the War of 1812, the British continued to view close affiliation with them as quite necessary. In order to maintain connections with the tribes living within the American Midwest, and with very deliberate intentions of influencing their loyalties, the British Indian Department continued its generous distribution of presents to the Indians at Drummond Island, at the north end of Lake Huron near the St. Mary's River, and at Fort Malden, near Amherstburg, across the border from Detroit. In 1828, when the International Boundary Commission gave Drummond Island to the United States, the British moved their northern gift-giving post to Penetanguishene, on Georgian Bay. Thomas Anderson, a British Indian agent, described how in one year at Drummond Island, the "issu[ing] of Indian presents commenced in June; and at the end of October . . . [he] had made issues to five thousand Indians from all points of the compass, including the Mississippi and Red River countries."[70] Likewise, there was a large procession of Indians from the United States who annually made their way to Malden. They regularly included people from Saukenuk. In 1828 a total of 9,422 Indians were given presents at both Malden and Drummond Island, with 5,906 receiving theirs at the Amherstburg post. In reporting that information to Sir John Colborne, then the chief British administrator of Upper Canada, Sir James Kempt, his counterpart in Lower Canada (Quebec), indicated at least four-fifths of all those Indians were from the United States and that they persisted in making their annual trips over the border in spite of repeated threats from American authorities to stop them.[71] The next year, when considering budget cuts, Colborne adamantly opposed any reduction of expenditures for Indian presents. "No alteration can yet take place with propriety, in the amount of the presents issued to the Indians who resort annually to Amherstburg from the United States, or to those who have been accustomed to visit Drummond's Island," he concluded.[72] The present-giving program was far more than a matter of mere charity. The British considered it prudent defense insurance, and Colborne and his colleagues undoubtedly agreed with James Kempt when he declared, "There is little doubt that by a continuance of kindness they [the Indians from the United States] will be disposed again to take up the Tomahawk when required by King George."[73]

The popularity of those programs among the Indians, especially those residing within U.S. territory, made American officials suspicious of British motives and designs. The old distrust, deeply internalized by the

Revolution and the War of 1812, could hardly be expected to simply disappear after 1814, especially among the men who had fought against the old archenemy. As a consequence, officials like Cass and Calhoun were virtually incapable of seeing anything the British did in Upper Canada as being primarily defensive in nature. In their minds, the building of forts and courting of Indians was all part of an ongoing British plot designed to do harm to the American Republic, and they were completely convinced the British remained entwined in malevolent conspiracies with the savages.[74] Indeed, John Quincy Adams concluded that the "bitter experience of thirty years had proved that all the Indian Wars" so cruelly inflicted on the innocent, good people of America "had been kindled by the pestilential breath of British agents and traders."[75] The paranoid style was very much the psychological leaven in their ideological worldview, and Great Britain was still the evil empire conspiring for their destruction.

Lewis Cass was especially distrustful of the British, and after the War of 1812, according to the historian Colin Calloway, "it would be several years before Americans in general, and Cass in particular, ceased to be haunted by the specter of a powerful Indian confederacy, revived by the [Shawnee] Prophet and supported by the British."[76] In a letter to Secretary of War Calhoun, who equally distrusted the British, Cass argued vigorously in the summer of 1819 that it was in the vital interests of the United States to prevent all further contact between the British and the Indians living within American territory. Concerning those Indians who persisted in making annual visits to Malden and Drummond Island, he contended they were "kept in a state of feverish excitement." "Their minds," he declared, "are embittered and poisoned toward us!"[77] Two years later, while on his expedition with McKenney to the west end of Lake Superior, Cass bitterly complained that the deeper they penetrated into the wild country, the more amazed and distressed he became by discovering just how strong and extensive British influence remained among the tribes. He attributed that influence mostly to the annual distribution of presents at Malden and Drummond Island and concluded, "There will be neither permanent peace nor reasonable security upon this frontier, until this intercourse is wholly prevented."[78]

In 1822 Cass had composed a speech for distribution among the Indian agents in the Michigan Territory, to be read to the Indians in their areas of jurisdiction. In that speech the Indians not only were to be told that their

"Great Father," the president of the United States, greatly disapproved of their visiting the British posts, but were also to be warned that the British agents would trick and deceive them in order to gain power over them for evil purposes. "When you leave the United States, persons are ready to whisper into your ears. Like bad birds they are flitting about you, telling false stories of us, poisoning your minds, and giving advice injurious to you and us," they were to be told.[79]

Some Indians were discouraged from going to Canada by that message, and during the same summer American military forces at Mackinac Island turned back Indian canoes on their way to Drummond Island. The few Ojibwa and Menominee who managed to get through told British agents they were fearful of being imprisoned and whipped when they returned home.[80] American attempts to stop the annual visits to the British posts appear to have been successful for at least a while. When the important Winnebago chief Four Legs arrived at Drummond Island from his village in northeastern Wisconsin in July of 1828, it had been four years since his last visit. In the meantime, he said, the muskets of his warriors and hunters had become broken or worn out and they had been without powder and shot for a long time. Four Legs explained, "The Americans have placed Great Guns to oppose our passage." Then in colorful language he explained to Thomas Anderson what had happened when they had set out on their current trip to Canada: "When we wished to come to our English Fathers, the Americans endeavored to persuade us not to come, saying 'what will you go there for?—I have trampled the Red Coats into the ground and nothing remains of them to be seen but their hands!'"[81]

"Notwithstanding the repeated threats of the American authorities and their having in one instance been actually fired upon, [the Indians] persevere in forcing their way to our posts," reported James Kempt in February of 1829. Certainly one major reason for that persistence was the opportunity of obtaining much-needed goods from the British. The U.S. federal government, eager to cut expenditures, had drastically slashed the budget for the Indian service by 50 percent in 1821 and then cut it even more in 1829.[82]

In 1815 Sir John Coape Sherbrooke, the governor-general of all British North America, ordered the Indian agents to inform their former tribal allies "distinctly and explicitly" that the British government would no longer assist them in their disputes with the Americans. That, however, was not the message delivered to them.[83] Rather, British officials in Upper Canada remained convinced it might still be necessary for the Indians "to take up the Tomahawk, when required by King George," as Kempt had put it. Those men undoubtedly continued to suggest to the tribesmen that the soldiers of the king would provide reciprocal armed support to them if they remained loyal to their true "fathers."

Beyond the mercenary manipulations indulged in by both sides, there appears to have been sincere affection and loyalty expressed by many of the tribes toward the British in Canada. Because of that, the Americans found it very difficult to replace the British and become their new "fathers." In 1816, when American military forces began moving in and building forts, a Winnebago chief from Wisconsin traveled to Drummond Island, where he declared, "I detest the Big Knives from the bottom of my heart" and then went on to say to the British commander, "Father, I know of no other Father but you!"[84] The second statement sounded almost like a profession of religious faith, and in some ways it was, simply because many of the tribal groups of the central woodlands attributed almost godlike powers to the British king, who, they believed, felt a warm paternalistic affection for his Indian "children." Those Indians sought to align themselves with his great power and draw upon it for their own well-being and protection. The British, in turn, skillfully played upon those feelings and beliefs to bolster their own interests. In the summer of 1823, for example, the Indian agent at Malden told a group of visiting Indians from across the border that "Americans were not the real Fathers of the Indians, and all the Americans wanted was the Indians' lands." Their "real Father," he said, was "the British King, . . . living over the great waters," and although he was then at peace "with all the world," he was "always prepared for any thing that may happen."[85] A year later, also at Malden, the message of implied military support must have seemed even more reassuring to the Indians, for they were told that even though "their Great Father the British King was at peace with all the world . . . at the same time he was prepared for war."[86]

For a time it had been British strategy to keep the Indians calm and restrained, discouraging them from stirring up trouble with the Americans, which might provoke retaliatory attacks against Canada. But, following the Winnebago War of 1827, as more Americans poured into the upper

Mississippi region and political pressures increased to have the Indians removed, more and more of the tribal leaders looked to the British for help. For example, when Four Legs arrived at Drummond Island in the summer of 1828, he described the country from which he had come as being "enveloped in a dense cloud" and said that he and his people had been "bent down (in great trouble) for two years by the Americans. . . . The Fire vessels are continually going up and down the River and we are in constant dread," he informed the Indian agent Thomas Anderson. But Four Legs feared the situation was much more foreboding than the mere disturbance of the peace by the intrusions of the Americans and their steamboats. He actually feared for the very physical extermination of all the Winnebago. He told Anderson, "It appears, my Father, from what I have heard from a Menomini friend that we have but a short time to live, this friend told me that when the Grass would get to a certain height (about mowing time) we would be cut off by the Americans." He wanted help from the British, especially from the king. "I speak with tears in my eyes [and] I am anxious indeed to hear from My Great father." In summarizing the conversation with Four Legs, Anderson told his superiors that the Winnebago had great confidence in themselves as warriors and Four Legs had assured him that if the British were to provide them with ammunition, "they would not hesitate to attack their vaunting enemy." In undertaking such an attack, the chief had said, it would "involve most of the western tribes on their side [and] they would immediately commence a massacre on the unprotected inhabitants of the extensive American Frontier, which would probably end in the [Indian] nations being restored to their rights of territory." With all this in mind, Four Legs told Anderson he expected he would "soon be called upon by his English Fathers to raise his war club against these Americans."[87]

That very same summer of 1828, the woodlands west of Lake Michigan must have been alive with rumors, and a group of Potawatomi—most likely those living at Milwaukee—sent out war belts to many other tribal bands living within Wisconsin, as well as to the Ottawa at L'Arbe Croche in Michigan. They did so with the intention of rallying the tribes against the Americans, in order "to crush the Big Knives," said Anderson. Many of the Indians who traveled to Drummond Island that season reported those activities to him and asked his advice about what they should do.[88]

About a month before Four Legs paid his visit to Drummond Island, Forsyth reported to William Clark that a man named Posseron had visited the Sauk on the Rock River. He identified Posseron as a French-Canadian who had been a lieutenant in the British army during the War of 1812 and who, after the war, had gone to work for the American Fur Company. Even then he had remained a troublemaker and during his visit to Rock Island had talked to the Indians in "very improper language," said Forsyth. He told Clark that Posseron, upon seeing the American flag flapping above Fort Armstrong, pointed to the banner and told the Indians it was just "a dirty piece of cloth, and fitting only to wipe a person's A[rs]e with it." More important, however, he also assured the Sauk that "British Troops were coming in from Canada to assist them [the Indians] to keep possession of their Lands, where their villages are."[89]

Just a short time before Monsieur Posseron's visit, Forsyth had been talking with the Sauk about the need for them to resettle themselves beyond the Mississippi. They had made an angry response and told the Indian agent "they would not move from the place where the bones of their ancestors lay, and that they would defend themselves against any power that might be sent to drive them away from their present villages."[90] Therefore, they must have derived considerable encouragement from what Posseron had to say, and felt reassured their British fathers still cared for them and were willing to come to their support.

Maybe it was just loose talk that had come from Posseron's mouth, or maybe he was a participant in an extensive and quite deliberate British strategy of anti-American agitation among the tribes, for, between 1821 and 1826, British agents from Canada were reported to be working among the Indians within the midwestern region as far south as the Arkansas Territory.[91] Tensions were increasing between the governments of Great Britain and the United States over interests in the Caribbean, and, in the late spring of 1827, reports circulated among the tribal villages concerning a quarrel between the two countries over "an island in the sea" and the impending outbreak of war between them. On hearing those reports, a delegation of Indian leaders from various tribes of the upper Mississippi valley set out for Malden in order "to hear the straight story from the British Indian agent." At the same time another delegation went off to Drummond Island for the same purpose.[92]

The next summer, as international tensions continued to escalate, a Fox warrior by the name of Naro-te-waig went to St. Louis and told Clark that the "Sauk Indians had been listening to bad birds who lived toward the sun rising (the British in Canada) and that they (the Sauks) intended to make war against the United States." Naro-te-waig also identified the Sauk chief Bad Thunder and a Sauk brave named Ioway (or Ihowai) as the ringleaders who planned to soon make war against the white people.[93] Later the same month, a passenger on board the steamboat *Indiana* reported to Forsyth he had received a warning from a Dr. Garland, who lived on the Henderson River. In their conversation the doctor had told him that more than three hundred Sauk and Fox Indians had gone to Canada to "compel the British to fulfill their promises made to the Indians formerly, to protect them and their lands." Dr. Garland had also said, according to the traveler, that he had reliable information indicating "the British would send troops, arms, and ammunition etc. to assist the Indians to drive away all the Americans out of the country." He expected the invasion to occur sometime that autumn, he told Forsyth.[94]

At the time, Forsyth knew for certain that a group of about one hundred Sauk men, women, and children had departed Saukenuk for Malden.[95] But there was nothing unusual about that. Almost every summer a party from Saukenuk made the trek to Malden by way of what had become known as the Great Sauk Trail. But perhaps this particular summer the doctor's tale made the old Indian agent somewhat more uneasy than he had been in the past. However, whatever his concerns may have been, they were greatly diminished when the Sauk returned in late August, and Forsyth happily reported to Clark that the Indians were far from pleased with the reception they had been given at Malden. "They were but illy received by the British, by their receiving but a few goods and very little civility shown to them in that country," he told the Indian superintendent.[96] That was good news for Americans officials, but it did not end their nervous speculations about conspiracies being plotted by the British and the savages. Later it was learned that Kinnekonnesaut, an important Sauk chief, had spent the winter of 1828 near Niagara Falls for the purpose "of uniting the Indian tribes of that country in behalf of the Sac band of Indians at Rock River."[97]

Early in 1829 James Kempt told Colborne he thought it inadvisable to reduce the quantity of presents given to the Indians in the coming summer.[98] Their attachment to the British remained too important. Then, quite late in the year, in early November in fact, a Sauk chief identified as Ayoroay (probably Ioway) visited Colborne in Kingston, at the east end of Lake Ontario. He was accompanied by a number of other Sauk braves, all "worn out with the fatigues of a long journey." Ioway or Ihowai was an important pro-British Sauk leader very active in attempts to create a wide-spread resistance movement among the tribes in order to prevent any further American expansion. As early as the summer of 1823, Forsyth had informed Secretary of War Calhoun that Ioway had returned home from Malden, having spent two or three years among the British, and had immediately begun telling the people of Saukenuk how generous and caring the British were toward the Indians. He encouraged them to go to Canada, and many of them did so, accompanied by a large number of Kickapoo and Delaware.[99]

In the summer of 1830 Black Hawk himself, then in his midsixties, traveled to Malden to seek the advice of the British fathers. The issue of the land had weighed heavily on his mind ever since the white people had first occupied the area in and around Saukenuk and pressure was exerted on the tribe not to return to the old village. After he spoke with British officials at Malden, he claimed they had advised him and his followers to remain peacefully upon their land and assured him the U.S. government would treat them fairly if they did so.[100]

When trouble arose the next summer, Clark told General Gaines the British most definitely had a hand in stirring it up. Because the Sauk persisted in making their annual treks to Malden, he told the general, the British had managed to retain a powerful influence over them, and that was especially the case with the Black Hawk faction, which he referred to as the "British party." It was the British connection, asserted Clark, that accounted for the American agents having so little influence with them.[101] Gaines concurred and was convinced there existed among the troublesome Sauk "a deep rooted infatuation toward England & relentless enmity toward the United States. . . . Their English friends," he told Adjutant General Roger Jones, "had spoken to them of an intended war" with the United States and sought their support.[102] Gaines regarded Upper Canada as a nest of enemies where the Sauk received their annual rewards for "their former treachery and [their] continued hostility toward the United States."[103] Because of his concern about this assumed conspiracy, the

Articles of Agreement and Capitulation he dictated to the Sauk after driving them out of Saukenuk required them "to abandon all communication & cease to have any intercourse with any British Post, Garrison or Town, & never again to admit among them, any [British] agent or trader."[104]

A few weeks later Gaines must have felt even more justified in having taken such action when the *Niles' Weekly Register* reported on some ominous disturbances occurring among the Indians of western Michigan. The savages there, the article indicated, had been holding hostile councils, and there was growing concern about their intentions to attack Chicago. But the article identified the real culprits behind those developments as shady individuals from across the Canadian border, stating without equivocation that "those hostile movements are ascribed to the intrigues of British emissaries among the Indians."[105]

While all this was taking place, and completely unknown to Gaines, the young Sauk war chief Neapope was on his way to Malden. Forsyth described him as "a smart and active young man of about twenty-eight or thirty years old." He was also an important tribal leader, with a well-deserved reputation for being a courageous warrior, and enjoyed much personal prestige on account of being a descendant of some of the Sauk's most important hereditary chiefs. Like Black Hawk, Neapope was a traditionalist, for, according to Forsyth, "he had never tasted whiskey or smoked tobacco." But, on the other hand, and somewhat out of character for a man of his culture, he was "passionate for an Indian [and] very talkative" and had an unusually "blustering way" about him, Forsyth mentioned.[106]

The details of his visit to Canada are not known, but when Neapope returned to Illinois in the fall of 1831, he stopped to visit Wabokieshiek at his village on the Rock River and there learned for the first time how General Gaines had driven Black Hawk and his band out of Saukenuk. The young chief remained with the Prophet throughout the winter, and at some point in the season, he later testified, Wabokieshiek sent him upon an errand across the Mississippi to Black Hawk's camp in central Iowa to invite the old leader and his people to come to the Prophet's village in the spring to grow corn there during the summer.[107] But, according to Black Hawk, Neapope's message was about much more than "making corn." By Black Hawk's account, when they met, Neapope offered him encouraging words from the British, who, the young chief said, had confirmed the right of the Sauk people to reside in their old village because the land there could only be sold "by the voice and will of the whole nation." The British fathers, he went on to say, felt sure the Americans would not force them out if they returned peacefully to Saukenuk. However, "in the event of war," declared Neapope, "we shall have nothing to fear! as they [the British] would stand by and assist us."[108]

As Neapope delivered his message, Black Hawk had every reason to be extremely pleased with the word from Canada. The talkative young war chief informed him that Wabokieshiek too had received a message from the British fathers. The information sent to the Prophet, he said, indicated the intentions of the British to send the Sauk "guns, ammunition, provisions, and clothing, early in the spring," and the vessels carrying that cargo would "come by way of Mil-wa-ke."[109] Neapope also reported that the Prophet had received wampum and tobacco from the Ottawa, Chippewa, Potawatomi, and Winnebago along with their solemn pledges to join with the British in the fight to support the Sauk in defense of their land. And even if they were defeated in their war with the Americans, Black Hawk and his band would be given safe refuge within the Selkirk settlement in Canada, Neapope assured him.[110]

Those messages must have seemed the fulfillment of Black Hawk's deepest wishes and most earnest prayers. Neapope's words must have reinforced his faith in the British fathers and renewed his hope for the preservation of the Sauk way of life, which he believed could not survive without Saukenuk. "During the night," he later said, "I thought over every thing that Neapope had told me, and was pleased to think that, by a little exertion on my part, I could accomplish the object of all my wishes."[111] He was deeply gratified the British fathers intended to stand up and protect them from the injustices of the Americans, and said he felt a great surge of revived optimism that his people "would be once more happy." Referring again to the happiness of the people, he said, "This has always been my constant aim; and I now begin to hope that our sky will soon clear."[112]

In the cold darkness of that winter night it must have seemed to Black Hawk that the Great Father, the British king, was about to awaken from his long sleep, perhaps stirred from his slumber by the cries of hungry Sauk women and their naked children. As the times had grown more troubled, and the conditions of life more miserable, the paternalistic intervention of the British—a possibility always implicit in the speeches of the king's agents at Malden—must have seemed the Sauk's last remaining hope of redemption. The news of such intervention being at hand must have been so remarkably reassuring for Black Hawk to hear that he could not permit himself to doubt its veracity. And, of course, he believed the British would never lie to their Indian children.

Months before Neapope's visit to Black Hawk's winter camp there had been new rumors of impending war between Great Britain and the United States. In a letter written to Lewis Cass in the late summer of 1831, Joseph Street remarked that many of the Sauk and Fox were "warmly attached" to the British and were "prepared at any auspicious moment to join the Standard of Great Britain, if raised against the United States." He then told Cass that those "ignorant and infatuated" people were "anxiously expecting such [an] event" to take place in a short time.[113] During the winter, rumors of war were heard once more upon the hunting grounds. In one instance, the Indians at the trading post operated by Joshua Palen on the lower Iowa River heard reports "that the English had sent a message to the Sauks . . . to keep possession of their lands & that they would help them as the English were going to war with the Americans."[114]

According to Felix St. Vrain, Billy Caldwell had brought such a message to the Sauk. Caldwell was a controversial man of chameleonlike qualities. He was the abandoned métis son of Captain William Caldwell Sr. of the British army and had been born in a Mohawk village near Niagara in Upper Canada in 1780. Since early adolescence he had made his way in the world by his wits and by adjusting his identity to fit his changing circumstances. Sometimes he was an English-Canadian or an Irishman, sometimes an Indian or a soldier of the king, and at others a British Indian agent or fur trader. But around 1820 he moved to Chicago and soon became a justice of the peace and an interpreter for the local Indian agents and traders. Then, in 1829, he radically changed his identity once more by becoming Sauganash, chief of the Prairie band of Potawatomi in northern Illinois.[115] Caldwell certainly had all the connections needed for transmitting such a message from the British to the Sauk or to Wabokieshiek, and in the spring of 1832 he was irritated enough with the U.S. government to want to cause trouble for it. In a letter to Forsyth he mentioned the government's plans to remove his Potawatomi band beyond the Mississippi and suspected "some underhanded work may be put in practice" against them. "The thunder storm looks black to us," he said, referring to the turbulence brought on by their impending removal, and then went on to lament that the Indians had "always been the dupes." Time was passing so swiftly, and he regretted, he told Forsyth, he was "probably never to act the part which . . . [he] was created for." What he meant by that is unclear, but it probably referred to his long-frustrated ambitions to become an important man. He was clearly upset about his situation, but there is no hard evidence to indicate either that he had contact with the British during the winter of 1831–32, or that he tried to instigate trouble for the Americans by telling either the Sauk or the Prophet that the British were coming to their rescue with military force.[116]

But whatever Billy Caldwell did or didn't do that winter, Major John Bliss, the garrison commander at Fort Armstrong, along with Felix St. Vrain, identified him as the rogue messenger. Referring to Black Hawk's followers, Bliss informed General Atkinson, "His band generally believe the Caldwell story that the British will help them whenever those Indians may get into war with the United States." He also reported that one of Keokuk's followers had come up from their Iowa River village to inform him about Black Hawk and Neapope holding talks with some bands of the Potawatomi, Kickapoo, and Winnebago, telling them "that the Canadian French and British will join them & that they can get as much powder & lead as they want two days march from" Rock Island.[117] At the same time, Nathan Smith, a trader who ran a post on the Des Moines River, told Atkinson that Black Hawk's band would soon be heading for the Prophet's village. He also informed him, "They have stated to me that they are going to the British."[118] The *Galenian* also reported Black Hawk's band had been "promised succor from the British—and that they expected their ammunition etc. from the British."[119]

Whoever the source of such information may have been, the story about the British coming to the support of the Sauk was well known, widespread, and generally believed throughout the upper Mississippi region. Equally evident was the fact that Black Hawk and his followers also believed it to be true. When they left their winter camp in Iowa in April to return to the Rock River valley, they carried with them a British flag.[120] The Potawatomi chief Shaubena said it was the flag Black Hawk had been given two years before on his last visit to Malden.[121] In addition to the flag, some Sauk men wore medals bearing the likeness of King George IV, others carried certificates signed by British officers, and one old woman took with her a copy of a speech made by General George Provost, at Quebec City in March of 1814. In that address the royal governor had declared to his Indian allies, "We must continue to fight together for the King, our Great Father [who] considers you as his children."[122] As Black Hawk and his "British Band" moved northward toward their old homeland that early spring, they must have felt a powerful sense of exaltation believing their Great Father would soon arise and join them in their righteous fight to reclaim the center of the world and all that had once made the Sauk a great people.

7

THE ROAD TO WAR

_____

Fare thee well. We go to fight
For the tribe's protection,
Yet we know the road to war
Ever is a long journey.

Chippewa song (translated by Frances Densmore)

SPRING CAME TO the lead mine region with stingy reluctance in 1832, bringing on cold winds and hard rains. Creeks and rivers rose and flooded their banks, and snow fell much later than usual. Nevertheless, the white people living there looked forward to a new season of hope and prosperity. There had been tough times for them ever since the Winnebago troubles of 1827. Persistent anxieties about Indian problems put life on a constant uneasy edge. Then all was made worse when lead prices plummeted, pushing the entire region into a severe economic slump. Conditions in Mineral Point, within the Michigan Territory, were typical of those in virtually all the other mining settlements. When Daniel Parkinson first moved there in 1829, it had been a boomtown with miners and merchants and settlers swarming in, all with high expectations and inflated hopes of almost instantly striking it rich. "The town grew up with great rapidity, and every thing wore a most pleasing and encouraging aspect," wrote Parkinson. Within a year, however, the bottom fell out of the lead market. Profits crashed, costs and prices rose, and, according to Parkinson, "in consequence of the great depression of the times, many persons became discouraged and left the country, many more gave up business, and the country at that period, and during the years 1830 and 1831, presented a most gloomy and unpromising appearance."[1] But it was not only tough times among the diggings; grain prices also collapsed, so that farmers too suffered major setbacks. Then everyone was hit and hurt by the scorching drought that prevailed through the long, punishing summer of 1831; there was an almost total absence of rain and a prolonged spell of stifling heat, resulting in dreadfully meager harvests and paltry supplies of grain. But in early April of 1832, everyone again hoped for better days as they caught scent of the musty dampness that floated on the winds. As the editor of the *Galenian* proclaimed, "This spring seemed to open prospects in the most flattering manner, and every man, woman, and child seemed to gladden as the spring approached. . . . It was a common exclamation here," he continued, "that our hard times were at an end."[2]

Many of the region's problems had been blamed on the Indians. The clouds of war had seemed to gather and thicken, and the unrelenting agitations of the Black Hawk band had seemed destined to be bringing on a devastating storm. But in the spring of 1832 all that seemed to have passed away. General Gaines had put those troublesome renegades sternly in their place and banished them once and for all beyond the Mississippi. Only one problem with them remained, arising from the aftereffects of the Sauk and Fox massacre of the sleeping Menominee encampment at Fort Crawford the previous July. It had been a particularly vicious attack, and the Menominee were determined to take their revenge. In midwinter Joseph Street warned William Clark that Menominee warriors were already gathering from their hunting camps between the Black and Chippewa rivers and were assembling a formidable force of about three hundred well-armed fighting men. "Their avowed intention," he told Clark, was "to go against the Sacs and Foxes in the Spring, if the Murderers of Prairie du Chien [were] not before that given up." He also told the Indian superintendent the Menominee had sent wampum belts among the Sioux, Ottawa, and Potawatomi, and informed him of the many indications that "an extensive combination of tribal forces was taking shape."[3] Then, at the beginning of February, Street wrote to Thomas Burnett, his subagent then on leave in Kentucky, reporting, "The Menominees and the Sioux are preparing for a retaliatory War this Spring, and if [the] government is not early in stopping them they will certainly go [at it], in considerable force."[4] Billy Caldwell was also well aware of the impending prospects for an unusually ferocious intertribal conflict and in a letter to Thomas Forsyth predicted the Sauk and Fox would have "their handfull" with the forces he felt certain would move against them from out of the north as soon as the rivers were free of ice.[5]

Just the possibility of such a conflict deeply concerned officials in Washington. It could rock the stability of the entire upper Mississippi region and would surely involve more and more tribes once it began. An accumulation of long-standing resentments, repeatedly irritated and inflamed by aggressive miners, dishonest traders, and conflicting intertribal relations could pour forth with contagious fury if the government failed to take decisive action to get control of the situation. In mid-March Elbert Herring, McKenney's replacement at the federal Indian Office, took steps to head off trouble and instructed Clark to take whatever measures he considered necessary to bring about the immediate surrender or apprehension of the Sauk and Fox men who had participated in the massacre of the Menominee at Fort Crawford. If he could not get them all, Herring told him, he was to at least take enough of them captive to set a proper example. If there were problems accomplishing that, he was to take hostages—maybe four or five of them from each tribe—and hold them until the Indians came to their senses and handed over the actual murderers. Herring was convinced those firm actions would prevent war. Therefore, he ordered troops from Jefferson Barracks to move up the Mississippi to assist Clark in whatever measures he chose to undertake.[6]

The job of applying military pressure, if needed, was given to Brigadier General Henry Atkinson, a meticulous, middle-aged officer who had acquired a reputation for being careful, cautious, and unusually well organized. Steady and dependable, without so much as a hint of personal flamboyance, Atkinson was a decidedly uninspiring leader. But at least he was no glory seeker with heroic aspirations, who might exploit the trouble with the Indians to advance his own reputation. In fact, he was well respected among the Indians for doing his duty with a rare, evenhanded fairness, not favoring the whites over the natives when enforcing treaty stipulations or government policies. All in all, Atkinson was a safe choice and had already proven himself by his coolheaded handling of the 1827 Winnebago disturbances, which he had brought to a conclusion without spilling any blood. He felt certain he could do the same in apprehending the Sauk and Fox fugitives who had murdered the Menominee, and was convinced that just a show of force would be quite sufficient to head off any further trouble. In fact, Atkinson seemed the ideal man for that job.

Two days after Indian commissioner Herring had written to Clark, Alexander Macomb, commanding general of the entire U.S. Army, ordered Atkinson to proceed to Fort Armstrong with an "efficient force." There, he told him, if the Sauk and Fox did not hand over the murderers—at least eight or ten of them—he was to then use force "to apprehend them or to take hostages." Macomb emphasized the importance of taking fast and aggressive action to head off the attacks planned by the Menominee and their allies against the Sauk and Fox, but also stressed that force was not to be applied "til it become absolutely necessary." Furthermore, he made it unmistakably clear that any Indians taken into custody were to be "humanely treated."[7]

General Macomb's orders did not reach Atkinson until the first of April—two full weeks after being sent. But once received, Atkinson immediately set to work. On April 3 he responded to his commander, assuring him that an appropriate-sized force would be ready to move out within three or four days, and promised Macomb the situation would be properly handled. Confident of his ability to deal with the Indians, he informed Macomb, "From a personal acquaintance with many of the principal Indians, among the Sacs and Foxes, & a knowledge of the country, and of their character, I am persuaded that I shall be able to carry your views into effect without much difficulty."[8]

It was a straightforward assignment. Atkinson quickly assembled his soldiers and supplies and, on Sunday, April 8, set off upriver from Jefferson Barracks with six companies of the Sixth Infantry regiment. Three of those companies were under the command of Major Bennet Riley, and they departed on the steamboat *Chieftain,* while the other three, headed by Captain Zalmon Palmer, were on the *Enterprise,* which also carried Atkinson and his staff. Colonel Albert Sidney Johnston, who served as Atkinson's aide-de-camp, set the total strength of the force at "about 220 men."[9] In setting out, they all assumed they had a well-defined and somewhat modest task to perform, which would not take much time or require much effort.

However, at that very same time, and completely unknown to Atkinson and his men, Black Hawk had already gathered a very substantial number of followers on the west bank of the Mississippi River, just a few miles above the mouth of the Des Moines River, where Fort Madison had once stood. There were men, women, and children, including a considerable number of elderly people, and, according to Black Hawk's own account, their aim was to "rescue" or "secure" their old village of Saukenuk. He also indicated that earlier in the season he had asked Keokuk to intercede for them with Clark to arrange a meeting between himself and the "Great Father" in Washington so he and the other chiefs might better explain to the president why it was necessary for them to retain possession of their old village. He hoped that such a meeting would enable them to settle their differences with the Americans in an amicable manner.[10] It was a naive hope, and when nothing came of it, Black Hawk felt compelled to act. Encouraged by Neapope, who had assured them of British help, the members of the determined band commenced their journey up the Mississippi. "Our women and children," explained Black Hawk, were "in canoes, carrying such provisions as we had, camp equipage, etc., and my braves and warriors on horseback, armed and equipped for defense."[11]

About sixty-four miles downstream from Rock Island, at Yellow Banks (now Oquawka, Illinois), they crossed over to the east side of the Mississippi, probably on April 6. The Indian agent Felix St. Vrain, then at Keokuk's camp on the Iowa River, became aware of what was happening and wrote to William Clark, on April 8, telling him, "Black Hawk and Napope with their bands are about crossing the Mississippi near the Yellow Banks."[12] But Atkinson knew nothing of any of that until the afternoon of April 10, when he reached the Des Moines Rapids, near the confluence of the Iowa and Mississippi rivers. There he was informed by an unidentified source that the Sauk band, consisting of four or five hundred heavily armed horsemen, as well as a large number of armed men and boys paddling canoes, had crossed over into Illinois. He was also told there were numerous women, children, and old people. Altogether Colonel Johnston figured the entire group consisted of about "two thousand souls." Johnston also estimated there to be somewhere between six to seven hundred warriors.[13] As soon as he acquired that information, Atkinson sent a dispatch to General Macomb apprising him of the situation.[14] When Atkinson and the *Enterprise* passed Yellow Banks two days later, all he had been told was confirmed by other informants, who also told him the Sauk had been joined by a substantial number of Kickapoo and Potawatomi.[15] All of that, of course, greatly complicated Atkinson's assignment. He was no longer sure what to do, and surmised in his letter to Macomb that the forces he had brought along were "not sufficient to contend successfully against eight hundred or a thousand well armed Indians."[16]

The *Enterprise* and General Atkinson reached Fort Armstrong around midnight on April 12. They had passed by Black Hawk and his people without even knowing it, but the Sauk had seen them and had become alarmed over the prospects of having to contend with the soldiers upon reaching the Rock River.[17]

Well before Atkinson's arrival, Fort Armstrong was awash with rumors and anxious speculation. On March 29 Felix St. Vrain had already received a warning from Keokuk and Pashipaho (Stabbing Chief), delivered by his own brother, Charles St. Vrain. It was the opinion of those two chiefs that Black Hawk and his followers intended to return to Saukenuk to grow corn during the summer. They said they had tried to persuade them to give up that foolish idea and remain in the West but had been rebuffed in their attempts. Charles St. Vrain knew by then of the band's determination to ascend the Mississippi and reported to his brother what he had overheard of a conversation between Black Hawk and the fur trader Russell Farnham at the Lower Rapids, near the mouth of the Des Moines River. In that exchange Black Hawk had told Farnham he indeed intended to "return and raise corn at the old village on Rock river," and that it was also his plan to kill Felix St. Vrain, Rinnah Wells, and George Davenport once he got there. Furthermore, during his stay at the Lower Rapids, Charles St. Vrain observed the warriors of the band "danced only War dances."[18] All that news caused a stir at Fort Armstrong, but the interpreter Antoine LeClaire attempted to calm fears by dismissing Black Hawk's murder threats as nothing more than the idle boasts "common to all Indians," and predicted the old man and his band would not even attempt to reoccupy Saukenuk but would instead take up summer residence in the new village on the west side of the Mississippi established two seasons before by the Fox refugees from Dubuque's Mines. On the chance LeClaire might be right, Felix St. Vrain had the cornfields there plowed in preparation for their arrival.[19]

The nature of the situation, as understood by the people on Rock Island, was given a new twist on Sunday, April 1, when Wabokieshiek, the Winnebago Prophet, wandered into Fort Armstrong and, without even being asked, told Felix St. Vrain he had sent two young men over the

Mississippi during the winter to Black Hawk's camp to invite him and his people to come to his village on the Rock River in the spring, where they could grow their corn in peace. When St. Vrain explained to him how the articles of capitulation imposed by General Gaines prohibited the Sauk from recrossing the Mississippi ever again, the Prophet claimed he knew nothing about any such rule and would not have extended the invitation if he had. Wabokieshiek then wanted to know who had signed such an agreement, and when St. Vrain answered by showing him the actual document, he abruptly said the Black Hawk band "might stay on their own side of the Mississippi"—meaning the west side of the river—and that "he would not meddle with them any more."[20] The conversation between the Prophet and the Indian agent was both frank and friendly, and even as it was ending, Wabokieshiek remained convinced he had done nothing wrong and "did not think [there had been] any harm in asking the Sacs to come to his village, believing that they had only agreed to not return to the village near the mouth of the Rock River."[21]

The next morning St. Vrain informed the commander of Fort Armstrong, Major John Bliss, of his conversation with the Prophet. Bliss was furious. He called Wabokieshiek in and subjected him to a stern interrogation, confronting him with a series of terse and probing questions clearly accusatory in tone. Bliss made threats and suggested all the inhabitants of Prophet's own village could be compelled to moved west of the Mississippi if he did not give him his full cooperation. The mood of the exchange was tense and hostile, and, in time, Wabokieshiek grew uncomfortable, then angry, and then finally stalked out of the room refusing to say anything more to the overbearing major. Upon leaving, he gave no indication of his plans. Bliss was convinced he was a troublemaker who was deliberately plotting to cause a violent disturbance between the Sauk and the U.S. government. He wanted him arrested and sent downriver to St. Louis in chains, but St. Vrain urged restraint, thinking such rash action would surely cause more trouble than it might prevent. All the same, the hotheaded Bliss began making preparations for war.[22]

At the same time Wabokieshiek was visiting Fort Armstrong, Joshua Palen, a fur trader who worked for Russell Farnham at a post near the mouth of the Iowa River, came in and told Bliss that Black Hawk and his people were preparing to move upriver to Yellow Banks, "where they would detach their families to what he called the Iron river . . . where they would be safe." After that, said Palen, "they would be at liberty to reoccupy their village & to commit any mischief."[23]

Two days later Charles St. Vrain wrote to William Clark from Keokuk's village, confirming what Palen had reported about the planned crossing at Yellow Banks, as well as the Indians' intentions to "re-establish themselves near the old village." Furthermore, the same day—April 8—a Sauk man by the name of Blacksmith arrived at Fort Armstrong from downriver and told Bliss that the Black Hawk band had already crossed over into Illinois and predicted they would reach the Rock River in four or five days. Their ultimate destination, he thought, was the Prophet's village rather than Saukenuk.[24]

Also on April 8, John Spencer crossed the Rock River and rode southward, and along the way came upon two members of the Prophet's village returning home. In a brief conversation they told him that "the British band did not intend to raise corn" that year. When Spencer returned to Fort Armstrong and reported to Bliss what he had heard, the major informed him that the settlers in the area had all come to the conclusion that Black Hawk was "determined to strike a blow and retreat across the Lakes to Canada." Bliss later told Atkinson he agreed with the settlers and said he too was convinced the hostile Sauk had been plotting hostile actions for some time.[25]

Three days later Keokuk, Pashipaho, and other Sauk and Fox chiefs friendly toward the Americans arrived at Rock Island. Keokuk indicated Black Hawk's band was larger than his own, and that a majority of the Sauk people had become followers of the old man. Then more information came in later from which Bliss deduced that Black Hawk was heading north along the east bank of the Mississippi, with a force of as many as six hundred warriors, which included about one hundred Kickapoo and Potawatomi. He also found out from another Indian who had been with Keokuk that Black Hawk and his warriors planned "to go to the Prophet's Village & remain there until their families have got out of reach, then to attack the settlements in small parties & run off to Malden."[26] This information seemed to validate all his previous suspicions.

Benjamin Pike, a leader among the settlers at Saukenuk, returned home on April 12 from a trip downriver and reported to Bliss there were 1,500 people with Black Hawk. He also said they had told him they intended to "take peaceable possession of the Prophet's village, but if the Whites want[ed] War they shall have it."[27]

All those rumors and reports, coming from diverse sources and alleging different motives and intentions to the Sauk, caused considerable consternation among the growing crowd of people gathering at Fort Armstrong. Where was the British Band going? What did they intend to do? Was Saukenuk their destination, or did Black Hawk and his followers intend to go on to the Prophet's village? And would there be war? Definitive answers were virtually impossible to get not only due to the incomplete and inaccurate nature of the information acquired by the Americans but also because of the apparent uncertainty and indecision among the leaders of the British Band itself. Indeed, from time to time it was difficult to tell who was actually in charge of the migration. When Keokuk and the friendly chiefs arrived at Rock Island on April 11, they stated the band was then "under the direction of some young chiefs one of whom is Black Hawk's son."[28] And later in the month, in a reply to a message sent to him by General Atkinson, Black Hawk asked: "Why do the whites enquire of me the reason for my coming here? I do not command the Indians. The Village belongs to the Chiefs." Black Hawk then identified Neapope as the "principal Chief of the Band."[29]

During the winter, Black Hawk had said his plan was to "rescue" their old village in the spring,[30] but in early April, after crossing the Mississippi, there was considerable confusion within the band about its destination and plans. When William and Erastus Deniston, two brothers who lived near Yellow Banks, met the Indians along the trail, their uncertainty was made quite evident. The Denistons informed Bliss: "They told different stories about their future residence. Some named Rock river, Some Illinois & other the sweet ground. The Bighead said he should raise no corn but should hunt on the head of Rock river & then go off."[31] A brief time later, John Spencer went to see the Sauk as they drew near the Rock River. He talked with Black Hawk's son Nasheweskaska, and asked him where they were going. His answer was imprecise. Perhaps it was a deliberate attempt to mislead the whites, or maybe just a reflection of the band's continued indecision, but Nasheweskaska answered that "maybe they should go over to their old village, or they might stop where they were, or go up Rock River to Prophetstown [the Prophet's village]."[32]

Nevertheless, as they drew close to the Rock River, Wabokieshiek paid them a visit shortly after his own disconcerting meeting with Bliss. When he left the fort, officials there wanted him to intercept the British Band and persuade them to turn back. Instead he did just the opposite. He urged them on, telling them they had every right to go wherever they wished as long as they remained peaceful. And as long as they remained peaceful, he argued, the American soldiers would not dare "molest" them.[33] It was after that when Blacksmith identified the Prophet's village as their destination, as did Benjamin Pike and Keokuk.[34] But even that did not settle it. Toward the end of April, when the band was already camped near the Prophet's village, Black Hawk himself, in answering a message sent to him by General Atkinson, said they had been "invited by the Winnebagoes at Peketolica to go and live with them," and implied his intention of doing so.[35] Therefore, precise knowledge about the British Band's plans remained hard to pin down, and, indeed, even Black Hawk may not have been sure where they were going and what they intended to do.

Such confusion must have caused considerable anxiety and irritation among the many people who, in good faith, had followed Black Hawk on this dangerous venture. In setting out, they undoubtedly believed they were heading for Saukenuk—returning home to the fertile fields and the graves of their ancestors—to regain their ancient way of life, which, until very recently, had brought them such happiness and abundance. They longed for all they had once shared, and that was especially true for the women who hauled the heavy burdens along the trail and tended to the needs of their families. But as their journey seemed to become more aimless, they must have grown ever more disgruntled, particularly as their provisions dwindled. The warriors on horseback also must have worried more and more about the safety of the slow and cumbersome band and wished for their leaders to settle on a decisive, clear-cut plan before they all bumbled their way into disaster.

In the meantime, Atkinson landed at Rock Island on Thursday, April 12. It had taken him five days to make his way upriver from Jefferson Barracks. As he had been preparing for that voyage, Black Hawk's band was departing from the site of Fort Madison. They crossed into Illinois and covered the sixty-four miles from Yellow Banks and the Rock River in about a week, for it was April 13 when Andrew Hughes, the subagent of the Iowa River district, discovered the band "only a few miles below the mouth of the Rock river."[36] Spencer, who had observed their progress, later recalled, "The Indians did not make more than ten miles a day, but came along regularly, reaching here [Rock River] soon after the General."[37] During a meeting at Fort Armstrong on April 13, Taimah's son, Apanosokeman, said he had visited their camp, which was then located near the last rapids on the Rock River, where they had moved after spending the previous night near the blockhouse constructed the year before by General Gaines a few miles south of the river.[38] That concurred with what Spencer recalled, which was that the Indians "went up Rock River about two miles and camped for the night."[39] The location of that camp was about five or six miles south of Fort Armstrong.

Atkinson certainly knew they were there. Black Hawk was also well aware of Atkinson's presence, and it caused him great concern. He and his followers felt sure the soldiers would try to prevent them from moving farther upriver. Black Hawk worried that they "might be taken by surprise." "Consequently," he said, "we commenced beating our drums and singing to show the Americans that we were not afraid."[40] Spencer heard them. "The next morning, at the old fort, we could hear them beating their drums and singing so plainly that they seemed but a short distance from us," he wrote.[41]

The morning after his arrival at Fort Armstrong, Atkinson broke into a flurry of activity, seeking to better assess the situation he would have to manage. Foremost, he wanted to know the size of Black Hawk's fighting force. He was also more than just a little curious about their plans and quite eager to find out if Black Hawk had alliances with other tribes. In seeking such information, he consulted the very best experts at hand and sent out his own agents to gather further intelligence. The answers he received were surprisingly consistent.

On the question of force size, Major Bliss said that there were "six hundred warriors, including one hundred Kickapoos & some Potawatomies."[42] George Davenport was more vague, saying only that Black Hawk had "induced a great many of the young men to Join them" and had "crossed about five hundred horses into the State of Illinois and sent about seventy horses packed, accompanied by their old men, women & children." Davenport also suspected they would be "joined by the Winnobagos, Pottawato[mies] and Other Indians."[43] A few days later, Felix St. Vrain, who was getting intelligence directly from the scene, indicated there were "at least six hundred warriors, among which are Kickapoos, Potowatomies, Winnebagoes," and also pointed out that the "unfriendly band of Sac Indians were constantly recruiting their forces."[44] Only Daniel S. Witter, a settler who had fled from the advancing Indians at Yellow Banks, made an exaggerated claim, saying that Black Hawk's force consisted of "1000 warriors," all of whom were "determined to fight."[45]

The experts were all in agreement about the primary intentions of the Black Hawk band. Every one of them was sure the Sauk had crossed the river with warfare on their minds. Davenport told Atkinson he had been informed by one of his traders who had wintered with them "that the British Band of Sack Indians is determined to make war on the frontier Settlements." They would first establish a stronghold in the swamps of the upper Rock River, he claimed, where their Winnebago and Potawatomi allies would join them, and then, predicted Davenport, they would "make a descent and murder all the Settlers on the frontiers."[46] A similar warning came from Andrew Hughes, who had actually followed the band after it made the crossing at Yellow Banks. The day after Atkinson arrived at Rock Island, Hughes wrote and informed him, "That those indians are hostile to the whites there is no doubt, that they have invaded the state of Illinois to the great injury of our citizens is equally true." Then the subagent urgently recommended "that *strong* as well as *speedy* measures should be taken against Black Hawk and his followers."[47] Nathan Smith was another man at Rock Island that April who knew a great deal about the Sauk. He was a longtime fur trader who, in fact, had just wintered in the Black Hawk camp on the Des Moines River, and because his wife was Sauk, Smith was quite fluent in their language. He told Atkinson that during the winter he had become well aware "that they intended to commence hostilities on the Americans in the Spring." Smith further reported that one of the Sauk men had told him "he would rather kill Genl. Gaines than any other being on earth," and in all his conversations with other members of the band "they always appeared to have a wish to fight the Americans."[48]

All those suspicions and warnings seemed fully confirmed by Apanosokeman and François Labussier, a well-educated, French-Sauk métis who often worked as Keokuk's interpreter. At the request of Keokuk and Wapello, those two men paid a visit to Black Hawk's camp near the rapids on the lower Rock in mid-April, to see if they could talk enough sense into those people to persuade them to turn back before they were in serious trouble. When they arrived, they were given a hostile reception. An angry and agitated member of the band accosted Labussier, knocking off his hat and accusing him of coming to tell lies. At the same time, "one of the Menommenie Murderers, brandished a Lance, saying that it had only served to kill some of the Manommenies at Prairie du Chien, but he hoped to brake, or wear it out on the Americans." Even Black Hawk himself told them "he would be prepared to die in twenty days." After hearing their report, Felix St. Vrain concluded, "Everything goes to show that they are determined, for war against the United States."[49]

Most observers on the scene were convinced the Indians had to be stopped and driven back across the Mississippi before there was serious bloodshed. John Spencer had been in their camp and noticed Black Hawk's warriors all "had fine looking guns, and seemed to be well armed." He also stated, "We all supposed the General would stop the Indians at this point."[50] The subagent Andrew Hughes advised strong action be taken to turn back the band while it was still near the mouth of the Rock River. Also, some months later, when reflecting back on the events of that spring, Colonel Zachary Taylor, who joined Atkinson's forces at Fort Armstrong, told his friend Quartermaster General Thomas Sidney Jesup: "I thought at the time I joined the Genl & still am of the opinion he ought not to have permitted the indians to have ascended rock River . . . without making the attempt to stop them, which I am under the impression he could have done."[51] Black Hawk himself nervously expected the American soldiers to use force to drive the band back across the Mississippi.[52]

Some historians of the Black Hawk War agree with Taylor. Roger Nichols, for example, thinks Atkinson should have at least met with Black Hawk, held a parley, and warned him what the consequences of his actions would be if he persisted in Illinois. That might have persuaded the band to withdraw to the west side of the Mississippi.[53] Cecil Eby also believes more decisive action should have been taken before the Sauk continued up the Rock River, and dismisses Atkinson as merely "a paper general, unwilling to proceed until all risk had been eliminated."[54] All the same, at the time those events were unfolding there were a number of very knowledgeable individuals who thought Atkinson's force was in fact far too small to take on the British Band by itself. William Clark, for one, told the secretary of war that he was convinced that "a very considerable force, and properly concerted measures" would be "indispensably necessary to drive those hostile Bands from the Lands they . . . invaded."[55] Atkinson had no such strength at his disposal, and Thomas Forsyth, who often differed with Clark, agreed that the troops at Fort Armstrong lacked the capacity to deal with Black Hawk. Exaggerating the numbers for sarcastic effect, he asked his friend John Connolly: "What is one hundred & fifty men under Genl Atkinson to do with 2000 Indians? . . . It is a farce!" he declared.[56]

But there was no hesitancy on Atkinson's part in deciding what to do. Rather quickly he made up his mind not to move against Black Hawk while the band was still encamped near the mouth of the Rock River, telling General Macomb his forces were "not sufficient to contend successfully against eight hundred or a thousand well armed Indians."[57] Even after finding out the Indians were not nearly as numerous as first thought, he held fast to his decision. Again he wrote to Macomb, reporting there to be about five hundred warriors who had "assumed a hostile attitude," but once again stated he "thought it most advisable not to pursue them" since his own force was "too small to oppose to them with a prospect of success without great risk." If he attacked and failed, "that would only give them confidence and add to their numbers the wavering and disaffected" from among the other tribes. Atkinson also pointed out that the Indians had committed no hostilities whatsoever since crossing the Mississippi, but felt sure an attack from him would provoke a violent response from them, which might precipitate an outburst of vicious assaults upon the unprotected frontier.[58]

It should be recalled that General Atkinson had at his disposal only the 220 men he had brought upriver, along with Bliss's two undersized companies stationed at Fort Armstrong. All were infantry soldiers, while the Sauk warriors were on horseback and hence able to cover considerable distances at rapid speeds. The slow-moving foot soldiers would be at a decided disadvantage when chasing after such a highly mobile enemy force well acquainted with the terrain. Furthermore, no one in their right mind, with even a superficial knowledge of the Sauk, should have underestimated the courage and ferocity of their warriors, especially if called upon to defend their women and children. Henry Atkinson had been on the frontier since the summer of 1819. He knew the Indians better than most men in his profession, and his considerable knowledge and experience led him to conclude that caution was the better part of valor in the situation he faced.

But all the same, he was not idle or ambivalent. The same day he informed Macomb of his decision not to attack the Sauk, he met with Keokuk, Wapello, and the other friendly chiefs at Fort Armstrong. Immediately he set the tone for the council with some tough talk and blunt warnings. Atkinson told his audience that if Black Hawk and his followers did not come to their senses and recross the Mississippi, measures would eventually be taken to compel them to do so. And if they resisted, there would be hell to pay. "I will treat them like dogs," he declared. "They can be as easily crushed as a piece of dirt," said Atkinson, standing before them in his full-dress dark blue, brass-buttoned uniform, with his sword at his side and dirt in his hand, sternly asserting, "If Black Hawk's band strikes one white man [,] in a short time they will cease to exist!"[59]

After that, during the next few days, he sent messages to virtually every official of any importance in the entire region, apprising them of the situation and alerting them to be on their guard. He wrote Governor Reynolds, ordered more supplies for his own troops, and then sent letters to Henry Dodge, Henry Gratiot, and Joseph Street, as well as to John Kinzie, the Indian subagent at the Fox-Wisconsin portage, William Ferguson, the subagent at Galena, and Samuel Stambaugh, who was then in charge of Indian affairs at Green Bay. Orders and information were also sent to Captain Gustavus Loomis at Fort Crawford and Captain Joseph Plympton, who was then the commanding officer at Fort Winnebago. Then, on April 14, Atkinson boarded the *Enterprise* and set out for Fort Crawford, where, two days later, he inspected the troops in the morning and met with Loomis and Street in the afternoon to decide on what measures were needed to prevent the Menominee and Sioux from carrying out their plans to attack the Sauk and Fox villages to the south. On his way back to Rock Island, he stopped and met with Henry Dodge in Galena. Together they formulated a plan for the defense of the mining region. And as soon as he arrived back at Fort Armstrong on April 18, he began preparations for another meeting with the friendly chiefs. That council convened the next morning, and three of those who had murdered the Menominee were surrendered into his custody. The other fugitives, he was told, had taken refuge in the British Band. Five days later, Atkinson sent two Indian runners to Black Hawk's camp with a message for the old man himself, and the day after that he dispatched orders to Fort Crawford, commanding Captain Loomis to send him three companies of soldiers as quickly as possible.

The general's letters to Governor Reynolds were the most important business he turned his hand to during those hectic mid-April days, for they set in motion a chain of developments that had unanticipated, far-reaching consequences.

In his first letter to Reynolds, written on April 13, Atkinson set a tone that was sure to alarm and provoke him. An emotionally volatile man, the governor frequently jumped into ill-considered actions and was strongly inclined to read into even the most insignificant of Indian disturbances sinister designs and diabolical threats. He was easily agitated, and Atkinson seemed to deliberately play upon Reynolds's phobias and prejudices. While most of the letters he sent to other people were almost clinical in their exactitude, those he wrote then to Reynolds exaggerated the dangers and bristled with phrases sure to excite strong emotions. That appears to have been his purpose. With insufficient forces of his own, Atkinson may have intentionally tried to spur Reynolds into making a hotheaded reaction to the Sauk band's incursion into Illinois, so that once again, like the summer before, he would call the militia into action. Atkinson knew full well how much the Indians feared the militia, and probably reasoned that just the threat of its involvement would be sufficient to panic the Indians into crossing back over the Mississippi.

The general and the governor were made of decidedly different stuff. Atkinson was a stable and methodical individual with all the qualities of self-discipline one would expect of a man who had spent his entire adult life in military service. The sixth son of a North Carolina plantation family, he was polite, gracious, and of an amiable disposition, but not inclined to become chummy or gregarious. Nor was he a drinker in a profession that had more than a fair share of drunkards. Henry Atkinson was a responsible person with a low tolerance for disorder of any kind, a rather anal-retentive sort of fellow who meticulously planned his every assignment and carefully calculated his every move. He was dependable but dull, and had made his way in the army—all the way up to the lofty rank of brigadier general—by being competent and conscientious, and survived repeated budget cuts and force reductions by not sticking his neck out and by remaining loyal to patrons who looked out for his interests. But he was also fair-minded and decent to the men who served under him and was strongly inclined to settle conflicts by the most peaceful means possible. Indeed, he had much more the temperament of a peacemaker than a warrior, and by 1832 he had managed to spend twenty-four years in the army without ever once having led men in battle.[60]

John Reynolds, by contrast, was a person unusually eager to be known as a man of bold and decisive action. He was certainly more a man of action than one of intellect, for Thomas Ford, later to become the governor of Illinois himself, remarked that Reynolds was "a man of good talents in his own peculiar way," but "no one would suppose from hearing his conversation and public addresses that he had ever learned more than to read and write and cypher to the rule of ten."[61] In politics he was a moderate Democrat who favored internal improvements and was therefore not completely an orthodox adherent to the Jacksonian persuasion. But he related well to the voters and, according to Ford, "had learned all the bye words, catch-words, old sayings, and figures of speech invented by vulgar ingenuity and common among a backwoods people," and they comprised the essence of his political discourse.[62] But, even with all those "good ole boy" skills, many people perceived him as being only the lesser of the two evils presented to them in the election campaign of 1830. His opponent was William Kinney, then the lieutenant governor. Kinney was a semiliterate Baptist preacher and a "whole-hog" Jacksonian—which meant he did not favor either banks or internal improvements—and, according to Thomas Ford, Kinney "went forth electioneering with a Bible in one pocket and a bottle of whiskey in the other" so he "could preach to one set of men and drink with another, and thus make himself agreeable to all."[63] By comparison, Reynolds was a pillar of respectability and refinement. But perhaps William Orr, editor of the *Kaskaskia Republican*, reflected the opinion of a great many people when he admitted to a friend he had voted for Reynolds not "from the conviction of his entire fitness" for the office but mostly because he "believed him to be better qualified *in point of education* than the gentleman by whom his election was opposed."[64] Without claiming too much, Reynolds was in fact better educated than Kinney. He had actually attended a college, at least briefly. At the invitation of an uncle, young John had gone off to Knoxville at the age of twenty-one with all his backwoods rough edges conspicuously showing, intent upon becoming a college man. He enrolled for classes. He tried but failed, and in the process appears to have suffered a "nervous breakdown," for according to one historian, young John Reynolds was sent home to Cahokia by his physician, who warned him "never to study again, lest it damage his mind."[65] He deviated from that advice just enough to read the law and to be admitted to the bar. Only later, after his time as a mounted ranger in the War of 1812 and after his marriage to a French "Creole" widow with exceptionally good social and political connections, did his career as a lawyer and land speculator begin to prosper. Reynolds also got into the dry-goods business in Cahokia and in 1819 was appointed to a judgeship. He was a good-looking, good-natured man made of "easy and pliable material,"[66] as Ford put it, except he was possessed by a near-fanatical loathing of the British and was "a well known Indian hater."[67]

In his first letter to Reynolds of April 13, Atkinson informed the governor that Black Hawk had crossed the Mississippi with a fighting force of about five hundred mounted men and was heading up the east bank of the Rock River toward the village of the Winnebago Prophet. While he pointed out that the Indians had not yet engaged in any hostile activities, he did declare, "I think the frontier is in great danger." He also admitted to Reynolds that his own force was simply "too small to justify" him "pursuing the hostile party," but assured the governor he would use all means at his disposal to "co-operate" with him in the "protection and defense" of the frontier.[68]

Reynolds undoubtedly already knew about the British Band's movements, but Atkinson's letter, and especially his declaration of the frontier being in "great danger," gave him ample justification to do what he must have been itching to do: to once again call up the militia. Atkinson had not asked for that, and had no authority at the time to request it, but it was an election year. He surely knew that Reynolds lusted for the opportunity to use the "crisis" to acquire for himself a heroic reputation as the courageous man who saved the state from the bloodthirsty onslaught of a savage invasion. Not reacting boldly enough to such a threat, and perhaps appearing too slow, indecisive, and unmanly, would diminish his popularity and thereby hurt his chances for reelection. On the other hand, killing Indians was sure to stimulate considerable public interest. It would certainly be popular among his constituency and enhance his vote-getting appeal. In replying to the general, Reynolds thanked him for making him aware of "the necessity of energetic movements to protect the frontier settlements."[69]

In his next letter, sent on April 18, Atkinson continued to sound the alarm, to which Reynolds reacted with all the predictability of a well-conditioned Pavlovian dog. "They are so decidedly hostile," declared the general, "that nothing short of punishment will bring them to a proper sense of their misconduct."[70]

Nine days later he turned up the heat even higher with yet another letter, raising the possibility of the Winnebago, Kickapoo, and Potawatomi joining forces with Black Hawk, which would give him a force "amounting to 1000 or more men," asserted Atkinson. Adding to that, he informed Reynolds that the subagent Henry Gratiot had been to Black Hawk's camp and, according to him, said Atkinson, the old warrior had declared "that his heart is bad, and he will not return [across the Mississippi], that if I send after him, he will fight, and that *he can whip us.*"[71] No such phrase as "he can whip us" ever appeared in Gratiot's report,[72] and Atkinson used it in no other correspondence except for that one single letter sent to Reynolds. With the governor, that remark, along with Atkinson's warnings of dire danger, produced a predictable reaction: Reynolds mobilized the militia and prepared for war.

On the other side of the situation, Black Hawk's plans remained quite murky. After reaching the Rock River on April 13, he and his followers had continued upriver in the direction of the Prophet's village. A few days before that, Wabokieshiek had joined the band somewhere "below Rock River." He was still upset from his meeting with Bliss but told Black Hawk the "American war chief" would not harm them while they remained peaceful, pointing out how that would buy them some much needed time "since they were *not yet ready* to act otherwise." And then the Prophet said, "We must wait until we ascend Rock river and receive our reinforcements, and we will then be able to withstand an army."[73] In that statement he was undoubtedly referring to the assistance he anticipated getting from the British, as well as the support from other Indian tribes in the region. Nevertheless, it remains unclear whether Black Hawk planned to initiate a war or simply enhance his ability to defend his people against anticipated American attacks.

Shaubena, the Potawatomi chief, said that sometime during April one of Black Hawk's sons and a Sauk warrior by the name of Little Bear left the band's encampment near the mouth of the Rock River and met with a large gathering of Potawatomi warriors at a place identified as "Indian town" for the "purpose of inducing the warriors to become their allies."[74] A few weeks later, when the band had established another camp about twenty-five miles above Dixon's Ferry, Shaubena met with Black Hawk himself. After dinner, he said, the old leader took him and other Potawatomi chiefs off to a nearby grove of trees to talk with them in private. There Black Hawk warned that the Potawatomi too would soon be forced by the Americans to leave their homes and "be driven westward toward the setting sun to find a new home beyond the Father of Waters." He then explained that "he was on the war-path, and if his friends gave him support, the whites would treat on favorable terms and return to him his village." He also told his guests he had sent runners to many other villages far and wide, and that if the Indians of the region would unite, "they would be so strong the troops would not attack them, but would make overtures for peace."[75]

On April 24 Atkinson sent a message to Black Hawk, which was paternalistically condescending in tone, and addressed him as if he were some naughty child. He began by declaring that the "great father"—meaning the president—would be angry with them for violating their agreement with General Gaines. Then in admonition—more an urging than an order—he wrote: "I advise you to come back and recross the Mississippi without delay. It is not too late to do what is right—and what is right do at once." If they chose not to act on his advice, he warned, he would write their "great father" and tell him of their "bad conduct," and then chided, "You will be sorry if you do not come back."[76]

At the very same time, Henry Gratiot was paying a visit to Black Hawk's camp. He had made his way down from Turtle Village, a Winnebago community on the Rock River just within the southern boundary of the Michigan Territory, and traveled 160 miles by canoe with some of the "principal men" of that village who were not in favor of what Black Hawk was doing. They reached the Prophet's village on April 24 and found the Sauk encamped nearby. Gratiot and his party received a cold reception, and an altercation soon flared up when Gratiot hoisted a white flag over his tent. Black Hawk had it taken down and replaced by a British flag. Gratiot responded. He took down the British flag and put the white one back on the staff, only to have a group of irritated Sauk men pull it down again. In the end the dispute was terminated by leaving both banners flying. Soon after that Gratiot learned that Black Hawk's people, together with all the Prophet's followers, planned to move still farther upriver in order to spend the summer among the

Winnebago living on the Pecatonica River. Meanwhile, he observed most of the Sauk men in camp spent most of their time "in dancing their war dance."[77]

It was while he was there that Atkinson's message to Black Hawk arrived. Gratiot read it aloud, having it translated and explained to Black Hawk, who then made a brief but firm reply. In reporting what Black Hawk said, Gratiot wrote, "He says that, he intends to go further up Rock river—his heart is bad, and if you send your officers to him he will fight them." Gratiot also noted that Black Hawk treated the general's message "with apparent contempt."[78]

Henry Gratiot's account was at odds with one delivered to Atkinson just the day before by two Sauk messengers sent by the chiefs of the British Band to explain to the general their position and plans. In that message, Neapope—identified as their "principal chief"—wanted Atkinson to know they "had no bad intentions" but were nonetheless determined to move on and settle with the Winnebago on the Pecatonica. The messengers indicated that about twenty Winnebago had come to their camp and "invited them to go on." Furthermore, Black Hawk himself communicated through the same messengers, saying, "I have no bad feelings."[79]

Although clearly an attempt to reassure the general of their lack of belligerent intentions, that same evening, soon after the messengers departed, Keokuk warned Atkinson not to trust anything they had said. "The Indians are decidedly hostile," declared Keokuk, saying that "they will go up Rock river to get among the swamps, and that their object was mischief."[80] From this information it would appear that both Keokuk and Gratiot were each attempting to manipulate the situation in order to precipitate violent action against Black Hawk and his followers. And in fact they appear to have succeeded. The very next day—April 27—Atkinson wrote to General Macomb. In his brief dispatch he reported the incident about the British flag and the war dancing in Black Hawk's camp, and then declared, "They must be checked at once, or the whole frontier will be in a flame."[81]

In the meantime, Governor Reynolds had risen to the bait dangled before him by General Atkinson and had sounded the alarm, proclaiming, for all to hear and read, that the Indians had "assumed a hostile attitude," had "invaded" the state, and were taking "possession of the Rock River country, to the great terror of the frontier inhabitants." He also told the public he considered "the settlers on the frontier in imminent danger" and was therefore calling upon the militia to arise and defend the country. He hoped his brave fellow citizens would respond "with promptitude and cheerfulness" and instructed them to gather at Beardstown, on the Illinois River, by April 22. From there they would hunt down the offending savages.[82]

Events, which eventually proved disastrous, were thereby set in motion by a flurry of vague rumors and ill-informed guesses, and an already confusing situation was made even more problematic by the mixed motives and personal agendas that had already caused so much trouble throughout the region. And in that fog of ambiguity, fearful imagination began to take control of leaders on both sides, driving them faster and farther down the road to war.

8

A MARTIAL PEOPLE

*The people of the backwoods: "Bred from generation to generation
in the forest, they were as expert as the Indians, in all the arts of the
hunter and all the devices of savage life. . . . Acquiring hardihood
and courage by these manly exercises, they became a martial people,
enterprising and fearless, careless to exposure, expert in horsemanship, and trained to the use of arms."*

Judge James Hall, *The Indian Tribes of North America,* vol. 3

ONCE BLACK HAWK and his British Band had crossed the Mississippi,
and once the Illinois militia was on the move, the two forces were on a col-
lision course, which neither seemed able or willing to alter or escape.

Even though it was plowing time on the farms, the response to
Governor Reynolds's call to arms was immediate and enthusiastic. There
was both anxiety and excitement in that, but at the very heart of it all was
an intense hatred for the Indians. When the militiamen had set out the
previous spring, Reynolds had remarked that they had "entertained rather
an excess of the Indian ill-will." In April of 1832 that "ill-will" was back
with a vengeance, and many of the same men, who the year before had
been forced to settle for burning some lodges and desecrating some
graves, were more eager than ever to kill some savages.

Indian hating was part of the very character of society in the West, and
its very essence was distilled down and presented in a powerful, highly
popular short story written by Judge James Hall, who lived in Vandalia,

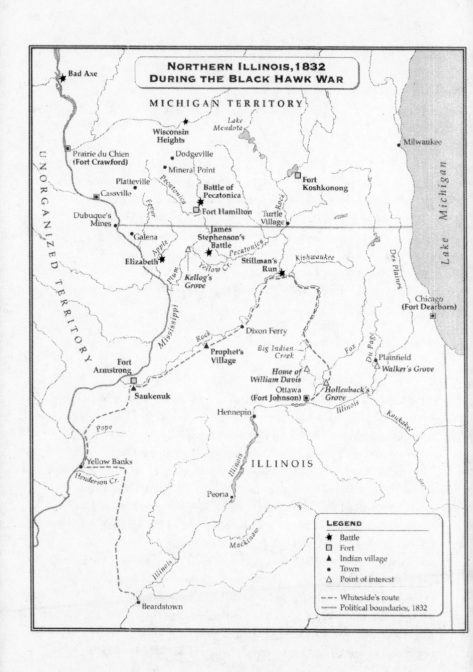

NORTHERN ILLINOIS, 1832
DURING THE BLACK HAWK WAR

MICHIGAN TERRITORY

Bad Axe

Lake Mendota

Milwaukee

Wisconsin Heights

Prairie du Chien (Fort Crawford)

Dodgeville

Mineral Point

Fort Koshkonong

Platteville

Cassville

Battle of Pecatonica

Fort Hamilton

Dubuque's Mines

Turtle Village

Galena

James Stephenson's Battle

Elizabeth

Kellog's Grove

Stillman's Run

Kishwaukee

Des Plaines

Chicago (Fort Dearborn)

Dixon Ferry

Rock

Prophet's Village

Big Indian Creek

Fort Armstrong

Home of William Davis

Plainfield

Walker's Grove

Saukenuk

Ottawa (Fort Johnson)

Hollenback's Grove

Illinois

Hennepin

Pope

Illinois

Yellow Banks

Henderson Cr.

ILLINOIS

Peoria

Mackinaw

LEGEND

★ Battle
□ Fort
▲ Indian village
• Town
△ Point of interest
--- Whiteside's route
Political boundaries, 1832

Beardstown

UNORGANIZED TERRITORY

Lake Michigan

Fever

Apple

Plum

Pecatonica

Yellow Cr.

Mississippi

Rock

Fox

Du Page

Illinois

Kankakee

Pecatonica

Illinois, where he operated the *Illinois Gazette*. Published in 1828, he titled it simply "The Indian Hater."

The brief tale began with the narrator stopping into a general store in a small Illinois frontier town, where he encountered a group of local people. After talking with them for a while, he noticed a solitary man, about fifty years old, slender, tanned, muscular, and perceptibly different from the other customers. "In his eyes," said the narrator, "there was a look of watchful, sagacious self-possession. . . . He was dressed," he continued, "in a coarse, gray hunting-shirt, girded round his waist with a broad leather belt, tightly drawn, in which rested a long knife, a weapon common to the western hunter."[1]

After a time, some Indians entered the store. The appearance of the man clad in the hunting shirt was immediately transformed by their intrusion. His muscles became rigid and taut, his cheeks flushed, and his eyes gleamed with a strange ferocity as his hand tightened around the hilt of his large hunting knife. The Indians, upon catching sight of him, abruptly turned and departed.[2]

Soon after the Indians had left, the man followed. In asking the other customers about this mysterious figure, the narrator learned he was Samuel Monson and that he had a particularly deep hatred for all Indians. Monson sometimes went to their hunting grounds, where he lay in wait for them, he was told. And it was said that Monson could actually "scent a red skin like a hound." He hunted them "like wild beasts," declared one customer. But at the same time, the people in the store described Monson as an exceptionally good neighbor and an honest man who worked hard, paid his debts, and was always willing to extend a helping hand to a fellow settler. Throughout the conversation it was also quite apparent that all of those who spoke shared Monson's attitudes toward the Indians, for many of them said they had lost family members in Indian raids. Furthermore, explained the narrator, "all who have been raised in the backwoods, have been taught to fear and dislike them."[3]

Eventually the narrator resumed his journey over the green vastness of the prairie. Along the way, some distance from the town, he unexpectedly came upon the body of a newly slain Indian. Monson soon appeared and took credit for the killing, and then, by way of explanation, recounted the tragic tale of his own unfortunate family. He described how one autumn evening, after a long day of gathering corn, he was taking his ease by his hearth while his children played in the cabin and his wife busied herself with some chores. All of a sudden their tranquillity was shattered by a bloodcurdling yell that came from out of the nearby forest. Going to the door to investigate, he discovered his haystacks on fire; then, bolting out of the darkness came a party of "yelling savages," rushing toward his home like a pack of "howling wolves." The "monsters," said Monson, then set fire to the cabin roof and stood back laughing. Monson sped from the house with his rifle and ax, and although he managed to kill several of the attackers, he was soon overpowered and struggled in vain to loose himself as his entire family perished in the flames. He witnessed their agonies and heard their cries but was unable to help. When later he managed to escape, he vowed to make the killing of Indians the central purpose of his existence.[4]

Hall's story was widely read and firmly embraced by people in the West, for it reflected some of their strongest feelings and deepest fears and its main character was, to them, a heroic figure with whom they could easily identify. In their own folk culture, Monson—the Indian Hater—was an *Everyman,* while the Indian played a role similar to that of the *Wild Man* in medieval folklore. In the medieval imagination, the Wild Man had been the dark and repulsive predatory figure who lurked in the shadowy places beyond the boundaries of civilized order and Christian goodness, waiting to prey upon the innocent and vulnerable. It was particularly the women and children he victimized, catching and carrying them off into the wild places to slake his demented thirst for blood and carnage and satisfy his other perverted desires. He was the grotesque personification of human depravity at its worst—dwelling beyond decency, beyond order, beyond all hope of redemption, and living in a loathsome state in which passions and appetites had gained full ascendancy. He was clearly the negative archetype of what proper men could surely become outside the restraining influences of social order where their own sinful drives and desires might take over their lives.[5] The Indian—at least the image of the Indian that prevailed in the imagination of the trans-Appalachian West—was such a Wild Man within an American context. He was seen as the archenemy of everything good and decent, and the Indian Hater, like some Beowulf in buckskin, championed the right and set the proper example for what a true man should strive to be. Indeed, both the wild Indian and the Indian Hater were major and necessary figures in the regional mythology from which the people there derived both their collective and personal identities.

The entire country was absorbed in issues of identity at this time. The Revolution, and the sudden and complete rejection of the old English identity, had brought on a compelling need to create a new one in order to describe and define what an "American" was. But that was no simple undertaking, because, especially following the War of 1812, the whole country was caught up in rapid and radical change, explosively growing in numbers and size and being transformed by the tumultuous forces of its own massively expanding market system. That onward rush of change swept aside many of the old social restraints and dissolved long-standing bonds and loyalties that had previously held communities together. People felt confused and disoriented. More and more of them were leaving behind the old and familiar places in the East and moving in waves of mass migration westward, so that by 1830 28 percent of all the country's people lived in the region between the Appalachian Mountains and the Mississippi River. Feelings of anxiety and insecurity ran rife throughout society and were made all the more severe by the passing of the Revolutionary generation. The founders had long provided the entire nation with a shared sense of purpose and direction. But in dying, and thereby passing from history into mythology, they left what seemed an unfillable void in the public life of the country and a disturbing sense among their progeny of being cut off from the sacred time of the nation's origins. Furthermore, the inheritors of the Revolution felt anxious about and unsure of their own adequacy to hold together and lead the nation their fathers had made, or ever approach the standards of virtue and valor attributed to them. Therefore, in the years following the War of 1812 all those feelings and developments made the need for a clear sense of national identity seem all the more urgent.[6]

As a scholar of nationalism, Benedict Anderson pointed out how modern nations are for the most part "imagined communities."[7] That has been especially true for the United States, and at no other time in the nation's history were those imaginative efforts more intense than in the span of years between the Battle of New Orleans and Lincoln's delivery of the Gettysburg Address. During those decades, much of what was thought and believed concerning the meaning of being American was articulated by the country's newly emergent intellectuals, particularly the writers and artists of the urban Northeast. They, more than anyone, were most vehement about the need for the United States to declare its cultural independence from Great Britain and the entire Old World, and immersed themselves in efforts to present a distinctive American voice, style, and perspective, which accurately reflected the country's unique collective character. Nevertheless, what writers like James Fenimore Cooper, William Cullen Bryant, Washington Irving, Ralph Waldo Emerson, and artists such as Thomas Cole and Asher B. Durand, along with a host of lesser lights, came up with proved to be a primarily regional vision which saw the country from a decidedly eastern point of view. All the same, they sought to project that vision upon the entire nation and imagined themselves to be the spokesmen for an all-encompassing national identity.

One strong characteristic of this myopically eastern perspective was its depiction of the American wilderness. Driven by a romantic abhorrence of urbanization, industrialization, and the complex and disturbing forces of modernization, as much as by their declared mission of giving expression to the national identity, writers like Cooper and Bryant saw in the expansive, unmolested wilderness of the West the very elements and influences that most made America American and most distinguished it from Europe. To them the West was the natural homeland of liberty and a vast verdant region free of what Bryant called "the sorrows, crimes, and cares" of a society grown too civilized, confining, and artificial. They saw the state of nature between the Appalachians and the Mississippi as the New World Garden, an unspoiled place of new beginnings and untrammeled opportunities—a place to begin the world over again, as Thomas Paine had suggested—and a realm of beauty and adventure that inspired a rebirth of wonder.[8]

Although effusive in their praise of the western state of nature, they found the westerners themselves far less admirable than the land they inhabited. Their image of the people residing in the interior was that of a crude, backward, unrefined lot who lived a low and slovenly and almost barbaric existence. Indeed, for easterners, the westerner became the negative "other"—a Wild Man of sorts—who enabled them, by comparison, to feel good about themselves and quite superior to the people they envisioned dwelling in the smoky cabins beyond the old mountains. It was from just such people, with their axes and plows and all their irritating mess and clatter, that Natty Bumppo fled ever deeper into the far-off territory. And in the nostalgic reveries of eastern intellectuals, they were the people guilty of the wanton destruction of the pristine American wilderness. They were, in the eastern version of the American identity, a national embarrassment and the source of moral and cultural degradation in the heartland.

As one might expect, westerners had a decidedly different sense of who they were and what made the United States a distinctive nation. They had their own myths of collective identity, which were articulated by the region's newspaper editors, political orators, and writers, such as Judge James Hall, who saw the westward-moving pioneers, as they saw themselves, as a hardy, courageous people in the very vanguard of an expanding republican civilization. They had marched over the mountains, confronted dangers and uncertainties, and made the wild country bloom into a garden of abundance. "The American backwoodsmen [were] a class of men peculiar to our country," wrote James Hall in his 1828 book, *Letters from the West,* suggesting they were perhaps the most authentically "American" of all the citizens of the Republic. By leaving the East and removing themselves into the wilderness, they had become "a race of husbandmen [who] were transformed into bold, adventurous, military people," declared the judge.[9] They were, he went on, "brave, generous, and patriotic; poor but not sordid," and through "manly exercise" had become "enterprising and fearless, careless of exposure, expert in horsemanship, and trained to the use of arms."[10] Besides all that, Hall found them to be true democrats, far different and much more liberated than those who were members of the mindless human herds inhabiting the eastern cities. "Their mode of life induced independence of thought, and habits of self-reliance; for as there was but one class, and one occupation, all were equal, and each was thrown upon his own resources," concluded Hall.[11] In all those admirable ways he saw them as being fundamentally different from the men who remained in the East, and in the West, he asserted, they were engaged in the creation of an unmistakably American way of life. Out beyond the "ragged ridges" of the Appalachians, separated from the East by an "immense wilderness," "every man was a politician, a soldier and a patriot, ready to make war or to make laws, to put his hand to the plough or to the helm of state, as circumstances might require," proclaimed Hall in a stirring outburst of mythological adulation.[12]

It was the myth of the yeoman farmer American-style, and a fantasized realization of the "new man" envisioned in the poetic musings of Hector

St. John de Crèvecoeur—highly flattering and shamelessly idealized, and in blatant contrast to the coarse and slovenly stereotype that easterners portrayed westerners to be. It was an identity many westerners uncritically embraced, and some of them, like Andrew Jackson and John Reynolds, saw themselves to be the very fulfillments of that myth.

Those contrasting views of the West and westerners were also accompanied by radically divergent images of the Indian.

Numerous scholars have discussed how Americans characterized the natives in ways that are actually inverse images of themselves. One of them stated: "As fundamental White ways of looking at themselves changed, so too did their ways of conceiving of Indians. Since the description, interpretation, explanation, and manipulation of the Indian as image and person were and are inextricably combined in White minds, the . . . understanding of past and present White images becomes but the latest phase of a centuries-old White effort to understand themselves through understanding Native Americans."[13] Viewing the Indians during the early nineteenth century produced both positive and negative images, reflecting the ambivalent views Americans had of themselves.

During the 1820s, for example, when the national identity crisis was unusually intense, eastern writers and a good deal of the literate eastern public took a keen interest in the native people and saw in them much of what they themselves longed for and wished to be. In their view, the Indian was a natural man, part of the unspoiled splendor of the American state of nature, and free from all the confusion and corruption of a society that seemed determined to make itself into something far too complex and impersonal. Also, for a country with so little history of its own, and so insistent upon renouncing its own Old World past, the Indian provided a uniquely American past that reached far back into the depths of time beyond even the rise of Rome.[14] And in a figure such as Uncas of Cooper's *Last of the Mohicans,* and in the central charismatic character of *Metamora,* a highly popular play about King Philip's War, there was also the powerful sensual appeal of a muscular, masculine virility, and an admirable model of natural nobility. So it was that the Indian was seen as authentically "American," possessing qualities with which many Americans eagerly wished to associate themselves. "Without its aboriginal heritage," writes the historian Jill Lepore, "America was only a more vulgar England, but with it, America was its own nation, with a unique culture and its own ancestral past."[15]

That was certainly the case among many of the articulate people of the East. But in the West the images were quite different. For while in New York and New England, the Indian was romantically associated with "us," in the scattered settlements beyond the Appalachians, the Indian was emphatically "other."

As most westerners saw it, there were no noble savages except for those envisioned by the overactive imaginations of misguided easterners. Most of the people of the interior agreed with Matthew Fitch of Mineral Point, in the Michigan Territory, who referred to them as "savage monsters" whose unfortunate victims, he said, ranged "from the hoary head of age down to the babe that hung fondly to the mother's breast."[16] The origin of this Indian hating, so widespread and strong throughout the West, could be traced back, claimed Judge Hall, to the very real and traumatic historical experiences shared by many westerners, which were perpetuated in the regional collective memory by the stories they were told from early childhood on. Those were terrifying tales of "painted savages" and "midnight conflagrations" and "bleeding scalps torn from the heads of gray-haired old men, of infants, and of women—[and] of mothers and children carried away into captivity." Such stories, said Hall, accurately reflected the cruel and cowardly nature of the savages, and the constant retelling of such vivid narratives filled the mind with deep dread of the loathsome natives.[17] As a consequence of such emotional conditioning, the men of the West were strongly inclined to see their mission in life as essentially destructive. "The savage was to be expelled; the panther, the wolf and the bear to be exterminated; the forest to be razed," declared Hall.[18]

The East's positive image of the Indian rather predictably reinforced anti-eastern views in the West. Those feelings were clearly put into words by Dr. Addison Philleo, a medical doctor who was also the editor of the *Galenian,* the newspaper he published in Galena, Illinois, during the 1830s. In an 1832 article Philleo said that when he first "emigrated from the East," he was "astonished at the prejudice existing in the Western country against the eastern population." But after living in Illinois for only a short time, he too grew to resent what he called "the ignorance which so generally prevails among the Eastern people relative to this country, and our relations with the neighboring tribes of Indians." Soon, he admitted, he no longer wondered why "the West should wish to be separated from such a people." But the easterners Philleo despised most of all were "a certain class of religious fanatics in many of the New England states" who, he claimed, "look upon barbarous savages as they would upon angels, and never speak of them without using the inappropriate name of 'poor Indians.'" He then observed that if they only knew the Indians as westerners knew them, or personally witnessed any of their cruel and barbaric deeds, they would not hold them in such high esteem or express such soft-hearted sympathies for them.[19]

Such anti-eastern feelings ran unusually strong, for what was at stake were fundamental feelings of self-worth and even the defense of one's own manhood. The historian George Mosse explained how the process of forming nation-states also required a major redefinition of masculinity throughout Western civilization. The old aristocratic ideal was no longer appropriate to the needs of the great masses of men mobilized and made members of the newly emerging national societies. Therefore, a new definition of *maleness* had to be devised, and the revised model of masculinity that eventually took shape arose out of an era of war and revolution, heavily influenced by romanticism. As a consequence, observed Mosse, there was a "militarization of masculinity," resulting in the new "manly virtues" placing heavy value on physical courage and heroic self-sacrifice, and in the belief that true manhood could be most fully realized on the battlefield.

That, of course, required there to be external enemies to war against—forces and foes believed to threaten women and children and even the life of the nation itself—and in the collective imagination such adversaries became the great monsters young men were called upon to battle and slay. In bravely taking on such fights, eager youths might prove to the nation and themselves their true manliness. At the same time, this affirmation of masculinity also required a much sharper distinction between the "male" and "female" spheres and characteristics of life, as well as what Mosse described as "countertypes that reflected, as in a convex mirror," the image of what a good man was not supposed to be. Those negative roles invariably fell to people and groups marginalized by modern society: Jews, Gypsies, aliens, vagrants, criminals, religious nonconformists, homosexuals, and anyone regarded as weak or degenerate or thought to be a threat to the nation's social and moral order. Hatred of them, said Mosse, was most intense when "good" men, for whatever reasons, were most insecure about their own masculinity.[20]

This was most certainly occurring in the United States as well as western Europe. However, the peculiar conditions of the early Republic made it all the more difficult to be a man. When the Revolution and the expanding economy rejected paternalism and then proceeded to dissolve the connecting bonds of family, community, and cultural traditions, men were cut loose as autonomous equals in a republican marketplace where they had to sink or swim, succeed or fail on their own efforts and merits. The personal freedom and opportunities that went with this development gave rise to furious motion and immense productivity, as well as an unusually competitive society in which each man, as Alexis de Tocqueville observed, was thrown "back forever upon himself alone" and confined "entirely within the solitude of his own heart."[21] In that state of individual isolation American men became preoccupied with self—with self-reliance, self-control, self-improvement, and self-promotion—and for them the only valid form of masculinity was that of the self-made man. Personal worth was determined almost exclusively by individual achievement, measured in money and fame and the acquisition of power. To successfully compete and amount to anything of any importance demanded ceaseless activity, endless striving, and the avoidance of all the debilitating and effeminizing influences associated with aristocracy, luxury, and unproductive ease. And amid the roar and commotion of it all, each man was required to create his own identity and prove his manhood again and again.

The young Republic was a remarkably productive place but was also a highly agitated society churning with anxiety, restlessness, envy, and insecurity, and its people searched for scapegoats upon whom to blame their failures, and enemies to destroy in order to affirm their masculinity and power. As a consequence, observed the historian Michael Kimmel, the primary "emotions that seem to have animated Jacksonian America were fear and rage."[22]

It was in that context that western men declared themselves to be better, braver, stronger men than their eastern countrymen, who they believed were weak and unmanly by comparison. Furthermore, they used the Indians, who they denigrated and dehumanized, as convenient enemies against whom they could display their own masculine prowess for everyone to see. Thus, somewhat like the Englishmen of an earlier era who defined themselves in contrast to the "effeminate" French and the "beastly" Scots, the men of the trans-Appalachian West formed an identity by comparing themselves to the foppish fellows out East and the wild, cruel savages of the unsettled frontier.[23]

Nowhere was that more evident than in the troubled region of Illinois and the southwestern corner of the Michigan Territory, especially among the eager militia volunteers heading for Beardstown in late April of 1832. Reynolds had called for as many of them as he could get for a thirty-day term of enlistment, offering them pay of twenty-one cents a day. Samuel Whiteside was appointed to be their commander. A native of North Carolina, Whiteside was a tall, forty-nine-year-old man with a flat face, high forehead, and a wide thin-lipped mouth, all of which gave him a resemblance to one of the great stone-face megaliths of Easter Island. He was a natural choice due to his well-known reputation as an Indian fighter acquired during the War of 1812, and because he had been a brigadier general in the state militia since 1819.

From the very start, the whole operation was in confusion and off schedule. Supplies were hard to come by, especially grain for the horses, and because of the heavy spring rains the provisions for the troops were extremely difficult to move by wagon. Matters were further complicated by the fact that there were many more volunteers than had been anticipated, although it was difficult to tell just how many there actually were. On April 30 Reynolds told Congressman Joseph Duncan he had a force of "about 1500 mounted men," yet the very same day, in a letter to General Atkinson, and in what appears to have been a deliberate lie, the governor informed the general he had 2,200 men "mostly mounted."[24] John Wakefield, a scout or a "spy" with the expedition, said there were 1,600 horsemen and 200 infantry, and that they were organized into four regiments and one spy battalion.[25] After seeing Reynolds's army, Atkinson reported that it consisted of "1700 state troops of which some 1500 are mounted volunteers."[26]

Politics played a major role in the internal dynamics of the militia. Most of the companies arriving at Beardstown had already elected their officers, but Reynolds appointed his own staff, all at the rank and pay of colonels, choosing men who could advance his own political interests. It was, after all, an election year, and the governor was running hard for reelection. But Reynolds was not alone in using the situation for political purposes. Indeed, a good many of the officers were candidates for the legislature or county offices and did not hesitate to take advantage of having so many voters all together in the same place to carry on a great deal of electioneering among the volunteers. The back-slapping, speech-making, favordoing, and especially the passing out of free whiskey weakened further the already slack discipline within the militia, and political self-interest made officers reluctant to issue or enforce unpopular orders. William Orr, who was a private in a volunteer company from St. Clair County, as well as the editor of the *Illinois Advocate* of Edwardsville, was shocked by much of what he witnessed in that regard and wrote to a friend commenting about how "the shameful and ludicrous principle on which places were filled on the one hand, and electioneering importunities and solicitations on the other" made many of them pause and wonder whether they "were not going on some frivolous holiday excursion, and not to encounter hostile Indians."[27]

Yet, from the very beginning, it was evident to most of the volunteers that they were on no joy ride. The weather made sure of that. Orville Browning, who much later became secretary of the interior for Andrew Johnson, was then just a lowly militia private from Adams County, Illinois, who kept a detailed diary in which he commented about the trials and discomforts of the troops. On April 25, as Browning's company was still on its way to Beardstown, it rained heavily throughout most of the afternoon. The next day was "warm and sultry," and at the end of the march they found their "encampment much infested with rattle snakes." That same evening he described how the weather once again turned nasty, jotting down the following brief notation: "[It] commenced raining & continued without intermission during the night—had no tents—could not sleep. Stood in the mud ankle deep till day." The downpour persisted throughout the next day, and Browning remarked that they "marched thro mud knee deep on" their horses.[28]

Shortly after that journal entry, all the companies encamped at Beardstown were ordered to form up and move out. They did so on April 30, eight days behind schedule. On May 1 William Headen, a medical doctor with the troops, wrote to his brother from Beardstown: "All is confusion and bustle," he said, telling him that the last of the militia companies had been ferried across the Illinois River that morning. They were to be issued five days' rations and armed with what he called "Harpers Ferry muskets." All the men were in good health and full of enthusiasm, he reported, in spite of the fact they had already "suffered a great deal of hunger, fatigue and wet since" starting out.[29]

The militia was to march about eighty miles northwest to Yellow Banks, the very place where Black Hawk and his band had crossed the Mississippi nearly a month before. They set off on a Monday, and that Wednesday night camped in an open prairie, two miles away from both wood and water, which irritated them greatly. The weather was "cold and tempestuous," and they were without fuel for their fires or water for themselves and their horses, and that gave rise to "much dissatisfaction and murmuring among the troops," wrote Browning.[30] On May 3 they reached the Henderson River, which was greatly swollen by the heavy rains. Reynolds estimated the stream to be between forty and fifty yards wide, but there was neither a bridge nor boats for their crossing.[31] Therefore the men felled trees and made crude rafts on which they and their equipment were ferried across, while their horses swam the fast-flowing stream. "The army crossed in great disorder," and "two or three horses drowned," noted Browning.[32] Reynolds also indicated a supply wagon or two toppled into the water and were swept away by the powerful current. Yet all the men made the crossing in only about three hours and camped at Yellow Banks that night.

There they waited. Reynolds had ordered two steamboats—the *William Wallace* and the *Java*—to bring supplies up from St. Louis, and had anticipated they would already be at Yellow Banks when the troops arrived. That was not the case. The volunteers, most of whom had already carelessly consumed or thrown away their rations, were forced to forage. Some of them shot the hogs on a nearby farm, and the rest made out as best they could until the *William Wallace* arrived on May 6. The steamboat came "barely in time to save the disaster of disbanding the army," wrote Reynolds.[33]

The next day, Reynolds, Whiteside, and their disorderly congregation of amateur soldiers marched on to the mouth of the Rock River.

During the time the militia had been on the march, decisions were made in Washington about what action needed to be taken to deal with the Indian problem in Illinois. It was an election year for the people in power there as well, and they wanted the mess handled quickly, before

Indian policy became even more of an issue. The government already had enough of a fight with Chief Justice John Marshall and the stand taken by the Supreme Court in the case of *Cherokee Nation v. Georgia* (1831), as well as the more recent decision handed down in the case of *Worcester v. Georgia*. In both decisions Marshall and the Court had favored the Indians, which not only raised more controversy over the administration's removal policy but also caused problems for President Jackson with his political base. He did not want those controversies to cause political trouble in the Midwest. Therefore, on May 5 General Macomb sent clear instructions to General Atkinson. "The Executive has determined, that something decisive must be done in regard to those Indians," he told Atkinson. Only then did he authorize Atkinson to call on the Illinois militia for assistance, if he thought it necessary. Of course, Reynolds had already jumped the gun, but Macomb's orders provided formal authorization, and that, in turn, made the volunteers eligible for federal pay of $6.66 a month for privates, and triple that if the private provided his own horse. Atkinson was also told by Macomb to demand the surrender of all the Sauk and Fox murderers of the Menominee without further discussion or delay, and that all the Sauk and Fox who had crossed the Mississippi be returned to the western territory immediately. "Should they refuse promptly to comply with your demands you will forthwith attack them and force them to obedience," Macomb sternly declared, instructing Atkinson about how the whole matter needed to be handled quickly and decisively, before it became more complicated or controversial. The time for talking was over. Firm action was needed. All the same, care was to be exercised. "In case any of their women or children should fall into your hands, it is the Presidents particular wish that they should be treated with kindness and humanity," stated General Macomb.[34]

With his marching orders in hand, Atkinson wrote to Colonel Zachary Taylor, who had just returned to his command at Fort Crawford after a lengthy leave of absence in Louisville, Kentucky. The general told Taylor to bring soldiers down in four Mackinaw boats and to join him at Fort Armstrong as soon as possible, as he intended to move up the Rock River in pursuit of the Indians on Thursday, May 10, which was only four days away.[35]

Taylor and his troops arrived on May 8. Reynolds and the militia had reached Fort Armstrong just the day before, and Atkinson had promptly put them all under federal command as a means of controlling them. Two days later—May 9, and a full day ahead of schedule—Atkinson began his pursuit of Black Hawk, moving his 340 regular soldiers along with the 160 militia volunteers who had no horses up the Rock River as far as the rapids near Saukenuk in keelboats and Mackinaw boats, towed behind the steamboat *Java*. At the same time, Whiteside, Reynolds, and the mounted militia rode along the south bank of the river. The next morning, the faster-moving militia was sent on ahead, with orders to go as far as the Prophet's village. But they were also given the option of pressing on ahead and to "move upon the Indians should they be within striking distance."[36] In the meantime, the regular troops and infantry volunteers, under the immediate command of Colonel Taylor, commenced their slow and arduous ascent of the Rock River, hauling, lifting, and sliding their five ninety-ton Mackinaw boats and the two thirty-ton keelboats, all packed full of equipment and provisions, through deep water and over exposed rocks. The weather that May was unusually cold. The wind blew hard, there were torrential rainstorms, and Colonel Albert Sidney Johnston wrote in his diary, "The soldiers strained every nerve to get on rapidly with the boats."[37] Captain Henry Smith, in charge of one of those companies, said, "For many days the troops . . . had not a dry thread on them, compelled to wade against the rapid stream, dragging or lifting the boats along from daybreak until night."[38] But try as they might, even with all their exertion, progress was painfully slow.

The mounted militia raced on ahead. Reynolds was extremely eager to overtake and attack the Indians, grabbing all the glory for himself before any of the federal forces could become involved. It would be good for his political reputation, and, according to William Orr, "the electioneering mania" seemed to have "taken possession of him."[39] Reynolds, rather than Whiteside, appeared to be the man actually running the operation, and he ordered John Wakefield and Colonel John Ewing to scout ahead and find the trail taken by the Black Hawk band. Even for Ewing and Wakefield it was tough going, and Wakefield complained that the country they passed through was "an almost continual swamp."[40] Nevertheless, the army of volunteers kept up a fast pace, which put them far ahead of their own baggage wagons, of which there were eighteen or twenty, each pulled by two or three pairs of oxen. Because of the mud and water, the wagons were able to cover only a few difficult miles each day.

In no time, those wagons became a source of irritation, especially to the men in the ranks, not only because of their slowness but also because they were being used to haul the officers' gear. Orr was particularly indignant that their equipment and baggage were loaded on the wagons and that "the officers could not be prevailed on to pack even their great coats, whilst the men were compelled to pack not only their personal baggage, but their rations for eight or ten days ahead, together with their cooking utensils." Private Orr had only scorn for the self-centered, office-seeking, militarily incompetent militia officers, and declared, "Our officers availed themselves of every privilege their rank could give them; and were *hated* and *execrated*."[41] What was even worse was how those strutting, self-important fellows neglected even their most fundamental duties; never drilling the men or giving them even elementary instructions in the most basic of military matters. "The whole time that I was out I never witnessed a company drill, a battalion drill, a regimental drill, nor a Brigade drill—and what will still more demonstrate the absence of all military usage, I never heard a roll call in the whole Brigade from the time of its organization," protested Orr. The entire operation, in Orr's opinion, was a slovenly, disorganized, undisciplined mess, and whenever he was on sentry duty he invariably found men "snoring on their posts." Throughout the army "there was a total absence of discipline; orders were obeyed or disobeyed as suited the pleasure or convenience of the men," observed William Orr with considerable disgust.[42]

On May 11 Whiteside and his rambunctious horsemen reached the Prophet's abandoned village about noon and remained only long enough to burn some lodges.[43] While there, Wakefield and Ewing returned with a Potawatomi prisoner. Under interrogation, the captive revealed that Black Hawk and his band were only a two-day march farther upriver. That was exciting news to the troops and their leaders, and as a result, Whiteside, at Reynolds's urging, ordered the militia to move on to Dixon's Ferry at top speed rather than waiting at the Prophet's village for Atkinson to catch up. The game was afoot, and there was no time to lose. To hasten their progress, Reynolds "decided to leave the onerous and cumbersome baggage [wagons]" behind.[44] Then, at forced-march pace, they managed to reach Dixon's Ferry the very next morning. Nevertheless, the great hurry "caused the total failure of many of our horses," reported Orr, who doubted the sense of the entire effort. "Was not this forced marching the quintessence of folly when the provisions were following at the tardy rate of not more than from five to ten miles per day?" he asked.[45] And, in fact, at Dixon's Ferry the army had to stop and rest while Whiteside and Reynolds sent an urgent message back to Atkinson, imploring him to hurry since their troops were hungry and virtually out of provisions.[46]

While the militia waited impatiently at Dixon's Ferry and the regulars stopped and burned what was left of the Prophet's village, Black Hawk was confronting some disturbing realizations about his own predicament. He too was running low on provisions, and there was growing dissension within his band. Wacomme and Packenoi, two Sauk men who had visited Black Hawk's camp in late April, informed Atkinson of that situation. They observed growing hunger among the people of the band and noticed "there was a lodge of women that wanted to come back" and cross over the Mississippi again.[47] Shortly after their visit, at least six canoes loaded with people deserted the band, determined to rejoin the Sauk who remained in the West. Atkinson met those people on May 12, while on his way upriver, and decided to take three of their men along to guide him to Black Hawk's encampment.[48] At the same time, Thomas Owen, the Indian agent at Chicago, wrote to Reynolds, telling him he had it on good authority that the Sauk, who he said were about thirty miles beyond Dixon's Ferry, were "in a state of Starvation" and "anxious to recross the Mississippi, but dare[d] not . . . for fear of being intercepted by the Militia & indiscriminately slaughtered."[49]

Nothing seemed to be turning out in accordance with the old man's vague expectations. The Winnebago had not come to his support as they had promised with the wampum belts they had sent him during the winter. The Potawatomi, who he felt certain could be counted on, also disappointed him. A delegation of their chiefs came to his camp on the Kishwaukee River, near the northern border of Illinois, and informed him that they had no corn to spare to feed his people. While they were present he asked them "if they had received any news from the lake from the British." They told him they had not. Nor had they heard anything about "a chief of the 'British Father' coming to Mil-wa-ke with guns, ammunition, and provisions."[50] All of that came as a demoralizing shock to him, and suddenly he realized he had been "deceived" and "all the fair promises that had" been sent to him "through Neapope, were false."[51]

In one last desperate effort to salvage his disintegrating situation, Black Hawk arranged for yet another meeting with a different group of Potawatomi chiefs. He made elaborate preparations for them. A large bower decorated with flowers and evergreen boughs was erected, and he had a choice dog killed for a special feast.[52] But even before his guests arrived, he had decided to be candid with his own people and tell them "that if the White Beaver [Atkinson] came," they would go back across the Mississippi, "as it was useless to think about stopping or going on without provisions."[53]

The day before Black Hawk's dog feast with the Potawatomi, Major Isaiah Stillman left the militia camp at Dixon's Ferry with a mounted force of about 275 volunteers and every intention of finding and attacking the British Band. Stillman was a forty-year-old Yankee from Massachusetts, who had migrated to Illinois in 1824, first settling in Sangamon County, and six years later moving north to Fulton County, where he became a merchant of pots and pans in Canton. Soon after learning of Black Hawk's return to the state, Reynolds had sent him orders to raise a mounted force of four companies, each company to consist of fifty volunteers, and to range the frontier area from the Mississippi eastward, being on a constant lookout for hostile Indians.[54] On April 28 John Dixon, who operated the ferry on the Rock River, also sent a message to Stillman, informing him that Black Hawk and his band had passed through his place that morning and planned to continue on upriver for another twenty miles or so.[55] The next day Stillman was on the move with his force of one hundred men.[56] By May 3 he was drawing near to Dixon's Ferry with an enlarged troop of 130 men, still expecting even more volunteers to join him. Major David Bailey, another New Englander with a similar force recruited from Macon, Tazewell, McLean, and Peoria counties, was in the same vicinity.[57] Stillman sent a dispatch to Reynolds on May 4, telling him he was probably within thirty miles of Black Hawk's camp and had sent out scouts and rangers to discover its precise location. However, because he was low on both provisions and ammunition, he was proceeding with caution, he informed the governor.[58]

When Reynolds reached Dixon's Ferry eight days later, both Stillman and Bailey were awaiting him there with a combined force of 275 mounted volunteers, none of whom had yet been mustered into federal service. In his later written account Reynolds asserted, "The officers and privates of these battalions solicited me warmly to permit them to reconnoiter the frontiers, and report where the enemy were lodged, if they could discover it."[59] Although that assertion was probably true—both Stillman and Bailey were certainly excited about the prospects of confronting the Indians—it was also true that Reynolds himself had a most ardent desire to attack and defeat Black Hawk before Atkinson ever arrived on the scene. The governor did not want to share any of the spotlight nor applause with the general, nor did he want to be restrained by Atkinson, whom he considered excessively cautious. Since neither Stillman's nor Bailey's troops were yet under Atkinson's authority, Reynolds asked Whiteside to "take command of those men, and give them marching orders," and send them forth against the Sauk.[60] Whiteside refused to comply, saying he was already under orders from Atkinson and had no authority to command any troops other than those of his own brigade.[61] Furthermore, Whiteside made it quite clear he did not approve of the proposed expedition, saying that "if it was necessary to order out 2,000 men to whip these Indians, it was certainly erroneous policy to order out 200 men to make an attack."[62] Reynolds was undoubtedly irritated by Whiteside's refusal but, not wanting to miss an exciting opportunity to enhance his political fortunes, the governor made Brigade Major Nathaniel Buckmaster issue the order, which they fraudulently attributed to Samuel Whiteside, directing Stillman and Bailey to "forthwith proceed with four day's rations" to Old Man's Creek (now called Kyte River), where it was believed Black Hawk was camped, and to "coerce said Indians into submission."[63]

What happened after that is not so clear. There was a great deal of disagreement and inconsistent reporting of important details, and even substantially different accounts of what actually transpired. But what began with deceit and duplicity ended in disaster for all concerned.

What was clear from the very beginning, and what Reynolds admitted to Henry Dodge in a letter he wrote to him at the time, was that Stillman's force was "to kill as many Hostile sacks as they may meet."[64] Even the *Galenian* reported that Stillman "commenced his march up Rock river with a fixed determination to urge a war of extermination where ever he might find any part of the hostile Indians."[65] What was equally clear was that none of the Black Hawk band, nor any other Indians in Illinois for that matter, had committed any hostile actions whatsoever since crossing the Mississippi in the first week of April. Indeed, Thomas Forsyth later observed that because Black Hawk and his warriors "were hampered with many women and children . . . [they] had no intention to make war."[66]

When Stillman left Dixon's Ferry, early Sunday morning, May 13, 1832, he had three companies containing a total of 130 men. Those units were under the command of Captains David Barns, Asel Ball, and Abner Eads. Major David Bailey also had three companies led by John G. Adams, Merritt L. Covell, and James Johnson, with a total of 151 men. That made it a force of 281 mounted militiamen, all eager for action.[67]

The sky was dark when they departed, and in a short time it began to rain. It poured throughout the day, and, before long, the men and horses were drenched and cold. The next day, however, it turned warm and sunny and pleasant, and they trudged along until about an hour before nightfall, reaching Old Man's Creek, about thirty-five miles up Rock River from Dixon's Ferry. Along the way, as before, the slower-moving baggage wagons, being "too heavy," became mired in the mud and were left behind by the faster-moving horsemen. Andrew Maxfield, who was a private in Asel Ball's company, said the wagons were abandoned about ten miles from Old Man's Creek. But before moving on, "one barrel of whiskey was therefore, unheaded, and all . . . canteens filled."[68] What remained in the barrel after that was consumed on the spot. Hours later the militiamen crossed Old Man's Creek and made camp on the plain beyond its north bank. "The camp entirely filled a small open wood, which was on every side surrounded by open and clear prairie slightly undulating," said Captain Henry Smith, who went on to claim "the strongest fortress could hardly have been more effectively defended" than the campsite they chose.[69]

There are numerous inconsistencies in the descriptions of what happened after that, due, in part, to the varied vantage points of the observers, as well as to the strong desires of the participants to be seen in favorable light. The fact is, all the eyewitness accounts were transparently self-serving. Also, many of the reports have an almost surrealistic quality to them. Therefore, what really happened in the battle that became known as Stillman's Run will forever remain something of a mystery.

According to Stillman himself (who never filed an official report but instead published a self-serving account in the *Missouri Republican* more than a month after the fact), one of his scouts sighted two Indians on horseback around two o'clock on the afternoon of May 14. The Indians immediately fired on him and then tried to get away by swimming across the Rock River. They never made it. The scout took aim and fired, killing both. When the Sauk riders fell into the river, their horses turned and swam back. The unidentified scout brought them into the militia camp around six o'clock that evening.[70]

Late that same afternoon, at his camp on Sycamore Creek, Black Hawk held his dog feast and met with the delegation of Potawatomi chiefs. The feasting was just ending when a messenger rushed in and reported that "three or four hundred white men, on horse-back, had been seen about eight miles off. . . . I immediately started three young men, with a *white flag*, to meet them, and conduct them to our camp, that we might hold council with them, and descend Rock river again," Black Hawk later indicated. After those three braves had departed on that mission, he sent out after them another "five young men to see what might take place."[71] Interrogated after the war, Neapope claimed he had been the person who had given the dog feast for the Potawatomi chiefs, and when he had learned "some Americans" were nearby, he said, "I prepared a *white flag* to go & see them, and sent two or three young men on a hill to see what they were doing."[72] Shaubena, who did not attend the feast but was in Dixon's Ferry at the time, later reported that from what he learned from those who had been there, it was Black Hawk (not Neapope) who had "immediately dispatched two warriors, with a *white flag*, to meet the army," and had also sent out "four others to follow behind, to see what became of the flag-bearers."[73] Mention was also made of the white flag in an article published in the *Niles' Weekly Register* on June 9, 1832.

According to Stillman, he and his men had just begun setting up camp when they sighted "a small party of men" coming toward them. At first they assumed they were members of their own advance guard. As the riders came closer, Lieutenant Asahel Gridley, a miller and merchant from Bloomington, Illinois, and a member of Merritt Covell's company, who was still on his horse, decided to ride out to see for himself who they were. Most of his comrades in Covell's company soon followed. It did not take long before they discovered the approaching riders were Indians. When they did, there was an exchange of gunfire. Stillman said three Indians were killed and another three taken prisoner. One militiaman was also killed, he reported. The Covell company then took off in pursuit of the fleeing Indians, who were heading in the direction of Sycamore Creek, which Stillman estimated was about five miles away.[74]

Andrew Maxfield, of Asel Ball's company, also reported that soon after they commenced establishing their camp, they saw "a party of 8 or 10 mounted men, about half a mile distant to the north on an eminence." Some of the militiamen thought they were part of their own advance guard, others thought they might be Indians, and Maxfield, who was eager to ride out and see for himself, was nevertheless cajoled by his comrades into unsaddling his horse and turning it loose to graze so he could lend a hand with setting up the camp. But no sooner had he done so than Lieutenant Gridley came rushing in raising the alarm. Maxfield quickly caught his horse and mounted it, and, "with about five or six others . . . rode with rapid strides in the direction of the enemy, who instantly disappeared, behind the hill." At that point, he said, Covell's company was coming back with "two prisoners mounted." Maxfield then said he and his companions galloped on for about another five miles upriver, finally catching up to the fleeing Indians. Those Indians, he said, were well armed with bows and arrows, spears, and rifles, and were carrying "a *red flag*." When they refused to surrender, the militiamen opened fire on them and "brought down three Indians and one pony."[75]

Captain James Stephenson of Galena also wrote an account of that initial confrontation. He had caught up with Stillman just before nightfall, as the camp was being prepared, and later reported to the *Galenian* that "three Indians delivered themselves up—their object being doubtless, to parley with the whites." Shortly after they came in, he "saw a few Indians standing on an eminence" and "two or three men went out, but seeing that they held forth no flag of truce, they suspected their hostility."[76]

None of the reports from members of the militia make any mention of the Indians coming in with white flags.

Maxfield, the only reporter among the initial pursuers, said that once they had caught up with and commenced firing at the fleeing Sauk riders, the Indians rallied and counterattacked. The militiamen fell back. Soon, however, their comrades from the camp, who came riding up with Major Stillman in the lead, reinforced them. Then they all moved back across a bog and formed a battle line, he said. It was at that point, as night was descending, when "a deputation bearing a *white flag*, was seen advancing,"

Maxfield reported. Stillman, himself, indicated that when he and his men caught up with Gridley and the others, "an Indian appeared, and made signs of peace." With Captain Abner Eads as their interpreter, Stillman and a few other officers advanced and were told "the Indians would surrender, in case they could be treated as prisoners of war." Stillman promised they would be treated as such, so he claimed, but went on to say that the Indians behaved in such a suspicious manner he was soon convinced they were not sincere about surrendering and were, in fact, engaged in "treachery."[77] Maxfield also claimed the Indians deceitfully used the white flag only to lure Eads and the others into an ambush, "from which he narrowly escaped," and that the whole parley was a "sham . . . to give the Indians time to send out their flankers." Only after realizing this, said Maxfield, did Stillman pull his troops back to a safer position on a hill about a mile away.[78]

Black Hawk's version of what occurred is quite different from the accounts presented by Stillman, Maxfield, and Stephenson. He claimed that the three men he sent out with the white flag went all the way to Stillman's camp, where they were taken prisoners. Then a militia party of about twenty mounted men intercepted the five observers he had sent out after them. There was shooting, and two of the Indians were killed, stated Black Hawk. The other three made it back to the Sycamore Creek camp and raised the alarm, but Black Hawk claimed he had only about forty warriors still in camp at the time, for nearly all "his young men were absent, about ten miles off," hunting for desperately needed game. Those he had with him mounted their horses just as they saw a large group of white riders rushing headlong toward their camp. Black Hawk claimed he then declared to his men: "Some of our people have been killed!—wantonly and cruelly murdered! We must revenge their death!" Although greatly outnumbered, they charged directly at Stillman's force, his warriors fully expecting to be cut down and killed. "Every man rushed and fired," claimed Black Hawk, "and the enemy retreated! in the utmost confusion and consternation, before my little, but brave band of warriors."[79]

Stillman asserted it was the Indians who commenced the attack. But no matter how it began, it soon turned into a wild melee of panic and confusion for the militiamen. Suddenly they seemed beset by the intensity of their own fight-or-flight response, becoming disoriented and under attack by their own fear-induced hallucinations. Amid the shadows of twilight, in the tall grass of that unfamiliar terrain, the eyes of the militiamen seemed to play terrifying tricks on them, and their growing fears greatly magnified the actual perils of that night. James Stephenson told of how, "as if by magic, each tree and stump appeared to send forth a band of savages," so that in his startled state of mind he estimated there "were at least 1000 Indians." The whole scene soon became a chaos of terror—"the swampy ground, the surprise, the retreat of the whites, threw everything into confusion."[80] The Indians were "seen by the glittering moon light, on three sides like swarms of summer insects," and all the members of the militia were instantly swept up in panic, admitted Maxfield. The officers tried to make their men hold the line, but their sense of dread was so strong "all the exertion of the officers was insufficient to arrest the flight."[81]

Stillman, on the other hand, provided a much more orderly, albeit exaggerated, picture of events, saying he saw the Indians suddenly appear in "martial order; their line extended a distance of near two miles, and under rapid march." Their "war-whoop," he claimed, "was heard in almost every direction—their flanks extending from one creek to the other." Night descended. After that the only light came from the flashing of the guns, he said, which may have created something of a strobe-light effect. Whatever the case, it was frightening. But in contrast to both Stephenson and Maxfield, Stillman insisted that his officers and men acted with "prudence and deliberation, until compelled to give ground to a superior foe." A brief but heroic counterattack by Captain John Adams and his men gave them time to make an orderly retreat back across Old Man's Creek, he claimed. Unfortunately, in crossing over, said Stillman, many of the men got their guns wet, which made further retreat absolutely necessary.[82]

The distortion of actual events by Stillman becomes obvious by comparing his account with the reports of most other participants, but his claims seem almost credible when measured against the descriptions of that night's events written by Colonel James H. Strode, who, like Stephenson, was a militia leader from Galena. Strode was an attorney from Kentucky with a bigger than average ambition to become a war hero. At the time, he was also a candidate for the state senate and especially anxious to look good in the eyes of the voters, or at least eager to tell a tale that would save him from embarrassment. But he tried too hard. Recounting his experience for the newspapers, he said they were all encamped a little above Old Man's Creek at twilight "in the gloaming of the evening." Suddenly, they became aware that Black Hawk and his "army" were coming down upon them in a "solid column," and then in an amazing military maneuver, he claimed the Indians "deployed in the form of a crescent upon the brow of the prairie." In doing so, said Strode, they proved themselves "equal to the best troops of Wellington in Spain." There were hundreds of them in Strode's dramatic narrative, in which he waxed almost poetic in telling his readers, "It was a terrible and a glorious sight to see the tawny warriors as they rode along our flanks attempting to outflank us with the glittering moonbeams glistening from their polished blades and burnished spears." But while the scene filled him with awe, it also struck terror into the hearts of Stillman's men, who, said Strode, began to break into small groups and head for the protection of the "tall timber." But, alas, it was soon a general rout, and even though he and Stillman and a few other gallant men risked their lives to cover the retreat, they could not hold out for long. Soon he found himself all alone on the darkening plain, shots whistling about his ears, so that he too was compelled to flee for his life as the ferocious savages closed in upon him.[83]

But no matter how hard Colonel Strode and the others tried, they could not make the embarrassing, panic-stricken rout seem the least bit heroic. Zachary Taylor called it a "disgraceful affair," in which the troops lost all self-control, "became panic-struck & fled in the most shameful manner that ever troops were known to do."[84] Men who only a short time before had declared with such bravado what they intended to do to the Indians once they had caught them had been reduced to timid cowards by some phantom images in the moonlight. They raced through the night as fast as they could beat their horses into running the thirty-five miles back to Dixon's Ferry. Maxfield arrived there about two thirty in the morning, and Stillman came in about a half hour later. At first roll call the next morning, fifty-two men were still missing and feared dead. But over the next two days most of them came straggling back, and when Whiteside took his force to the place where the battle had happened, he set the final casualty count at eleven dead and five wounded. But the loss of face was incalculable.

Their humiliating defeat made the national news, and in an article in the *Niles' Weekly Register*, on June 9, 1832, it was reported that the militia's pursuit of the Indians "had been conducted without any regard to discipline," and that the Indians had completely outsmarted them and drawn them into a fatal trap.

Reynolds, who, against the wishes of Whiteside, had set the whole catastrophic mess in motion, took none of the blame and attributed the "disaster" to the "want of discipline, subordination, and the proper previous arrangements of the officers." He also suggested, pointing to the empty kegs found abandoned at their campsite, that "fire water" was "a partial cause of the disasters."[85] William Orr would not let Reynolds off the hook and asserted that sending Stillman out in the first place had been a "capital error" and a "grand blunder," which he blamed entirely on the governor, whom he described as being a "slippery article in political trade" who wriggled about, evading all responsibility and blame. But Orr was also critical of the "irregular and unmilitary conduct of the Battalion" and the "incapacity of those who would be officers."[86]

On the morning of May 15, Whiteside took his whole force out to where the fiasco had happened. All were deeply disturbed by what they found. One of the soldiers said they were surprised by the large number of dead horses they saw scattered around, and then felt downcast and sickened by the state in which they found the bodies of their slain comrades. "They were mutilated beyond description," he wrote, going on to say that "their heads [were] cut off—their tongues cut out by the roots—their bodies opened and their hearts torn out—their limbs separated from their bodies, and many of them literally chopped to bits."[87] The remains were gathered, and nine of the dead were buried in a common grave just below the ford on Old Man's Creek, while the other two were laid to rest in individual graves.[88] They also discovered the Indians had looted the camp and "taken all the baggage and stores," including "6 or 8 kegs of powder, and 2 or 3 hundred pounds of lead."[89]

Much had been lost by Stillman's Run. A severe blow had been dealt to the manly pride of the militia and to the tough image the western men had so aggressively sought to project for the entire nation to admire. They had been humiliated. After that, many of those who had set out from Beardstown with a keen desire to kill Indians lost heart for the entire enterprise and wanted no more of it. And, as one historian pointed out, Stillman's defeat soon became "so humiliating, so shocking to their sense of manhood, a cloak of censorship dropped over the battle."[90] But before it did,

Major Stillman and his men became laughingstocks, and even though he raged back against the "sapient wiseacres and electioneering demagogues" who were having so much derisive fun at his expense, it did little good.[91] Their reputation was beyond redemption. Zachary Taylor confessed to General Atkinson, "The more I see of the militia the less confidence I have of their effecting any thing of importance; & therefore tremble not only for the safety of the frontiers, but for the reputation of those who command them, who have any reputation to lose."[92] But even worse than that, when Atkinson learned of the blundering defeat, he told Henry Dodge how he deeply regretted that Stillman had ever been sent out, for the results of his ill-advised adventure "closed the door against settling the difficulty without bloodshed."[93]

9

THE GREAT FEAR

A wide frontier had been laid naked by this unexpected disaster, and more substantial evils were preceded by a thousand fanciful and imaginary dangers.

James Fenimore Cooper, *The Last of the Mohicans*

FROM THE VERY first bloodshed of the Revolution, the citizen-soldier in the ranks of the militia—the minuteman at Lexington and Concord—became a vital figure in the country's emerging national mythology. The thousands of common men, who appeared to emulate the brave and admirable example of Cincinnatus, and who left their plows and families behind to take up arms to defend the homeland against the English king's mercenary thugs, were thought to be ideal citizens who arose to become ideal soldiers, inspiring pride and patriotism throughout the land. They became the ideological metaphors that made the defense of life and liberty every man's responsibility, at the same time democratizing the honors of war by offering ordinary men the opportunity to become heroes. Although highly idealized, the winning of the Revolution, through what appeared to be the triumph of the armed common men over the professional armies of the British state, seemed to validate the whole romantic notion about the superiority of the citizen-soldier fighting for a noble cause, and that belief soon became an important influence on the way Americans thereafter viewed war.

Those views were strongly reinforced by the tales told about the Battle of New Orleans, which described how ordinary American farmers and sharpshooting frontiersmen, although greatly outnumbered and under-equipped, took on a grand force of the British king's most elite troops. The rigorously trained and disciplined invaders, in fancy uniforms, were said to be veterans of Wellington's wars against Bonaparte. All smartly marching in well-disciplined step to the sound of the pipes and drums, they were led into battle by one of the king's most accomplished generals. And yet once again it was the citizen-soldiers who triumphed. In the smoke and fury of that armed struggle only seventy Americans were lost, while more than two thousand British soldiers went dead, wounded, and missing. It was a euphorically inspirational moment for the young Republic, and in accounting for the great victory considerable credit was given to the strong character of self-made American men, whose very lack of discipline and regimentation, along with their rebellious attitudes toward authority, were all hailed as virtues that contrasted them with, and made them better men than, the rigid and obedient redcoats who marched unwaveringly like sheep to the slaughter.[1]

Those images shone brightly in the imaginations of the men who rode with John Reynolds and Samuel Whiteside up the valley of the Rock River in pursuit of Black Hawk and his British Band. They fit their own mytho-logical illusions of themselves. They were, after all, soldiers of the most amateur sort, without uniforms, without drill, discipline, or training, and under the command of men like themselves, democratically elected to their positions of authority and possessing little knowledge or experience in the difficult business of organizing and leading large numbers of men in the perilous work of mass violence. But they were prideful, even arrogant, about all they were not, and that arrogance was energized by the intense hatred they felt toward the Indians, much of which had been acquired early in life from the "nursery stories" Thomas McKenney said were told to them as children. "In our infant mind," observed McKenney, the Indian "stood for the Maloch of our country. We have been made to hear his yell; and our eyes have been presented with his tall, gaunt form, with the skins of beasts dangling round his limbs, and his eyes like fire, eager to find some new victim on which to fasten himself, and glut his appetite for blood."[2] In those militiamen the two myths converged, and in their hatred and pride, they were determined to emulate the manly examples of their brave fathers at Lexington and New Orleans, to leave the plow in the field and rise up in arms to destroy the monsters who dared to endanger their homes and their rights as free men.

However, Zachary Taylor's critical opinion of the militia was shared by virtually everyone in the regular army. Nevertheless, the scorn was mutual. Juliette Kinzie, the highly articulate wife of the Indian subagent at the Portage, personally observed the discord between the army and the militia and indicated, "The regular troops looked with contempt upon the unprofessional movements of the militia; the militia railed at the dilatory and useless formalities of the regulars," and each was convinced "that matters could be much better conducted without the other."[3]

But in the early twilight of May 14, 1832, on the prairie near the Kishwaukee River and Sycamore Creek, where the myth of the citizen-soldier confronted the realities of war, the fears deeply implanted by those "nursery stories" mentioned by McKenney seemed to all come to life with a terrifying ferocity, and the volunteers fled in panic. They lacked the self-control to stand their ground. On hearing the news of Stillman's "run," Colonel Albert Sidney Johnston, a West Point graduate, attributed the hysterical route of the militia to "the incapacity of their leader, and total absence of discipline in his battalion, and consequently a want of confidence in each other, [so that] these troops . . . had not the courage to face the Indians at Kishwaukee."[4] All things considered, they were not *real* soldiers, and that made all the difference.

Fear, when unchecked, can sow confusion, confound reason, and invite peril. It can unravel armies and reduce otherwise orderly societies to anarchy, and when deliberately spread, terror can leap out of control like a runaway brush fire, gathering momentum, even enhancing the power of those who unleashed its fury. Stern-willed discipline induced by firm authority and a strict regime of training and drill can preserve soldiers from its disintegrating blows. Civil societies beset by terror require confident, reassuring leaders and capable, courageous security forces to hold them together and maintain their collective sanity. But there was very little of any of that in northern Illinois and the mining district of the Michigan Territory in the spring of 1832.

The inability of Stillman and his volunteers to control their own fears altered the nature of the campaign and its consequences. In looking back at those events, Thomas Forsyth observed, "Black Hawk and [his] party had no intention to make war against the white people when they crossed over to the Eastside of the Mississippi River, but when attacked by Major Stillman's detachment, they defended themselves like men, and . . . thus the war commenced."[5] Whatever Black Hawk's original intentions may have been were unclear (perhaps even to himself). But Stillman's attack provoked an Indian reign of terror upon the farms and small settlements along the frontier. With the complete collapse of their myth-inspired bravado (especially after viewing the mutilated bodies of the dead), the men of the Illinois militia immediately lost interest in the war. Nothing was turning out as they had expected. As their time in the field lengthened and their conditions grew increasingly uncomfortable, they became more disgruntled and discouraged. And when they tasted the bitter humiliation of defeat, they completely lost heart, wanting only to return home and be forever done with soldiering.

Even while the *Galenian* histrionically "called down the God of War," and appealed to every good man in the region to "glut his steel and dye his hunting shirt purple with those monsters' blood,"[6] most of the volunteers at Dixon's Ferry had no interest in doing battle with anyone. They complained about everything from the lack of provisions brought about by their own irresponsible abandonment of their supply wagons, to the discomforts caused by the wet spring weather, the incompetence of the officers they had elected, and the inadequacy of their equipment. The bellyaching continued even after Atkinson and the regulars arrived on May 17 and fed them from the supplies brought up in the boats. What Atkinson saw disturbed him, for conditions in the camp were almost out of control. He soon issued an order forbidding "the frequent firing of Arms in and about the vicinity of the encampments."[7] Indeed, the regulars wanted nothing to do with the militia and established their camp on the north side of the Rock River, thereby separating themselves from the unruly mess of the amateur soldiers by the entire width of the stream.

After only a day at Dixon's Ferry, Atkinson had the militia up and on the move, ordering Whiteside and his troops to draw ten days' rations and get prepared to set out the very next morning in pursuit of the Indians.[8] The general, Colonel Taylor, and a contingent of regulars accompanied them. Once they all reached Sycamore Creek, the two forces separated, the volunteers being ordered to move up the creek and "scour the country in that direction for the enemy,"[9] while the regulars pressed on to a Potawatomi village at the confluence of Sycamore Creek and the Kishwaukee River.[10] Left on their own, the militiamen displayed little interest in searching for the elusive Black Hawk band, and when William Hamilton returned to Dixon's Ferry after being with them, he informed Colonel Johnston that all but a few were simply ignoring their orders and conducting no search whatsoever.[11]

While most of the volunteers were in the field, Stillman and his men remained in camp on the Rock River, where they became increasingly uneasy as messages came in telling of Indian attacks along the frontier. Many soon began to desert. Stillman wrote to Atkinson, informing him of what was happening: "Many of our men are hearing of depredations committed in other places, have left us with precipitation [and are] making fast speed to protect their families." He claimed he was using every means he could to prevent them from leaving but told the general he could no longer keep them at their post for any more than another day.[12]

Attitudes were soon the same among Whiteside's troops. Having started out in a glum and apathetic mood, they grew increasingly discouraged in what seemed to be a futile search for Black Hawk. Reynolds said it was "like following a shadow," and that the "men became disheartened and murmured considerable."[13] William Orr, who usually found a lot to be critical of, complained that during their march they had changed course numerous times, "seemingly at a loss [as to] what direction to take."[14] Even Nathaniel Buckmaster, the brigade major on Whiteside's staff, expressed his dissatisfaction in a letter to his wife: "This thing of being a soldier is not so comfortable as it might be." In fact, he was totally weary of the entire campaign and simply wished to return to her and the comforts of home as soon as possible.[15] But when Buckmaster and the other volunteers came upon a small deserted Potawatomi village, between the juncture of the Kishwaukee and the South Branch rivers, they reached their emotional low point upon discovering "a number of scalps of [white] men, women, and children."[16]

"While the army lay at this village," said Reynolds, Major William G. Brown and the governor's own brother, Thomas Reynolds, after having been out all night searching for runaway horses, reported they had almost collided with a large Indian force heading north in the darkness. They felt certain those Indians were members of the Black Hawk band. An officers' council was convened that same morning. Everyone above the rank of

lieutenant was included. The discussion was boisterous and full of acrimonious disagreement until Governor Reynolds put the main question to
a vote—whether to turn north and track down the Indians, or move southward along the Fox River and head for home. Many of the officers, indicated Reynolds, were adamantly opposed to "pursuing the enemy any
longer," and when the vote was taken, it was a tie.[17] Whiteside, who
presided over the council, had the deciding vote and cast it in favor of giving up the chase, declaring his personal refusal to lead men whom he had
come to regard as cowards. As a result, the whole campaign fizzled, and
the demoralized army of disgruntled citizen-soldiers began making its way
toward Ottawa, Illinois, where it would disband.

Reynolds would claim he vigorously opposed breaking up the militia
force and that he urged the men to stay on for at least a while longer to
protect the otherwise defenseless frontier. Zachary Taylor, in fact, angrily
insisted they continue northward in pursuit of the Indians. But their
efforts were of no avail. Whiteside tried to explain the situation to
Atkinson. He told him that when the men had mustered in, they had
agreed to serve for "no particular length of time" but had been "under the
impression that they would be retained only about three or four weeks."[18]
By late May they were tired of it—tired of the marching and the rations,
tired of the officers, and of being ordered about. And having entirely lost
their sense of adventure following Stillman's disaster, they simply wanted
to be civilians again. Even before the officers cast their tie vote, the men in
the ranks were thoroughly fed up, and some began to slip away on their
own. Harriet Buckmaster reported to her husband, Nathaniel, how volunteers were drifting back home, two and three at a time, and how she suspected they must have been "runaways and cowards."[19] News of the
discontent within the militia even reached St. Louis, where Thomas
Forsyth wrote to George Davenport saying he had heard reports that
"many of the volunteers were returning home and are already sick of the
campaigning." Then he wondered sarcastically what would have ever
become of them "once the flies and mosquitoes arrived in [the] next
month?" There would have been some loss of blood then, and how could
the brave soldier boys have ever withstood such threats and discomforts?
he asked Davenport, poking fun at the militia that had already done so
much on its own to make itself seem ridiculous.[20]

By the time Forsyth was writing those remarks, Whiteside was struggling to prevent the premature dissolution of what was left of his army. He admitted that "the great disorder in the Brigade occasioned by the men's quitting their places in the line and stattering [scattering] over the country" finally made it necessary for him to punish those who were caught trying to desert.[21] Due to that action, at least some of the force remained intact for the last four days of the journey down to Ottawa, but they marched on, remarked Reynolds, "with deep feelings of mortification," as well as with "irritable and bad feelings."[22] On May 28, at Ottawa, what was left of what had once been a large and enthusiastic fighting force stood down without ceremony, barely a month after setting out from Beardstown with such brave intentions.

While most of the men took off for home, about three hundred agreed to stay on for another twenty days to provide at least some minimal protection for the otherwise completely unprotected frontier region.[23] The young, twenty-three-year old Abraham Lincoln, a captain in one of the Sangamon County companies, remained among them.

In late May someone from Canton, Illinois, wrote to the *New York Mercury*, remarking about the widespread feelings of insecurity felt by the inhabitants of that area. "The people here," he declared, " are now greatly alarmed at the news of the Governor's discharging the Militia."[24] Indeed, the breakup of the militia caused a surge of panic to rush through the entire region, made even more alarmed by spreading rumors of Indian attacks.

Indian raids did in fact increase. They were widely dispersed and opportunistic, rather than part of any orchestrated grand strategy, and many were carried out by warriors who were not members of Black Hawk's band.

On Monday, May 21, a raiding party from west of the Mississippi River struck the small settlement of Savanna, on the Plumb River, about thirty miles south of Galena. Some enterprising young braves from Keokuk's village or the Fox village at Dubuque's Mines, eager to steal some horses and perhaps collect a scalp or two, probably carried it out. When the attack came, there were only three men in the settlement. Another man, out hunting at the time, was discovered by the attackers, who chased after him throughout the afternoon. However, he eluded his pursuers and eventually managed to escape without harm. In fact, no one was injured or killed in this incident, and, for all their efforts, the Indians were only able to get away with three horses. Even then, one of the horses was killed and the other two were badly wounded by the gunfire of the defenders.

News of the raid soon reached Galena, where Colonel James Strode, who had put himself in command of the town, sent a party of mounted militia to the rescue. They traveled down to the Plumb River aboard the steamboat *Dove*. But by the time they arrived, the Indians were long gone and all the Galenian volunteers found were a great many bullet holes in the houses and in the door of the blockhouse the settlers had built. Not needed in Savanna, the militiamen continued downstream on the steamboat to Fort Armstrong, where it picked up a cargo of muskets and rifles, and then returned to Galena without incident.[25]

Around that time, Captain James Stephenson dispatched from Galena a party of six militia volunteers to take a message to General Atkinson, still at Dixon's Ferry. En route, they were attacked by a small war party at Buffalo Grove, about twenty miles from their destination. One of the volunteers, William Durley, a young man who had migrated north from Bond County to mine lead, was shot. When hit, he exclaimed, "O God!" as he toppled from his horse. He was dead by the time he reached the ground.[26] A musket ball also blew through the hat of another of the volunteers, coming within a half inch of his brain, but he and his four surviving companions managed to spur on their horses and escape with their lives. A few days later, Durley's remains were found by a group of seven travelers led by the Indian agent Felix St. Vrain. They were heading toward Rock Island from Dixon's Ferry. On finding the corpse, they discovered that young Durley had been shot just above his left groin. He had also been scalped, his nose cut off, and his head almost severed from his neck. It was a gruesome spectacle, and they buried what was left of the poor man in a shallow grave near the edge of the grove.[27]

St. Vrain's party consisted of Thomas Kennedy, Aquilla Floyd, Alexander Higginbotham, John Fowler, Aaron Hawley, and William Hale, most of whom lived in the southwest hill country of what would become Wisconsin. They had all set out from Dixon's Ferry on May 23, carrying a message from General Atkinson to Henry Gratiot, and after burying the body of William Durley, they pushed on to within about a half mile of Kellogg's Grove. There, to their great surprise, they came under fire from a party of about thirty Indians, who suddenly appeared out of nowhere. While their attackers were still about three hundred yards away, St. Vrain and his comrades quickly turned their horses to get away, since only four of them were carrying guns. But the Indians followed fast after them, and during the chase only Kennedy, Floyd, and Higginbotham managed to escape.[28] Three days later, a militia troop under James Stephenson reached Kellogg's Grove, on its way to Dixon's Ferry, and stopped to search for both the living and the dead of St. Vrain's group.[29] They found no one, and it was not until June 8, when Stephenson and his men returned to Kellogg's Grove with Alexander Higginbotham, that the search was resumed. On their second attempt they found the bodies of St. Vrain, Hale, and Fowler in the tall grass about four miles south of the grove. Hawley's remains were never located. All three corpses had been gruesomely mutilated. The *Galenian*, in its June 13 edition, reminded its readers that Black Hawk had vowed to kill St. Vrain, and reported that the Indian agent had been shot through the neck. The article went on to describe in horrible detail how his head had been cut off and carried away, along with his severed feet and hands. The shocking appearance of that corpse, along with those of Hale and Fowler, deeply disturbed the men who discovered them, and the gruesome newspaper report surely intensified the dreadful sense of vulnerability felt by people throughout the mining district.

Black Hawk made only brief mention of those attacks in his own account. However, soon after Stillman's Run, as he was moving the band northeastward, he met up with a party of Winnebago warriors, who, he said, "seemed to rejoice in our success" over the soldiers and offered him their services. It is not clear from which of the many Winnebago villages they had come, but they arrived at the Sauk camp near the source of the Keshwaukee River looking for action. Black Hawk conferred with them and then "arranged war parties to send out in different directions," which included warriors of his own band as well as those eager Winnebago volunteers. After a few days had passed, six of the Winnebago returned to Black Hawk's camp with a single scalp, most likely the scalp of William Durley. Four days later, Black Hawk indicated, more of his Winnebago allies came in and reported how "they had killed four men, and taken their scalps; and that one of them was Keokuck's father (the [Indian] agent)." That was clearly the war party responsible for the killing of St. Vrain and his companions.[30]

While the slaughter of the St. Vrain party deeply disturbed the white people of the region, it had nowhere near the terrifying impact of the raid on the William Davis homestead, along Big Indian Creek, on May 21.

In the spring of 1830 William Davis, a blacksmith from West Virginia, settled with his wife and six children on Big Indian Creek, about twenty miles above Ottawa. There he set up a blacksmith shop and sawmill within a substantial grove of trees. His place sat right on the Great Sauk Trail and was about six miles downstream from a substantial Potawatomi village. A number of other families soon moved into the same general area. William Hall and his family were among them. The Halls were from Kentucky, but William had already been to the lead region for the better part of three years before giving up the quest for fortune and taking a homestead in LaSalle County, about two and a half miles east of the Davis place. He and his wife, Mary, had three daughters and three sons with them. There were also the Pettigrews—William, his wife, and two children—who had also arrived from Kentucky in the early spring of 1832. They were living with the Davises until they could get a place of their own. Next to Davis's, John H. Henderson had a farm. Henderson was from Tennessee and had a family as well as a hired man, Robert Norris. Henry George, who worked for Davis, had a cabin on Bureau Creek a few miles to the west.

In April of 1832 there had been an incident between Davis and a man from the Potawatomi village upstream. When Davis had built his sawmill, he had also constructed a dam across the creek to power the mill. It worked fine for him, but it impeded the migration of fish upstream, which greatly upset the Potawatomi who depended on the fish for their sustenance. They protested to Davis, but Davis rudely dismissed their pleas. Not long after that confrontation, a member of the Potawatomi village, a man by the name of Keewassee, took it upon himself to commence the destruction of Davis's much-hated dam. Davis caught him in the act and gave him a severe thrashing with a hickory rod. Keewassee went away bruised and angry, but he was far from finished with Davis.

Right after Stillman's Run, Shaubena, the chief of the large Potawatomi village near Paw-Paw Grove about a dozen miles northwest of Davis's, set out on horseback to warn the settlers above the Illinois River about the possibility of attacks from the Sauk. After he left the Hall farm, William Hall gathered his family, loaded up his wagon, and set out for Ottawa.[31] On the way, during the morning of May 21, the Halls met William Davis returning home after doing some business in Ottawa. When told of Shaubena's warning, Davis proclaimed his refusal to be run off his land by any Indians and persuaded the Halls to abandon their flight and return to his place with him. The Pettigrew and Henderson families were already there, along with a Mr. Howard and his son, as well as the hired men, Henry George and Robert Norris.

That afternoon, William Hall and his son John went to work on a shed adjoining the blacksmith shop, while inside the shop Davis and Norris were busy at the forge repairing a broken musket. At the same time, Henry George and William Davis Jr. made repairs to the mill dam, just south of the shop. The women and children were all in the main house sewing, and William Pettigrew and his infant son were with them. Edward and Greenberry Hall, Mr. Howard and his son, and two of the Davis boys, along with Henderson, were in the field south of the creek planting corn. It was an unusually hot afternoon, and everyone went uncomfortably about their business at a lethargic pace.[32]

The door and windows of the Davis house were wide open in order to catch whatever breeze might move the heavy air. At around four thirty in the afternoon Rachel Hall, the seventeen-year-old daughter of William and Mary Hall, was startled when she looked out one of those windows and saw a party of about seventy Indians coming over the fence and into the yard only about eight to ten paces away. William Pettigrew saw them too. He quickly arose from his chair, his baby still in his arms, to bar the door. He was shot down where he stood, and the door remained open. There was no chance for escape. Both Rachel and her nineteen-year-old sister, Sylvia, made a futile attempt to hide, but the Indians soon seized them and carried them both out into the yard, while back in the house other members of the raiding party hastily set about the macabre work of massacring all the women and children.[33] Hearing their screams, the men in and around the blacksmith shop began rushing toward the house. Indians in the yard and still on horseback opened fire. William Hall was hit in the chest and killed instantly. The others then turned and fled. Norris and George were both shot while trying to cross the creek. William Davis Jr., after briefly hiding behind the blacksmith shop, managed to make his way to safety. John Hall also escaped. He concealed himself under the deep bank of the creek and slowly made his way downstream for about two miles, then arose and sped across the open prairie toward

Ottawa. In time, he overtook John Henderson. The two of them went on together until they were within about four miles of Ottawa, where they met up with all the men and boys who had been working in the cornfield. All eight got safely away.[34]

Back at the Davis place, fifteen people had been butchered in what Rachel Hall estimated to have been the duration of about ten minutes. Their bodies were obscenely mutilated. All were scalped. The men and children were chopped to pieces, and the dead women were hung up by the feet and the "most revolting acts of outrage and indecency practiced upon their bodies," one report stated.[35] After that, the war party burned down the house and all the outbuildings and wantonly slaughtered the livestock.

All of that took place while the militia was in a state of near mutiny on its way to Ottawa to be discharged. The simultaneous occurrence of those two developments—the Indian attacks and the dissolution of the region's primary defense force—caused terror to spread like a uncontrollable blaze throughout the sparsely settled countryside of northern Illinois and up into the mining region of the Michigan Territory. The perilous situation even distressed the people of western Michigan and Indiana. Reynolds noted that the entire region "was in a panic on account of Indian murders being committed in every direction,"[36] and Reuben Holmes, a colonel in the militia, informed a friend, "The alarm and distress of the frontier cannot be described; it is heartrending to see the women and children in the agony of fear, fleeing their homes and hearths, to seek what they imagine is but a short respite from death."[37] And the *Galenian* protested, "The Illinois militia are disbanded, and have left us to fight our own battles, defend our own country, or fall sacrifice to the tomahawk and scalping knife."[38]

For settlers living on solitary homesteads or in small isolated clusters of farms, there was an almost overpowering sense of dread. Even under the best of circumstances those people felt vulnerable. They were small, almost insignificant specks within an immense, open landscape, which spread out in all directions as far as the eye could see. Above them the huge vault of the sky, unobstructed by either trees or man-made structures, must have seemed an immeasurable space, surrounding and enveloping them in its vastness. They all felt diminished in the presence of such immensity, and such feelings must have become overwhelming when the sky turned the harsh color of dark slate and then rumbled and shook with the fury of a prairie thunderstorm, ripping open the scowling heavens with jagged slashes of lightning. There had been many such storms that spring. But even without their frightful power, the land itself could disorient a person amid its undulating expanses of waving grass, and with winds howling at all hours, one could come to have the deeply distressing sensation of being absorbed into and merged with the surrounding environment. Caleb Atwater experienced such a feeling when he came onto that prairie in the summer of 1829, and felt "a flood of absorbing sensations" rush into his soul as he stood in "breathless silence," almost hypnotically entranced by the landscape. Feeling submerged and assimilated into infinite space and time can bring on a sudden desperation to remain conscious of self and objective reality.[39] Perhaps the people living upon those open plains and among the tree-sparse hills knew such feelings all too well, and whatever sense of personal significance or autonomy they might have struggled to retain may have simply been overwhelmed by the vastness of their environment, leaving them with a sense of powerlessness born of the awareness that the natural world had little need of them and they had little control of it.[40]

Such insecurities were of course exacerbated considerably by the threat of Indian attacks, which seemed to come out of nowhere and left behind misery, death, and mutilated bodies. Imaginations became wildly agitated, conjuring up frightful images of phantom savages driven by a maniacal lust for bloodshed and cruelty. As Thomas Owen, the Indian agent at Chicago, observed about such threats, "Some of the intelligence was greatly exaggerated, and much of it, the mere vision of fancy produced by the fears of a few individuals."[41] John Wakefield alluded to the same fear-distorted reactions and remarked that "the mind of man, when there was cause of fear or suspicion of danger, was frequently apt to suffer his imagination to lead [him] astray, which was the case at this time."[42]

That exaggerated and disorienting sense of terror was most certainly the reaction the Indians deliberately sought to create with their atrocities. Of course, it was intended to supplement their limited numbers and modest resources, while weakening the settlers' will to stand firm. Zachary Taylor saw that as a direct consequence of the massacre at the Davis farm. "You have no idea, nor can I describe the panic & distress produced by this," he told a friend, pointing out that not just women and children were terrified by the horror of it all, but extreme fear also "prevailed among a large portion of the men . . . who fancied they saw an Indian in every bush, or behind every tree or stump, whenever they were out of sight of a Fort."[43]

That sense of panic was especially strong in the area just west of Chicago, in the Fox River valley near the Davis place. It also happened to be the same region where friendly Potawatomi riders traveled out to farms and small villages to warn settlers of the possibility of more such attacks. From both the Potawatomi and fleeing settlers seeking refuge in Chicago, Thomas Owen received information that led him to conclude the Sauk were preparing for a major campaign. Accordingly, he wrote on May 24 to James Stewart, a subagent in western Michigan, and told him, "The Sacs are concentrating at the Big Woods about 40 miles from this place, and it is probable, they will make an effort to reduce this Post."[44] That report proved to be pure erroneous speculation. The Sauk had no such plans. Instead, they were moving northward into the Michigan Territory. But fear had a reality all its own.

Plainfield, a small settlement on the Du Page River, was right in the midst of the area between the Big Woods and Lake Michigan. Reverend Stephen R. Beggs, the community's Methodist minister, later recalled how settlers to the west of them, fleeing from the Fox River valley, had hurriedly passed through Plainfield on their way to Danville, down near the Indiana border. "They came with their cattle and horses, some bare headed and others bare footed, crying 'The Indians! The Indians!'" wrote Beggs. Some of the refugees were from Hollenback's Grove, which the Indians had looted and burned a few days before, and some of the men among them reported "how the Indians were killing and burning all before them." Such warnings deeply disturbed the inhabitants of Plainfield, many of whom also wished to escape to safety somewhere farther east. A little later, however, some friendly Indians came to town and informed the inhabitants how the refugees had wildly overstated the dangers. After that, most of the town's people decided to remain right where they were. They built a fort of fence rails and barn timbers around Beggs's house, and even some of the people from the Fox River decided to stay on with them. There were 175 of them in all, but they had only four guns among them and their ammunition was in very short supply. Fearing an attack might come at any time, they frantically made preparations to defend themselves as best as they could. "All our pewter spoons, basins, and platters were soon molded by the women into bullets. As a next best means of defense, we got a good supply of axes, hoes, forks, sharp sticks and clubs," hoping their makeshift arsenal would enable them to hold out until relief might come from Chicago, wrote the Reverend Beggs.[45]

The people of Plainfield huddled nervously in their small stockade for four days. On the fourth day, which was a Sunday, a mounted force of about twenty-five white men, and as many friendly Potawatomi, arrived from Chicago and remained a short time. Before departing, some of the militia riders almost cruelly mentioned they had heard reports about the intentions of some hostile Indians to attack the community that very night or perhaps the next. After hearing that, the townspeople spontaneously decided to abandon Plainfield and seek refuge in a more secure place. Beggs observed that even "the stoutest hearts failed them, and strong men turned pale, while women and children wept and fainted." Although they all agreed on the urgent need to leave the town, there was much heated disagreement about where they ought to go. Should they make their way to Chicago, or run off to Ottawa, which had a sturdy fort, or should they simply scatter and hide out in the woods until the danger passed? The debate went on inconclusively for some time until the exasperated people decided once more that their safest option was to remain right where they were.[46]

On Wednesday, the company of Chicago volunteers, which had arrived and departed the previous Sunday, returned. They brought with them gruesome stories of what had transpired at the Davis homestead, just a few miles west of Plainfield. On hearing that, everyone in town then resolved to get to Chicago as soon as humanly possible.

They departed the next morning under the protection of the militia company and traveled the entire forty miles in that single day, reaching Chicago by sundown. By then the otherwise small community at the bottom of Lake Michigan had become an overcrowded refugee camp. John S. C. Hogan, the local postmaster, wrote to Lewis Cass, telling him how the town was "filled with refugees from the country in all directions, flying from scenes of bloodshed and devastation," and because there were so many of them, the settlement had become dangerously low on food and all other supplies. Indeed, there was a mounting threat of starvation, warned Hogan.[47]

But amid all that fear and confusion, Mrs. Beggs gave birth to their first child.[48]

Prospects of hunger in Chicago were quite real, and, in fact, there were growing concerns about the shortage of grain throughout much of Illinois. The harvests had been disappointingly small the previous fall, and food supplies were reaching the bottom of the bin after another unusually hard winter. Because the spring had been so cold and wet, the winter wheat had not fared at all well either. One man from Lewistown, on the west side of the state, remarked that not only did the people there live in terror of Indian attacks, but many were also "quite destitute of provisions." He went on to say, "Wheat is nearly all winter-killed, and unless there is soon a favorable change in the weather, the corn crop will fail again."[49]

The Reverend Adam Payne, an itinerant preacher from Pennsylvania, was among the people who had gathered at Plainfield. Payne was a large, imposing man of striking appearance. He had dense raven-black hair, which had grown well below his shoulders. He also had a great bushy black beard covering his face and extending all the way to his waist. Also, befitting a man of his profession, he had a powerful booming voice, exceptional oratorical skills, and had preached with great success among the Indians. For that reason he had little fear of them. He had ridden out from Chicago to visit friends, but when everyone in Plainfield fled to Chicago, he decided to push on westward for Ottawa. He simply ignored the warnings of possible Indian attacks, and his journey was uneventful until he drew near Holderman's Grove, a little over halfway between Plainfield and Ottawa. As he approached the grove, a small war party of Indians dashed out in his direction firing their guns. Almost immediately Payne was shot in the chest. He managed to turn his horse and take flight, but the horse too had been wounded and soon went down and died beneath him. The Indians then closed in. Payne, who was unarmed and helpless to defend himself, was soon killed. One of the attackers cut off his head, with all its bushy black hair and beard, and carried it off. After that, none of the white people of the entire area felt safe.[50]

While a wave of terror swept through northeastern Illinois, a deep current of anxiety surged into the mining region as well. The June 6 edition of the *Galenian* reported that the Black Hawk band was heading for Four Lakes (site of present-day Madison, Wisconsin). It was news that caused "great alarm among all the inhabitants throughout the mining part of the territory," said the newspaper. At many of the "diggings" people erected forts, while still others departed in hast for Galena. Within Galena itself, Colonel James Strode proclaimed a state of martial law and then put every able-bodied man to work on the construction of a stockade. All were required to work from nine in the morning until six at night, and anyone selling or giving away spirituous liquors during work hours could be brought before a court-martial and severely punished.[51] That action did not sit well with the people of the community and, furthermore, it greatly upset General Atkinson. The general fired off a letter to the dictatorial militia colonel, declaring, "I cannot but admonish you against the course you have adopted of declaring martial law, pressing personal property, coercing personal labor, [and] hiring Steam Boats by the day etc." He also warned Strode that the federal government was unlikely to pay for any of it.[52]

About the same time, Atkinson had three hundred muskets and a considerable supply of ammunition sent up to Galena from Jefferson Barracks.[53] But in spite of the stockade and the weaponry, people remained suspensefully on edge, so that when a warning alarm was sounded around midnight on Monday, June 4, the entire community exploded into panic. People left their beds and houses and sought refuge in the nearly completed fort. Horatio Newhall described some of the scene that night in a letter he wrote to his brother, Isaac, "Men, Women & children flying to the Stockade. I calculated seven hundred women & children were there within fifteen minutes after the alarm gun was fired. Some with dresses on, and some with none; some with shoes and some barefoot . . . [and] women and children were screaming from one end of the town to the other."[54] As it turned out, it was a false alarm. But the collective fears that rumbled just beneath the surface of life were so strong that the warning shot had caused them to erupt with great force. The day after, however, when the towns-people discovered Strode and his staff officers had intentionally set off the alarm to test the people's readiness, their fears turned to rage. "When the people learned how cruelly their fears had been played upon, their indignation knew no bounds," remarked one writer, who went on to report how all business was suspended and an angry mass meeting was held. While it was in session, Strode and his staff left town and ran for their lives.[55]

The sense of terror was intense and widespread. "Travel east, west, north, or south, we see nothing but waste, destruction, and dilapidation," the *Galenian* declared, and then elaborated: "Fields half ploughed for sowing and planting; some just planted; gardens partly made; hogs, cattle, fowls etc. running wild; houses vacated, and left with all their furniture within them, and not an inhabitant within 60 miles, presents an aspect too gloomy for reflection." Other people, who still waited in agonizing uncertainty within the many small forts quickly constructed throughout the region, were dangerously short of food and other provisions. The *Galenian* warned, "Should this war continue, famine, without some relief from the lower country, must be the result."[56]

In mid-May, after learning of Stillman's defeat, Henry Dodge sent a letter to General Atkinson from his own fort at Dodgeville. "The people of the Mining Country are badly prepared to receive so great a shock as a Defeat of the Illinois Militia is calculated to produce," he told him.[57] Once news of that began to get around, along with the reports of vicious Indian attacks, the region north of the Illinois border was soon in a fearful frenzy. It reached all the way north to Green Bay. Elizabeth Baird, the métis wife of the town's prominent young Irish attorney, Henry Baird, later recalled just how apprehensive the whole community had become during early summer on account of the "daily alarming reports of the Indians and their doings." Their concerns were compounded by the fact that, at the time, the fort there was under reconstruction and thereby in no condition to provide anyone with much protection. One night, after an unusually anxious day, the Bairds, too nervous to eat supper, went to bed only to be awakened with a jolt by the sound of two guns firing in the darkness. That was the community's agreed-upon alarm signal. Henry and Elizabeth had slept in their clothes in case of such an emergency. Hastily arousing their children, who they did not take time to dress, they all ran off to the Indian Agency house, which soon became crowded with other panic-stricken families. They remained there in fearful anticipation until the first rays of sunlight appeared over the east rim of the bay. It was then a military officer informed them that it had all been a mistake, and that the shots they had heard had not been an alarm at all but just guns being fired in the predawn darkness to awaken the militia encamped near the town.[58] A silly mistake, but one that revealed just how fearful people had become, even at a considerable distance from where the violent events of that summer were transpiring.

The brutal attack on the Davis farm added yet another dimension to the crisis. During the raid, the Indians had taken captive the Hall sisters,

Rachel and Sylvia—"two young and beautiful women . . . taken prisoner by those monsters in human shape," as John Wakefield put it.[59]

Ever since Mary Rowlandson had been carried off during an Indian attack on Lancaster, Massachusetts, in 1676, stories of women taken captive by Indians had evolved into a distinctively American literary genre, which served as a vehicle for the mythology pertaining to Anglo-America's relations with the native people.

While each individual captivity account had its own particular tale to tell, collectively they shared themes and characteristics to the point of becoming so prescribed they repeated many of the same phrases, images, and metaphors. The plots too were highly formulaic, so that if you read one captivity narrative all the rest were quite predictable. Nevertheless, they provided a rare look into the female frontier experience and presented some women as strong and courageous individuals able to survive the perils of savage captivity without the care and protection of white men.[60]

Such narratives were highly popular reading in early America. Virtually all were based on the actual experiences of real women, which gave them a high degree of authenticity and credibility. The earliest ones sprang almost exclusively from New England and were heavily religious in theme and symbolism, depicting the captivity as some awful pilgrim's progress from which the sorely tested victims were rescued and redeemed by the grace of God. But, in time, writers such as Cooper adapted the form to fiction with great success, as in *The Last of the Mohicans* with its dramatic capture and rescue of Alice Munro. Also, by Cooper's time, most captivities had become secularized and sentimental, and used to reinforce the values and assumption of patriarchal society and the territorial expansion of the country at the expense of the native people.[61]

But beyond religious and ideological concerns, all those narratives reflected a deep fear of the loss of "self"—an anxiety about being absorbed by the wilderness and transformed from a white civilized person into a wild and degenerative savage.[62] That was vividly illustrated in the tale of Eunice Williams, the daughter of the Reverend John Williams of Deerfield, Massachusetts, who was captured by Indians and carried off to Canada in the winter of 1704. A young girl, only seven years old at the time, Eunice remained with her captors for the rest of her life, becoming the "unredeemed captive," who lost her culture, religion, and even her English-American identity. She became, to the horror of all who had known her in

Deerfield, a Roman Catholic wench, married to an Indian man, and the mother of a dirty brood of half-breed children. In the mind of many New Englanders, poor Eunice suffered a fate worse than death.[63]

In their melodramatic plots the Indians were always villains, portrayed as the monstrous agents of evil and frequently referred to as "devils in human shape." Their deeds were diabolical: slaying little children, smashing their brains out on tree stumps, inflicting almost unimaginable pain and cruelty upon innocent people, cold-bloodedly killing all those unable to keep up with the march into the darkness, and subjecting the victims they allowed to survive to lives of anguish and humiliation. In other words, the captivity narratives totally dehumanized and vilified the native people, turning them into objects of disgust and hatred, and by doing so providing readers with a highly charged emotional justification for wanting to see them exterminated. In that way the stories served the interests of imperial expansion and freed white people from any guilt they might otherwise feel over the destruction of Native American cultures and the seizure of their resources.

According to the historians Richard Slotkin and Christopher Castiglia, the same tales also reveal some sexual and gender concerns that deeply bothered early America. The plots strongly suggest that Indian men were sexually attracted to white women, lusting after their bodies, and engaging in raids with rape very much on their minds. Furthermore, the defenseless white women, whose lives were spared, were often doomed to a disgustingly degenerate existence as sex slaves to the dark-skinned wild men who carried them off into the night. But not far beneath the surface of such images lurked the fear that white women might actually prefer Indian men as sexual partners to men of their own race and culture. The muscular, agile, passionate warriors of the wild country might be more erotically tempting and sexually pleasing than almost any woman could possibly resist, and once they had known such savage ecstasy—once white females had been sexually liberated from the repressive confinement of Anglo-American culture—there would be no turning back. They would be lost in the raging torrent of their own primal drives and desires. Therefore, on the frontiers of early America, the Indian man was seen as the greatest threat to the moral purity of white womanhood, as well as the white man's most formidable sexual competitor. And thus the narratives imply that war against Indians was warfare for the protection of white woman (even against themselves) and all that was decent, as well as a brave defense of the proper and necessary patriarchal order of civilized society.

Christopher Castiglia further points out how "the captivity narrative flourished during periods of gender and social tensions," which were precisely the times, he says, in which "the established interlocking hierarchies of race and gender" were most in need of reinforcement and reassertion, at least from the perspective of white men.[64] There were some clear indications that gender tensions were a virtually inescapable aspect of the settlement process of the Midwest and Great Lakes regions, where, it would appear, many women were reluctant and discontented participants. Arriving in Upper Canada in the summer of 1832, Catherine Parr Traill, a well-educated Englishwoman, moved into the forest country just above Lake Ontario with her husband and commenced the pioneering life. There she observed among the settlers that, while the men were in good spirits and full of enthusiasm for the adventure, the women generally were not. "The women," she wrote, "are discontented and unhappy. Few enter with their whole heart into the settler's life. They miss the little domestic comforts they had been used to enjoy; they regret the friends and relations they left behind in the old country; and they cannot endure the loneliness of the backwoods." She also noted that "the men complain that their wives are always pining for home."[65]

Those feelings were not peculiar to the Canadian experience, nor was that emotional discord reserved for men and women who migrated to North America from across the sea. It also happened among the people who moved west from the northeastern part of the United States. Caroline Kirkland was such a woman, and she made observations virtually identical to Traill's when she settled in the wilderness of Michigan, west of Detroit, also in the 1830s. "Women are the grumblers in Michigan . . . [and] many of them have made sacrifices for which they were not prepared and which detract largely from their every-day stores of comfort."[66] And concerning the settlement of Illinois, a well-known woman writer from New England, Margaret Fuller, who toured the Lake Michigan region in the summer of 1843, remarked: "It has generally been the choice of the men, and the women follow, as women will, doing their best for affection's sake, but too often in heartsickness and weariness. Beside it frequently not being a choice or conviction, of their own minds that it is best to be here, their part is the hardest, and they are least fitted for it."[67]

Such observations certainly suggest there probably was stress and strain between men and women—especially husbands and wives—over their contrasting expectations and experiences relating to life on the frontiers. The resentments and unhappiness these tensions produced in the women may very well have fostered defensive and guilty reactions in men. That, in turn, may have left men feeling an even more urgent need to assert their patriarchal authority and take control in order to prevent their efforts to prosper in the new life from being undone by the complaints and protests of discontented women. Then, with the Indian attacks, the slaughter of women and children, and the captivity of attractive, young women like the Hall sisters, conflicting emotions on both sides of the gender divide were undoubtedly exacerbated considerably. In that context, the story of Rachel and Sylvia Hall became a complex metaphor for all the troubled relationships of gender and race that existed along the frontier, and the girls themselves were symbols of the threats, both real and imagined, the Indians posed to white women and the American family.

For the Hall girls, as well as everyone else gathered at the Davis place that terrible Monday afternoon, the Indian attack came by complete surprise. There had been the warnings of Shaubena, shrugged off by Davis, who defiantly refused to be frightened off by a few rumors. When the attack came, everything occurred so furiously that neither of the Hall sisters had any clear memory of distinct events. "The confusion in the house was so great and the terror inspired by the firing of the guns and the shrieking of the dying prevented me . . . from knowing the manner in which they were killed," said Rachel.[68] Sylvia later claimed that, although she had witnessed little of the killing, she unfortunately saw her own mother "sinking under the instruments of death" just as she, herself, was being pulled through the door and out into the yard by one of the attackers.[69]

Much later—in September of 1867—Rachel and Sylvia collaborated in the writing of a memoir of their captivity experience. In that account the girls embellished their earlier reports a little by telling, for example, how they had seen an Indian seize the Pettigrew baby, who had been in his father's arms, and bash his brains out on a tree stump. That was a stock captivity narrative image, but neither sister had mentioned it in the reports they made soon after the events of that day.[70] Even in a very badly written narrative, published in 1832, in which the anonymous author erroneously referred to the girls as Frances and Almira Hall, there were also no details of the bloody events that took place in and around the Davis house. What was said about the violence was only that "no language can express the cruelties that were committed."[71] John Wakefield was also at a loss for words on that subject, saying that "the imagination can only think [of] the pain they suffered, but it is impossible to write it."[72] In his account of the Big Indian Creek massacre, Thomas Ford stated he would not describe the actual events of the day, but did mention how some of the Indians involved "afterwards related with infernal glee how the women had squeaked like geese when they were run through the body with spears, or felt the sharp tomahawk enter their heads."[73] Though very little was reported about the actual killing—in fact, very little was known of it—almost everything that was said focused on what supposedly had happened to the women and children.

Considerably more, on the other hand, was written about the mutilation of the dead bodies. John Hall, Rachel and Sylvia's twenty-three-year-old brother who escaped death that day, returned to the scene of the slaughter the next morning. He was the first to see what the attackers had done. According to his account, among the bodies there were "some with their hearts cut out, and others cut and lacerated in too shocking a manner to mention or behold without shuttering."[74] Other descriptions, made soon after the events, included grisly details especially about how the women had been "hung up by the feet" and indecent acts committed upon their bodies.[75]

In contrast to the diabolical characterization of the Indians—"savage monsters," as the 1832 "Narrative" called them—the Hall girls were described as "two highly respectable young women,"[76] "two young and said to be beautiful females,"[77] and "two weak and feeble young women."[78] John Wakefield waxed melodramatic as he related how they were "torn with violence, by frightful savages, from the abodes of peace and innocence," and he lamented how they were carried off by "butchers" into a "wilderness, where no friendly voice could salute their ears, no soothing comforter to pour the oil and balm of consolation into their swelling and almost bursting hearts."[79]

The girls themselves told how they were taken north across Big Indian Creek and then forced to run as fast as they were able for about two miles until they reached a woods in which the Indians had left their horses. There, said Rachel, they were "placed upon two of the poorest and most

indifferent horses they had," and led by the Indians, they all set off northward at a full run.[80] They continued on at a very fast pace until about midnight, when they stopped to rest the horses. The Indians were uneasy.
They were concerned about being followed. Therefore, they paused for
only about two hours. When the journey resumed, both Rachel and Sylvia
were placed on the same horse. They galloped on until late morning. "We
by this time were almost fatigued to death, and faint from hunger,"
recalled Sylvia.[81] They were given an unappetizing breakfast of scalded
beans and roasted acorns and ordered to eat. During that stop, said
Rachel, the Indians also busied themselves dressing the scalps taken in
the raid, stretching the gruesome little pelts upon small hoops. Because of
that, and the fear of their own impending deaths, neither girl ate much of
the food provided by their captors. When the journey recommenced, the
sisters were once more put on separate horses. On that leg of the trip,
Rachel's horse gave out and she was placed on another—a horse that had
belonged to the Hendersons—and was seated behind an Indian man.
They went on, stopping only once before arriving at Black Hawk's camp
around nine o'clock in the evening. Rachel estimated they had traveled
about ninety miles in twenty-eight hours.[82]

The entire camp gave them a warm welcome. When they first arrived,
several Sauk women flocked around the girls, helping them down from
their horses, and then giving them some decent food to eat. Rachel
reported, "There was great rejoicing and feasting" in the camp that night.[83]
Neither Rachel nor Sylvia witnessed that revelry, however. They were
nearing exhaustion from their arduous journey, and when they retired for
the night, some of the same women who had greeted their arrival accompanied them to a lodge and slept beside them throughout the night.
Although they slept "a confused and disturbed sleep," in the morning their
"fears of being killed began to abate," said Rachel.[84]

Rachel described the camp as being located on the bank of a small
stream and surrounded by low swampy ground in the midst of a grove of
small oak trees. They were probably on Turtle Creek, in the area above the
Winnebago village at the confluence of the creek and the Rock River. By
then they were clearly within the region of what would become Wisconsin.

The day after the girls arrived—May 23—the entire band packed up
and moved on about five miles to the north. Once they were resettled, a
large number of warriors congregated and began to dance. They were soon

joined by some of the women. A pole was erected in the middle of the camp, upon which they placed two red flags and all the scalps they had taken in the raid, and around it they performed the Scalp Dance with great enthusiasm. The Hall girls looked on in disturbed amazement until some of the women came over to them and proceeded to paint their faces. One side was painted red, the other black. Once they had been decorated so, the warriors came and led the two young women around the encampment several times. Eventually they were placed on a blanket and required to lie facedown while the men continued to dance around them, "singing and yelling in the most horrid manner," Sylvia later recalled.[85] While they danced, they waved their war clubs, tomahawks, and spears. Then, even before the dancing was done, Rachel and Sylvia were taken away by two "old looking" Indian women.[86]

In the days after that, the Sauk men repeated the same ceremony every afternoon, each time with the girls facedown on a blanket at the very center of the ritual. That gave Sylvia great concern, and she later indicated, "Here once more, from their actions, we thought we were going to be killed."[87] On the other hand, the two older women who had been assigned to look after the girls treated them with warm affection, and all the time they were in the Black Hawk band's camp they were fed well. Rachel reported that their meals typically consisted of fried cakes, boiled corn, fried venison, and fried leeks, and they were given coffee to drink,[88] which had been taken from the Davis house.[89] The generous meals they were served not only displayed the Indians' concern for their comfort and well-being, but also revealed that the Black Hawk band had plenty of provisions at the time, although Rachel did mention that they ran out of flour on the fifth day of their captivity.

Each day they moved on another few miles deeper into the Michigan Territory. On the fifth day of their journey—May 28—(Sylvia recalled it as being the sixth day of their captivity) they made camp on what Rachel described as "a tolerably large river . . . with a number of large lakes immediately in its vicinity."[90] Perhaps, by then, they were on the Rock River near Lake Koshkonong. On that very day, Henry Gratiot, who had "learned that the Saukees had taken and were holding in captivity two white women," wrote in his diary, "I immediately sent a runner to White Crow & Little Priest, with a promise of the highest reward that should be offered if they would bring me those women unhurt."[91] Gratiot knew of the captivity of the Hall girls because General Atkinson had written him about it the day before he made that diary entry. Atkinson informed him about the massacre at Big Indian Creek and of what had become of the girls. "This heart-rending occurrence," Atkinson had said, "should not only call forth our sympathies but urge us to relieve the Sufferers." Therefore, he ordered Gratiot either to make his way to Turtle Village or to send someone he trusted to that Winnebago community, and to "prevail on the head chiefs and Braves of the Winnebagoes there to go over to the hostile Sacs and endeavour to ransom the Prisoners." He also instructed Gratiot to offer them a reward of $500 or $1,000 for the freeing of each girl.[92]

Gratiot contacted the Winnebago, who sent a delegation to Black Hawk's camp. Rachel later recalled that when the Winnebago first arrived, the older women looking after them became "much distressed" at the possibility of the girls being taken away. The Winnebago envoys tried to explain to Rachel and Sylvia that they had come to rescue them, but neither girl understood what was said, and pessimistically "supposed," said Rachel, "they were going to take us entirely away where we would never again see our friends and countrymen."[93] Soon a lengthy discussion commenced between four Winnebago spokesmen—who the girls later learned were White Crow, Little Priest, Whirling Thunder, and Spotted Arm— and the Sauk leaders. After a time, a Sauk man came and took Sylvia by the hand and led her to the council. Only later was Rachel taken to join her. A great deal of hard bargaining ensued before both girls were turned over to the Winnebago, and, according to Rachel, the Sauk "exhibited much unwillingness to suffer us to leave them." A few days later, in a meeting at Porter's Grove, White Crow told Gratiot and Dodge about the negotiations. Soon after they arrived at the Sauk camp, he said, they had been able to buy one of the girls but not the other. It was the seventeen-year-old Rachel the Sauk wanted to hold on to. "They said no we shall not give her up, and we said we must have her," explained White Crow, adding that "the Sacks answered[,] we have Lost too much Blood, and we will keep her." Intense negotiations continued. "It took us almost all day before we could obtain her," said White Crow, who complained that he had to give up his much-valued, last horse to clinch the deal.[94]

The talks concluded around sundown. The Winnebago put the Hall girls on horses and prepared to move out. But before they were able to depart, "a Sauk came," said White Crow, "and wanted to cut off one of the girls Hair, and I caught his hand and prevented him[,] but afterward I allowed him to cut off a small Lock."[95] Rachel, in her 1834 account, mentioned the same incident but said that locks of hair were cut from both herself and her sister.[96] In their much later joint memoir, the sisters recalled the lock-cutting episode in considerable detail: "We were both placed on horses, while one of the young Indians stepped up, and with a large knife cut a lock of hair out of Rachel's head over the right ear, and one out of the back of the head and said to the old chief White Crow that he would have her back (as we afterwards learned) in three or four days. One of the Indians also cut a lock of hair out of the front of Sylvia's head."[97]

After that, the Winnebago negotiators and the Hall girls rushed off into the night. They rode at a full run for over an hour, "the Winnebagoes expressing fears . . . the Sacs would pursue and overtake" them, Rachel later recalled.[98] White Crow said both girls were also very anxious. Both looked very bad and cried all the time, and one of them was sick to her stomach during the journey, he reported.[99] In due time, however, they reached the safety of the Winnebago village on Turtle Creek. There the Winnebago women comforted the girls and cared for them, giving them new clothes. Among the Winnebago, said Rachel, they "slept more comfortably and sounder" than at any time since the beginning of their captivity.[100] A few days later they were taken west and turned over to Henry Dodge.

In his autobiography, Black Hawk put a highly self-serving spin on the entire incident of the Hall girls' captivity. He claimed the Potawatomi had instigated the raid on the Davis farm, and it was the Sauk members of the war party who had saved the girls' lives during the attack. He also took credit for initiating contact with the Winnebago. "A Messenger [was] sent to the Winnebagoes, as they were friendly to both sides, to come and get them, and carry them to the whites," he stated, referring to the Hall girls and their release from captivity.[101]

The anonymous author of the 1832 "Narrative" harkened back to older New England themes in his tortured account and gave all the credit for saving the girls to God. He referred to the intervention of the Winnebago as being "commissioned by Heaven, to rescue them from their perilous situation," and in mentioning the Hall girls themselves, declared, "Yet however great their afflictions, it was evident that they were supported and protected by that Supernatural Being, who has power alone to soften the savage heart."[102] Wakefield also expressed the conviction that Rachel and Sylvia Hall had escaped from the savages only because "an all-wise Providence . . . had watched over them." In the end, when their ordeal was over and their pilgrim's progress completed, Wakefield went on to say, "The guardian angels of heaven had prepared a second father to take them by the hand." That "second father" was the Reverend Reddick Horn, a friend of the Hall family who lived a few miles outside of Beardstown, and who, according to Wakefield, "with the affections of a father . . . flew to them to administer comfort to their heaving bosoms."[103]

Even though Rachel and Sylvia Hall were returned to the patriarchal protection and control of American society, the unusually brutal murders of the families on Big Indian Creek and the girls' captivity among the savages vividly dramatized the nature of what the struggle between the Sauk and the settlers had become, at least in the anxious imaginations of the white people. What had happened to the Hall sisters summoned up old and fearful collective memories and brought into play compelling images that magnified the feelings of vulnerability felt throughout the frontier region. Because of the terrible deeds done at the Davis homestead and the captivity of the girls, Black Hawk and his allies came to be thought of as "the worst of inhuman butchers that probably the earth affords," observed Wakefield.[104] They had dared to attack the American family and to threaten the security and sanctity of white womanhood, and because of that, in the minds of the white people of the region, nothing short of their utter extermination would be enough.

10

A HERO AROSE

The hero arose, surrounded closely by his powerful thanes . . .
And standing on the hearth in webbed links that the smith had
woven, the fine-forged mesh of his gleaming mail-shirt, resolute in
his helmet, Beowulf spoke: " . . . So every elder and experienced
councilman among my people supported my resolve to come here to
you . . . because they all knew of my awesome strength. They had
seen me bolstered in the blood of enemies when I battled and bound
five beasts, raided a troll-nest and in the night-sea slaughtered sea-
brutes. I have suffered extremes. . . . Now I mean to be a match for
Grendel, [and] settle the outcome in single combat.

Beowulf (Seamus Heaney translation)

AS THE COLD, wet spring of 1832 moved unrelentingly on toward the
heat and humidity of early summer, the terror set in motion by the Indian
raids grew more intense and widespread throughout the upper Mississippi
region. The disbanding of the militia and the almost total inactivity of the
regular army deeply disturbed the people there. They wanted something
done to alleviate the threats to their lives, and during the first week of June
an anonymous settler from Jo Daviess County, Illinois, declared in a letter
to the *Galenian,* "A wound has been inflicted in the vitals of the country,"
and "the voice of our country calls loudly for vengeance."[1] But his was an
unheeded voice. No action was taken. No help was offered, no leader
arose to offer any reassurance, and the Indians continued their vicious
attacks with impunity.

The same day that call for vengeance appeared in the newspaper, Indians killed William Griffith Aubrey, a miner who worked for Ebenezer Brigham at Blue Mounds, in the Michigan Territory. Aubrey was shot twice in the body and stabbed in the neck by a spear. The incident occurred about a mile and a half away from the fort Brigham had built near his diggings. Aubrey's companion, Jefferson Smith, had also been hit three times by gunfire but had managed to escape and return to the settlement to raise the alarm. People there suspected the Winnebago were responsible for the attack, and feared many more of them would soon join with Black Hawk to greatly expand the war.[2]

Two weeks later another attack was made on Blue Mounds, where Emerson Green and George Force were killed by a war party of considerable size. One eyewitness claimed it consisted of between fifty and one hundred warriors.[3] Later, when the army interrogated Indian prisoners, two young Winnebago braves, who were members of the Prophet's band, boastfully took credit for the deaths of Green and Force.[4]

On June 9 a party of Indians crossed over from the west side of the Mississippi, about fifteen miles south of Galena, looting some farms and stealing twelve or fourteen horses grazing just outside a small stockade about two-thirds of the way up the Apple River.[5] A few days later another, similar raid occurred in the same area, and although no one was killed or even injured, anxiety levels escalated and Captain James Stephenson rushed down from Galena with a dozen volunteers determined to put a stop to any more such menacing incursions. He picked up more men once he reached the Apple River fort, then headed eastward until he caught up with the war party in open country beyond Yellow Creek, about twelve miles east of Kellogg's Grove. But before he and his men had a clear shot at them, they disappeared into dense woods. Unable to flush them out, the volunteers dismounted and charged into the thicket. Guns were fired from both sides, but in his report of the incident Stephenson stated: "We got into such close quarters as to be constrained to use the bayonet and butcher's knife. We killed five or six of the d[amn]d scoundrels and lost three of our own men." Nevertheless, there proved to be more Indians in the underbrush than Stephenson and his men could handle, and the volunteers ended up pulling out, taking most of the horses the Indians had stolen with them. That afternoon they returned to Galena, triumphantly bearing two scalps they had cut from the Indians they had killed.[6]

Stephenson had been wounded in the encounter—shot in the chest by a musket ball—but was well enough to boast of their bravery to the newspaper. When ordered to charge, he said, "every man obeyed as coolly as if going to a drill," and "every one was determined to conquer or die."[7] They had boldly struck back at the enemy and drawn blood but, unfortunately, they had done little to end the threats posed by marauding Indian bands, which seemed able to strike whenever and wherever they wished.

At about the same time Black Hawk had a vivid dream. He was then traveling west with a force of about two hundred of his warriors, heading away from his main camp above Turtle Creek, just north of the Illinois border. The dream came to him during the second night of the journey, and in the morning, without ever revealing any of its specific contents, Black Hawk acted decisively on the message he was convinced had been sent to him by the supernatural powers. After that he and his men headed in great haste for the Apple River, which he referred to as Mos-co-ho-co-y-nak.[8]

On Sunday night, June 24, Black Hawk and his large war band attacked the fort along the Apple River. Arriving in the afternoon, the Sauk had remained concealed among the trees for some time, sizing up the situation. While they were doing so, four mounted men came riding in from the north and entered the fort. Those men, whom Colonel James Strode had sent down from Galena, were Frederick Dixon, George W. Harkleroad, Edmund Welch, and a young man by the last name of Kirkpatrick. Their ultimate destination was General Atkinson's headquarters on the Illinois River, but they stopped at the fort to take refreshments and rest their horses. When, a short time later, they reemerged from the stockade intending to continue their journey, they got only a few hundred yards before they were fired upon by the well-concealed Sauk war party.[9] The sound of musket fire was immediately followed by a loud, blood-chilling yell from the attackers. Edmund Welch was shot in the left thigh just below the hip. He tumbled from his horse but returned fire on the Indians as he went down. Then, ignoring all danger to himself, Dixon rode up and pulled Welch from the ground, hoisted him up onto his horse behind him, and then retreated in great haste toward the fort, alerting the settlers on his way. "Lucky was it that he did so," reported Addison Philleo, the editor of the *Galenian*, who indicated most of the people there were then still outside the palisade—virtually all the women and children were, in fact, leisurely picking berries along the river, suspecting nothing—and surmised that the place would have surely become another "scene of revolting massacre" had not Dixon warned them of the danger.[10]

But once the commotion began, everyone rushed headlong for the fort, and all managed to get safely inside and close the gates just as a large "numbers of savages [began] pouring in from all sides."[11] Within the palisade there were only twenty to twenty-five men under the command of militia captain Clack Stone to hold off the attack. At first, according to one of the defenders, Oliver Emmell, "the women and children were panic-stricken, crying and wringing their hands," until Elizabeth Armstrong took control of the situation. Emmell described how she gave them all a stern talking-to and told them "it was worse than folly to give up to fear."[12] After that, the people got a grip on themselves, all joining in the defense of their small stockade, and the *Galenian* later reported: "Thus the women were all occupied as well as the men—girls of eight years old took their part, some made cartridges, some run balls, some loaded muskets, all were engaged."[13] Elizabeth Armstrong took charge of the women's activities and set a coolheaded, courageous example.[14]

During the fight, George Harkleroad, as he climbed above the picket to get a better shot at an Indian, was himself shot in the head and instantly killed.[15] Black Hawk mentioned the killing of Harkleroad in his own account: "One of their braves, who seemed more valiant than the rest, raised his head above the picketing to fire at us, when one of my braves, with a well directed shot, put an end to his bravery."[16] The only other casualty within the fort was Josiah Nutting, a settler who was wounded in the upper right arm. He eventually recovered.[17]

The attack went on for three-quarters of an hour. Firing on both sides was incessant, and the hot air hung heavy with the acrid smell of gun smoke. "Finding that these people could not be killed, without setting fire to their houses and fort," observed Black Hawk, "I thought it more prudent to be content with what flour, provisions, cattle and horse we could find." It was not that he was squeamish about burning them to death, as much as concerned about the firing on the fort, houses, and barns attracting attention. Night was falling, and a blaze of such magnitude would have been quite visible in the darkness for a great distance and might have prompted a large military force being sent down from Galena to investigate.[18] Therefore, the Sauk war party broke off the attack and turned to the looting of the cabins and the driving off of a large number of the settlers' livestock.[19] After dark, Kirkpatrick managed to slip out of the fort, elude the enemies, and ride all the way to Galena, where he reported what had transpired that day on the Apple River.

The very next day, while once again moving eastward, Black Hawk and his band managed to shoot up a militia force led by Major John Dement, at Kellogg's Grove. They killed five of Dement's men, wounded three others, and also killed about fifty of their horses.[20] Then, toward the end of the same week, other Indians struck George Wallace Jones's mining settlement at Sinsinawa Mound, located between Hazel Green and the Mississippi River within the Michigan Territory, killing two men out working in a cornfield.[21] When a militia troop from Galena arrived at Sinsinawa Mound a few days later, they found the bodies of James Boxley and John Thompson "most shockingly mutilated." "The heart of Thompson was taken out and both were scalped," the *Galenian* reported. The next week the newspaper further observed, "All the inhabitants north of us, and on the Mississippi, this side of Cassville, have come in today, and intend to remain until the war is ended."[22] Everyone felt vulnerable.

Addison Philleo, editor of the *Galenian*, was outraged by the cowardly dissolution of the militia and accused Reynolds of abandoning "the [mining] country to the ruthless savages, and the defenseless inhabitants to the scalping knife and the tomahawk." He vehemently protested the total lack of protection provided the region and became even angrier in late June when he grew suspicious about why that was the case. People were dying almost daily, even though he believed (quite erroneously) there were more than enough regular troops to defend the frontier. Nevertheless, Philleo, plainly suggesting someone was up to no good, complained that the soldiers were all "mysteriously kept away from this endangered [mining] country, for causes, as we think, well known to us, and which will, at some future time, be properly developed to this much injured community." Atkinson's cautiousness made him furious, and he sarcastically claimed that the regulars may as well "be stationed in Boston for the protection of [the mining district] . . . as at the mouth of Fox river." Philleo was appalled that the Indians could freely roam about the countryside "carrying death and destruction with them wherever they passed," and never "meeting a defeat" from the army.[23]

A contributor to the *Galenian*, identified only as "M," joined Philleo in the criticism of General Atkinson, declaring that "a great majority of the people" in the region had grown increasingly dissatisfied with the general's handling of the entire situation. "M" thought it high time to express some "indignation at the conduct of a commander, by whose ill contrived movements, the lives and property of ten thousand inhabitants were placed in great peril." He, like Philleo, also took strong exception to the fact the regular troops, who were being "paid by the government, for the express purpose of defending the frontier settlements," were stationed at such a great distance from where the Indian attacks were actually occurring. The soldiers were safe and secure, while the citizens on the frontier were left exposed to the cruel fury of the savages.[24]

Very similar opinions were held by Stephen Mack, a fur trader who had a post at Bird's Grove, on the north bank of the Rock River close to where it and the Pecatonica joined. In a letter to his sister, Lovicy Cooper, written in early June, Mack indicated, "I can by no means approve of the tardy operations of our chief officers, for it gives time to the nimble footed Indians to ravage our frontier settlements and bathe their hands in the blood of helpless women and unsuspecting infants."[25] Indeed, the dissatisfaction with Atkinson became national news when the *Niles' Weekly Register* published a letter from the West in which the author reported how "the frontier inhabitants" had grown "exceedingly exasperated" with the "slow movements" of General Atkinson and his soldiers.[26]

Even President Jackson lost patience with Atkinson. On June 12 John Robb, Cass's chief clerk and temporarily the acting secretary of war, wrote a stinging letter to Atkinson, informing him that the president viewed, "with utter astonishment, and deep regret," the state of affairs on the frontier. Robb went on to scold Atkinson by declaring, "The President had a right to anticipate promptness and decision of action, and a speedy and effectual termination of Indian hostilities, and the capture or death of Black Hawk." Decisive action against the Indians was overdue and absolutely necessary, concluded the acting secretary.[27]

As confidence in General Atkinson plummeted, Henry Dodge began attracting more attention and praise and, according to Moses Strong of Galena, "by common intuitive feeling, was regarded as the leader of the people of the lead mines."[28]

Dodge had been born in Vincennes, Indiana, in October of 1782, and by 1832, at the age of fifty, was a man who had come far in life. His father,

Israel Dodge, from Canterbury, Connecticut, had been a soldier in the Revolutionary War and had been severely wounded in the chest by a British bayonet during the Battle of Brandywine. After the war, like so many other New Englanders, the Dodges headed west, first to Indiana and then, in time, Israel deserted the family and set off on his own for the Spanish territory just west of the Mississippi. There he settled in Ste. Genevieve. In the meantime, his abandoned wife, Nancy Ann, and young Henry went to live in Louisville and then settled for a time in Bardstown, Kentucky. In 1796, at the age of fourteen, Henry joined his father in Spanish Louisiana. Later, he returned briefly to Kentucky, where he read law, and then, in 1805, he returned to what, by then, had become the Missouri Territory, where he was appointed deputy sheriff of the Ste. Genevieve District under his father's authority. When Israel Dodge died the very next year, Henry, then twenty-four, moved up to take his place as sheriff.

Young Dodge advanced even more during the War of 1812, when he was appointed federal marshal for the entire Missouri Territory and given the rank of major general in the Missouri militia. Once the war was over, he set out to make his fortune in the salt-making business at the mouth of the Saline River and did quite well until 1817, when the steamboats began shipping salt in from the East and the price plummeted from five dollars a bushel to seventy-five cents. Dodge then did some lead mining and smeltering in Jefferson County, Missouri, until 1827, when he moved north to the Fever River with his wife, Christiana, their nine children, and his slaves. His intention was to make a fortune in the lead rush, which was then at full flood tide.

Early that summer Dodge sent Christiana and the family on ahead aboard the steamboat *Indiana*, while he and the slaves moved more slowly up the Illinois side of the Mississippi on horseback, driving a large herd of cattle and horses before them.[29] That November they moved again, departing Galena for land claimed by the Winnebago within the Michigan Territory, where he established a mining and smeltering settlement he somewhat immodestly named Dodgeville. There he constructed a substantial stockade containing twenty log buildings and assembled a large work crew of at least 130 rough, well-armed men.

Dodge himself was a tough and attractive man, with a strong personality and some decidedly charismatic qualities. He was ambitious and pushy, but people respected him and there were a good many men in the mining district eager to work for him and, in time, eager to follow him in fighting the Indians. He was tall and strong, with a long, thick mane of dark hair. Dressed in a tanned buckskin hunting shirt, he carried two pistols in holsters and a sword on a broad belt around his waist. He was very much the image of a weatherworn frontiersman, made muscular and resourceful by life in the backwoods. When Lieutenant Joseph Steel Gallagher of the regular army met him during the Black Hawk War, he described Dodge in a letter to his wife as "a good looking man of about 40, dark complexion, good features, and of a very decided, but not stern, expression of countenance."[30] Dodge was actually fifty years old at the time but must have been in very fine physical condition, and Gallagher also added, in a letter to his brother, that he was a man of "great personal bravery."[31]

During the Winnebago disturbance of 1827, Dodge had stepped forward and taken the lead in raising a fighting force at Galena, and had done so again in the spring of 1831, when Black Hawk and his followers had briefly returned to Saukenuk. At Dodgeville the whole family and work crew lived in conditions very much like those of a fortified medieval manorial outpost amid the windswept wild country of what would eventually become Wisconsin. According to his daughter Selina, they all lived within "a small blockhouse, whose walls were pierced with loopholes and which were surrounded with a stockade made of logs, with heavy barred gates, which were kept always locked." There, in that isolation, a foreboding sense of apprehension prevailed, and everyone got on with life armed to the teeth.[32]

When word reached the mining region in early May of 1832 that Black Hawk and his British Band had once again crossed over the Mississippi, Henry Dodge, concerned over the "defenseless situation of the country," raised a small force of twenty-eight mounted men from among his own work crew, and on May 14 the *Galenian* reported, "Gen. Dodge with a Spartan band of about 30 men" rode off to Dixon's Ferry to join the other forces already assembling there with intentions of driving the Indians from the land.[33] In the course of the next few weeks, Dodge added more members to his armed band, building it into a substantial force of about two hundred tough and eager volunteers. John Fonda rode with them and said there was "a free-and-easy, devil-may-care appearance about them" and never before had he seen a "wilder, more independent set of dare-devils."[34]

They soon became the most elite and successful frontier fighting force of the entire conflict, and their aggressive and determined leader, Henry Dodge, outdid his would-be rivals such as John Reynolds, James Henry, and William Hamilton, to emerge as the war's preeminent heroic figure.

Addison Philleo admired Henry Dodge a great deal and used his news-paper to promote his reputation. "Gen. Dodge," he wrote in early June, "is certainly one of the most indefatigable & efficient men in this or any other country. He is consistently on the alert; one day he is found at home plan-ning and adopting means of defense in case of attack, and the next day he is found pushing his little force of mounted Spartans into the very heart of the Indian country."[35] That image of Dodge as a man of thought as well as bold action—as a rugged, smart, self-disciplined leader of few words, shrewd strategies, and bold deed—won for him considerable public ven-eration. So confident was Philleo in his character and leadership that he asserted in his June 13 edition, "We believe, had Gen. Dodge possessed sufficient force, he would have ended the war, and completely vanquished the enemy before this time."[36]

While already well known in the mining district even before the Black Hawk War, Dodge quite deliberately sought to enhance his reputation in the early stages of the conflict by involving himself in the rescue of Rachel and Sylvia Hall. The captivity of the girls had evoked some very powerful emotions and carried great symbolic significance for everyone living along the exposed frontier. Dodge cleverly identified himself with all those feel-ings and symbols when he took the initiative to meet with the Winnebago chiefs who had secured the release of the girls from the Black Hawk camp. His meeting with them took place at Blue Mounds, on Sunday, June 3. Dodge arrived there with a large party of armed men, in the early evening. Moses Strong claimed he had as many as two hundred mounted riflemen with him, which made a most impressive show of force to the Indians, who were already encamped and awaiting his arrival. Upon reaching Blue Mounds, Dodge immediately took charge of the situation, purchasing a steer from Ebenezer Brigham, which he presented to the Winnebago for a feast, and then procured for them comfortable quarters in the miners' cabins. But because it was already late in the day, no formal talks were held, and Dodge, after amiably mingling with the feasting Indians for some time, retired for the night.[37]

No sooner had he fallen asleep, however, than Bion Gratiot, Henry Gratiot's brother, came rushing to his cabin urging him to "rouse up! rouse up!" and warning that the Indians were about to attack. In a state of great agitation, Gratiot hurriedly explained how the Winnebago had left their cabins to hold a rabble-rousing meeting in the forest, and identified White Crow as the ringleader of what he described as a rapidly emerging plot to massacre Dodge and his men. According to Peter Parkinson, who was also there as a member of Dodge's troop, White Crow (Kaurahkawsee) was a very clever and influential leader. He estimated him to be about fifty years in age, described him as straight and dignified and about five feet, ten inches tall, and called him "a Cicero among Indians for his power of oratory and eloquence."[38] White Crow's appearance was also made distinctive by the black handkerchief he wore over his missing left eye. Around a great fire, which flashed and crackled in the darkness of the forest clearing, this spellbinding leader whipped his followers into an emotional frenzy, Gratiot reported to Dodge. In his harangue, said Gratiot, the highly animated chieftain had ridiculed the white soldiers and dismissed Dodge as being of "no great shakes of a fighter," and then declared that Black Hawk would soon "make mince-meat of him and his handful of men, as he had done of the 'soft-shelled' Maj. Stillman and his men at Kishwaukee." Indeed, White Crow described all American men as a "soft-shelled breed" who were timid fighters, and "when the spear was applied to them they would squawk like ducks" and "would run upon the first approach of danger . . . like turkeys and quails." Those derisive remarks, said Gratiot, were accompanied by clever mimicry and dramatic gestures, which threw his audience into a hilarious uproar. At the same time this performance was being given, two young warriors were dispatched to the large Winnebago community at Four Lakes to rouse reinforcements, while, according to Gratiot, the warriors with White Crow were busy "grinding and whetting their knives, toma-hawks, and spears."[39]

Dodge remained calm and attentive as Gratiot delivered the news. Then, after indulging in only a little "severity and invective," he called for the officer of the guard and his interpreter and, accompanied by just six other armed men, strode off quickly to where the Winnebago were gath-ered, determined to demonstrate as dramatically as possible that he was not part of any "soft-shelled breed" of men.[40] Immediately upon reaching the Indians, still gathered around the fire listening to White Crow, Dodge audaciously took action. He placed White Crow and five other chiefs under arrest and "marched them off without ceremony" to one of the cabins. There he bluntly ordered them to lie down and remain quiet for the rest of the night, placed a strong guard around the place, and then laid himself down next to the prisoners, intending to remain with them until dawn.

In the morning he ordered everyone, including the rest of White Crow's party and the Hall sisters, to move to James Morrison's farm at Porter's Grove, about fifteen miles to the west. Henry Gratiot, along with his interpreter (Catherine Myott) and his assistant (George Cubbage), met them there. A full council was held. The Hall girls were turned over to Dodge and Gratiot, who then warned the Winnebago of the grave consequences that would surely befall them if they were even tempted to give any support or encouragement to Black Hawk and his renegade band.[41] When the council concluded, Dodge kept hostage three chiefs—Whirling Thunder, Spotted Arm, and Little Priest—as insurance in case the Winnebago had any second thoughts about testing the softness of American shells anywhere in the mining district. A few days later, William Campbell, a close personal friend of Andrew Jackson's and assistant superintendent of the lead mines on the Mississippi, wrote to the president, proclaiming with great exuberance that the Hall girls had been "redeemed from captivity by Genl. Dodge."[42]

Although Henry Gratiot thought Dodge had overreacted to the situation with White Crow and the Winnebago, and misunderstood some of what had been said for "want of a good interpreter,"[43] Dodge's firm action at Blue Mounds and Porter's Grove did much to demonstrate the strength of his character and reinforce his reputation among both the Indians and the inhabitants of the mining district. Like Hawk-eye, who, in Cooper's romantic tale of woodland warfare, rescues Alice and Cora Munro from their cruel captivity among the savages, Dodge's "saving" of the Hall sisters from what must have seemed an identical fate greatly enhanced his identification as a courageous defender of those who could not defend themselves.

Following the Porter's Grove conference, Dodge and his men were in almost constant motion for the better part of the next fortnight. First they were off to Gratiot's Grove, then back to Blue Mounds, and then they made their way to Kirker's farm near the headwaters of the Apple River, about fifty miles northwest of Dixon's Ferry. The plan was to rendezvous with General Hugh Brady and the regular troops he was bringing down from Fort Winnebago. They made camp at Kirker's farm around noon on Thursday, June 7, and once they were settled in, Dodge called an assembly and addressed the men with what Daniel Parkinson described as a "spirited speech."[44] In his remarks Dodge characterized Black Hawk and his band as a "faithless banditti of savages" who were the "enemy of all people, both the whites and Indians."[45] A bloodthirsty lot, they sought to engage other tribes in their malevolent conspiracy against the helpless American settlers, declared Dodge; "like the pirates of the sea, their hand is against every man, and the hand of every man should be against them." He then focused on what he believed was really at issue in the struggle. "Our existence as a people is at stake," he asserted, then sternly told his men, "The security of the lives of our people depends on our vigilance, caution, and bravery."[46] In his view—a view that appeared to reflect something of his own New England background—their struggle was actually against the power of evil itself, which threatened all they valued, and, therefore, their mission was an undertaking of the greatest importance.

With Stillman's panic-stricken catastrophe implicitly in mind, Dodge urged his men to be "vigilant, silent, and cool." Orderly self-control was absolutely essential if they were to escape a similarly shameful fate, he told them. "Discipline and obedience to orders will make small bodies of men formidable and invincible," he claimed, and warned that "without order and subordination the largest bodies of armed men are no better than armed mobs." That had been the failing that had undone the Illinois militia and left the frontiers vulnerable to attack. If they were to save the people from slaughter and their society from ruin, it was up to them to summon up their courage, subordinate their individuality to the higher cause, and become much better men than those who had followed John Reynolds and Samuel Whiteside in pursuit of the Indians. They could triumph, Dodge told them, if they remained coolheaded and carried out his orders without hesitation or timidity.[47]

In that short but inspiring oration, Dodge deliberately emphasized attitudes and behavior that would contrast his men and their methods of warfare from the pusillanimous example set by the Illinois militia. He was eager to demonstrate what brave western men could accomplish when well led and properly disciplined. By doing so he hoped to redeem their badly damaged reputation and perhaps even repair the region's severely wounded collective pride. In the end, of course, he wanted to defeat the Indians—to break them and reduce them to submission—and to thereby rescue the region from the reign of terror let loose upon it by Black Hawk and his war parties. Then, too, the idea of acquiring fame and glory for himself was also among his aspirations.

From Kirker's farm they pushed on to Dixon's Ferry, where they met up with General Brady and his two companies of regulars. Brady was a crusty, sixty-four-year-old veteran, who somewhat arrogantly underestimated the caliber of his enemy when he boastfully declared he could, with just two companies of mounted infantry, "whip the Sauk out of the country in one week."[48] He and Dodge got on quite well together during their journey to General Atkinson's headquarters at Ottawa. Upon arriving there, Dodge and Atkinson conferred about the campaign still being planned, and on June 11, with clear authority from the general to handle military matters in the mining region, Dodge headed for home, arriving in Gratiot's Grove three days later "much worn down and fatigued."[49] There he dispersed his men to the many small forts scattered throughout the area and then rode on alone to Fort Union at Dodgeville.

Before leaving Gratiot's Grove, however, Dodge wrote a public letter to the *Galenian*, warning readers to be on their guard for Sauk war parties, which, he said, were prowling the countryside. "They watch from the high points of timber our movements in the day light, and at night pass through the prairie from one point of timber to another, and communicate with their main body, which are in the swamps of Rock river," he informed them. He also pointed out how the Sauk, because of their intimate familiarity with the land, could continue their menacing mode of warfare for years to come, and declared, "I am convinced, that we are not to have peace with this banditti collection of Indians until they are killed up in their dens."[50]

The death of William Aubrey at Blue Mounds on June 6, while Dodge had been away, offered chilling proof of the very threats he warned about in his public letter. Moreover, just as he was arriving home, another such murderous attack occurred just south of Dodgeville. On Thursday morning, June 14, six men were out working in a cornfield on Omri Spafford's farm, about six miles southeast of William Hamilton's place, on the east bank of the Pecatonica River. Besides Spafford himself, the work crew consisted of Francis Spencer, Bennett Million, Abraham Searles, James

McIlwaine, and John Bull. According to Spencer, who survived the attack, they had just begun to work when suddenly a band of Indians, concealed among some nearby trees, opened fire on them. All the crew members immediately dropped their tools and headed for the river, crossing it quickly. But four of them were gunned down as they attempted to climb the opposite bank, and only Spencer and Million managed to escape. Million was able to get back to Fort Hamilton, while Spencer made his way up a deep ravine. Later, when the coast was clear, he crawled off into the thick underbrush of the forest, where he remained hidden for nine days. Meanwhile, the attackers proceeded to scalp and mutilate the bodies of the men they had murdered on the riverbank.[51]

News of the attack soon reached Fort Defiance, located on Daniel Parkinson's farm, about five miles southeast of Mineral Point. There, a force of thirteen men was assembled, and setting off to hunt down the war party, they reached Fort Hamilton about midnight.[52] The next morning Million took them down to the farm, where they found the headless body of Omri Spafford and the grotesquely mangled corpses of Searles, McIlwaine, and Bull. A short time later, they came upon Spafford's severed head, which had been scalped and tossed into the tall grass along the river. Throughout the day they hunted high and low for Spencer's remains, assuming he too had been slain. Before giving up the search and returning to Fort Hamilton for the night, they solemnly interred the dead in a common grave.[53]

Dodge also soon learned of the assault on Spafford's farm, and he too set out for Hamilton's with Thomas Jenkins and John Messersmith Jr. They stopped along the way at Blue Mounds for fresh horses and then rode on to Fretwell's Diggings, where they spent the night. The next morning, after leaving the main road to take a shortcut, they met Henry Apple, a German settler heading home from Fort Hamilton. Dodge and Apple exchanged some brief remarks, then went in opposite directions. Unfortunately, Apple had not gone far before being entrapped in an ambush the Indians had actually set for Dodge, who undoubtedly would have been their victim had he stayed on the main road. Dodge and his companions heard shots and then saw Apple's horse gallop by with gunshot wounds to an ear and its neck, and a great deal of blood on its saddle. When the riderless horse reached the fort, Daniel Parkinson later recalled, "all was instantly wild excitement and disorder" as a number of men quickly "mounted their horses . . . and were upon the act of rushing indiscriminately after the Indians." That did not happen, however, because Captain James H. Gentry kept his wits about him and ordered the overeager militiamen to halt, threatening to shoot the first man who dared disobey him by attempting to leave the fort. In doing so, he reminded them of the helter-skelter confusion that had brought about Stillman's disaster. Cool heads prevailed, and a few minutes later Henry Dodge rode through the gates and took command.[54]

It was then just a little after eight o'clock in the morning of June 16. On entering the fort, Dodge hardly paused. After barking out a few terse instructions, he and twenty-nine other riders galloped off together, determined to hunt down the Indians before they got away. They rode past the scalped and lifeless body of Henry Apple, pushed on through a thicket of tangled underbrush and vines, and then once more broke out onto open prairie, where they caught sight of the fleeing war party. No sooner had they done so, however, when the Indians managed to cross over the east branch of the Pecatonica and enter what William W. Woodbridge, one of the pursuers, described as an "almost impenetrable swamp."[55] Dodge and his men also crossed the Pecatonica, swollen by the heavy rains of the night before, and then struggled to get their horses up its steep bank on the other side.[56] On reaching the swamp into which the Indians had vanished, they all dismounted. Four men were left with the horses, four others were posted on high ground to watch for the Indians if they tried to slip away, and the remaining twenty-one men followed Dodge, who moved with all deliberate speed into the woods.[57]

According to Charles Bracken, a young lieutenant with the attack party, Dodge briefly halted the squad and gave anyone who might have qualms about proceeding into the tangled underbrush the opportunity to fall out.[58] No one did. All twenty-one then advanced in an extended line into the "dense thicket," not knowing where the enemy might be lurking. After Dodge's group penetrated the woods about two hundred yards,[59] Peter Parkinson reported, the "stillness and suspense of the occasion was suddenly broken" when the Indians, who were hiding behind the bank of an oxbow lake of the Pecatonica, let out a terrible yell and opened fire from about sixty feet away.[60] Three of Dodge's men—Samuel Black, Samuel Wells, and Montaville Morris—went down. Dodge then ordered the rest of the party to charge. They did so without hesitation and got to

within about six feet of the Indians before letting loose with a blazing volley upon them. They "literally shot the Indians all to pieces," said Dodge.
What then followed was an intense physical struggle at close quarters.
The charge had brought the volunteers and Indians "face to face, and
breast to breast," said Parkinson, and after discharging their guns they all
became entangled in a brutal hand-to-hand melee—spears and tomahawks,
bayonets, musket butts, and bare hands.[61] There were eleven Indians altogether, and Dodge later reported to Atkinson that "nine of them were
killed on the spot and the remaining two killed in crossing the lake."[62]
Then, when the rage and fury of the conflict was spent, Dodge's men proceeded to scalp the enemy dead, procuring for themselves trophies that
would prove they had outdone the Indians at their own savage form of
warfare. Francis Gehon, who participated in the battle, told a friend, "The
men behaved with grate Grate Galantry and bravery on this accation."[63]
By winning the battle and scalping the dead, "[we] showed the Indians
that we were not the soft-breed, as they had said we were," declared Peter
Parkinson.[64]

"Glorious Victory," proclaimed the headline on the *Galenian's* front
page, which went on to characterize the "Battle of Pecatonica," as it called
the skirmish, the first important American victory of the war, and proudly
pointed out that in their attack on the Indians, Dodge and his men had
"killed and scalped them all."[65] Also, in the same edition of the newspaper,
there was a letter by an anonymous writer that reflected a growing public
confidence in Henry Dodge. The writer admitted he had previously wondered why Philleo had lavished so much praise on Dodge, who, he said,
was then "a man untried, and, as yet, somewhat inexperienced in Indian
warfare." However, he rejoiced over how the Battle of Pecatonica had radically altered his opinion, and admitted to the editor, "The victory which
has just been achieved, and the manner in which the battle was conducted by Gen. Dodge has inspired me, and I believe convinced the whole
community, that your confidence was not misplaced." Then, offering his
own enthusiastic vote of confidence, he wrote, "With such a Commander
as Gen. Dodge, and such men as have proved their valor in the late charge,
I would not fear to go and face the enemy, though twice our numbers."[66]

In retrospect, public reactions seem rather exaggerated to what
amounted to little more than a modest encounter along the Pecatonica
River. After all, Dodge's force consisted of only twenty-nine members, while

just eleven Indians were involved in the clash, and the struggle, although strenuous and bloody, was over in a matter of minutes. Nevertheless, the anxious people of the mining region were not alone in attributing great significance to this event. Most of the early chroniclers of the Black Hawk War did so as well. For example, Thomas Ford, in his history of early Illinois, said that "this little action will equal any for courage, brilliancy, and success in the whole history of Indian warfare."[67] Moses Strong also claimed that what had happened that day at the oxbow of the Pecatonica was "for daring bravery and cool undaunted courage, . . . not excelled in the history of Indian warfare."[68] And Charles Bracken, who participated in the fight, later credited their "gallant conduct" with proving "that American volunteers, when individually brave," would indeed "follow to their death, a brave and determined leader, in whom they had confidence."[69] And still another participant—Peter Parkinson—asserted conclusively that as a result of this single victory "the tide of war" was turned against the Indians; calling it "a remarkable battle," he declared, "At any rate, it was the turning point of the war, and had more to do with its final termination than all the other circumstances put together."[70]

While actually only of minor military importance, the Battle of Pecatonica was nevertheless an event of very considerable psychological and symbolic consequence. It occurred at a desperate time. Nothing in the war had been going in favor of the settlers. The militia had abandoned them, the army was disengaged and seemed indifferent to their fate, and the Indians seemed able to strike and kill whenever and wherever they wished. Also, the atrocities committed by the war parties seemed so much the work of utterly depraved minds that people sensed they were dealing with enemies more demonic than human—enemies who appeared and disappeared at will and ghoulishly reveled in the sadistic tormenting of their helpless victims before finally putting the poor wretches out of their misery. On top of all that, there were the painfully embarrassing questions about the masculine toughness and personal courage of western men. Then, just as everything seemed overwhelmingly bleak, Henry Dodge appeared, first to rescue the Hall girls and then to fashion a redeeming victory out of his armed clash amid the underbrush along the Pecatonica River. It was not much, but it proved the Indians could be beaten, and that the common men of the West could indeed be brave. It revived hope and rekindled confidence. People made the most of it—maybe more than what seems warranted—because it was all they had of a positive nature with which to reassure themselves, and for that reason Henry Dodge began to take on the image of a heroic leader.

The *Galenian* poured out profuse praise, and Addison Philleo appeared to engage in deliberate mythmaking concerning Dodge's reputation. Other expressions of high regard came from Thomas Burnett, the Indian affairs subagent at Prairie du Chien. Burnett complimented Dodge on his "patriotic efforts" to defend the mining region. "Your sacrifice, zeal, energy, and success in defending our exposed frontier, almost without means, will not be forgotten by the Government, and will live in the grateful recollections of your fellow-citizens," he assured Dodge.[71] At the same time, the leading inhabitants of Prairie du Chien, in a spirit of "high respect and admiration," sent Dodge a double-barreled gun in appreciation for what they described as the "bold and energetic course of conduct" he had displayed in defending their "suffering country."[72] Furthermore, a committee of women in Galena, who identified themselves as the "Daughters of the Lead Mines," fashioned a distinctive flag for Dodge and his band to carry into future battles. They presented it on June 21, in gratitude for his "unwearied exertions" on their behalf. In their statement of appreciation the women referred to him as "Our Father War Chief" and said they hoped and trusted "the God of battles" would strengthen his hand and give him complete victory over the "common enemy."[73] Dodge graciously accepted the banner on behalf of his "gallant little band" and promised to press on with the fight, in which, he said, they were contending for everything dear to them as a people.[74]

Into those rituals of recognition people projected some of their deepest hopes and most enduring fantasies, and their belief that a hero had arisen to save them from some of their worst fears wrought a remarkable change in the psychological climate of the territory. But, of course, such sentiments associated with warrior heroes have very ancient roots in Western civilization, but during the early Republic it was Cooper's Natty Bumppo—Hawk-eye, Deerslayer, Pathfinder, the Longue Carabine of the *Leather-Stocking Tales*—who emerged as the heroic metaphor for American culture.[75] Dressed in buckskin and armed with a long gun, this self-made, self-sufficient hunter-hero escaped from the forces that held most other men down and back and was a truly free individual in the unspoiled state of American nature. But there, in the wilderness, by necessity he became a warrior caught in inescapable conflict with the wild savages of the land. As a result, American heroic narratives were then mostly stories of Indian wars, and the much-repeated tale of King Philip's War, says the historian Richard Slotkin, became "in many ways an archetype of all the wars which followed."[76] Indian wars were peculiar to the American experience, and in the stories told about them the hero invariably triumphed over the wild men through the courageous, coolheaded exertion of his indomitable will and the deadly accuracy of his marksmanship. But these stories were complex narratives involving more than the clear-cut clashing of the "us" and "other," for the hero possessed a great many Indianlike qualities of his own that made him authentically "American" and enabled him to beat the natives at their own violent game in order to displace them and thereby become the rightful lord of a land that had not been his own.[77]

It was a myth that became a vital ingredient of the newly emerging national identity, and like all myths, it tapped into and gave expression to some very powerful collective emotions, and in the interplay of symbolism and experience, the myth actually seemed at times to come alive through the exploits of certain men.[78]

That is what happened in the early summer of 1832 along the Pecatonica River. Henry Dodge appeared to possess many of the qualities that were then characteristically heroic. He was tall, rugged, and physically strong, with handsome features and long dark hair. He was dressed in a "buckskin, sassafras tanned, hunting shirt, and Kentucky jean pants."[79] Moreover, he was courageous, decisive, and very much a self-made man of stoic discipline and self-control. He rode hard, shot straight, and displayed a manly indifference to hardship, danger, and even death itself. And with his emergence the people in the mining district were suddenly filled with hope that he would slay the monsters that stalked their land and rescue them from the terror that gripped their lives.

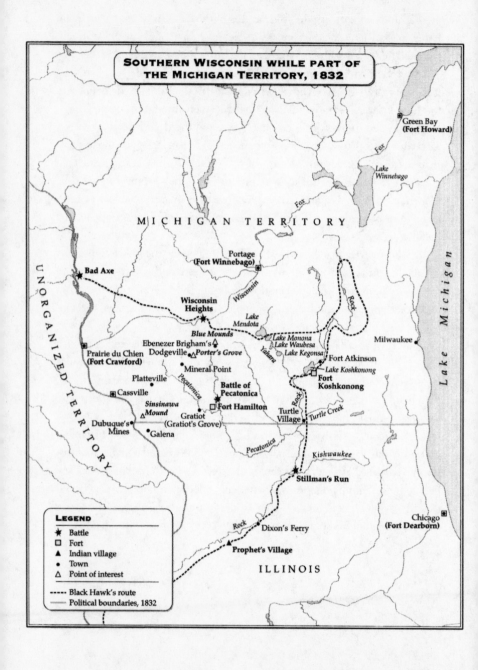

SOUTHERN WISCONSIN WHILE PART OF THE MICHIGAN TERRITORY, 1832

Green Bay
(Fort Howard)

Fox

Lake Winnebago

MICHIGAN TERRITORY

Portage
(Fort Winnebago)

Bad Axe

Wisconsin

Wisconsin Heights

Lake Mendota

Milwaukee

Blue Mounds

Ebenezer Brigham's

Dodgeville *Porter's Grove*

Lake Monona
Lake Waubesa
Lake Kegonsa

Prairie du Chien
(Fort Crawford)

Mineral Point

Fort Atkinson

Lake Koshkonong

Yahara

Fort Koshkonong

Platteville

Pecatonica

Battle of Pecatonica

Cassville

Fort Hamilton

Sinsinawa Mound

Gratiot
(Gratiot's Grove)

Turtle Village

Turtle Creek

Dubuque's Mines

Galena

Rock

Pecatonica

Kishwaukee

Stillman's Run

Rock

Dixon's Ferry

Chicago
(Fort Dearborn)

Prophet's Village

ILLINOIS

UNORGANIZED TERRITORY

Lake Michigan

LEGEND

★ Battle
□ Fort
▲ Indian village
● Town
△ Point of interest

- - - - Black Hawk's route
········· Political boundaries, 1832

11

HUNTING A SHADOW

On the 4th of July the main army lay on the banks of Lake Koshkonong . . . and experienced a melancholy and sadness of feeling indescribable. The provisions wasting away—almost gone— and the enemy not chastised. Two or three thousand fine soldiers under arms and nothing done, caused reflections in the breasts of the officers, and many privates, that were extremely mortifying and painful. But what could be done? We were almost hunting a shadow.

John Reynolds, *History of Illinois, My Own Times*

AS HENRY DODGE'S reputation grew ever more heroic, and General Atkinson slowly and carefully made preparations to resume the campaign, Black Hawk and his British Band vanished into the dense forests and treacherous swamps of southern Wisconsin. Following their attack upon the Apple River settlement, and deeply disappointed when other tribes did not join their cause or even provide assistance, Black Hawk led the band northward up the Rock River valley and into the great dismal swamps around Lake Koshkonong. He took to the mosquito-infested wetlands knowing full well the Americans would soon be after them again, and hoped the almost impenetrable morasses of the place would conceal and protect them until their adversaries gave up the chase. After all, the members of the militia had demonstrated just how short their interest span could be when dealing with difficult missions, and none had displayed much tolerance for discomfort or hardship. Besides that, there were few other options left to the Sauk, who were fast running out of ammunition and supplies.

All along the trek, from first crossing the Mississippi, Black Hawk had often seemed oddly inconsistent in his actions and strategies. On some occasions he was brilliantly clever and very much in charge of the situation, while on others he seemed indecisive, even bumbling and dumbfounded, and naively credulous about advice offered by the likes of Wabokieshiek and Neapope. His intentions were seldom clear. Then, too, he sometimes seemed relegated to the margins of the decision-making process by the young chiefs. He could be personally courageous and seemed willing to sacrifice himself for the good of his people, but his lack of an overall plan threatened their very survival. Furthermore, his decision to hide among the reed beds and trembling bogs of Lake Koshkonong seemed a desperate, last-ditch effort to stave off disaster, but one that might prove a dead-end strategy from which there was no escape. While Black Hawk vacillated, avoiding confrontation, and seemed at a loss as to how to extricate his people from their worsening predicament, Henry Dodge, by contrast, was decisive, direct, and determined to hunt them down.

However, it would be inappropriate—even incorrect—to judge Black Hawk by the same standards used by the Americans to measure the mettle of their leaders. Although personal courage and manly valor were much admired by the Sauk, they did not embrace the leadership style so admired by their white enemies. Indeed, their cultural approaches to war were quite different, and Black Hawk thought the British and Americans foolish in the manner they fought their battles. "Instead of stealing upon each other, and taking every advantage to *kill the enemy and save their own people,* as we do (which, with us, is considered good policy in a war chief), they march out, in open daylight, and *fight,* regardless of the number of warriors they may lose," he somewhat disdainfully observed.[1] Because of such cultural differences, it would be more fitting to understand Black Hawk and his behavior by considering the figure of the trickster, an important mythological character prevalent in the narratives of all the woodland tribes. Known by various names, such as Naanabozho, Nanabush, and Winnabajo, the trickster was part human, part supernatural. He was also the revealer of truth and an inveterate liar, both a killer and a healer who was simultaneously tragic and comic, spiritual and carnal, good and evil, foolish and wise, and often an exceedingly sly buffoon. Along with all his contradictions, the trickster possessed the magical power to change his shape and form, transforming himself, for example, from a man into a tree or a bear or a gentle breeze that blew up the skirts of shy young women and gave them orgasms. A brilliant creation of native imagination, he was a highly complex figure whose ambiguities more accurately reflected the truth of life than the clear-cut and opposing categories used by white people to explain existence. Above all else, the trickster was an unusually clever gambler and con man, rather than an idealistic hero upon some quest to defeat evil in a head-on clash of strength and will.[2]

Black Hawk embodied the trickster in many ways, and throughout most of June and July of 1832 he appeared and disappeared, fought and fell back, changed appearances, strategies, locations, and at times seemed to vanish altogether. And all along the way he frustrated and fooled the Americans who hunted him. As a result, the campaign of early summer, which was largely a contest between the old Sauk leader and Henry Dodge, became a cat-and-mouse game engaged in by a hero eager to join battle and end the ambiguity forever, and a trickster who sought to survive by stealth and deception.

The trickster strategy first worked well on William Hamilton. Hamilton was the thirty-five-year-old son of the great Alexander Hamilton, who, like his father before him, was eager to acquire a heroic reputation. In an effort to do so, he decided to fight fire with fire by assembling a fighting force of Sioux and Menominee warriors, with whom he intended to catch and destroy the British Band. Young Hamilton, a fine-featured, diminutive man of aristocratic bearing, had spent a year at West Point before moving west, where he eventually became the U.S. surveyor of public lands in Illinois. Then, in 1828, with riches on his mind, he moved to the Michigan Territory, where he established Hamilton's Diggings, a mining settlement that Juliette Kinzie described as "a group of log cabins, low, shabby, and unpromising in appearance."[3] When war came, he saw it as an opportunity to create his own personal legend as a frontier Indian fighter, and hit upon the idea of the Indian brigade as a means of achieving that.

The warriors were recruited by the Indian affairs subagent Thomas Burnett and John Marsh. About 170 of them were turned over to Hamilton at his own village. Once they were assembled, Hamilton insisted, in no uncertain terms, there be absolutely no ambiguity about his absolute authority over this force.[4] Nevertheless, because Black Hawk and his raiding parties remained so elusive, and because neither Hamilton nor Atkinson devised any plans for the purposeful use of his Indian brigade, the Sioux and Menominee soon lost interest in the entire operation. Hamilton led them around for a time, unsuccessfully searching for the enemy, and then, not knowing what else to do, they all lazily loitered about Fort Hamilton for a few weeks. Finally, in late June, Hamilton informed Atkinson, "The inactivity of our service has so disheartened the Indians under my command that they have almost all returned to their homes."[5] When Joseph Street confronted the Sioux on their homeward journey, after accomplishing nothing with Hamilton, one of their chiefs by the name of L'Arc (or Lark), referring to Hamilton as the "little man," declared, "He did not use us well!" He then complained that Hamilton had wandered aimlessly around the countryside, making no attempt to join up with the larger army. "Our feet are sore and our moccasins worn out; we want to see our families," said L'Arc, expressing the group's collective exasperation. Although unimpressed with Hamilton, the Sioux voiced real admiration for Dodge, whom they described as the "man with much beard," and praised him for the manner in which he had dealt with the war party on the Pecatonica. In fact, they had all gone out to the scene of that battle once it was over and mutilated the bodies of the dead Indians in something of a gruesome celebration before heading home. "He is a brave man, and there are brave men along with him; but they are very few," declared L'Arc.[6]

While Hamilton's efforts fizzled and Dodge's fame grew, Atkinson was once again attempting to assemble a new army of Illinois militia. At his headquarters on the Illinois River, where he received supplies directly from St. Louis and Jefferson Barracks, he accumulated provisions and made ready to renew the campaign as he awaited the arrival of the militia. Reynolds had issued a new call for three thousand fresh volunteers at the end of May, ordering them to gather at Ottawa on June 14.[7] Somewhat surprisingly, given the experience of the first militia, a good many men once again responded to the call. But they were anything but prompt or orderly in getting to Ottawa, and when they arrived it was obvious the new force was very much like the one it replaced. William Cullen Bryant, visiting his brother in Illinois at the time, heard complaints about the new volunteers and described something of their character in a letter: "Some of the settlers complained that they made war upon the pigs and chickens," and that "they were a hard-looking set of men, unkempt and unshaven, wearing shirts of dark calico, and sometimes calico capotes."[8] A young second lieutenant, Philip St. George Cooke, a West Point graduate who eagerly volunteered to transfer from Fort Leavenworth to Atkinson's command, was even more critical. He referred to the militia as "that prosopopoeia of weakness, waste, and confusion," and said that soon after reporting for duty he found himself "in the midst of the multitude of citizen volunteers, who were as active as a swarming hive; catching horses, electioneering, drawing rations, asking questions, shooting at marks, electing officers, mustering in, issuing orders, disobeying orders, galloping about, 'cussing and discussing' the war and rumors thereof." He also mentioned how the task of bringing any order into that chaos was "painfully slow," and complained about those "raw fellows" having no "idea of the first principles of military respect and subordination."[9] Even John Reynolds, who described the volunteers as "intelligent, hardy, and patriotic citizens," had to admit there was a severe "want of discipline and organization among them."[10]

Eager to get on with the campaign, Atkinson began imposing some structure upon that unstable mass on June 15. That day a brigade of 962 volunteers was organized and put under the command of Alexander Posey, a medical doctor from Gallatin County who also happened to be Joseph Street's brother-in-law. Posey had been elected brigadier general two days before.[11] On June 16, and then four days later, two more brigades were assembled: one of 959 men under Milton K. Alexander, a merchant from Edgar County, and another containing 1,275 volunteers commanded by James Henry, the sheriff of Sangamon County.[12]

At noon on June 20, after drawing ten days' rations, Posey's First Brigade, along with Hugh Brady's two companies of regulars, set out for Fort Hamilton, and five days later Atkinson and the rest of the regulars, as well as Henry's Third Brigade, departed Ottawa for Dixon's Ferry. On June 26, Alexander and his men left for the Plumb River valley, located between Galena and Rock Island on the far western side of the state. After an embarrassingly long delay, the military was finally on the move again.

The march to Dixon's Ferry was an exasperating experience for young Lieutenant Philip St. George Cooke. The ground was wet and soft from successive days of pounding rain, and their "progress with heavy laden wagons was tedious," he complained. On their second day out someone in the militia raised an alarm by shouting "Indians! Indians!" and suddenly several hundred volunteers, without being given any orders, galloped off in all directions eager to confront and kill some savages. While chasing phantoms with reckless abandon across the prairie, they threw away all their provisions in an attempt to ride all the faster, but, in the end, no Indians were ever sighted.[13] After that, the citizen-soldiers were decidedly on edge, and Reynolds later recounted an incident in which a sentry fired off his musket in the night, claiming he had seen an Indian holding a torch moving through the darkness toward the camp. The sound of his gun had aroused the entire encampment, but before the situation got out of hand it was quickly determined that the sentinel had simply been confused by some shadows in the moonlight. "At times the imagination will work wonders," admitted Reynolds.[14]

A few nights after their arrival in Dixon's Ferry Cooke reported hearing the heavy and continuous discharge of muskets coming from the militia camp around nine o'clock. The reason for all the shooting remained a mystery to him, but as a consequence of the great racket, "the horses broke loose, and more than a thousand of them ran scampering over the prairie hills," he complained. The next day was spent hunting for runaway horses, many of which had been injured in the darkness by colliding with Dixon's fences.[15] Nothing much had changed from the first time around. The new militia was no different from the previous one, and not much had been learned from former mistakes. In a letter to General Macomb, Atkinson described his new force as consisting almost "entirely of new levies" except for the four hundred regulars, and admitted that it was "difficult to say with certainty" what the outcome of the campaign might be.[16]

The very first real encounter between members of the new militia and the Indians only reinforced such feelings of uncertainty. Twenty-eight-year-old Major John Dement, state treasurer and the commander of a spy battalion that was part of Posey's brigade, came in contact with a Sauk war party near Kellogg's Grove on Tuesday, June 26. In fact, some of Dement's scouts, well out ahead of his main force, fell into an ambush set for them by Black Hawk, who was then returning from his raid on the Apple River. Shocked to see his vanguard under attack by what he estimated to be about two hundred warriors, Dement aggressively went to their assistance. One report described how the young major and his men "bravely stood their ground until they were in danger of being surrounded," and only then fell back to a defensive position near their camp.[17] Even Black Hawk expressed admiration for how those men handled themselves. "They acted like braves," he said.[18] At the end of the day, Posey and the rest of the brigade arrived, and then the Sauk withdrew. Before the encounter was finished, five of Dement's men were dead, "three or four others" wounded, and at least fifty of their horses killed by Indian gunfire.[19] On hearing the news, and in spite of the examples of personal bravery, Joseph Street called it "another disastrous skirmish" and concluded that such "ill-fought battles" only gave encouragement to the Indians.[20] Many other anxious bystanders undoubtedly agreed.

By the end of June Henry Dodge still remained the only ray of hope in an otherwise dismal state of affairs. Heading north from Dixon's Ferry, Atkinson continued on his slow and plodding pace up the Rock River valley and by July 4 reached the muddy margins of the Lake Koshkonong area. There, according to Reynolds, the entire army "experienced a melancholy and sadness of feeling indescribable." For them, it became their own personal "Slough of Despond," where they were dragged down and nearly overwhelmed by their feelings of futility and failure, and caught in a confusing maze of mud, water, impenetrable reed beds, and rain-swollen streams. Their provisions were fast wasting away and almost gone, and their enemy infuriatingly elusive. It was as if they "were almost hunting a shadow," complained Reynolds.[21]

As Atkinson had moved toward that morass, Dodge set out from Fort Hamilton to join him with five mounted companies made up of about two hundred rugged men from the mining region.[22] Posey and his First Brigade also left Hamilton's heading eastward with the same intentions. And at the same time, Milton Alexander's Second Brigade, which had been in the Plumb River region, was also ordered to rendezvous with Atkinson near Lake Koshkonong.[23]

For Henry Dodge the journey commenced with a confrontation with William Hamilton. He arrived at Hamilton's Diggings with George Wallace Jones on June 30. "As we rode together," Jones later recounted, "I saw a man run into Colonel Hamilton's house and fort, and soon [after] saw Hamilton . . . emerge and run after us, hallooing to us to stop." When Jones suggested to Dodge that they ought to pause to find out what he wanted, Dodge snapped back, "Damn him, I do not care about seeing him!" But when Jones persisted, Dodge became more irritated and reined in his horse, without ever turning to look at his pursuer, who continued yelling at the top of his voice. When Hamilton caught up to them, he furiously declared how adamantly he objected to being put under Dodge's command. Dodge listened to his complaint only briefly and then, completely losing his temper, he leaped from his horse and drew out both his pistols. He advanced toward Hamilton extending the butt ends of those weapons toward him, sternly declaring: "Take your choice, sir, take your choice!" Hamilton held up his hands and backed off. "General, I do not want to fight," he protested, and Dodge sharply retorted, "Damn you, obey my orders hereafter!" That settled the matter. Dodge, with his dominance over Alexander Hamilton's son firmly established, remounted his horse, Big Black, and rode off with Jones to Posey's camp.[24]

When they reached the camp, another contest of wills and authority ensued. Even before arriving, Dodge had told Jones he had been given orders by General Atkinson to take command of Posey's brigade. This impending adjustment in the chain of authority was also plainly implied in a letter Atkinson sent to Posey on June 28, in which the general told him, "You will report and receive the orders of Genl. Dodge as soon as practicable, who is an officer of great experience & merit & is acquainted with the country."[25] The same day, Atkinson also wrote Dodge, informing him that Posey had been instructed to report to him.[26] What was to be done was quite clear in Dodge's mind, but much less so for Alexander Posey. When Dodge arrived at his encampment, Posey simply refused to turn over the First Brigade to Dodge when he requested he do so. Although annoyed by the rebuff, Dodge shrewdly indicated he would not force the matter or even try to assume authority over the Illinois volunteers unless they elected him their leader.

The troops were then drawn up in a hollow square and informed of the situation. According to George Wallace Jones, Dodge opened the proceedings by declaring, "If you choose to elect me as your commander, I will lead you to victory, if we can overtake Black Hawk and his army."[27] Many of the Illinois men were eager to put Dodge in charge. Daniel Parkinson, who was present that day, said that John Dement and his battalion were strongly in favor of electing Dodge.[28] Indeed, Jones said he overheard Dement telling his men that General Dodge "would lead them on to victory and retrieve the honor which a short time before they had lost in an

Indian fight under Posey."[29] In that statement, Dement was referring to Posey's refusal to use his large force against Black Hawk's raiding party, which had attacked Dement's spy battalion at Kellogg's Grove. It was a decision deeply resented by many of the troops at the time. And it was precisely that lack of courage and aggressive leadership the *Illinois Herald* of Springfield cited as the main reason why Posey ought to be removed from his command and replaced by Henry Dodge.[30]

In his own defense, Posey made what Jones characterized as "a pathetic appeal to his command, imploring them not to disgrace and forever ruin him by voting for a stranger to be their commander."[31] In the end, observed Daniel Parkinson, it came down to "a matter of state pride," and Posey retained his position "by a small majority."[32] Once the outcome of the voting was known, Dement was so enraged with disappointment he tore up his commission papers, threw the shreds on the ground, spat on them, and resigned his command of the spy battalion.[33]

With issues of command more or less settled, Dodge and his men rode out of Fort Hamilton and headed east on the morning of July 1, 1832. They camped the first night of their journey on the east branch of the Pecatonica River, which was very high from recent rains. They had considerable trouble crossing it the next morning and had to swim their horses and raft over their baggage. At the end of that second day, they stopped on the Sugar River, where James Stephenson and a company of sixty mounted volunteers from Galena joined them. Later that night Stephenson was elected Dodge's second-in-command.[34] William Hamilton also joined Dodge there, coming into camp with a small party of about twenty Menominee warriors and a few volunteers he had gathered from his own mining crew. On the third day, while cutting through the Four Lakes region, White Crow and a few of his Winnebago warriors joined the accumulating force. Although Dodge did not completely trust White Crow, he was glad to have him along as he claimed to know exactly where Black Hawk's mysterious camp was located. Dodge might have been willing to deal with the devil himself to obtain such information. They then crossed the Yahara River, just below Lake Kegonsa, and slogged on through what Daniel Parkinson described as an area of "almost impassible swamps."[35]

There among that marshland, Dodge received an express message from Atkinson, ordering him to report immediately to his headquarters on the Bark River. Dodge was furious. From the very beginning of the march it had been his intention to find and destroy Black Hawk's band all on his own—to dramatically end the war and have all the glory for himself—and Daniel Parkinson described how "Col. Dodge felt somewhat vexed to be thus thwarted in his purpose, and remarked that he was crippled in every movement he wished to make, by untimely expresses."[36] But despite his irritation and disappointment, he obeyed orders. Along with his little army, he completed the journey to Atkinson's headquarters during the evening of Thursday, July 5.[37] The day is recorded as having been one of dark, brooding skies and heavy rain.[38]

Throughout most of the march, Dodge and his troops, even though technically under Posey's command, did their utmost to keep themselves quite separate from Posey and his brigade. They resented the awkward situation, and toward the end of the journey, according to Charles Bracken, many of Dodge's men began voicing their dissatisfaction with Posey and his chaotic, undisciplined band of militiamen. While all admitted Posey himself was a "gentleman," they were nevertheless convinced "he did not possess the firmness requisite to command volunteers . . . [and] his want of decision rendered his men insubordinate and disorderly." Furthermore, Dodge's men were worried that Posey and his militia would desert them if and when they ever became embroiled in a serious encounter with the Indians. The men from the mining region did not trust the Posey brigade, and when they reached Atkinson's camp Dodge took immediate action to have his force reassigned to work with Milton Alexander, who had just arrived at Lake Koshkonong the day before.[39]

Dodge accomplished that objective even while angrily confronting Atkinson about some other prickly matters. When they arrived at the Bark River camp, Dodge and his men were irritated, hungry, and almost exhausted. In starting out they had carried only "scant rations for two or three days," wanting to travel as lightly and fast as possible, assuming they would be well fed once they caught up with the main force. Their provisions were therefore completely gone well before completing their trek. When Dodge met with Atkinson, the general not only was unresponsive to the men's need for food but actually ordered Dodge and his troopers to directly "go to work at building fortifications." At that Dodge blew up. According to John Ryan, a volunteer from the mining region, "General Dodge told him he did not come there to build forts, that he had come to fight Indians, and flatly refused to employ his men in building forts, much to the indignation of Atkinson who in turn refused to furnish Dodge with any provisions, a thing that looked to us almost inhuman."[40] In time, however, tempers cooled, and their disagreements were resolved. Dodge got what he wanted: His force was reassigned to work with Alexander, Atkinson relented and gave them whatever provisions he could, and there was no further mention of fort building. All of that made the power of Henry Dodge's personality and his increasing importance to the campaign unmistakably evident.

The days that followed were spent in a most frustrating search for Black Hawk and his band. "Indian sign[s] plenty, find mats kettles steel traps," scribbled Nineveh Shaw in his journal on July 7.[41] Nevertheless, the Indians themselves seemed invisible. "Scouts were out in every direction to discover their trails; as yet however, they were unsuccessful owing to the nature and frequency of the swamps and muddy creeks," reported the *Galenian*.[42] Indeed, the conditions the soldiers were required to contend with pushed them beyond the limits of their patience and endurance. From accounts provided by men in the field, the *Galenian* informed its readers that "hundreds of the army were frequently compelled to dismount, during their march, and wade through mud and water, to keep their horses from miring in the swamps." Even the governor and other officials of the state accompanying the expedition were "wading thro' mire and water, sometimes as deep as the armpits," noted the newspaper.[43] At some places it was necessary to cut brush and the long, coarse swamp grass and lay it down on the soggy ground so the heavy baggage wagons could pass on. "There were plenty of scythes, and men to use them; so it was an easy job to make a temporary bridge," observed John Wakefield of Henry's brigade.[44] But crossing such bridges was not always as easy as constructing them, and Philip St. George Cooke remarked that in traveling "over these trembling causeways, each horse seems to consider his passage an adventure; and many a rider, too"[45] Their ordeal in that treacherous marshland became especially difficult when part of the army attempted to cross the Whitewater River on July 9. There, said Wakefield, "many a horse mired down, and threw his rider into the water, where he and his gun were literally buried in mud and water."[46]

Two days before the crossing of the Whitewater, violent events were added to their troubles. Early in the morning of July 7, one of the regular soldiers and a member of the militia went down to the river to do some fishing. Just before that, and unknown to them, according to Lieutenant

James J. Justice, "Two or three of the young Winnebagoes that were with us crossed over the white water before the fog had dissipated and fired on one of the Regulars & and one of the militia and wounded the former."[47] Wakefield, too, reported that the soldier was hit twice and his wounds were quite severe.[48] But that was not the end of bloodletting for the day. That night, after dark, Captain Charles Dunn, a member of Posey's brigade and the officer of the day, was, according to Daniel Parkinson, "going around to relieve the guard [and] was unfortunately shot by one of the sentinels and dangerously wounded."[49] Wakefield indicated that Dunn was struck in the groin, and "when examined his surgeons pronounced it mortal."[50] Captain Dunn did not die, but the incident disturbed everyone deeply. Philip Cooke made note of the event by simply stating, "One of the militia sentinels was so nervously vigilant as to shoot a friend." He then added scornfully, "This is not a very uncommon occurrence among them; and they are supposed by some ill-natured persons to be generally more dangerous to their friends than to their enemies."[51] Those incidents, of course, contributed to the worsening of a situation in which everyone was worn down and their nerves were badly frayed.

Everything about the swamp campaign was miserable, and the *Galenian* said the men were confronted at every turn by "almost insurmountable obstacles, which, in the shape of swamps, creeks, want of provisions . . . and jaded horses, presented themselves."[52] In time, more and more of the volunteers simply refused to participate any longer. By July 10 Governor Reynolds and his staff had had enough and departed for home, thereby setting an example that only encouraged other men to do the same. In fact, observed Reynolds, a great many men in the militia had by then become convinced that all their efforts were accomplishing nothing, and because of the apparent futility of the campaign "a great many worthy and respectable individuals . . . returned to their homes."[53] In his history of the war, Thomas Ford was somewhat critical of the militia members who deserted the cause, asserting that far too many of them had unrealistically joined up looking for fun and adventure, and then, when the going got rough and they became exposed to "the unexpected hardships and privations of a soldier's life," they were not tough enough to take it. As a result, he noted, there were "rapid reductions in the numbers of every regiment."[54]

Sickness also took a toll. Without elaboration, Atkinson mentioned the increasing number of "sick who were accumulating," and that the regular soldiers "threw up" some crude shelters for them. Dysentery was perhaps the most serious illness with which they were afflicted.[55]

To make matters even worse, they were rapidly running out of provisions. Atkinson blamed the militia at least in part for that; "But for the waste of provisions by the volunteers, and the unavoidable losses in swimming rivers and the miring down of horses in creeks and swamps[,] the supply would have been ample," he told a colleague.[56] Lieutenant Cooke, always more critical of the militia than his commander, noted, "The volunteers had been improvident and wasteful to the degree of leaving in certain camps rations that had been issued, by the barrel in unbroken bulk!" Besides that, he complained, "the militia convoys were incredibly timid," and drivers sometimes abandoned their wagons "in consequence of their having imagined that they had seen an Indian or two."[57] No matter who was to blame, the situation grew quite serious. James Justice noted in his journal, "The soldiers was [sic] now becoming quite discontented . . . [being] entirely without provisions."[58] Years later, Abraham Lincoln, who was a participant in this swamp campaign, remarked about it somewhat humorously: "I had a good many bloody experiences with the mosquitoes; and although I never fainted from loss of blood, I can truly say I was often very hungry."[59] Many of his comrades in the ranks experienced the same problem. In fact, the supply situation became so severe by early July that, "by the advice of a council of war," Atkinson temporarily suspended operations. On July 9—the very next day—he sent Henry Dodge, Milton Alexander, James Henry, and their men to Fort Winnebago, at the portage between the Wisconsin and Fox rivers, to procure twelve days' additional rations and to return with them to Atkinson's camp "without delay."[60] That same day, he sent Posey and his volunteer brigade back west to Fort Hamilton. To reduce the drain on the meager supplies that remained, that day he also sent most of the Potawatomi, who had joined his force, back to Chicago, telling General Winfield Scott that while they were dependable guides, they unfortunately ate a great deal.[61] The next day Henry Gratiot noted in his diary that "in consequence of the scarcity of provisions Genl. Atkinson discharged all of the Winnebagoes except White Crow and his son."[62] The two of them guided Dodge through the wilderness to Fort Winnebago.

The journey to the portage was uneventful. Atkinson had estimated the distance to be about thirty-five miles,[63] but, in fact, it turned out to be almost double that, and Dodge, who struck out well in advance of both Alexander and Henry, covered nearly half the distance the first day.[64] The Illinois brigades went only ten miles the first day and took three whole days to reach their destination.

Fort Winnebago was then hardly a real fort—more an isolated military outpost without a palisade or artillery, where a few wooden buildings had been arranged in a rectangular formation upon a hill along the north bank of the Fox River. It looked down upon a broad open prairie and was directly across the river from the portage road, which extended for a little more than a mile southward to the Wisconsin River. Canoes and Mackinaw boats were carried along that road between the two rivers on ox-drawn wagons. In fact, people had been hauling their vessels and cargoes along the same trail well before Father Marquette and Louis Jolliet traversed it in 1673. During the 1830s one of the men in charge of moving crafts and cargoes between the rivers was Pierre Paquette, an unusually large métis man of legendary physical strength, who was also the local agent for the American Fur Company. He was held in very high esteem by whites and Indians alike, and, as soon as Dodge arrived, he contacted Paquette, hoping to get some information about the whereabouts of the Sauk. There were a great many Winnebago people then encamped at the portage. They were refugees, trying to stay out of the way of the war, not wishing to be implicated by either side. Because they had left behind their gardens and hunting grounds, they had fallen into what the Indian agent John Kinzie described as a "state of demi-starvation."[65] Dodge figured they would know where Black Hawk was. And because Paquette, whose mother had been Winnebago, was fluent in their language and had great influence among them, he assumed Paquette could get the information if anyone could. Paquette asked around and reported back to Dodge that the Sauk band was encamped on the upper Rock River at a place called Hustis' Rapids (Hustisford), just below Cranberry Lake (now Horicon Marsh).[66]

Alexander and Henry arrived with their brigades late in the evening of Thursday, July 12, having traveled about twenty miles that day.[67] Weary from the journey, they bedded down soon after getting there, but whatever hopes they had for a good night's sleep were soon dashed. "We were soon Rousted from our slumber by the Running of the horses which had taken flight," James Justice noted in his journal.[68] The horses—more than a thousand of them—stampeded through the camp, and the sound of their hooves pounding upon the ground was like the heavy rumble of thunder, observed Satterlee Clark, a sutler at the fort.[69] Justice said the incident was life threatening, declaring they were all "in great danger of being run over and killed." Nevertheless, he added, "the horses passed through the encampment without hurting any person."[70] Regrettably, the same could not be said for the horses themselves. Wakefield reported that the panic-stricken animals all ran northward for about thirty miles before stopping,[71] and Clark observed that over sixty of them were found dead the next morning.[72] Many more were injured, quite a few were never found, and it took the better part of two days to round up the surviving animals and drive them back to the fort.[73]

Dodge, so impatient to be off in pursuit of the Black Hawk band and so extremely eager to strike the blow and claim the victory, simply had to cool his heels and bide his time. But while he formulated his plans and waited, conditions among the Sauk became truly desperate. They, like the soldiers who hunted them, had also exhausted their provisions. "Situated in a swampy, marshy country," observed Black Hawk, "there was but little game of any sort to be found—and fish were equally scarce." There were at least a thousand people to feed, including a great many women and children and old people. They had been on the move for fourteen weeks, and in the swamps, as their situation worsened, they ate their dead horses and were forced to dig roots and strip bark from the trees to obtain anything to nourish themselves. The old people began to die. Faced with the mounting crisis, Black Hawk decided to make a hazardous attempt to break out of the swamp country around Lake Koshkonong, head west, and, with some Winnebagos to guide them, reach the Wisconsin River, descend it, and escape across the Mississippi into the region that afterward became Iowa.[74]

The information Dodge obtained from Paquette led him to believe the Sauk were moving in exactly the opposite direction—fleeing eastward—and he wrote to Atkinson, telling him that if the enemy Indians continued "to retreat in the direction of Lake Michigan," he felt certain he could still catch and defeat them.[75] There were other people who also assumed the Sauk would head east, convinced that their ultimate destination was still Canada. Thomas Forsyth was one of them. He told George Davenport that he supposed "the old Hawk and some of his principal friends will go to Munnito-walk, or Shebuygun, on Lake Michigan, get Birch Canoes from the Chippeway Indians and push on to Canada."[76] Much closer at hand than Forsyth, John Kinzie wrote to Governor George Porter of Michigan during the time Dodge was still at Fort Winnebago, telling him, "The Sac & Fox Indians, I understand are making for Milliwalkie and that vicinity, and it is conjectured [they] intend making good their retreat in canoes (which they can procure along the Lake) to Drummond Island."[77] A few days later, Addison Philleo, then serving as the army surgeon with the Twenty-seventh Regiment, wrote back to the readers of his newspaper, informing them that William Hamilton had arrived at the portage from Green Bay and told everyone there the "hostile Indians had moved in the direction of Mil-wa-ki, on Lake Michigan."[78]

Their orders from Atkinson made it unambiguously clear that they were to pick up the supplies and return to his headquarters "without delay"; nevertheless, with victory and fame appearing to be so close at hand, Dodge attempted to persuade both Alexander and Henry to ignore those orders and join him in hunting down Black Hawk instead. Knowing Stephenson, his second-in-command, was a close friend of James Henry's, he sent him to talk with Henry. Stephenson was persuasive, and Henry agreed to join Dodge in the pursuit of Black Hawk. After that, Dodge convened a general council of officers. He revealed the intelligence he had acquired from the Winnebago refugees, through Paquette, and proposed they return to Atkinson's camp circuitously by way of Hustis' Rapids on the upper Rock River, where they could finally attack and defeat the renegade Indian band that had so long eluded them. Alexander and his officers rejected Dodge's proposal outright, refusing to consider bending the letter of their orders even slightly. They would return directly to Lake Koshkonong with the supplies.

Dodge accepted their decision but immediately made preparations for moving out. He was excited by the prospects and became, said Peter Parkinson, "the main-spring, the life and energy of the army, suggesting and planning all its movements."[79] He culled the force, and all the men with worn-down horses unfit for a fast-riding chase were discharged. That included Stephenson and most of the volunteers from Galena, as well as a good many members of Henry's brigade. When the weeding-out process was finished, a total of about six hundred men remained.[80]

On Sunday, July 15, Alexander and his brigade left Fort Winnebago with the supplies, returning south by the way they had come. That same day, Dodge and Henry also left the portage, taking Paquette as their interpreter, along with seven or eight Winnebago guides to pilot them through the unfamiliar territory. They headed due east toward the Rock River.

Dodge and Henry rode hard for three days, but when they finally reached Hustis' Rapids all they found were a few emaciated Winnebago, who informed them the Sauk were farther upstream at Cranberry Lake.[81] James Justice was suspicious of the Winnebago and quite cynical about the information they were providing. There were undoubtedly a great many more members of the expedition who felt the same. After all, it would not have been the first time in the war that the Winnebago had deliberately deceived the Americans. In fact, later, when army officers interrogated members of the Black Hawk band, the Sauk prisoners admitted White Crow and numerous other Winnebago men had given them considerable assistance during their journey through Wisconsin.[82]

Dodge was of course deeply disappointed in not finding the Sauk there, and although it was still early in the day, he decided to make camp and reconsider their options. From there he wrote to General Atkinson a somewhat misleading letter explaining where they were and what they intended to do. He then sent this message off with his adjutant, William W. Woodbridge, accompanied by Dr. Elias H. Merryman of Henry's brigade, and Little Thunder, one of the Winnebago guides. According to Wakefield, the couriers left about two o'clock in the afternoon and planned to ride hard without stopping in order to reach Atkinson's camp that night.[83]

Woodbridge, Merryman, and Little Thunder had traveled only about eight miles, however, when they came upon a fresh, well-traveled trail heading west, and upon further investigation found bark had been removed from trees and some digging had been done in search of wild potatoes.[84] They concluded that a large group of Indians had recently passed that way, and surmised it must have been the Black Hawk band. But night was coming on by then, and Little Thunder, using sign language since neither Woodbridge nor Merryman understood Winnebago, tried to discourage them from any further travel. Ignoring his advice, the two of them decided to head back as fast as their horses could run. They rushed off into the darkness, crashing noisily through the forests, and when they reached the camp a startled sentry opened fire upon them. Fortunately for them, they passed unharmed into the camp and with great excitement delivered their news to Dodge. That information, said Wakefield, "seemed to give new life to every heart; as now there appeared to be a prospect of bringing our toils and troubles to a speedy end."[85] Indeed, the discovery of that trail changed everything.

The troops were up and eager to go well before dawn the next morning. In order to make maximum speed, it was decided to leave behind five baggage wagons, sutler's stores, and all the cumbersome camp equipment. However, even though they traveled light and got an early start, the journey itself proved arduous, as, once again, they had to move through dense thickets and treacherous swamps. What's more, in the early afternoon they were caught in an unusually fierce thunderstorm. But in spite of it all, observed Wakefield, "there was no murmuring, no excuses made; none getting on the sick report," for "the men had something now to stimulate them."[86] James Justice also indicated they all "felt as if they would shortly overtake the savage foe and give him a scurging and then Return home."[87] The rain stopped toward evening, but only briefly, and then resumed again after dark when, noted Wakefield, it once more "commenced thundering, lightening, and raining tremendously."[88] Most of the men were without tents, having left them behind with the baggage wagons. "The next morning we arose[,] the most of us leaving a puddle of water where we had lay," wrote Justice in his journal.[89]

Before setting out from Hustis' Rapids early on Thursday, July 19, both Dodge and Henry wrote to Atkinson explaining what actions they intended to take. Their messages were delivered the same day, and the next morning the general sent his reply. Atkinson was clearly excited by the new developments and very much approved of the decision Dodge and Henry had made. "I have to urge and direct that you will press on with all haste and never lose sight of the object till the enemy is overtaken, defeated & if possible captured," he told them.[90]

With confirming orders in hand, they reached Four Lakes on the second day. Along the way some of their scouts had taken a Winnebago man captive, and, upon interrogation, he had told them Black Hawk was only a few miles ahead of them.[91] On learning that, Dodge sent out Captain Joseph Dickson with a few men to see if they could actually find the Sauk.

Dickson "returned in a very short time," said Wakefield, "and stated that he had seen the enemy's rear guard about one mile and a half distant."[92] The news excited everyone. But because it was already quite late in the day, and on the advice of Pierre Paquette, who worried about them getting lost or ambushed in the thick forest after dark, they made camp on the east end of Lake Monona. After securing their horses and eating what Wakefield described as a "frugal supper,"[93] the bone-weary men, many still wet from the storms of the previous day, retired for the night. Some did not sleep easy, fearing a sneak attack from the treacherous Sauk. "We were under arms the greater part of the night," wrote James Justice.[94]

On Saturday, July 21, they were up and on horseback as early as possible. They traversed the isthmus between Lake Monona and Lake Mendota, with Colonel William Ewing's spy battalion, of which Wakefield was a member, taking the lead. Dodge and his men were next in line, and Henry's brigade brought up the rear. It was a fine summer morning, and James Justice was quite impressed with the country he saw around the lakes and regretted that they "had only time to take a passing view of the Romantic beauties of the wilderness, and passed on from the beautiful sandy shores of the lakes."[95]

Moving northwestward, they then passed into a region Wakefield described as a "Broken and Barrony Woods." He surmised the Sauk were deliberately leading them into country where the forest was so thick they could "turn neither to the right nor left."[96] Justice wrote in his journal, "From the top of one stupendious hill we could view nothing but the savage wilds of high hills and narrow Vales."[97] Numerous horses broke down along the way, their riders continuing on foot as best they could.

About ten o'clock that morning, some of the scouts discovered and killed a Sauk man who had given up the struggle and was disconsolately sitting upon the fresh grave of his dead wife.[98] Shortly after that, advance riders discovered three more Sauk men, who had fallen behind the main band. Two were killed outright, and the other managed to escape. Addison Philleo was with that advance party, and when the first Indian was killed while passively sitting on the grave, Philleo leaped from his horse and proceeded to scalp the man. He was also involved in the incident with the other three Sauk, stalking them for some time, and then, when they "got them into a good position for attack," he sent back for reinforcements.

Dodge sent up ten more men. In the account printed in the *Galenian* (undoubtedly written by Philleo himself), it was reported that Philleo "came up within 20 paces of the hindmost Indian, and shot him through the body, the ball entering immediately under the heart." But the man was not dead. He staggered backward a few paces, briefly propped himself against a tree, and then as he was falling to the ground he fired off his gun, hitting Isam Hardin, one of the reinforcements sent by Dodge. In fact, three musket balls hit Hardin. One went through his thigh, another penetrated his lower leg, and the last one struck him in the foot.[99] Hardin lived, but the Sauk man did not. And when it was certain he was dead, Philleo strode up and slashed off his second scalp of the morning.

That initial taste of blood only heightened the anticipation of the troops and whetted their appetite for more. They knew they were getting close and that the Indians were in a state of panic, for the trail was strewn with their mats and kettles and other goods, apparently cast aside in their fearful haste to escape their pursuers.[100] Also, according to Charles Bracken, after those first Indians had been killed, Dodge's men became "dissatisfied with the slow gait at which Ewing's battalion led the pursuit, reasoning among themselves that it was safe to dash ahead, overtake the enemy, and fight them" before they reached the Wisconsin River.[101] They therefore sped up, passing Ewing, who, in turn, ordered "his men forward with blows and curses," and thereby managed to keep up with Dodge, who rushed onward at full gallop.[102]

By late afternoon more and more horses were breaking down and giving out. Also, it began to rain once again, and care had to be taken to keep muskets dry. What's more, Neapope and the Sauk rear guard were feinting attacks in an attempt to slow down the advance of the troops, so that Dodge and Ewing were forced to stop from time to time and form their men up into defensive battle lines. But by early evening they were drawing near the Wisconsin River. Most of Black Hawk's people rushed on toward the river, intending to cross over to an island in midstream where it would be difficult for the soldiers to attack them. As they did so, many warriors took up a defensive position on the high ground, about a mile from the river, determined to hold back the soldiers and buy time for their people who had already begun the crossing. "We were now compelled to fight," said Black Hawk, "or sacrifice our wives and children to the fury of the whites!"[103]

It was about six o'clock when the foremost militia riders discovered the Indians forming up for battle. Dodge halted and dismounted his men, quickly organizing them into two columns on either side of Ewing's troops, who by then were also on foot and moving forward. But they had hardly commenced approaching the heights when the Sauk came dashing down toward them. "We had scarcely time to form on foot, before the Indians raised the war-whoops, screaming and yelling hideously, and rushing forward, meeting us with a heavy charge," wrote Wakefield.[104] Dodge said the Sauk warriors got to within thirty yards of them before his men fired off their first volley, killing one attacker, wounding one or two others, and forcing the Indians to halt and fall back.[105] Henry, who did not arrive on the scene until after that initial confrontation, later reported to Atkinson how both Ewing's and Dodge's troops had "gallantly withstood the shock and drove back the survivors in confusion and dismay."[106]

After their charge had been repulsed, the Sauk attempted to outflank the combined militia force, which, by then, was under the overall command of James Henry. Wakefield observed that the Indians held a very strong position and that most of them became almost invisible in the dim light, among the tall grass and dense underbrush from which they fired upon the troops.[107] Philleo described how "the heads of the Indians above the grass, resembled stumps in a newly cleared forest."[108] The exchange of fire went on at least a half hour. During that time Thomas Jefferson Short of Henry's brigade was killed and one of Dodge's men was wounded. Throughout it all the rains continued to pelt down upon them. Finally, growing frustrated with the lack of decisive movement, Dodge and Ewing asked Henry's permission to rush the Indians with a bayonet charge. Permission was granted, and the charge, said Henry, was carried out "with the greatest promptitude, and in the most gallant style."[109] The volunteers rose and ran up the rising ground. As they came on, the Sauk jumped to their feet amid the high grass, and soon, said Henry, "the enemy was driven from the heights, fleeing down the precipitous declivities, and took refuge in the swamps, thick woods and high grass in the bottom of the Ouisconsin."[110] Dodge was more succinct, simply reporting to Atkinson, "The enemy then gave way in every direction retreating to the river."[111] Black Hawk described how they had been forced to give ground under the pressure of that attack: "The enemy succeeded in gaining this point, which compelled us to fall back into a deep ravine, from which we continued firing at them and they at us, until it began to grow dark."[112]

Throughout the battle, Black Hawk was mounted on his white horse, positioned on a high hill from which he gave directions to his warriors in a loud voice. His horse, twice struck with gunfire, was bleeding badly, and in time Black Hawk, too, was forced to retreat down into the swampy region along the margin of the river, but in doing so, he said he went with a feeling of satisfaction, "knowing" that the "women and children had had sufficient time to reach the island in the Ouoisconsin."[113]

Once the battle for the heights was over, the victors began hurriedly searching through the grass and underbrush for fallen Indians. "The Winnebagoes scalped eleven Indians killed by the whites, and the whites took thirteen scalps," reported Dodge.[114] Satterlee Clark, the sutler from Fort Winnebago who had gone along on the expeditions, provided a little detail on some of what transpired once the fighting was finished. "Then came the struggle for scalps," and "every man who could run started down the hill at top speed," he wrote. Each of them hoped to gain some grisly trophies for himself, and Clark shared that ambition. Paquette rushed past him on his horse, and Clark caught hold of the horse's tail and held on until he had been pulled up the hill, where they found four dead Indians. "Pauquette took one scalp, I took one, and the Indian scouts took the other two," he reported.[115]

Dodge estimated they had killed at least forty Indians, and suspected many of the slain had been removed from the battlefield by the Sauk in an effort to conceal the magnitude of their losses.[116] Henry claimed a body count of between thirty or forty and said it was hard to be exact since the dead were "scattered over a wide tract of country covered with thick woods."[117] Wakefield set the number much higher: "We killed sixty-eight of the enemy, and wounded a considerable number; twenty-five of whom, they report, died soon after the battle."[118] Black Hawk claimed—he was clearly mistaken—that only six of his men had been lost in the fight.[119] From information gathered later from the interrogations of Indian prisoners, it was revealed that the Kickapoo, who had joined Black Hawk's band, had put up an especially ferocious fight on Wisconsin Heights, and virtually all of them had been killed. One Indian woman prisoner told Joseph Street that sixty-eight warriors had lost their lives in that battle.[120] While Black Hawk minimized his losses, he was convinced, on the other hand, that his warriors had inflicted some serious damage on the Americans. "The loss of the enemy could not be ascertained by our party; but I am of opinion that it was much greater, in proportion, than mine," he claimed. The fact was, only one American had died—Thomas Jefferson Short— and just eight others had been wounded.[121]

In commenting about what had happened on the heights that day, Satterlee Clark wrote, "That battle made many heroes, and so it should."[122] But none got or took more credit for the victory than Henry Dodge. The account of the battle published in the *Niles' Weekly Register* claimed that Dodge had been in command of the whole army, and described the violent clash to be "another defeat of the Indians by Gen. Dodge."[123] Also, in his report to Captain Gustavus Loomis, at Fort Crawford, Dodge made no mention of either Ewing or Henry and gave the very distinct impression that he alone had been responsible for the victory. The day after the fight, he told Loomis, "I will cross the Ouisconsin to morrow," suggesting that he was very much the moving force behind events.[124]

But regardless of who else deserved credit, a significant victory against the Indians had finally been achieved, and that had been due largely to the persistence, assertiveness, and obsessive ambition of Henry Dodge. Throughout the long and dismal days following the disbanding of the first militia, only Dodge had raised the hopes of the people, and only he had set an admirable example of personal courage. It was, therefore, only natural he should be hailed a hero.

On the other side, however, even in defeat, Black Hawk remained the trickster, mysteriously disappearing over the river and into the darkness, vanishing with his band into the uncharted wilderness stretching west- ward toward the Mississippi.

12

INTO THE VALLEY OF DEATH

The world is a dead thing to them
the trees and rivers are not alive
the mountains and stones are not alive.
The deer and bear are objects
They see no life.

They fear
They fear the world.
They destroy what they fear.
They fear themselves.

Leslie Marmon Silko, *Ceremony*

THE VICTORY IN the tall grass and midsummer rain on Wisconsin Heights brought to an end the frustrating succession of mistakes, failures, and embarrassments that had characterized so much of the American campaign against Black Hawk and his Sauk band. Moreover, the events of that warm July evening set in motion the final act of a drama that would conclude less than two weeks later along the east bank of the Mississippi River. The militia's success against the Indians, as qualified as it may have been, awakened in the troops a renewed confidence and eagerness to finish the job. But in their minds and those of the civilian population from which they had come, they were convinced that ending the trouble once and for all would require the complete annihilation of the offending Indians.

In his speech to his men at Kirker's farm just three weeks before, Henry Dodge had claimed that not only was the "future growth and prosperity" of the region endangered by the renegade Indians, but their own very "existence as a people" was at stake. He described the British Band as "the enemies of all people," whose "thirst for blood" was "not to be satisfied," and therefore, like rabid dogs or voracious wolves, they would have to be hunted down and exterminated.[1] It was, of course, a dramatic overstatement of the actual situation, but one reflecting the views held by most people then living along the upper Mississippi frontier. The conflict, in fact, had hardly begun when the *Galenian* called upon Governor Reynolds to "carry on a war of extermination until there shall be no Indian (with his scalp on) left in the northern part of Illinois."[2] As the struggle grew more protracted and widespread, the cry for annihilation became ever more adamant, so that in late June the *Galenian* declared the people of the mining region were "ready to exterminate the whole race of the hostile Indians, and restore a lasting peace" or "leave their [own] corpses on the field of battle."[3]

White people were convinced that the savages had brought this fate upon themselves, and therefore felt no sympathy or mercy was owed them. That harsh moral logic of extermination was explained by the Indian agent Joseph Street, in a speech to the Sioux, given at Prairie du Chien, on June 22, 1832. "The Great Father," said Street, wanted only what was best for his "red children," and desired them to live in peace with one another as well as his "white children." When they did not do so—when they were disobedient and misbehaved—he wished most of all to "reclaim them, and make them good [again]." In the case of the Sauk, however, Street explained how the Great Father's feelings were quite different, for they had "dared to kill some of his white children," and for that the Great Father could never forgive them. "He has tried to reclaim them, and they have grown worse," declared the Indian agent, who then concluded, "If they cannot be made good they must be killed."[4]

It was with such killing in mind that the militia moved from the heights down into the deep valley of the Wisconsin River the morning after the battle. Upon reaching the swampy, overgrown bottomland, they were disappointed to discover the Indians had escaped once again and vanished into the forest. Like the animals they hunted, the Sauk were masters of deception and evasion.

Following the battle, Black Hawk had been astonished when the soldiers had not continued their pursuit all the way to the river. But the cessation in their action was what enabled his band to make its escape.[5] According to one Sauk woman, it had provided time enough for the women and old people to get to the island and for the men to move the children from slough to slough on horses. Then too, when encountering a particularly broad and deep slough, they took time to fashion a raft of poles, mats, and skins to "put the children on and pushed it over [by] swimming."[6] Everyone was taken across the Wisconsin, even the wounded. On reaching the other side, Black Hawk held a brief council. According to another woman, the old leader had told them even before the battle that "if he got whipped he would cross the Wiskonsin push on to the Mississippi above prairie du Chien and cross that too."[7] He reiterated that plan when they regrouped after the fight. Unfortunately for some, however, they no longer possessed the means of making that journey, for it was decided by the council that only people who still had good horses could go with Black Hawk on the overland trek to the Mississippi. As a consequence, said the same Sauk woman, "all the women & children, old people & the wounded who could not ride were to go down the Wiskonsin and try to escape to the West side of the Mississippi."[8] "Some women who had good horses went" with the main band, as did some of the wounded from the battle, while those who would be going down the Wisconsin hurriedly made canoes. "They were only of Elm Bark stripped off & tied at each end," and all were "very frail and clumsy," it was reported.[9] The plan was for everyone to eventually meet up again west of the Mississippi, on the Cedar River, and from there to return to Keokuk's village to the south.

In the course of a single night those decisions were made and carried out. "The next morning," wrote James Justice in his journal, "we perraded and marched down to the River But the Indians had got across the River."[10] After the soldiers waded through the swamps and searched along the riverbank, Wakefield said it soon became evident the Indians had already "made their retreat . . . during the night, leaving a great many articles of their trumpery behind."[11]

Lieutenant Philip St. George Cooke was impressed with what the Indians and their leader had managed to pull off. "After all their boasting," he wrote, concerning the soldiers' self-congratulatory reaction to their own victory, "the simple fact was, that Black Hawk, although encumbered with the women, children, and baggage of his whole band, covered himself by a small party, and accomplished the most difficult of military operations—to wit, the passage of a river—in the presence of three regiments of American volunteers."[12]

Not lingering long among the muddy riverbank marshes, the soldiers soon returned to their camp. There they spent the remains of the day drying clothes, making litters in which to carry wounded comrades, and engaging in still more boastful banter.[13] But there was a strong undercurrent of anxiety, for all suspected Black Hawk and his braves would soon be back to attack them when they least expected. That uneasiness escalated when they were suddenly "alarmed early in the night by the horses which had taken a fright and Run up to the camp," noted James Justice in his diary.[14] They were certain that prowling Indians had intentionally spooked the horses. Therefore, as an additional precaution, General Henry increased the guard. He had fires set around the perimeter of the camp and kept them burning throughout the night. He also ordered every man to remain awake and fully armed.[15] Then, toward dawn, something quite eerie occurred. All was quiet. Suddenly the silence was shattered by "an unearthly sound."[16] Daniel Parkinson identified it as "the loud shrill voice of an Indian from the summit of one of the highest peaks in the vicinity."[17] Justice estimated that hill to be about half a mile away. However, the voice was clear, and it penetrated the darkness with what one soldier called "loud, distinct, and strange ejaculations. . . . The effect was almost electric," exclaimed the same anonymous trooper.[18] The phantom in the predawn gloom continued to call out for ten or fifteen minutes in a tone and cadence James Justice said he "never heard equaled by any human voice."[19] The men's hair bristled as they felt cold shudders of fear pass through their bodies. They gripped their muskets tensely in preparation for an attack. "We thought that Black Hawk's entire force was being brought to bear upon us in a night attack," said Daniel Parkinson.[20] Meriwether Clark, the son of Indian superintendent William Clark, who had reached the camp the night before, said the nocturnal speaker was "distinctly heard giving commands," as if he were directing the movements of a large fighting force.[21] Then, as suddenly as it had begun, the voice ceased calling. The woods reverted to a ghostly silence. No attack ever came from out of the darkness. Once it grew light, some soldiers were sent out to investigate. All they found were some hoof tracks in the dirt and the remains of a dead horse that had been killed in the battle, which the Indians had cut apart and carried away for food.[22]

The whole incident remained an unaccountable mystery until later, when several Indian captives revealed what had gone on that night.[23] The man who had cried out in the darkness, and who was never specifically identified, had spoken in the Winnebago language, assuming that Paquette and the Winnebago scouts were still among the soldiers. He was "making propositions of peace," wrote Daniel Parkinson, and was saying "that the Sauks and Foxes would surrender themselves up . . . and only asked protection for the lives of their woman and children."[24] Wakefield, who had a different source, gave a somewhat different version of the message. According to him, the man on the hilltop, speaking in Winnebago, had stated that "they had their squaws and children with them and that they were starving for something to eat, and were not able to fight us; and that if we would let them pass over the Mississippi, they would do no more mischief."[25] No matter what the contents of that message may have been, Paquette and the Winnebago guides had already departed for Portage the day before, and there was no one left in camp who understood what the man was saying. "Hearing no response," Parkinson reported, the Sauk band "concluded that their proposals were not acceptable, and no mercy would be shown them."[26]

In the morning, James Henry and Dodge determined that since they were once again nearly out of provisions, they should strike out for Blue Mounds, about thirty miles to the southwest. For Daniel Parkinson, and probably most of his comrades, the journey proved to be unusually tough, and he described it as "one of the most fatiguing days that was experienced during the war."[27] They had to go "over almost impassible creeks, through swamps, over hills, and through thick woods," he complained, and the encumbrance of the wounded men being lugged along in litters made travel all the more difficult. Parkinson himself took charge of John McNair, his orderly sergeant who had been shot in the thigh, carrying him in his arms over the many creeks that had to be crossed. Of course the day was excruciatingly difficult for McNair, himself, due to his painful wound and the discomforts he endured being jostled about in a litter slung between horses.[28] Along the way many of the already overworked horses simply broke down. But, in spite of the difficulties, everyone made it safely to Blue Mounds shortly after dark.[29]

At the same time, General Atkinson, with his regulars and Milton Alexander's volunteers, was also heading for Blue Mounds. They had left Lake Koshkonong on July 21 and the first day had trudged on, said Lieutenant Cooke, "in a cold and beating rain," fording the Rock River just below the lake, and then collapsed on the other side of the flood-swollen stream "half dead with cold and fatigue." They camped where they fell. Fortunately for them, conditions improved somewhat in the morning, and after an uneventful but arduous four-day march through the forest, they arrived at Blue Mounds in reasonably good shape.[30]

The reunited forces paused only briefly near Brigham's diggings, and after just a single night's rest, and with three days' rations in their packs, they all pushed on to Helena, a small sawmill settlement on the Wisconsin River about halfway between Portage and Prairie du Chien. They reached there on Friday, July 26. Posey and his men also came up to Helena from Fort Hamilton, where they had been posted earlier, and Dodge, who had briefly returned home to recruit more men, arrived at the village the next day.

There was, as usual, some complaining among the ranks of the militia. This time it came mostly from the men who had fought the battle on Wisconsin Heights—those men who had pushed themselves and their horses to extremes in order to catch and fight the Indians and who had just completed a most difficult journey to Blue Mounds. They were weary and wanted a few days to recuperate before undertaking yet another series of forced marches through rough country. Many of their grain-starved horses were lame, and most of their riders seemed in no better condition. "We thought it nothing more than Justice that we should be allowed to Rest a while and let the others take some active part in the war for they had hitherto done nothing," declared James Justice.[31] They even sent petitions to Atkinson demanding time enough to revive their strength, but he ignored their complaints and requests and continued making preparations for crossing the Wisconsin River.

His indifference simply made the volunteers all the more irritated. Furthermore, they were very skeptical about the general's plans and felt the entire expedition could very well become a futile wild-goose chase into the wilderness. Wakefield stated, "There was now more dissatisfaction prevailing than I observed during the whole campaign." Many in the militia, he said, were convinced they "would never again see an Indian" simply because Black Hawk and his band had gained such a huge head start. They were also concerned about traveling through unknown and uncharted country. Without Indian guides, they could become lost in a labyrinth of forests, swamps, and meandering streams.[32] But their weariness and low morale did not make them docile and subdued. In fact, Posey's brigade, already so well known for its lack of discipline and self-restraint, went wild, and Robert Creighton, a local farmer, angrily complained to Atkinson that they had destroyed his crops. They had senselessly ruined "ten acres of oats[,] four acres of corn, one half acre of Wheat, & three quarters of an acre of potatoes," and Creighton demanded compensation for his losses.[33]

Amid all the ruckus and vituperation, Atkinson continued making preparations for the chase. "I deemed it advisable," he later wrote, "to divest myself of all baggage, and select a body of the most efficient men and horses for the final pursuit."[34] Accordingly, all members of the militia with horses judged unfit for the journey were culled out and sent off to Fort Hamilton, and some members of the regular army were also assigned to remain at Helena to guard the baggage wagons and tend to the needs of the sick and wounded who were to be left behind. Once that winnowing of the ranks was completed, Atkinson was left with a force of four hundred regulars and nine hundred militia volunteers. This combined contingent barely equaled the size of a single brigade that had set out from Ottawa thirty-one days before.

The abandoned village of Helena was then quickly dismantled by the troops. Most of its buildings were made of pine timbers and planks, which were taken to be fashioned into rafts. The crossing of the Wisconsin began in the morning of July 27, with men "swimming their horses and carrying their Bagage across on Rafts," noted Justice. By noon the next day everyone was over.[35] The river, although shallow and filled with sandbars, was quite wide at that point, and because the rafts were small, it took considerable time to get everyone and everything across. Atkinson, in a letter to General Winfield Scott, apologized for the "tardiness" but explained that it was "unavoidable."[36]

Once on the other side, no one was sure where to even begin looking for the route taken by the fleeing Indians. But they were lucky. Having traveled only a few miles along the west bank of the river, they simply happened upon the trail. Philip St. George Cooke witnessed the moment of discovery. "Suddenly I saw Colonel D[odge]—who was riding in advance with the General—draw his sword and spur forward with great animation, riding hither thither—gazing on the ground, and uttering unintelligible exclamations," wrote Cooke. Soon Atkinson rode up and joined him. He was delighted.[37] Nineveh Shaw said they "found it about 5 miles up the river, the whoop was then given" and they all set off "at a brisk march."[38] The chase was on and, according to Wakefield, the soldiers were suddenly "not unlike a parcel of hounds after a fox."[39]

They forded the Pine River later the same day and made camp on the opposite bank.[40] In the days that followed, the journey became quite grueling. They entered a region that James Justice described as "one of the most dreadful pieces of Land" he had ever seen, where they penetrated deeper and deeper "into the Recesses of a savage wild of High Hills and low swamps overgrown with heavy timber."[41] The thorny underbrush was so dense in places as to be almost impenetrable, and it scratched the horses' flanks and ripped at men's legs. The many hills, which thrust upward across the land, were described by John Wakefield as "the tallest and steepest mountains" he had ever seen or climbed,[42] and Addison Philleo wrote: "Nothing but a deep ravine, with muddy banks, separated these mountains," and "the woods both upon the top of the highest mountains & at the bottom of the deepest hollows, was the heaviest growth."[43] In many places the men had to dismount and clamber up the slopes grasping at the grass and brush with their hands to keep themselves from tumbling downward to the bottom again.

Not only were the hills a challenge for the men, the entire terrain of the forested uplands was extremely hard on the horses. There was a problem finding proper fodder. For a long time there had been no grain for the horses, but among the hills there was not even much grass. James Justice noted in his diary that among the heavy timber there was nothing for the horses to eat except weeds and the leaves of small trees,[44] and Colonel Albert Sidney Johnston recorded on July 30, "We were compelled to cut small saplings of Maple & Elm for food for our horses which had suffered very much for grass since we entered these mountain forests."[45] At the same time, he observed the infantry soldiers no longer had trouble keeping up with the men on horseback "as the horses were much exhausted for want of food" and plodded along at a very slow pace.[46] On August 1 Nineveh Shaw scribbled in his journal, "Thirty horses gave out and had to be left."[47] Many more would go lame and be abandoned before the army reached the Mississippi.

Wakefield called that region "a lonely and disheartening place,"[48] and Cooke described how they all felt disoriented among its hills and forests: "All were in profound ignorance of our whereabout; as individuals, we were certainly all 'lost'; and perhaps none knew the distance or direction of the nearest point of the Mississippi."[49] Nevertheless, he remarked about how the entire army remained in high spirits throughout the ordeal. They felt certain they were gaining on their prey and would catch Black Hawk's band well before they were able to escape over the Mississippi.[50] "All now were once more satisfied," declared Wakefield, who added, "There was now hope once more of falling in with the enemy—all murmuring again ceased."[51]

That country, so treacherous and mysterious for the soldiers, was much the same for Black Hawk and his people. According to Makauk, a Fox man later interrogated by soldiers, it was Wabokieshiek, the Winnebago Prophet, and two other Winnebago men, who guided them through those unfamiliar hills and valleys. "The Prophet was the principal man who led us from the Wisconsin across to the Mppi. There were Winnebagoes always with us," said Makauk.[52] It seems the Prophet selected the route because it was the most direct way to the Mississippi, and also because it was through territory that would make it difficult for the Americans to find and catch them. Nevertheless, the trek was an extreme ordeal for a group already facing starvation and worn out by the forced march they had kept up since leaving the Lake Koshkonong swamps. Horses went lame and expired, men succumbed to wounds received in the battle on the Wisconsin, and more and more people simply became too weak to carry on. Many fell behind and were abandoned along the trail. Some died. And as the urgency of the flight intensified, people cast aside pots and mats, blankets, and all manner of gear in a frantic effort to pick up the pace. The army was therefore able to track the fugitive band by the debris it left behind, and to ascertain much about the condition of its members from the bodies found along the way. Even on the second day of the pursuit, Colonel Johnston noticed that the Indians were "hard pressed for provisions" and "forced to kill their horses for subsistence."[53]

The same day—July 29—Wakefield remarked that the trail was "strewed with the dead bodies of Indians," most of them of men who had been wounded at Wisconsin Heights.[54] Later, in a letter to his brother Larz, Robert

Anderson reported: "On our march across the country . . . I witnessed scenes of distress and misery exceeding any I ever expected to see in our happy land. Dead bodies males & females strewed along the road—left unburied, exposed—poor—emaciated beings—some dead from wounds recd in the engagement on the Ouisconsin—others by disease. The elms—the Linns along their routes were barked to give them food. Scattered along the route lay vestiges of [horses] tired out by travel—and killed to give life & sustenance to their masters."[55] The Indians were so desperately in need of nourishment that when they "killed a horse for food, there was no vestige of the animal left but the hair," remarked Charles Bracken.[56] All signs made it abundantly evident that the entire band was in severe distress. That, in turn, made the soldiers increasingly confident about their prospects of catching up with the fugitives. Also that day, army scouts captured a Winnebago man, who revealed to them that Black Hawk and his people were still about four days ahead on the trail.[57]

Two days after that, the army finally managed to emerge from the "gloomy forests" and move out onto a "vast high prairie," where there was plenty of lush grass for the horses. "No great change of circumstances ever had a pleasanter effect upon the spirit of an army," exclaimed Lieutenant Cooke.[58] The next day—August 1—they crossed the Kickapoo River. Near there they found an old Sauk man who had been left behind. When interrogated, he told his captors that the main band was not very far ahead, but that it had already reached the Mississippi and intended to cross over the next morning.[59] After hearing this, the army enthusiastically "moved on to complete the work of death upon those unfortunate children of the forest," observed Wakefield.[60]

But the angel of death did not descend upon the Indians alone that tragic summer. It swept westward into the Great Lakes region, moving from Quebec City and Montreal, down into New York, Pennsylvania, and Maryland, and then out into the interior of the continent on troop ships bound for the Black Hawk War. It came as a great cholera plague.

The cholera had already raged for some time throughout Asia and Europe, having devastating effects on places like Paris, where 7,631 people died of the disease in the first two weeks of June. In all it claimed more than an estimated fifty million lives throughout the Old World. Then, in early June, it appeared in Quebec, carried there, it was surmised, by immigrant ships. In Quebec City an average of forty people died each day throughout the month of June, and soon the plague moved on to Montreal. Late that same month, the *Niles' Weekly Register* reported, "The disease was raging in all its terror at Montreal—many died in the streets, after brief but horrid sufferings—death taking place before any medicine could be applied."[61] In fever and pain, violent vomiting and diarrhea, a person could be dead within a matter of a few terrifying hours. On June 15 the Montreal Board of Health revealed there had already been 1,204 reported cases of cholera in the city, 234 of which had been fatal.[62] The death count would go much higher before the plague had run its course. Catherine Parr Traill, an English immigrant on her way to the Lake Ontario region, passed by Montreal later in the summer and observed, "The cholera had made awful ravages, and its devastating effects were to be seen in the darkened dwellings and the mourning habiliments of all classes. . . . In some situations," she went on to say, "whole streets had been nearly depopulated; those who were able fled panic stricken to the country villages, while others remained to die in the bosom of their families."[63]

In what proved to be a futile attempt to keep the disease at bay, New York City prohibited immigrant ships from landing in its port, and upstate cities, such as Albany and Plattsburgh, likewise turned back immigrants coming down from Canada.[64] But, in spite of those efforts, the epidemic somehow seeped in, and during the two weeks ending on July 28, over fourteen hundred people were killed by it in New York City alone.[65] It soon spread to Philadelphia and then down to Baltimore.

While the epidemic was making its way along the East Coast, President Jackson—angry and dissatisfied with Atkinson's handling of the war—decided to make a change in the western command. In orders issued by the War Department on June 15, Major General Winfield Scott was put in charge and directed to go west with all deliberate speed and there find, attack, and destroy all hostile Indians in Illinois and the Michigan Territory, and then carry out whatever military measures he deemed necessary until all warring tribes were effectually subdued.[66] Scott immediately gathered soldiers from forts in the Northeast and assembled an expeditionary force of about a thousand troops, both infantry and artillery, and set out from Buffalo for Chicago in late June. All were packed aboard the steamships *Henry Clay, William Penn, Superior,* and the *Sheldon Thompson.*

By the time they reached Detroit, the plague had erupted among the soldiers on two of those ships. In a letter dated July 15, one unidentified army captain, who eventually reached Chicago, wrote: "We have traveled 600 miles in a steam boat crowded to almost suffocation, and the Asiatic cholera raging amongst us. The scenes on board the boat are not to be described. Men died in six hours after being in perfect health. The steerage was crowded with the dying, and new cases were appearing on the deck."[67]

The epidemic was so severe on the *Superior* and *Henry Clay* that both ships stopped at Fort Gratiot, above Detroit, where the St. Clair River flows from Lake Huron, and all passengers were evacuated before the vessels turned back for Buffalo. The army captain Augustus Walker said that "the disease came so violent and alarming on board the *Henry Clay* that nothing like discipline could be observed . . . [and] as soon as the steamer came to the dock each man sprang on shore, hoping to escape from the scene so terrifying and appalling." The soldiers scattered in all directions, and some headed south for Detroit. "Some fled to the fields, some to the woods, while others lay down in the streets, and under the cover of the river bank, where most of them died unwept and alone," reported Captain Walker.[68]

In a letter from the scene, dated July 16, one writer reported that the dead bodies of soldiers could be seen along the road between Fort Gratiot and Detroit, as well as men suffering from the sickness who would undoubtedly soon die. "A person on his way from Detroit here," said the author, "passed six lying groaning with the agonies of the cholera, under one tree, and saw one corpse by the road side, half eaten by the hogs."[69] The sickness soon reached the city itself. People in Detroit were seized by panic, and John Norvell, a traveler who was there at the time, reported, "The town is almost deserted by its laboring inhabitants; and the countenances of the remaining citizens . . . exhibit marks of unusual depression and melancholy."[70]

Among the troops aboard the *Henry Clay,* three artillery companies under Colonel David Twiggs were particularly hard hit. John Norvell also recorded some observations about what became of those men. "Of the three companies of artillery under colonel Twiggs, and two or three companies of infantry with them, few remain," he remarked on July 12. He then went on to explain that since their landing just below Fort Gratiot "a great number of them have been swept off by the disease. Nearly all the others have deserted. Of the deserters, scattered all over the country, some have died in the woods, and their bodies have been devoured by the wolves."[71] Of the 208 men under the command of Colonel Twiggs, 30 died of cholera on the ship and 155 deserted, and many of those deserters may have also succumbed to the cholera in time.

Carroll Gallagher was a young girl living in Fort Gratiot at the time. Later in life she said she could still vividly recall the soldiers pitifully ill with cholera and "seeing the death cart going around to collect the dead" each day. Her father, Lieutenant Joseph Steel Gallagher, was ordered to take his company to Chicago. At first he planned to go by steamship, but, she stated, "the cholera broke out among his men and no boat would take them." Therefore they had to march across country from Detroit to Chicago, and along the way a number of his soldiers died.[72]

General Scott, himself, continued on from Fort Gratiot into Lake Huron aboard the *Sheldon Thompson,* with four companies of soldiers. For a long time there were no signs of the disease on his ship, but as they approached Mackinac Island, four men showed symptoms of the dreaded sickness. Scott left them on the island and moved on toward Chicago. Everyone on board was "in high health and spirits" when they left Mackinac, but the next morning six more cases were reported. By the end of the day—July 8—fifteen more men had come down with cholera.[73] There was only one surgeon on the *Sheldon Thompson,* and he proved totally inadequate for dealing with the crisis. Scott said the man, "in a panic, gulped down half a wine; went to bed sick, and ought to have died."[74] Although the doctor survived, he was of no help. By the time they reached Chicago on July 10, of the 190 men on board, 80 had the disease, and "twenty odd" had died.[75] According to an anonymous soldier on the *Sheldon Thompson,* some of the dead were "buried" in Lake Michigan, as the ship lay offshore near Chicago. But the water there, "being so clear that their forms could be plainly seen," even at a great depth, that "unwelcome sight created such excitement, working on the superstitious fears of the crew," that the ship had to be moved.[76]

One officer on the *Sheldon Thompson* referred to the ship as a "moving pestilence" and described how he was himself struck down by the disease. They had reached Chicago and had just finished moving the soldiers ashore in small boats, when he was "thrown down on the deck almost as suddenly as if shot," he said. He had felt a growing stiffness in his lower legs but then remarked, "My veins grew cold and my blood curdled." He felt sick to his stomach, his "legs and hands were cramped with violent pain," and he experienced a "violent spasm." "The pain is excruciating," he exclaimed. The doctor gave him eight grains of opium and made him drink a full glass of brandy. In time he recovered.[77]

The *William Penn* finally reached Chicago on July 21. It had come through the plague almost unscathed. Among the four companies of soldiers aboard, there had not been a single case of cholera during the entire voyage. Only after they got ashore did some of them become ill.

At Chicago, Scott turned Fort Dearborn into a hospital and took great care to keep the sick soldiers separated from those who were still well. He also quarantined the entire army, keeping all his men isolated from the civilian population. Medical reports indicate that during the height of the epidemic in Chicago, two hundred cases were admitted to the hospital in a single week, and among those there were fifty-eight deaths. By July 26 the death count stood at two officers and sixty-five enlisted men.[78]

In spite of all General Scott's precautions, the epidemic provoked panic in the town. Scott wrote to Governor Reynolds on July 15 and informed him, "Most of the Inhabitants fled from this place on hearing we had brought the cholera with us."[79] Nevertheless, Scott's efforts to contain the disease must have been somewhat effective for, on July 22, he informed Lewis Cass that only three civilians had died of cholera. Inside the fort it was quite another matter. There, a great many soldiers died, and many more were laid low by the sickness. To prevent complications, the dead had to be disposed of expeditiously. One observer reported that the bodies were buried "without coffins or shrouds, except their blankets, which served as winding sheets, and there left, as it were, without remembrance or a stone to mark their resting place."[80] By early August, however, the grave diggers must have fallen behind in their work. On August 5 James C. Steele wrote in his diary, "Myself and some others went to Shicago for provisions, where I was astonished to see the ded boddys of the soldiers laying along the shore of the Lake, that had died with the chora."[81]

The epidemic prevented Scott from marching off to join Atkinson and taking charge of the war. Attempting that could have proven disastrous. The predicament was summed up well by George Boyd, the Indian agent at Green Bay. In a letter to Governor George Porter of the Michigan Territory, Boyd said he thought it highly inadvisable for Scott to bring his troops anywhere close to Atkinson's forces. "Would not the very rumor of Cholera under such circumstances, drive every militia man from the side of Atkinson?" he asked. Furthermore, he suggested the very risk of spreading the plague might increase the magnitude of the war itself. "Is it not within human probability," he asked the governor, "that Indian Tribes, at present luke-warm & indifferent as to the fate of this War, may not, by Witnessing the ravages made by the disease among our troops—at once and to the man, join the Sacs & Foxes, and raise the Tomhawk against us?"[82] Scott was of the same mind and told Lewis Cass he knew the militia would never allow itself to come anywhere near troops even suspected of carrying cholera. If he ever tried meeting up with Atkinson, it would undoubtedly result in "driving away all his mounted volunteers," he concluded. Even worse, he added, "we may, also, by joining him, infect with the dreaded disease, his regular force, and thus destroy all hope of subduing the hostile Indians for an indefinite period."[83]

So General Scott waited impatiently in Chicago until July 29, when, feeling certain the epidemic had run its course, he set off for Prairie du Chien. By then, however, it was already too late for him to join the campaign.

The various descriptions and discussions of the cholera plague included opinions about what had caused it to spread and who was most likely to catch the loathsome disease and die. Catherine Parr Traill observed that it was "the poorest sort of emigrants" who were most likely to get the sickness, especially those who "indulged in every sort of excess, especially the dangerous one of intoxication."[84] "A very large majority of the deaths at New York by the cholera, had been of persons of the most dissolute habits—prostitutes and confirmed drunkards," reported the *Niles' Weekly Register* in late July.[85] And later that summer, toward the end of August, when the plague erupted again among Scott's soldiers stationed near Rock Island, he told Zachary Taylor he was sure it would not "spread beyond a few drunken and worthless men."[86] It seems that Scott and others believed dissolute personal behavior made people most susceptible to the illness because there was an assumed moral dimension to its causation. Such an assumption convinced those who believed it that people who fell ill and died of cholera had probably brought it upon themselves and therefore deserved what they got.

A similar argument, with all its simpleminded and erroneous moral implications, was likewise applied to the Indians who were fleeing for their lives through the forests of western Wisconsin. Joseph Street had said as much in his speech to the Sioux, when he declared that "if they could not be made good they must be killed."[87]

As Atkinson and his army moved along to carry out their mission of moral retribution, they saw more and more signs of Indian distress. By the time they crossed the Kickapoo River on August 1, they knew they were closing in fast upon their quarry. The old Sauk man they had caught confirmed that. He told them he was certain Black Hawk and his band had already reached the Mississippi and would soon cross over to safety. Cooke, who had come to really despise the Illinois militia, said that once the volunteers "had extracted some information from him," they "then coolly put him to death."[88] Wakefield attempted to justify the cold-blooded killing of that old and defenseless man by asserting that he "deserved to die for the crimes which he had perpetrated, in taking the lives of harmless and unoffending women and children."[89] Guilt by mere association was apparently sufficient; the old man was held responsible for bringing his own death upon himself. That same distorted logic would later be applied to justify the slaughter of defenseless Sauk women and children.

As eager as the soldiers were to press on, they were nevertheless forced to stop for some rest around eight o'clock in the evening. "The horses being nearly broken down, and the men nearly exhausted from fatigue, Gen. Atkinson ordered a halt for a few hours," reported Addison Philleo in the *Galenian*.[90] They made camp in open country about ten miles from the Mississippi.

As they bedded down on the grassy prairie west of the Kickapoo River, Atkinson's army had no notion that the annihilation of the Black Hawk band had already commenced late that same afternoon.

Soon after the band had reached the east bank of the Mississippi, they heard and then saw a steamboat churning down toward them from out of the north. That disturbed them greatly, but Black Hawk said he told his men not to shoot. "I intended going on board," he later stated, "so that we might save our women and children."[91] He knew the captain—Captain Joseph Throckmorton—and because he intended to give himself up, Black Hawk waited until the *Warrior* drew near and then he took a small piece of white cotton cloth, put it on a pole, and called out to Throckmorton to send in a small boat so he could row out and surrender. Kish-kas-shoi, a thirty-five-year-old mixed Sauk-Fox woman, and the niece of Quashquame, said she was right beside Black Hawk when the *Warrior* pulled into sight. According to her testimony, Black Hawk said to the women, "Run and get me the white flag. I will go on board that boat"; at the same time, he instructed the men to put down their guns and the women and children to get behind trees. As the steamboat got close, Kish-kas-shoi said that Black Hawk waved his arms and shouted out quite loudly, "I am Black Hawk—and I wish to come and shake hands with you." She also reported that he had told the women, "Don't run—I will save you and the children by going on board and giving myself up."[92] Ana-kose-kuk, a middle-aged Kickapoo woman, corroborated Kish-kas-shoi's account, describing how Black Hawk, who she said took "pity on the women and children," had "sent for the white flag, and appeared to be very anxious to go to the steam boat to shake hands."[93]

Throckmorton later recounted how he had been returning from a visit to a Sioux village about 120 miles north of Prairie du Chien, when suddenly he and his passengers came upon a large group of Indians on the east bank of the river. The sighting occurred about two miles below where the Bad Axe River joins the Mississippi. "As we neared them, they raised a white flag," recalled Throckmorton, who said he already knew from information he had received from the Sioux that the Indians on the bank were members of the Black Hawk band. But, regardless of the white flag, Throckmorton admitted he was suspicious of their behavior and distrustful of their intentions. In fact, he saw the waving of the white flag as an attempt to "decoy" them into a trap and remarked that he was "a little too old" to fall for such a trick. Therefore, taking caution not to get his ship too close to the Indians, he dropped anchor near midstream and told the Indians to send someone out in a boat to parley with him. But they had no boat, and thus no one went out to talk. Assuming his invitation had been rejected, and after waiting about fifteen minutes so the Indians could "remove a few of their women and children," Throckmorton opened fire with his six-pound cannon and "a severe fire of musketry." The Indians returned the fire, and both sides battled on for more than an hour. Then, with night fast approaching, and the *Warrior* running low on wood for its boilers, Captain Throckmorton weighed anchor and headed for Prairie du Chien.[94]

Reuben Holmes, a West Point graduate and a colonel with the Illinois militia, was aboard the *Warrior* that day with Lieutenant James Kingsbury, who was in charge of a fifteen-man squad of regular soldiers from Fort Crawford. In a letter to General Atkinson, Holmes described how they had come upon the Indians and how their interpreter had told them the Indians on shore had identified themselves as Winnebago. Black Hawk later denied this, claiming that when asked whether they were "Sacs or Winnebagoes," he had instructed a Winnebago man who was with him to tell the whites they were Sauk.[95] Indeed, Wee-sheet, a thirty-five-year-old Sauk chief with the band, testified there was a man on the *Warrior* who spoke the Winnebago language and loudly asked who they were and if Black Hawk was with them. The Winnebago Prophet's nephew responded, clearly stating in Winnebago that Black Hawk was there and wished to surrender to the whites.[96] But there must have been confusion among the Americans about what was said, for Holmes explained they remained uncertain of the situation until "at last assured they were the hostile Sauks by a woman on board who knew their language." Holmes also indicated he saw two white flags raised by the Indians but, like Throckmorton, he and the other people on the boat remained "suspicious of their appearance & intentions." The unarmed Indians on the bank, he surmised, positioned themselves "apparently to cover the movements of some in the rear who could be seen preparing their guns & selecting trees to cover them." Everyone on the *Warrior* assumed the Indians were simply stalling for time as they set their trap, and so, rather than waiting to be caught in it, they opened fire.[97]

In the exchange of gunfire, a retired soldier from Fort Snelling aboard the *Warrior* was wounded in the knee,[98] and Throckmorton claimed that twenty-three Indians were killed and numerous others wounded.[99] The number of dead was later confirmed by a female Indian prisoner, who stated that "23 were buried in one place."[100]

Even before the grapeshot from the *Warrior*'s six-pounder ripped through those beleaguered refugees that early August afternoon, other members of the band were being killed on the lower Wisconsin River. After the Battle of Wisconsin Heights, hundreds of women and children, as well as a few men—all those without horses strong enough to make the demanding overland trek to the Mississippi—attempted to make their way down the Wisconsin River in crude, hurriedly made elm bark canoes. The day after the battle, Dodge had sent an express message to Captain Gustavus Loomis, the commander at Fort Crawford, informing him that some of the Sauk were heading downriver, and encouraging him to put a fieldpiece and some troops near the mouth of the Wisconsin to prevent any of them from escaping across the Mississippi.[101] Loomis acted on the suggestion and three days later informed Dodge he had anchored a large flatboat, with a six-pound cannon and twenty-five soldiers on board, at midstream near the mouth of the Wisconsin and had also sent another eight soldiers upriver to the ferry crossing.[102] Second Lieutenant Joseph Ritner was put in charge of those operations.

The trip down the Wisconsin was a disaster for most of the Indian people who attempted it. According to one woman survivor, "many canoes were upset and others sank—they were only Elm Bark stripped off & tied at each end—and a great many children were drowned, as there were few men along to save them."[103]

Sometime after midnight, July 29, Lieutenant Ritner and his men, waiting on the flatboat, heard and then saw "several canoes filled with Indians" attempting to slip past them in the darkness. "The Indians appeared to be all naked and painted warriors," Ritner stated in his report. The soldiers fired the cannon and opened up with their muskets. Some of the Indians fell into the water, but Ritner admitted it was difficult to see what was actually happening because of "the darkness, flashes, and smoke." However, he felt confident they had got them all, thus thwarting the Indians' attempts to escape.[104]

The following day, a soldier killed an Indian on the island above the ferry crossing and reported seeing "many fresh tracks of Women and children on the island."[105] The steamboat *Enterprise*, outfitted with a cannon, was sent to patrol up and down the Wisconsin, while bands of Winnebago and Menominee warriors were sent out to hunt down any Sauk refugees who may have gone ashore. The Indian mercenaries searched the riverbanks and woods by day and then at night by torchlight, and soon began returning with fresh scalps and prisoners. "The prisoners are the most miserable looking poor creatures you can imagine. Wasted to mere skeletons, clothed in rags scarcely sufficient to hide their nakedness. Some of the children look as if they had starved so long they could not be restored," reported Joseph Street to William Clark.[106] By August 8, the *Galenian* informed its readers that the operations on the lower Wisconsin had

"resulted in about 34 prisoners, 50 killed, chiefly women and children."[107]
Many more members of the band, too fearful of falling into the hands of
their enemies, undoubtedly remained hidden in the swamps and forests
along the river where they, too, likely died of hunger and exposure.

While Winnebago and Menominee warriors hunted the forested flood-
plain of the lower Wisconsin for those unfortunate people, Loomis and
Street called upon the Winnebago and Sioux villages farther up the Mississippi for help with the destruction of the main Sauk band. On July 30
Lieutenant James Kingsbury was sent upriver on the *Warrior* to confer
with the Winnebago chief Win-o-shec, at his village on the Black River.
After doing so, Kingsbury went all the way to Wabashaw's Sioux village on
the west side of the Mississippi, at Prairie aux Ailes. The Winnebago were
told to get themselves out of the path of the war and to bring all their
canoes down to Prairie du Chien.[108] They agreed, and as a result, Street
informed Clark, "the Sacs & Foxes . . . were cut off from any means of
crossing except on rafts, and two or three old canoes which were scarcely
able to float empty."[109] When Kingsbury met with the Sioux and informed
them that the Black Hawk band would try to get over the Mississippi, they
agreed "to stop their crossing until the army could come up with them."
Almost immediately, noted Loomis, a war party of about 150 Sioux warriors
started downriver in a flotilla of canoes and sped past the *Warrior,* which
had been pulled up about ten or fifteen miles above the Bad Axe River to
have its boilers scraped.[110]

In the early evening of August 1, soon after their clash with the *Warrior,*
Black Hawk urged his people to begin crossing the Mississippi. Some
commenced doing so right away and got safely over before darkness
descended. But according to Pama-ho, another Sauk chief with the band,
Black Hawk had previously argued strongly in favor of all of them going
together "up the river among the Winnebagoes." However, said Pama-ho,
"a great many would not listen to him, and plunged into the water to get
across."[111] Then, after dark, reported the Kickapoo warrior E-kish-kuk,
"B[lack] Hawk started off with the Prophet the night of the battle of the
steam boat, and he had not seen him since."[112] The young Sauk chief
Wee-sheet also mentioned Black Hawk's departure and said the old leader
had spoken with the chiefs before leaving and told them he would "go to
the head waters of the Wisconsin" and there hide himself "in the marshes
and thick woods."[113] In his own account, Black Hawk said that he

"intended going into the Chippewa country."[114] But no matter what Black Hawk's plans or intentions may have been, Wee-sheet made it clear how the band reacted to his running out on them: "None of us liked the Prophet and Black Hawk leaving us as they did. We said 'now they have brought us to ruin and lost us our women and children, they have run to save their own lives.'"[115] Neapope had already deserted them before the Battle of Wisconsin Heights, and with the departure of both Black Hawk and Wabokieshiek, all the leaders who had instigated the band's April return to east side of the Mississippi were gone. The people were abandoned to whatever fate might befall them.

That same night, about ten miles inland from the Mississippi, a bugle was sounded in the two o'clock darkness. Atkinson and part of his army were soon up and preparing to move out. Before taking their rest, the general had instructed all the troops to be prepared for that call to action, but apparently neither Alexander's nor Henry's brigades had heard the order or listened to what had been said. They had turned their horses loose to graze. As a result, observed Colonel Johnston, "they could not therefore get in readiness to move before it was light enough to distinguish their horses."[116] The rest of the troops did not wait. They set off without them, with Dodge's men forming the vanguard.

After traveling just a few miles, contact was made with the Indians. It happened about an hour after sunrise.[117] A small party of Dodge's scouts, under the command of Captain Joseph Dickson from Platteville, who had gone out ahead, suddenly came rushing back to report that the Indians not only were close at hand but were drawn up and prepared to fight. Dodge ordered Dickson to return to the scene and "to reconnoiter the enemy & occupy his attention" while the main force readied itself for battle. Upon their return, Dickson's men engaged the Indians in a brief skirmish and killed eight of them.[118]

By then Alexander's and Henry's troops were beginning to catch up. It had taken them an hour or more to find their horses, but once they were saddled up, said Nineveh Shaw, "we put spurs to our horses and pursued with all possible speed." Unfortunately for some, by the time they were getting close to Atkinson and the others, some of their long-abused horses were going lame, and Shaw stated, "We jumped off pulled off our saddles & baggage stripped off our coats and commenced running with all speed."[119] By then the rest of the troops had dismounted as well, and

Atkinson was arranging them for the anticipated battle. At the center of the formation were the 380 regulars under Taylor, along with Dodge's 150 men. Posey and Alexander were put to the right of them, and Henry to the left. They advanced in good order into the forest and soon sighted the river. Lieutenant Cooke noted that a heavy fog hung over the Mississippi "rising white as snow in the sunshine." It was about eight o'clock on "a bright rosy summer morn," and the soldiers were eager for battle.[120]

Fear must have gripped the people of the Sauk band once they became aware that their pursuers had finally overtaken them. They were caught— the broad, mist-covered river before them and more than a thousand, heavily armed soldiers moving in from where the sun still shone low among the trees. It must have seemed like some terrible dream, or like the end of the journey each soul takes after death. Upon dying, they believed, the soul undertook a long journey to the west, along the White River (the Milky Way) until reaching a great river flowing north to south. That river had to be traversed in order to enter the Afterworld, and the only way across was upon a long log guarded by the fierce doglike creature Pokitapawa, the "Brain Taker." At the approach of each new soul, Pokitapawa barked and howled, and the soul had to be swift and agile to make it past the Brain Taker's vicious teeth and knife-sharp claws, onto the log and over into the land of eternal feasting and joy that awaited beyond the water. The images of all that must have seemed far too real that morning to those weary and frightened people, caught between the Mississippi and an entire army of brain takers closing in on them from the forest.[121]

Some women were hurriedly making rafts, while many more sought hiding places with their children in the tall grass and dense underbrush. Others, including many men, plunged into the river intending to swim to the opposite bank.[122] Back among the trees, above the river, there was gunfire. Warriors of the rear guard, trying to buy time for the people on the bank, resisted and then fell back, and did so numerous times, retreating toward the river, where, said Wakefield, they eventually "sought refuge in their main army" and "joined in a body to defend themselves, and sell their lives as dear as possible."[123]

Before reaching the riverbank, some of the warriors tried to divert the army away from where the women and children had congregated. "The troops . . . in advancing had been drawn considerably to the right of the trail in following the movements of the retiring enemy," observed

Johnston. He also pointed out that Atkinson, "apprehending this to be a feint to divert him from his purpose & gain time," made some needed adjustments.[124] Henry was ordered to move straight ahead on the main trail all the way to the river, while Alexander and Posey were sent upriver to prevent the Indians from breaking out and fleeing away in that direction.[125]

Lieutenant Cooke indicated that the main force of the "enemy was driven across several sluices down the river bottom, which was covered with fallen timber, underwood, and high grass."[126] To get down there, the soldiers had to descend the steep bluffs that lined the river. Taylor said his regulars went down a "precipice so steep that the men were compelled to use their hands and Guns to aid them in their descent."[127] Henry and his men were the first to make it down and open the attack. On the river flats, among the fallen trees and tall grass, said Wakefield, "they all joined in the work of death."[128] And what happened then, Daniel Parkinson declared, was "more a massacre than a battle."[129]

Once Henry commenced the fight, Dickson and his scouts thrust themselves into the thick of the struggle. Shortly after that, Dodge, along with the regulars and some of Posey's men, made it down the bluff and joined in the killing.[130] There was some hard and brutal fighting. "Sloughs, deep ravines, old logs etc. were so plentiful as to afford every facility for the enemy to make a strong defense," reported Philleo. But the soldiers kept pushing them back toward the river.[131] John Fonda, from Mineral Point, witnessed some of what took place from the deck of the *Warrior,* which returned to the scene of the previous day's bloodletting once the fog had lifted. Fonda said he saw an old Indian with five sons crouched behind a fallen log, from where they were firing upon the regulars with lethal results. "The old man loaded the guns as fast as his sons discharged them, and at each shot a man fell," wrote Fonda. Dodge and his men soon caught sight of them and moved swiftly to take care of the problem. They rushed down the bluff, their muskets flashing in the smoke-filled air, and soon enough "each of the braves was shot down and scalped by the wild volunteers," Fonda remarked with enthusiastic approval.[132]

The Indians kept retreating, said Colonel Johnston, "disputing the ground step by step,"[133] and as they got closer to the riverbank the slaughter grew more frenzied. Concerning all that, Black Hawk declared, "Our braves, but few in number, finding that the enemy paid no regard to age or sex, and seeing that they were murdering helpless women and children, determined to fight until they were killed."[134] In an account printed in the *Niles' Weekly Register* it was pointed out how, as the Indians were pushed to the brink of the water, "men, women, and children were seen mixed together, in such a manner as to render it difficult to kill one, and save the other."[135] Lieutenant Cooke, who felt genuine sympathy for the women and children who were gunned down that day, said he hoped they were the unintended victims of random shots. However, he quickly added, "But it is certain that the frontiersman is not particular, when his blood is up, and a redskin [is] in his power."[136] Robert Anderson explained why the killing of Indian women was often unavoidable and sometimes even deserved. In a letter to his brother Larz he pointed out that because they were "fighting with an enemy who concealed themselves in the high grass and behind logs and the banks of the ravines and rivers—whose positions are designated by the flash and report of their guns [—] individual safety required that our fire should be directed to every point where an Indian appeared." And besides that, he declared to his brother, the Indian "women urged their warriors to an opposition to the U. States telling them 'that the warriors had become women and were no longer men.'" Furthermore, he claimed, some soldiers "were wounded by the squaws." Therefore, regarding the killing of Indian women, he concluded, "We may think it less to be regretted than under other circumstances."[137] In effect, they had brought it upon themselves and deserved to die.

At the same time, however, there are numerous indications that the killing of Indian women was sometimes quite cold-blooded and malicious. At one point in the battle, a young Indian woman, thought to have been about nineteen years old, arose from the high grass holding her little daughter in her arms. She was clearly unarmed and defenseless, but one of the soldiers—probably Abadiah Rittenhouse of Dickson's scouts—shouldered his musket and deliberately shot her down. The musket ball hit the child in the right arm, above the elbow, severely shattering the bone, and then penetrated the young woman's breast, killing her instantly.[138] It was also reported that Joseph Dickson, himself, quite deliberately shot an Indian woman who had fallen to her knees before him and begged for her life.[139]

Even Indian children, of no threat whatsoever to their attackers, were sometimes deliberately murdered. Amid the noise and chaos of the battle, a frightened little boy jumped out from his hiding place and ran for his life. As he did so, a volunteer named John House, who was also one of Dickson's scouts, was ordered by his commander to shoot the young boy down. "He did so and sent the bullet through his head," and then, almost immediately, reloaded his musket, took aim at another child, and, according to one eyewitness, "blew the top of his head off."[140] John House was apparently unusually coldhearted with regard to the Indian children. Later the same day, a Sauk woman, hoping to save her infant, tied the baby to a large piece of cottonwood bark and set it adrift in the river. According to one account: "The current carried the child near the bank, when House coolly loaded his rifle, and taking deliberate aim, shot the babe dead. Being reproached for his hardened cruelty, he grimly replied, 'kill the nits, and you'll have no lice'."[141] John Wakefield, the surgeon's mate and scout, was less hardhearted and even admitted "it was a horrid sight to witness little children, wounded and suffering the most excruciating pain." All the same, he did not refrain from mentioning that, like their parents, they "were the savage enemy, and the common enemy of the country."[142]

Along with the killing, there was a great deal of scalping done by men eager to carry home tangible evidence of their own bloody deeds against the hated savages. The English traveler Charles Latrobe, who was morally repulsed by the indiscriminate slaughter near the Bad Axe River, claimed that among members of the militia "scalp-taking was a subject of pride."[143] But some of Dodge's men went even beyond that in the taking of their trophies. John Fonda witnessed them killing Indians and then "cutting two parallel gashes down their backs[; they] would [then] strip the skin from the quivering flesh, to make razor straps of."[144]

Eventually the struggling Indians were forced into the river, where, as Street told Clark, the water became "tinged with the blood of the Indians who were shot on its margin & in the stream."[145] While some were being gunned down on the bank, Addison Philleo noted, "hundreds of men, women, and children plunged into the river, and hoped by diving, etc. to escape the bullets of our guns; very few, however, escaped our sharp shooters."[146] All of that became much worse once the *Warrior* got in on the action. Fonda described some of what took place then: "Some of the Indians, naked to the breech-cloth, slid down into the water, where they laid, with only their mouth and nostrils above the surface." Nevertheless, "by running the boat close in to the east shore, our Monomonees were enabled to make the water too hot for them." As a consequence, "one after another, they jumped up, and were shot down, in attempting to gain cover on the bank above."[147]

Some Indians did manage to escape, at least temporarily, to small islands in the middle of the river. The soldiers, however, were determined to deny them any refuge whatsoever. One group of regulars simply jumped into the water and waded over to the nearest of those willow-draped islands. In the vicious fight that ensued, the Indians were once again shot down or driven back into the river. But in conducting their cruel business there, the soldiers suffered a few casualties of their own. Five were killed and others seriously wounded.[148] Once the *Warrior* came close to shore, Taylor and another group of regulars, along with two companies of volunteers, went aboard. The steamboat moved out into the river, where it closed in and raked one of the islands with grapeshot from its cannon. Street told Clark, in a tone of grim gleefulness, that as the cannon rumbled and fired, Indian horses and men "fell like grass before the scythe."[149] Once the thunder of the cannon ceased and the smoke ascended into the air, Taylor and his troops went ashore. Lieutenant Cooke was a member of one of those landing parties. Once on the island, they searched high and low for Indians who might have survived the flying fragments of the lethal cannon barrages, but managed to find only two Indian men who had climbed a tree to get above the killing artillery fire. Once the volunteers sighted them, the situation soon came to resemble a hunting scene in which the quarry was treed and all the hunters pointed their guns skyward and blasted into the branches. "I saw them drop from limb to limb, clinging—poor fellows— like squirrels," wrote Cooke.[150]

In spite of all the soldiers did or tried to do, some members of the Black Hawk band made it across the Mississippi. Indeed, the water was full of Indian ponies thrashing about in panic, with men, women, and children trying to cling to them.[151] Among them was a young Sauk woman by the name of Na-me-sa. She said that once she and her baby were in the water "she kept her infant close in her blanket by the force of her teeth— seized a horse's tail, and got across the Mississippi."[152] According to Spencer, Wishita, another young mother, crossed over "on a pony, carrying a child about a year old before her,"[153] and E-kish-kuk, a young Kickapoo man, later testified that he "got across holding on to the mane of his horse."[154] According to Wee-sheet, the Sauk chief, who also managed to make it safely to the west bank, "more than 200 men, women, and children got across the M[ississi]ppi." But many more were killed or drowned in the attempt, and less than half the survivors were men, he added.[155] The day after the battle, the Indian agent Joseph Street, who was on the *Warrior,* observed a great many lifeless bodies of Indians and horses floating upon the water, being borne downstream by the current.[156]

After the battle, the soldiers rounded up the survivors still on the east bank. Women and children were flushed out of their hiding places in the tall grass and underbrush. Also, as Wakefield explained, "some had buried themselves in the mud and sand in the bank of the river, just leaving enough of their heads out to breath the breath of life."[157] They were rooted out and taken prisoner, but as one soldier who participated in that roundup later admitted: "We killed everything that didn't surrender."[158] The Indian prisoners were all women and children, and both Atkinson and Johnston reported there were just forty of them.[159] (There were actually only thirty-nine.) If, in fact, the size of the Black Hawk band had been well over a thousand people when it set out in early April (and some estimates put the number closer to two thousand),[160] then the fact that only thirty-nine women and children remained after the Battle of Bad Axe suggests a horrendous rate of attrition had occurred along the journey and that the battle itself was a work of mass slaughter. Yet all officials on the scene put the number of Indians killed in the actual fighting at a very modest body count of 150.[161] In most cases, however, they qualified their statements, as in Atkinson's report to Scott, in which he admitted, "The precise number could not be ascertained as a large proportion were slain in endeavouring to swim to the Islands."[162] In his account of the battle, Captain Henry Smith, another eyewitness participant, also referred to the figure of 150 Indian dead but went on to assert that "doubtlessly many more were killed in the river and elsewhere, whose bodies were never seen afterwards."[163] Just how many Indians actually died in the massacre will never be known, but what was clearly a bloodbath for them resulted in an extremely low casualty count for the Americans. While Wakefield, Philleo, and Nineveh Shaw all claimed there were twenty-seven American casualties (five killed and twenty-two wounded), Atkinson set the total at just twenty-four (five killed—all regulars—nineteen wounded), and Albert Sidney Johnston recorded just twenty-two.[164]

When the shooting ceased, Cooke reported seeing a "stray dentist from the East" prowling the battlefield, where he "gathered a rich harvest of teeth taken from the dead Indians."[165] Even in death there was no escaping the predatory greed of white people.

For some Indians, the dying went on well beyond that awful afternoon. Two days later, near the mouth of the Wisconsin River, Captain Glendower Price led a party of fifteen mounted militia volunteers from Cassville in an attack upon a group of Sauk refugees who had come downriver. They killed five or six and took six prisoners.[166] At the same time, the Winnebago and Menominee continued to hunt for Sauk stragglers along the Wisconsin, and did so with some success.[167] Meanwhile, on the other side of the Mississippi, it was the Sioux who eagerly pursued the surviving remnants of Black Hawk's band. The war party of about 150 Sioux warriors from Wabashaw's village tracked them deep into the territory of eastern Iowa. The Sauk fugitives may have numbered as many as two hundred people[168] and Na-me-sa and Wishita, the two women who had got over the Mississippi with their babies, were part of that group. Fearing the viciousness of the Sioux, they traveled fast, moving by both night and day. But on the seventh day of their flight, the Sioux caught up to them and fell violently upon their camp at sunrise. Wishita said they had spent the night in a valley and that it was a foggy morning. They were just preparing to resume their travels when suddenly, without warning, "the Sioux with great noise, whooping and yelling, broke into the camp, killing large numbers of them regardless of age or sex."[169] Both she and Na-me-sa managed to escape on horseback, but it had been a very close call. Most of those they left behind were killed. Makauk, a Fox brave with the group, said there might have been as many as eighty men in their party, but only about thirty survived the Sioux attack. "All the rest were killed completely," he said.[170] Street received a message from the Sioux, who said they tracked the Sauk for about 120 miles and finally overtook them at dawn near the juncture of the Cedar and Little Cedar rivers. They claimed the Sauk put up no fight at all but simply scattered in all directions. The Sioux boasted that they had killed two hundred of them and took another twenty-two prisoner. Street felt sure they were exaggerating for they brought back only sixty-eight scalps. Zachary Taylor thought so too. But no matter what the actual number of dead may have been, it was evident that those who had pursued the Sauk survivors were intent upon their extermination.[171]

During the heat of the battle below the Bad Axe, there were many indications that the soldiers—especially the "citizen-soldiers" of the militia—reveled in the massacring of the Indians. There had always been an eagerness among them for the killing of Indians, and whenever the possibility of doing so arose, their morale improved and their interest in the campaign increased. Fear, hatred, and imagination combined to convince them that the native people were the mortal enemies to all they held dear, and encountering those adversaries surely must have stirred up within them fantasies about the glories of battle. They also hoped that fighting Indians would provide them the opportunity to do brave deeds that would affirm and magnify their manliness. They rode on with heroic delusions, thinking of themselves as the protectors of the weak and defenders of the right, while, at the same time, they dehumanized and, indeed, demonized the Indian people. Most of the militiamen undoubtedly agreed with John Wakefield, who characterized the natives as being "like the wild beasts more than men," and asserted that by killing them they were "fast getting rid of those demons in human shape."[172] Furthermore, Wakefield may have spoken for virtually all of the volunteers when he summed up his feelings about the Battle of Bad Axe: "I must confess that it filled my heart with gratitude and joy, to think that I had been instrumental, with many others, in delivering my country from those merciless savages, and restoring those people [of the frontier region] again to their peaceful homes and firesides."[173]

The dehumanization of Indians and the entire "metaphysics of Indian hating"[174] made it easy and even enjoyable to slaughter native people—even women and children—and offered a ready-made moral justification for doing so. But the act of killing itself—the frenzied and ecstatic shedding of blood and the mutilating of bodies—set loose what the GI philosopher J. Glenn Gray referred to as the "monstrous desire for annihilation," which, he claimed, lurks within the darkness of every man and drives them to storm against their enemies "as if they are seized by a demon and are no longer in control of themselves."[175] It was that deep, disturbing, primal passion which emerged along the marshy riverbanks to turn the battlefield south of the Bad Axe River into a hellish place of murderous rage, where the winds of destruction howled. Such passions transformed especially the men of the militia into wanton killers every bit as diabolical as the imagined devils they so eagerly sought to destroy.

The savage intensity of that experience was also a manifestation of fears the men carried into combat. Concerning that, and the whole orgy of brutality that day, Charles Latrobe observed, "The cruelty of many of the militia toward the poor Indian when once in their power, was only to be matched by the fear which they showed at meeting the enemy."[176] Their fear soon mixed with rage, and then their very body chemistry changed. Hearts beat faster, respiration deepened and intensified, muscles tightened and grew instantly stronger, men became euphoric on their own adrenaline, and the almost palpable scent of testosterone drifted over the killing field. They were swept up into the ecstasy of battle.

Perhaps some of what happened that day could even be attributed to the revolutionary rage that had created the nation and led to its embittered rejection of the old identity. At the very core of the new identity, which afterward emerged, was a love of freedom and a glorification of violence that inspired a collective enthusiasm for republicanism and a driving desire for imperial expansion. It was a conflicted vision, producing an inner clash of contrary values, which was greatly magnified by the mass migration of people into the trans-Appalachian West after the War of 1812. There, between the old mountains and the Mississippi, that love of freedom and glorification of violence became highly exaggerated among the white inhabitants, who were the colonists of the Republic's internal empire. To them, violence seemed the prerequisite for their own freedom, and, as with imperialism in any place or time, it was an essential means of gaining possession of land and resources that were not rightly theirs. Beyond that, for the men of the trans-Appalachian West, bothered by nagging feelings of inferiority when compared to the people and culture back East, violence became an important measure of their manliness and a means of achieving superiority over at least the loathsome savages of the land.

For all those reasons, there should be little surprise about the slaughter that took place in the Battle of Bad Axe. What may be surprising, however, was the restraint and even compassion demonstrated toward the native victims by some of the American participants in the events of that day.

Philip St. George Cooke felt a sense of pathos for them all and regarded the entire war as an "ungracious errand" against a people who seemed "destined to atone in blood" only because they were guilty of loving their homeland far too much.[177] In numerous other cases, there were men that day who showed particular concern for the women and children caught in the tragic events which were not of their own making. Albert Sidney Johnston, for one, wrote in his diary about the devastating musket fire inflicted upon the Indians, killing "unfortunately some women & children which was much deplored by the soldiers."[178] Robert Anderson also lamented the death of the innocent and told his brother "the loss of squaws and children gives great cause of regret."[179] Even John Wakefield wrote almost apologetically about how Indian women and children, hiding in the grass, were unfortunately killed "contrary to the wish of every man, as neither officer nor private intended to have spilt the blood of those squaws and children."[180] Also, after the roundup of Sauk refugees along the lower Wisconsin River valley, Captain Loomis said it gave him "much gratification to state that those miserable beings [had] generally been received and treated with humanity" by the soldiers at Fort Crawford, declaring, "We war not with women and children."[181]

During the battle itself, Cooke intervened to protect a young Indian woman. He later wrote, "I rescued a little red Leila, whom I found in very uncomfortable circumstances . . . and I sent her by a safe hand to the rear."[182] When the battle was nearly over, Robert Anderson walked over to where a dead Indian woman had collapsed upon her own child. The child's arm had been badly wounded, and the little girl remained trapped beneath the dead weight of her mother. The *Galenian* reported, "Anderson went to the spot and took from under the dead mother her wounded daughter, & brought it to the place . . . selected for dressing wounds, and placed it there for surgical aid." The little girl was given a hard brisket to gnaw upon while a surgeon amputated her arm. She was cared for, and she survived.[183] Wakefield also wrote, "As soon as the battle was over, all the wounded were collected in one place, and with those of our enemy, were examined, and their wounds dressed; there was no difference here between our men and our enemy."[184] Street also took pity on the prisoners handed over to him by the Winnebago and Menominee search parties. He told Clark, "I shall endeavor to save the women & children if I can." He gave them food, covered their nakedness, and tried to restore their strength and health.[185]

Such acts of humanity may have been too few, but they were signs of something positive and good amid all the pain and death and brutality of the final ugly spasms of the war. In almost all cases, what compassion was shown came from members of the regular army, and most frequently from its officers, rather than from the volunteers among the ranks of the militia. That may have been mostly a matter of discipline. For, unlike the overeager and excitable amateurs, who wasted provisions and too quickly lost heart when facing hardship, the soldiers of the regular army—certainly no better men to begin with than most of those in the militia—were taught and trained, drilled and conditioned, to remain coolheaded under pressure and self-disciplined in the face of danger. Most of all, they had learned through hard lessons how to control their own fear and rage, and to value collective order over personal freedom. For them, imagination and insecurity were not allowed to become the dominant forces driving their actions. And perhaps because of that, the dark and primal impulses and the "monstrous desire for annihilation" did not achieve ascendancy. That may have been why they did not take scalps or cut the skin from men's backs for razor straps, and why they lamented the suffering of children, the wanton slaughter of women, and sometimes reached out to help the wounded and feed the hungry, even when those who suffered and hungered were Indians. In that plain stuff of discipline and self-control appeared the possibilities of something noble.

EPILOGUE

Memory believes before knowing remembers. Believes longer than recollects, longer than knowing ever wonders.

William Faulkner, *Light in August*

ONCE THE SOUNDS of gunfire stopped echoing among the high bluffs of the broad Mississippi Valley and desperate people ceased thrashing about in the water, the soldiers set about bringing the cruel chaos of battle to an orderly conclusion. Their passions spent, armed men, smelling of gun smoke, deliberately went about the business of rounding up prisoners, counting the dead, and getting the wounded to dressing stations above the riverbank. By late afternoon it was all over. What had begun as a defiant attempt in early April by Black Hawk and his followers to return home, to the very center of their world, and thereby save themselves from cultural extinction, had ended in unmitigated tragedy, which few survived. And on the eve of their destruction, Black Hawk had abandoned them to certain slaughter.

In an act of undisguised self-interest, Black Hawk, Wabokieshiek, and their families, along with Chakeepashipaho, Little Stabbing Chief, and perhaps as many as twenty-five others, deserted what was left of the British Band soon after sunset, following the lethal afternoon encounter with the steamboat *Warrior.* They made their way northeastward through Winnebago country toward the headwaters of the La Crosse River and eventually established a clandestine camp on Day-nik (Little Lake), a short distance southwest of present-day Tomah, Wisconsin. There they remained concealed by dense forest until inadvertently discovered by a Winnebago traveler named Hishoog-ka, returning home from a journey to the east. Soon after arriving back at his own village near the mouth of the La Crosse River, Hishoog-ka told his village chief, Karayjasaip-ka, what he had discovered. A council was held, and it was soon decided to send a delegation of three men, including Chasjaka (the Wave), Wabokieshiek's own brother, to Black Hawk's encampment to persuade the old warrior to give himself up and end his struggle with the Americans. The arrival of those messengers caused considerable consternation in the Sauk camp, and initially Black Hawk and the others adamantly vowed to never give up their fight. In time, however, they reluctantly smoked the calumet and agreed to return to Karayjasaip-ka's village. There they received a cordial welcome, but after only a few days, Black Hawk turned over his sacred medicine bag to the Winnebago chief for safekeeping and set off with Wabokieshiek for Prairie du Chien, intending to surrender to Joseph Street.[1]

When Black Hawk and the Prophet presented themselves at the Indian agent's house an hour before noon, on Monday, August 27, 1832, it was as if they had materialized out of nowhere. Once they were in custody, Street jubilantly declared, "The Indian War is over!"[2]

Certainly the armed violence of it all was at an end, but the contest for public opinion and for how the war would be remembered was only just beginning. According to the historian Jill Lepore, "How wars are remembered can be just as important as how they are fought and first described."[3] And in Black Hawk's case, from the time of his surrender to Street down to the hour of his death at age seventy-two in October of 1838, he waged a vigorous campaign to win that aspect of his struggle with the Americans after having lost everything else on the battlefield. Although so much of what happened in the war had been the unanticipated consequences of error, indecision, and happenstance, Black Hawk nevertheless made every effort to assign meaning and purpose to the tragic events in a manner that rehabilitated his reputation and vindicated his actions.

His surrender to Street was high drama in which he replayed some scenes very similar to those of Red Bird's capitulation to Major Whistler five years before. While in the Winnebago village, Black Hawk had had the women make him a special outfit, and when he presented himself at Prairie du Chien, Street said he "appeared, in a full dress of white tanned Deer-skins," fringed at the seams, and for all who witnessed the event it "was a moment of much interest."[4] Black Hawk was dignified, looking as a warrior ought to look, and one reporter described the famous Sauk leader as being of modest stature with a bristling scalp-lock of gray hair on the crown of his otherwise clean-shaven head, and appearing "much dejected," while still clearly assuming "the aspect of command." Wabokieshiek, by contrast, showed none of the old warrior's nobility but, according to the same writer, was a hulking figure "exhibiting a deliberate savageness" and was plainly seen to be the "priest of assassination or secret murder" who took no pride in "honorable war."[5] Just as had been so with Red Bird and Wekau, Black Hawk and the Prophet appeared to be the personifications of the light and dark sides of what white America assumed to be the Indian's paradoxical good-and-evil character, and by that contrast Black Hawk was made to seem all the more grand.

Before being taken away in chains by Zachary Taylor, Black Hawk delivered a powerfully poetic speech, which further enhanced his heroic image. Without even a hint of remorse or apology, he told his attentive audience he had "done nothing for which an Indian ought to be ashamed." Indeed, he declared, it was the white men—the scoundrels "who came year after year to cheat them and take away their lands"—who ought to feel shame, and it was against them, he said, he had "fought for his countrymen, [and] the squaws and papooses," who could not defend themselves. He lamented only his inability to fight on, wishing he had the power to destroy many more of his enemies, and, although he conceded defeat, he proclaimed that his heart had "swelled high in his bosom when he had led his warriors to battle." They had not gone down to defeat because they lacked courage. They had simply been overwhelmed, he asserted, by the white man's immense power. "The bullets flew like birds in the air, and whizzed by our ears like the wind through the trees in winter. My warriors fell around me; it began to look dismal. I saw my evil day at hand. The sun rose dim on us in the morning, and at night it sunk in a dark cloud, and looked like a ball of fire. That was the last sun that shone on Black Hawk," he told his captors in a burst of dramatic narrative. Maintaining he had done everything he could to save his people, he claimed that even in defeat he remained "a true Indian" who disdained "to cry like a woman." Then, keeping the focus entirely on himself and referring to himself in the third person, he ended the performance by declaring: "He can do no more. He is near his end. His sun is setting, and he will rise no more. Farewell to Black Hawk."[6]

The speech was patently self-serving and an unscrupulous distortion of the facts—he had, after all, run out on his people to avoid the final battle of a conflict he himself had set in motion—but it was nonetheless a clever rhetorical strategy worthy of the trickster himself, and deliberately designed to rehabilitate his reputation. By then he was the most famous Indian in America, and in the months ahead would become a living legend and the very symbol of courageous native resistance to the forces that were destroying their world and way of life.

From Prairie du Chien young Lieutenant Jefferson Davis took him and the Prophet by steamboat to Jefferson Barracks, where General Atkinson imprisoned them with other Sauk captives. There he spent the winter in chains with his two sons, along with Wabokieshiek and his brother and two sons, as well as Neapope, Wee-sheet, Ioway, Pama-ho, and Little Stabbing Chief. "The time dragged heavily and gloomily along throughout the winter," lamented the old leader.[7]

But their season of discontent was not entirely uneventful. Washington Irving paid them a visit in December, and George Catlin, the painter, spent a number of weeks at Jefferson Barracks sketching and painting portraits of all the Sauk prisoners, who, by then, were the objects of considerable public curiosity. Catlin was particularly impressed with Nasheweskaska, Black Hawk's oldest son, who he said was "a very handsome young warrior and one of the finest looking Indians" he had ever seen.[8] Then in March, Keokuk, Davenport, and Antoine LeClaire, along with several chiefs and braves, came to visit and brought with them Black Hawk's wife, Singing Bird, and his daughter, Nauasia. Davenport gave him a gift of dried venison, which pleased him much since it smelled and tasted of home. He was also delighted by the news that his old rival Keokuk had sent a petition to President Jackson pleading for the release of all the Indian prisoners. "I now began to hope that I would soon be restored to liberty, and the enjoyment of my family and friends," said Black Hawk.[9]

That hope proved premature. Rather than being set free, Black Hawk and his son Nasheweskaska, accompanied by Wabokieshiek and his son Pawasheet, and Neapope, Pama-ho, and two other minor chiefs, were sent east to Washington, D.C., in April. They were in the custody of Lieutenant Thomas A. Alexander and two soldiers, along with the interpreter Charles St. Vrain. It was a journey that would greatly enhance Black Hawk's fame and reputation.

They traveled first by steamboat up the Ohio River, stopping briefly at Louisville and Cincinnati where large crowds gathered to see them, and then on to Wheeling, where they boarded a stagecoach that took them along the Cumberland Road to Frederick, Maryland. There they were amazed when they boarded a railroad train, which sped them across the countryside to the national capital, arriving there on April 24. Two days later they were granted a brief audience with President Jackson, who had very little to say to them. Black Hawk attempted to explain why he had taken up the war ax against the Americans—saying that he had been driven to it by the many injustices committed against his people—but Jackson seemed disinterested and was extremely taciturn in his response.[10] They were soon dismissed and sent to Fort Monroe in Virginia, where they were to remain imprisoned until further notice.

At Fort Monroe they were under the custody of Colonel Abraham Eustis, who had been with Winfield Scott's army in Illinois, and who proved to be a most gracious host to his Indian prisoners, having their manacles removed and seeing to it that they were well fed and treated with respect. Indeed, he held dinners in their honor. Also, while in confinement there, an impressive procession of artists arrived to paint their portraits. It was an artistic who's who of the times and included James Westphal Ford, Charles Bird King, Samuel M. Brooks, John Wesley Jarvis, and Robert M. Sully. All were anxious to capture on canvas the images of the famous warriors, hoping to preserve them for the collective memory before the Indians had vanished forever.

Each of the portraits of Black Hawk is so distinctive it is difficult to tell they are all images of the same man. But all present him as a figure of great dignity and inner strength gazing pensively off into the distance, and as an "authentic" Indian uncorrupted by the artificialities and vices of civilization, and proud of who and what he was. Indeed, in the artists' renderings of him, Black Hawk became a reflection of some of American culture's most powerful myths and intriguing fantasies, evoking strong feelings of both admiration and pathos, which gave white America a bittersweet sense of heroic tragedy. That appealed deeply to the romantic sentiments of a great many people then living in the northeastern section of the country. Who Black Hawk really was and what he had actually done seemed almost irrelevant, for, by the time he reached the East, and especially after leaving Fort Monroe at the end of May, he became much less a man and much more a symbol that served the emotional needs of a society in search of self-definition and highly ambivalent about itself and its government's policies toward the native people.[11]

In fact, at the time of his eastern visit, the United States was awash with romantic notions about the natives. Between 1824 and 1834 forty novels were published in which the themes of the "noble savage" and "vanishing Americans" made up major portions of their plots. Cooper probably did it best, and the Indian characters of his *Leather-Stocking Tales*, along with those of dozens of lesser narratives, both reflected and influenced public consciousness, connecting readers to an imagined American past in which noble natives inhabited the continent's unspoiled, primal state of nature. The Indian—at least the mythological "noble savage"—became for many Americans an essential part of the national identity, and Black Hawk seemed to offer them confirmation of what they so eagerly wished to believe.[12]

The mythologizing of Black Hawk and his companions had begun early in the journey. One writer, who accompanied them on the steamboat up the Ohio River, seemed virtually entranced by them, and in an outburst of heroic prose presented in the *Niles' Weekly Register* he exclaimed, "We were immediately struck with admiration at the gigantic and symmetrical figures of most of the warriors, who seemed, as they reclined in native ease and gracefulness, with their half naked bodies exposed to view, rather like statues from some master hand, than like being a race whom we had heard characterized as degenerate and debased." To the writer those "sons of nature" seemed larger than life and more beautiful than art. But it was Black Hawk and his son more than any others who captured his most admiring attention. The old Sauk leader, he said, had a benevolent countenance with a "shade of sorrow" upon it, and was a "man of amiable disposition, kind in heart, and strict integrity"; his son emanated a "cultivated intellect" and was "the living personification of our *beau ideal* of manly beauty," he declared in a mood of near enchantment. It was as if Chingachgook and Uncas had come to life and were heading for the nation's capital.[13]

But it was after their release from Fort Monroe that Black Hawk and Nasheweskaska, and to a lesser degree their fellow travelers, became truly national celebrities, with thousands of people flocking to see them in a great public outpouring of curiosity and adulation that one writer called "Blackhawkiana."[14]

Clark and Atkinson had recommended to Lewis Cass the release of the Sauk prisoners after only four weeks at Fort Monroe. Cass agreed, but before the Indians would be permitted to return home, they would be required to take a tour of the major cities in the East in order to become acquainted with the immense size and power of the United States. That would convince them, reasoned Cass, of the utter futility of ever again contemplating any further violent uprisings against the Republic. Major John Garland was put in charge of the tour, which commenced on June 4 and soon turned into a triumphal progress for the Indians.

They began at the Gosport Navy Yard in Norfolk, Virginia, where they were taken aboard the seventy-five-gun warship *Delaware*. They were duly impressed. But after they returned to their hotel, a large crowd congregated in the street beneath their windows and called upon them to come out and make a public appearance. Black Hawk and the Prophet eventually consented. They emerged onto a balcony, bowed to the enthusiastic throng below, and addressed their cheering fans through the interpreter. "We will go home now, with peace in our hearts, towards our white brothers and our actions hereafter will be more satisfactory to you," promised Black Hawk.[15] The crowd loved it and responded with cheers and applause.

From Norfolk they moved on to Baltimore, reaching there on June 6. They were taken to the theater to see a performance of the play *Jim Crow* and found themselves sharing the spotlight with President Jackson himself. At the end of the evening, while leaving the building, the president walked up to Black Hawk, and shook his hand, and inquired about his health, having heard he had become seasick while on the trip from Norfolk. It was an important scene for both men, and each sought to enhance his public image by playing it to the fullest—the compassionate president showing paternal concern for the well-being of one of his native wards, and the dignified Indian leader from the wild American heartland meeting the chief magistrate of the nation on common ground. Orlando Brown, the Whig editor of the Frankfort, Kentucky, newspaper the *Commonwealth*, witnessed it all and made the observation: "It is really amusing to see what an infectious thing greatness is—Black Hawk attracts almost as great a crowd as the President, and resolving not to be outdone even by the General, he walks out upon balconies, and bows to the multitude with unceptionable [*sic*] grace." Brown went on to suggest that Jackson resented the public adulation shown toward Black Hawk, and informed his readers that the president's advisers had decided "that the two great men, must no longer travel the same road."[16]

After Baltimore it was Philadelphia, where they became caught up in a whirlwind of teas and dinners, public appearances and theater performances. There the Indians met Thomas McKenney and were given tours of the city waterworks, the mint, and the Cherry Hill Prison. They were also treated to the marshal splendor of a grand military parade. After watching the soldiers march, Black Hawk confessed that while he was no coward, he was sorry he had ever raised his tomahawk against the Americans. He then declared: "While the Great Spirit above keeps my heart as it now is, I will be the white man's friend. I will remain in peace. I will go to my people and speak good of the white man. I will tell them that they are as many as the leaves of the forest, very manly and very strong, and that I will fight no more against them."[17] Ever the trickster, he and his entourage were a big hit in Philadelphia.

That was even more the case in New York City. Even before landing at the wharf, "the crowd was so great that it was extremely difficult to effect a passage for their conveyance to their lodgings," reported Orlando Brown.[18] A reception was held for them at the city hall, and there, said Black Hawk, "we saw an immense number of people; all of whom treated us with friendship, and many with great generosity."[19] His son Nasheweskaska was the object of special attention, particularly from the women. During their stay in Philadelphia, one reporter had declared, "The son of Black Hawk is a noble specimen of physical beauty—a model of those who would embody the ideal of strength."[20] In New York he had the impact of a latter-day matinee idol, and another reporter observed, "Several of the ladies of that city, admiring the noble form and the handsome face of young Black Hawk, warmly kissed him."[21]

By then the tour was such a triumph for the Indians that officials in Washington decided to cut it short and send the Sauk home sooner than originally planned. But even as this exit strategy was implemented, "Blackhawkiana" continued at full force as far as Albany. Only after that did the cheering fade into the background. On June 30 the Indians boarded a steamboat in Buffalo, and by the time they reached Detroit they were in a profoundly different emotional environment. A large crowd gathered there as well, but in Detroit the mood was decidedly ugly and the throng resembled more a lynch mob than an admiring multitude. Effigies of Black Hawk and other members of his party were burned in a hostile display of collective hatred. Once again, the deep divisions between East and West were made dramatically evident. Furthermore, the malice in the voices clearly indicated that the myth of the "noble savage" flourished only in the part of the nation where real Indians had ceased to exist.

All the same, before returning to those harsh realities, Black Hawk had managed to stir up considerable public interest about Indians in general, and with stunning success had achieved celebrity status for himself. Upon returning West, he persisted in his efforts to further enhance his already legendary reputation. Late that summer he traveled to Fort Armstrong, where, in a series of long interview sessions with Antoine LeClaire, he dictated his entire autobiography. LeClaire, a huge hulk of a man, part-French, part-Potawatomi, and fluent in at least a dozen Indian languages, as well as English and French, was employed as the government interpreter for the Indian agency at Rock Island.[22] The manuscript he produced from the interviews was edited and prepared for publication by John B. Patterson, who had been the acting editor of the *Galenian* while Addison Philleo had been off with the militia killing Indians. The *Life of Ma-ka-tai-me-she-kia-kiak or Black Hawk* was published in Cincinnati in the fall of 1833 and immediately became a bestseller, going through five printings during its first year on the market. This small book provided a rare and authentic look into the Indian side of the racial and cultural conflict that had been raging within the heart of the young Republic. More than that, it firmly established Black Hawk's enduring fame as a spokesman for all Indians.

The eastern tour and his autobiography were important developments in their time mostly because they served the emotional needs of a significant portion of the American public. Both evoked strong feelings of support and sympathy for the Indians and created an illusion of a personal connection between the public and the imagined heroic figure of Black Hawk, who became for them a symbol of all the Native Americans. That affect, in turn, allowed those who experienced it to escape any sense of personal guilt or responsibility for what had been done to the Indians in their name. Guilt was thereby displaced and transferred to others and, as the historian Susan Scheckel points out, the mere act of reading the autobiography with empathy gave "each reader a personal sense of absolution from complicity in those actions" that had inflicted so much misery and death upon the country's aboriginal inhabitants. As a result, people had the delusion of doing justice to the victims of American expansion simply by feeling sympathy for them, while believing themselves to be morally superior to their own political leaders and those they regarded as their less civilized countrymen living along the western frontier.[23] Yet, all the while, they continued to accept with untroubled consciences the many benefits that accrued to the national society from the invasion, conquest, and colonization of the trans-Appalachian region. Black Hawk thereby unwittingly enabled white people to feel good about themselves. That, perhaps, more than anything, enabled him to rehabilitate his own reputation so that he was lionized and long remembered as a man of courage and noble character. In that the old trickster achieved his ultimate victory.

But removed from the public gaze, Black Hawk settled into his own personal decline. Forced to live in Keokuk's village on the last big bend of the Iowa River, he became, said George Catlin, "a poor dethroned monarch" who was "an object of pity."[24] In 1837 he moved his lodge down to the Des Moines River, in Davis County, not far from Fort Madison, where the British Band had congregated five years before in preparation for its fateful springtime crossing of the Mississippi. There the old warrior became a whiskey drinker and something of a dandy who dressed in American clothes, including a fine broadcloth shirt, a dignified wool military tunic given to him by President Jackson, and a high silk hat. He also wore medals on his chest and carried a silver-headed cane, a gift from Senator Henry Clay. To all his neighbors he appeared "meek and peaceable," and according to William Carroll Reed, who lived close by, he was "kind of dried up and shriveled, as though the sorrows and troubles he had had withered him like an old leaf."[25] He was clearly no longer the man he had once been nor even a faint reflection of the heroic figure of his many romantic portraits. Then, on October 3, 1838, upon returning from a trip to Rock Island to collect his government annuity, he died in a lodge near Iowaville after only a brief illness. He was seventy-two years old.

He was buried in a sitting position, clad in his military uniform, with his cane and two swords, and an extra pair of moccasins for the long journey to the land of the dead beyond the sunset. But even in death the white people would not let him rest. Less than a year later, his widow went to the grave and discovered that someone had dug up the body and taken his head. A few months later the rest of his remains were stolen away. The grave robber, in both cases, was a Doctor Turner, who lived in the area, and who had the bones cleaned and wired together so as to put the skeleton of the famous Sauk leader on display in his office. Black Hawk's relatives bitterly complained. Upon hearing the story, Governor Robert Lucas of the Iowa Territory ordered the skeleton seized and sent to his office in Burlington, where it was eventually put on public exhibition in the building of the Burlington Geographical and Historical Society. There the old warrior's bones remained until 1855, when they were lost forever in a devasting fire that consumed the entire building.[26]

The people he left behind fared little better. They too withered away like dead leaves. All their land east of the Mississippi was taken in the treaty imposed upon them by Winfield Scott and John Reynolds in that early autumn of 1832, and in a move that went well beyond the letter of the Jackson administration's Indian removal policy, the Sauk and Fox were also forced to give up a fifty-mile-wide strip of territory west of the Mississippi, running the full length of what would become the state of Iowa. That amounted to nearly 6 million acres and included the much-sought-after Dubuque's Mines. In exchange for that, they were promised a twenty-thousand-dollar annuity payment for the duration of thirty years, as well as forty kegs of tobacco and forty barrels of salt a year, and a four-hundred-square-mile reservation straddling the Iowa River. When it was all settled—when the submissive chiefs had marked the paper with quills—General Scott felt most self-satisfied with what he had achieved. But just before the actual document had been agreed to, he had asked his staff assistant, Lieutenant Joseph Gallagher, if he thought it was "a just and honorable treaty in the sight of God." Gallagher reassured him it was, adding, "on the whole, it might be considered quite liberal." The general was pleased, telling Gallagher "he did not wish to put his hand to anything which might cause him to blush hereafter."[27] There was never any indication that Winfield Scott ever blushed about what he did to the Sauk and Fox people.

Confined to their resource-poor reservation, under the authority of the vain and increasingly drunken Keokuk, the Sauk and Fox quickly deteriorated. Before the war their population had been increasing, and even after the terrible attrition of the campaign there were still more than 6,000 of them in 1833. By 1845, however, their Indian agent reported there to be a total of only 1,207 Sauk and 1,271 Fox remaining. They had suffered more than a 50 percent loss of population in just twelve years, and the wholesale depletion of game and other resources on their reservation made it impossible for them to sustain a way of life even vaguely resembling their traditional culture. They descended into abject destitution. Disease and drunkenness gained ascendancy over them, and their community was torn apart by angry discord.[28] In time they were moved on to Kansas and then eventually to Oklahoma, where they faded into oblivion until Jim Thorpe, Black Hawk's grandnephew, emerged at the time of the 1912 Olympic games to provide white America with a new "noble savage" to briefly admire.

While the Sauk and Fox descended into misery and seemed destined for extinction, the white people kept telling and retelling the story of the Black Hawk War. Although a military conflict of the most modest dimensons, lasting less than four months, claiming fewer than seventy-five American lives, and costing the U.S. government no more than a few million dollars, it was long considered a noteworthy episode that continued to arouse considerable public interest and debate. Beginning with Black Hawk's own autobiography in 1833 and followed one year later by John Wakefield's *A History of the Black Hawk War,* there have been eighteen books published about Black Hawk and the war, as well as a large number of biographies of the other major figures associated with the struggle. Additionally there have been scores of articles and essays, hundreds of newspaper pieces, two book-length epic poems, five novels, a play, numerous published memoirs and personal accounts of participants in the conflict, and an incalculable number of public lectures and orations. Furthermore, there are a great many monuments and plaques scattered across the countryside where those long-ago events had occurred. For such a minor violent encounter in the history of a country that has known as much conflict as this one, extraordinary efforts have been made to keep the memory of the Black Hawk War alive and important.

Of course, historical memory is always more a matter of reconstruction than simple recall and is indulged in because, as the historian David Thelen observes, the retelling of tales of things past is "profoundly intertwined with the basic identities of individuals, groups, and cultures."[29] "Every culture has five or six stories it tells itself over and over again as part of a pattern in self-recognition and sought-after cohesion," the historian Robert A. Ferguson tells us.[30] And for the upper Mississippi River region the story of the Black Hawk War is clearly one of those stories. Issues of identity are at the very heart of it. They were also the primary causes of the Black Hawk War itself. Nevertheless, the creating and maintaining of a collective identity is as much a work of imagination as the result of shared historical experience, and who people are or believe themselves to be changes over time. As a consequence, they reshape their historical recollections to reinforce the changing images they have of themselves.

In Illinois and Wisconsin, where so much of the local history remains recent and uneventful, the Black Hawk War is one of the few dramatic and memorable events that enable people there to feel an emotional connection and sense of identification with their own collective past. Without the war, towns like Dodgeville, Fort Atkinson, Dixon, Elizabeth, and Soldiers Grove would have seemed doomed to remain places almost without history, where nothing of interest or significance had ever happened. But because of the war—because blood had been shed and the passion and pathos of human tragedy occurred there—such places have taken on something of a sacred quality, becoming sites for monuments and shrines to which pilgrimages are still made, and the memories of heroes and martyrs and brave deeds remain vivid in the public consciousness.

That may be especially the case because the event itself was something of a rite of consecration. As the scholar Dudley Young points out, all such wars are "holy wars" because "the flowing of blood and the ripping of flesh consecrates the ground in the oldest and simplest sense we know." It is sacrifice, and *sacrifice* quite literally means "to make sacred."[31] In the American experience it has most often been the shedding of Indian blood that has transformed the profane wilderness—the land where white people were aliens who did not belong—into the sacred space of the Republic. Through the killing of the native people white men came to believe in their own power and superiority and their right to possess a land that was not their own.

For the most part, the story told of the Black Hawk War throughout the nineteenth century was about just that—about the triumph of white men over the wild country and its savage inhabitants. It was a narrative tradition begun by John Wakefield that culminated with Frank E. Stevens's *The Black Hawk War,* published in Chicago in 1903. Stevens's literary portrait of Black Hawk was that of a moody, neurotic man of the most meager talents, teetering on the brink of madness, and driven to reckless action by his own inner demons of hatred for the Americans and an insatiable lust for bloodshed. The American settlers, on the other hand, were characterized as hardworking, peace-loving "sturdy pioneers," who labored to cut small farms from the primeval forests in order to provide for the simple needs of their families. But when trouble came, when the Indians raised the tomahawk and firebrand against them, they left their plows in the field, took down their trusty muskets from above their hearths, and marched off together to defend their women and children and save their country from the vicious fury of the wild men.[32]

It was stirring, melodramatic stuff retold by Stevens in greater detail and with better documentation that ever before. But by the time his book was published, he was already fighting a losing battle. As the Midwest came of age following the great Columbian Exposition of 1893 in Chicago, where the famous Wisconsin historian Frederick Jackson Turner lamented the final closing of the frontier, the Black Hawk War was beginning to be perceived in a different light and was becoming a part of the region's past that evoked some feeling of collective discomfort. That was articulated quite clearly in August of 1898, on the sixty-sixth anniversary of the Battle of Bad Axe, when Reuben Gold Thwaites, the renowned scholar who was then superintendent of the State Historical Society of Wisconsin, delivered a public lecture on the very site where the battle had occurred. Rather than hailing it as a heroic moment in the state's historical experience, he referred to it as a "massacre" in which defenseless Indians had been "shot down like so many squirrels" or "so many rats," and characterized the entire war as "a tragedy with all the elements as such a drama as Shakespeare would have portrayed." It was, declared Thwaites, a regrettable episode that brought "dishonor to the American name." Henry Dodge was not even mentioned, and Black Hawk was referred to as "a patriot" to his people and "one of the noblest Romans of them all."[33]

The local historian Dr. C. V. Porter of Viroqua, Wisconsin, was in the audience that day. Twenty-eight years later he recalled Thwaites's lecture for an article he wrote for the *Crawford County Press*. In it he told his readers, "I believe it is all right to confess our sins and let it be known what a lot of criminals we Christian whites have been in our dealings with the Red men."[34] Since then the floodgates have been opened to a torrent of public mea culpas and apologies for what came to be regarded as the sins of the fathers committed during the Black Hawk War. In 1989 the

Wisconsin State Assembly, eager to be politically correct in minority matters, issued a formal apology and expressed its deepest, heartfelt "regret and sorrow" to the surviving members of the Sauk and Fox nations for the wrongs done 157 years before.[35]

Such confessions have also been accompanied by the idolization of Black Hawk himself. In the more recent stories of the war he has become a sympathetic tragic hero, and to many of the descendants of those who once demonized him he has emerged as the very epitome of the "noble savage." That is made evident by the heroic sculpture purported to be of him standing outside the Hauberg Indian Museum at Rock Island and even more so in Lorado Taft's magnificent forty-eight-foot-high stone figure of Black Hawk towering above the Rock River at Oregon, Illinois. In fact, throughout the region of northern Illinois and southern Wisconsin, Black Hawk has become something of a secular patron saint with a great many plaques and monuments erected in his honor. Everywhere there are banks and parks, savings and loans, schools, colleges, golf courses, counties, streets, and sports teams, including the Chicago Blackhawks, named after him, revealing just how closely the identity of the people living there is tied to the mythologized Sauk leader who once rode across their land. That imagined connection enables such people to fantasize and feel better about themselves—feeling perhaps more brave and heroic and "authentically" American by association—and also reveals their deep human desires to be something more than what they are.

Indeed, most of the reconstructed memory of the Black Hawk War has been designed to make white people feel good about themselves. While the public confession of past wrongs can be a good way for any society to begin some healthy self-examination, we have not yet become honest or introspective enough about this or any of our other wars against the Indians to face some truths about ourselves and the cycles of violence we seem doomed to repeat again and again. In many ways we remain too much like those cheering spectators who crowded the streets in Baltimore and Philadelphia in the spring of 1833, accepting the benefits of the conquest while confusing sympathy for contrition, idolization for justice, and seeking easy absolution without ever doing proper penance. As always it has been a problem deeply rooted in our collective identity and in the stories we keep telling ourselves about who we imagine ourselves to be.

NOTES

Prologue

1. Benjamin Drake, *The Life and Adventure of Black Hawk with Sketches of Keokuk, the Sac and Fox Indians and the Late Black Hawk War*, 7 ed. (Cincinnati: George Conclin, 1844), 74.

2. Richard Slotkin, *Regeneration Through Violence: The Mythology of the American Frontier, 1600–1860* (Middletown, Conn.: Wesleyan University Press, 1973), 79.

3. Joseph M. Street to William Clark, 3 August 1832, Ellen M. Whitney, ed., *The Black Hawk War, 1831–1832* (Springfield, Ill.: Illinois State Historical Library, 1973), vol. 2, part 2, 926. Referred to henceforth as *BHW*, vol. 2, part 2.

1: *The Beginning of Sorrows*

1. Lewis Cass to William Clark, 1 September 1825, U.S. Bureau of Indian Affairs, Indian Office Files, box 1 (photocopies from U.S. National Archives), State Historical Society of Wisconsin, Manuscript Collections. Referred to henceforth as Indian Office Files.

2. Thomas Forsyth to William Clark, 24 May 1827, Thomas Forsyth Papers and Letter Books, Draper Manuscripts, State Historical Society of Wisconsin, Manuscript Collections. Referred to henceforth as Forsyth Papers.

3. Ibid.

4. Forsyth to Lawrence Taliaferro, 28 May 1827, Forsyth Papers.

5. Forsyth to Clark, 30 May 1827, Forsyth Papers.

6. Ibid.

7. Forsyth to Clark, 24 May 1827.

8. Forsyth to Clark, 9 June 1827; Forsyth to Clark, 15 June 1827, Forsyth Papers.

9. William Snelling, "Early Days at Prairie du Chien and the Winnebago Outbreak of 1827," *Collections of the State Historical Society of Wisconsin* 5 (1868), 126, 128. Referred to henceforth as *WHC*.

10. Forsyth to Clark, 2 June 1827, Forsyth Papers.

11. James H. Lockwood, "Early Times and Events in Wisconsin," *WHC* 2 (1856): 125.

12. Snelling, "Early Days at Prairie du Chien," 147–51.

13. Adéle De P. Gratiot, "Adéle De P. Gratiot Narrative," *WHC* 10 (1888), 270.

14. Daniel H. Parkinson, "Pioneer Life in Wisconsin," *WHC* 2 (1856), 329.

15. Gratiot, "Narrative," 270.

16. Daniel Parkinson, "Pioneer Life in Wisconsin," 329.

17. Milo Milton Quaife, *Chicago and the Old Northwest, 1673–1835* (Chicago: University of Chicago Press, 1913), 315.

18. Herman J. Viola, *Thomas L. McKenney: Architect of America's Early Indian Policy, 1816–1830* (Chicago: Swallow Press, 1974), 157.

19. Daniel Parkinson, "Pioneer Life in Wisconsin," 331.

20. Thomas L. McKenney, "The Winnebago War," *WHC* 5 (1868), 179, 182, 186.

21. Quotation taken from Richard Drinnon, *Facing West: The Metaphysics of Indian-Hating and Empire Building* (New York: Meridian Book, New American Library, 1980), 169.

22. Lewis Cass, "Regulations of Indian Affairs in the Northwest Territory and Proposals for the Better Organization of the Indian Department," Detroit, 1815, a manuscript in the Edward E. Ayer Collection of the Newberry Library, Chicago, 36–38.

23. Lewis Cass, "Remarks on the Policy and Practice of the United States and Great Britain in Their Treatment of the Indians," *North American Review* 24 (April 1827), 29.

24. Lewis Cass, "Considerations on the Present State of the Indians and Their Removal to the West of the Mississippi," *North American Review* 30 (January 1830), 12–13, 45.

25. Ibid., 14.

26. Cass, "Remarks on the Policy," 10; Cass, "Considerations," 19.

27. Cass, "Remarks on the Policy," 10.

28. Thomas Forsyth, "An Account of the Manners and Customs of the Sauk and Fox Nations of Indians Tradition," in *The Indian Tribes of the Upper Mississippi Valley and the Region of the Great Lakes,* ed. Emma Helen Blair (Cleveland: Arthur H. Clark, 1911), vol. 2, 183–245; and Morrell Marston, "Letter of Major Marston to Reverend Doctor Morse, Fort Armstrong, November 1820," in *The Indian Tribes of the Upper Mississippi Valley and the Region of the Great Lakes,* vol. 2, 139–82.

29. Forsyth, "Account of Manners," 194.

30. Ibid., 195

31. Quoted in Alanson Skinner, "Observations of the Ethnography of the Sauk Indians," *Bulletin of the Public Museum of the City of Milwaukee* 5, nos. 1–3 (1923–25), 79.

32. Forsyth, "Account of Manners," 196.

33. Marston, "Letter to Morse," 162.

34. Ibid., 158.

35. Skinner, "Observations of Ethnography of the Sauk," 67.

36. Forsyth, "Account of Manners," 196.

37. Skinner, "Observations of Ethnography of the Sauk," 67.

38. Forsyth, "Account of Manners," 196; and Skinner, "Observations of Ethnography of the Sauk," 67.

39. Marston, "Letter to Morse," 158.

40. Ibid., 160–61.

41. Skinner, "Observations of Ethnography of the Sauk," 73.

42. Black Hawk, *The Life of Black Hawk,* ed. Milo Milton Quaife (New York: Dover Publications, 1916), 35.

43. See William A. McNeill, *Keeping Together in Time: Dance and Drill in Human History* (Cambridge, Mass.: Harvard University Press, 1995).

44. Black Hawk, *Life,* 35.

45. See Rene Girard, *Violence and the Sacred,* tran. Patrick Gregory (Baltimore: Johns Hopkins University Press, 1972).

46. Leroy V. Eid, "National War Among Indians of Northeastern North America," *Canadian Review of American Studies* 16 (Summer 1985), 125–54.

47. Forsyth, "Account of Manners," 237.

48. Black Hawk, *Life*, 9.

49. See Lucy Eldersveld Murphy, *A Gathering of Rivers: Indians, Métis, and Mining in the Western Great Lakes Region, 1737–1832* (Lincoln: University of Nebraska Press, 2000).

50. Stanley S. Graham, "Life of the Enlisted Soldiers on the Western Frontier, 1815–1845," Ph.D. diss., North Texas State University, 1972.

51. Edmund M. Coffman, *The Old Army: A Portrait of the American Army in Peacetime, 1784–1895* (New York: Oxford University Press, 1986), 43–44, 49.

52. Ibid., 152.

53. Charles Joseph Latrobe, *The Rambler in North America MDCCCXXXII–MDCC-CXXXIII* (New York: Harper and Brothers, 1835), vol. 2, 230–31; see also Francis Paul Prucha, "The United States Army as Viewed by British Travelers, 1825–1860," *Military Affairs* 17 (Autumn 1953), 113–24.

54. Graham, "Life of the Enlisted Soldiers," 17.

55. Patrick J. Jung, "Soldiering at Fort Howard, 1816–1841: A Social History of a Frontier Fort at Green Bay," Part 1, *Voyageur* 11 (Summer–Fall 1995), 27.

56. Coffman, *The Old Army*, 193.

2: The Center of the World

1. Jonathan Carver, *Travels Through the Interior Parts of North America in the Years 1766, 1767, and 1768* (London: John Cookley Lettsom, 1781; reprint, Minneapolis: Ross and Haines, 1956), 46–47.

2. R. David Edmunds and Joseph L. Peyser, *The Fox Wars: The Mesquakie Challenge to New France* (Norman: University of Oklahoma Press, 1993).

3. Black Hawk, *Life*, 1.

4. Claude Allouez, "Allouez's Account of the Various Tribes: From the Jesuit Relations of 1666–1667," *WHC* 16 (1902), 57.

5. Black Hawk, *Life*, 4.

6. Ibid., 42.

7. William Jones, "Episodes in the Culture-Hero Myth of the Sauks and Foxes," *Journal of American Folklore* 14 (October–December 1901), 234.

8. Ibid., 234, 235.

9. Ibid., 237.

10. Black Hawk, *Life*, 42.

11. Northrop Frey, *The Bush Garden: Essays on the Canadian Imagination* (Concord, Ontario: House of Ananis, 1995), 220.

12. Frederick Turner, *Beyond Geography: The Western Spirit Against the Wilderness* (New York: The Viking Press, 1980), 23.

13. Caleb Atwater, *Remarks Made on a Tour to Prairie du Chien Thence to Washington City in 1829* (Columbus, Ohio: Isaac N. Whiting, 1831; reprint, New York: Arno Press, 1975), 63, 64.

14. Ibid., 185–86.

15. Thomas Forsyth to Thomas McKenney, 25 August 1824, Forsyth Papers.

16. Forsyth to William Clark, 3 June 1817, *WHC* 11 (1888), 348; see also Forsyth to Thomas McKenney, 28 August 1824, Forsyth Papers.

17. Black Hawk, *Life*, 33.

18. Ibid.

19. Forsyth to Clark, 3 June 1817.

20. Forsyth to McKenney, 28 August 1824, Forsyth Papers.

21. Forsyth to Lewis Cass, 24 October 1831, Forsyth Papers.

22. Forsyth, "Account of Manners," 216.

23. Ibid., 237.

24. Marston, "Letter to Morse," 167.

25. Jeanne Kay, "The Fur Trade and Native American Population Growth," *Ethnohistory* 31 (1984), 277.

26. Black Hawk, *Life*, 34.

27. Forsyth to McKenney, 28 August 1824.

28. Forsyth to Cass, 24 October 1831.

29. Marston, "Letter to Morse," 151.

30. Murphy, *A Gathering of Rivers*, 144.

31. Forsyth, "Account of Manners," 214; Marston, "Letter to Morse," 166.

32. Forsyth, "Account of Manners," 215.

33. J. W. Spencer, *Reminiscences of Pioneer Life in the Mississippi Valley* (Davenport: Griggs, Watson and Day, 1872), in *The Early Days of Rock Island and Davenport: The Narratives of J.W. Spencer and J. H. D. Burrows*, ed. Milo Milton Quaife (Chicago: Lakeside Press, 1942), 32.

34. Marston, "Letter to Morse," 152–53; Murphy, *A Gathering of Rivers*, 145.

35. Black Hawk, *Life*, 36.

36. Murphy, *A Gathering of Rivers*, 105.

37. Ibid.

38. Moses Meeker, "Early History of the Lead Region of Wisconsin," *WHC* 6 (1872), 281.

39. Murphy, *A Gathering of Rivers*, 106.

40. Marston, "Letter to Morse," 153.

41. Black Hawk, *Life*, 36.

42. Ibid., 37; Forsyth, "Account of Manners," 230.

43. Marston, "Letter to Morse," 151.

44. Spencer, *Reminiscences of Pioneer Life*, 30–31.

45. Marston, "Letter to Morse," 151.

46. Forsyth to John C. Calhoun, 30 September 1824, Forsyth Papers.

47. Marston, "Letter to Morse," 149.

48. Spencer, *Reminiscences of Pioneer Life*, 29.

49. Black Hawk, *Life*, 38.

50. Marston, "Letter to Morse," 149.

51. Forsyth to Calhoun, 30 September 1824.

52. Skinner, "Observations of Ethnography of the Sauk," 32–33.

53. Ibid., 82.

54. Black Hawk, *Life*, 35.

55. Ibid.

56. Forsyth, "Account of Manners," 206.

57. Black Hawk, *Life*, 34.

58. Forsyth, "Account of Manners," 208.

59. Marston, "Letter to Morse," 175.

60. Forsyth, "Account of Manners," 223.

61. Black Hawk, *Life*, 34.

62. Ibid., 47.

63. James Merrell, *The Indians' New World: Catawbas and Their Neighbors from European Contact Through the Era of Removal* (Chapel Hill: University of North Carolina Press, 1989), 545.

64. John E. Hallwas, "Black Hawk: A Reassessment," *Annals of Iowa* 45 (Spring 1981), 609.

3: *Things Fall Apart*

1. Skinner, "Observations of Ethnography of the Sauk," 55; Cutting Marsh, "Documents Relating to the Stockbridge Mission, 1825–1848," *WHC* 15 (1900), 148–49.

2. Marsh, "Documents Relating to Stockbridge Mission," 125, 128.

3. Forsyth, "Account of Manners," 223.

4. Skinner, "Observations of Ethnography of the Sauk," 38.

5. Forsyth, "Account of Manners," 223.

6. Walter J. Ong, *Orality and Literacy: The Technologizing of the World* (London: Routledge, 1982), 31–77.

7. Forsyth to McKenney, 5 August 1830, Forsyth Papers.

8. Marston, "Letter to Morse," 155.

9. Forsyth to Calhoun, 24 June 1822, Forsyth Papers.

10. Meeker, "Early History of Lead Region," 272; James P. Beckwourth (as told by Thomas D. Bonner), *The Life and Adventures of James P. Beckwourth* (1856; reprint, Lincoln: University of Nebraska Press, 1972), 21–22.

11. Forsyth to Calhoun, 24 June 1822.

12. Quoted in John Denis Haeger, *John Jacob Astor: Business and Finance in the Early Republic* (Detroit: Wayne State University Press, 1991), 209.

13. Black Hawk, *Life,* 33.

14. Spencer, *Reminiscences of Pioneer Life,* 36.

15. Black Hawk, *Life,* 33.

16. See Frederick Turner, *Beyond Geography.*

17. Alexis de Tocqueville, *Democracy in America* (New York: Vintage Books, 1990), vol. 1, 292–93.

18. Kerry A. Trask, "Settlement in a Half-Savage Land: Life and Loss in the Métis Community of La Baye," *Michigan Historical Review* 15 (Spring 1989), 1–27; Patrick J. Jung, "The Creation of Métis Society: French-Indian Intermarriage in the Upper Great Lakes," *Voyageur* 19 (Winter–Spring 2003), 38–48.

19. Quoted in Trask, "Settlement in a Half-Savage Land," 27.

20. Alexis de Tocqueville, *Journey to America,* trans. George Lawrence and ed. J. P. Mayer (New Haven, Conn.: Yale University Press, 1959), 69.

21. Ibid., 182.

22. De Tocqueville, *Democracy in America,* vol. 2, 99.

23. Alexis de Tocqueville, "Fortnight in the Wilderness," in *Tocqueville and Beaumont in America,* ed. George Wilson Pierson (New York: Oxford University Press, 1938), 244.

24. Black Hawk, "Address to J.M. Street at Prairie du Chien, August 27, 1832," in *I Have Spoken: American History Through the Voices of the Indians,* ed. Virginia Irving Armstrong (Chicago: Swallow Press, 1971), 65.

25. James W. Oberly, *Sixty Million Acres: American Veterans and the Public Lands Before the Civil War* (Kent, Ohio: Kent State University Press, 1990), 9–10.

26. Lucius H. Langworthy, "Sketches of the Early Settlement of the West," *Iowa Journal of History and Politics* 8 (July 1910), 362.

27. Thomas Ford, *A History of Illinois: From Its Commencement as a State in 1818 to 1847,* ed. Milo Milton Quaife (1854; reprint, Chicago: Lakeside Press, R. R. Donnelley and Sons, 1945), 118–19.

28. William Cullen Bryant to Frances Bryant, 19 June 1832; Bryant to Frances Bryant, 12 June 1832; and Bryant to Frances Bryant, 19 June 1832, in *The Letters of William Cullen Bryant,* ed. William Cullen Bryant II and Thomas G. Voss (New York: Fordham University Press, 1975), vol. 1 (1809–36), 348, 343, 345.

29. Latrobe, *The Rambler in North America,* 152–53.

30. Philip St. George Cooke, *Scenes and Adventures in the Army or the Romance of Military Life* (Philadelphia: Lindsay and Blakiston, 1857), 16.

31. Atwater, *Remarks on Tour to Prairie du Chien,* 43, 47.

32. William Cullen Bryant to Frances Bryant, 4 June 1832, *Letters of William Cullen Bryant,* vol. 1, 339.

33. Cass, "Consideration on the Present State of the Indians," 65.

34. Murphy, *A Gathering of Rivers,* 162.

35. Ellen M. Whitney, ed., *The Black Hawk War, 1831–1832* (Springfield, Ill.: Illinois State Historical Library, 1973), vol. 2, part 1, note 2, p. 33. Referred to henceforth as *BHW*, vol. 2, part 1.

36. Quoted in Murphy, *A Gathering of Rivers*, 151.

37. Forsyth to Cass, 24 October 1831, Forsyth Papers.

38. Russell Farnham to Pierre Chouteau, 1 August 1830, *BHW*, vol. 2, part 1, note 2, p. 33.

39. William T. Hagan, *The Sac and Fox Indians* (Norman: University of Oklahoma Press, 1958), 13.

40. Forsyth to Cass, 24 October 1831.

41. Hagan, *Sac and Fox Indians*, 103.

42. Ibid., 115.

43. See Viola, *Thomas L. McKenney*.

44. McKenney to Cass, 17 September 1825, Lewis Cass Letter Book, Letters Received, 1817–31, State Historical Society of Wisconsin, Manuscript Collections. Referred to henceforth as Cass Letter Book.

45. McKenney to Cass, 18 April 1827, Indian Office Files, box 1. His emphasis.

46. Josiah Snelling to James Barbour, 23 August 1825, Indian Office Files, box 1. His emphasis.

47. Robert Stuart to Cass, June 1827, Cass Letter Book.

48. McKenney to Clark, 10 January 1828, Indian Office Files, box 1.

49. Forsyth to Clark, 24 June 1828, Forsyth Papers.

50. Forsyth to Secretary of War John C. Calhoun, 24 August 1824, Forsyth Papers.

51. Forsyth to Clark, 11 May 1825, Forsyth Papers.

52. Clark to James Barbour, 19 October 1825, Indian Office Files, box 2.

53. Forsyth to McKenney, 24 August 1824, Forsyth Papers.

54. Black Hawk, *Life*, 38.

55. Ibid., 47.

56. Lucius Langworthy, "Sketches," 363.

57. John Marsh to his father, 14 January 1827, in George D. Lyman, *John Marsh, Pioneer: The Life Story of a Trail Blazer on Six Frontiers* (New York: Charles Scribner's Sons, 1930), 106.

58. John Reynolds, *History of Illinois, My Own Times: Embracing Also the History of My Life* (Chicago: Chicago Historical Society, 1879), 169. Referred to henceforth as *My Own Times*.

59. Moses M. Strong, "Indian Wars of Wisconsin," *WHC* 8 (1879), 251.

60. Ibid.

61. Morgan L. Martin, "Narrative of Morgan L. Martin," *WHC* 11 (1888), 398.

62. Atwater, *Remarks on a Tour to Prairie du Chien*, 66.

63. Reynolds, *My Own Times*, 168.

64. Theodore Rodolf, "Pioneering in the Wisconsin Lead Region," *WHC* 15 (1900), 342.

65. Reynolds, *My Own Times*, 168.

66. Daniel Parkinson, "Pioneer Life in Wisconsin," 334.

67. *Miner's Journal* (Galena), 1 November 1828.

68. Juliette M. Kinzie, *Wau-Bun: The Early Days in the Northwest* (New York, 1856; reprint, Portage, Wis.: National Society of the Colonial Dames of America in the State of Wisconsin, 1989), 112.

69. Joseph Street to Ninian Edwards, November 1827, *WHC* 11 (1888), 358.

70. Street to the secretary of war, 15 November 1827, Joseph Mountfort Street Papers, State Historical Society of Wisconsin, Manuscript Collections. Referred to henceforth as Street Papers.

71. Street to Clark, 26 January 1828, Indian Office Files, box 2.

72. Forsyth to Clark, 10 June 1828, Forsyth Papers.

73. Meeker, "Early History of Lead Region," 290.

74. Quoted in Louis P. Masur, *1831, Year of Eclipse* (New York: Hill and Wang, 2001), 185.

75. Ibid., 188.

76. Spencer, *Reminiscences of Pioneer Life*, 23, 24.

4: A Tangled Web

1. De Tocqueville, "Fortnight in the Wilderness," 232.

2. Calvin Colton, *Tour of the American Lakes and Among the Indians of the Northwest Territories in 1830* (London: Frederick Westly and A. N. Davis, 1833), vol. 1, 217, 219, 218, xi.

3. Ibid., 224.

4. Ibid., 224, 225.

5. Ibid., 180, xiv.

6 Black Hawk, *Life*, 41.

7. Ibid., 42.

8. *Niles' Weekly Register*, 29 September 1832, 79; "Minutes of the Examination of Indian Prisoners," Fort Armstrong, 19 August 1832, *BHW*, vol. 2, part 2, 1030.

9. Street to Clark, 6 July 1831, *BHW*, vol. 2, part 1, 104.

10. Forsyth to Clark, 10 June 1828, Forsyth Papers.

11. Black Hawk, *Life*, 42.

12. Forsyth to Clark, 24 May 1828, Forsyth Papers.

13. Ibid.

14. Forsyth to McKenney, 5 August 1830, Forsyth Papers.

15. Forsyth to Clark, 24 May 1828.

16. Forsyth to Clark, 6 July 1828, Forsyth Papers.

17. Spencer, *Reminiscences of Pioneer Life*, 15, 17.

18. Ibid., 23.

19. Forsyth to Clark, 17 May 1829, Forsyth Papers.

20. Complete copy of the Treaty of 1804 in Frank E. Stevens, *The Black Hawk War Including a Review of Black Hawk's Life* (Chicago: Frank E. Stevens, 1903), 27.

21. Ibid., 28, 29.

22. Roger L. Nichols, *Black Hawk and the Warrior's Path* (Wheeling, Ill.: Harlan Davidson, 1992), 61.

23. Forsyth to Clark, 17 May 1829.

24. Black Hawk, *Life*, 41; Forsyth to Clark, 17 May 1829.

25. Forsyth to Clark, 17 May 1829.

26. Marsh, "Documents Relating to Stockbridge Mission," 138.

27. Ong, *Orality and Literacy*, 46.

28. Black Hawk, *Life*, 13.

29. Forsyth to Clark, 22 May 1829, Forsyth Papers.

30. William Clark to John Eaton, 20 May 1829, Indian Office Files, box 2.

31. Clark to Eaton, 1 June 1829, Indian Office Files, box 2.

32. Forsyth to Clark, 17 May 1829.

33. Forsyth to Clark, 22 May 1829.

34. Forsyth to McKenney, 5 August 1830.

35. Ibid.

36. Thomas McKenney and James Hall, *The Indian Tribes of North America; with Biographical Sketches and Anecdotes of the Principal Chiefs* (1844; reprint, Edinburgh: John Grant, 1934), vol. 2, 130–31.

37. Forsyth to Clark, 5 August 1821, Forsyth Papers.

38. Black Hawk, *Life*, 42.

39. Spencer, *Reminiscences of Pioneer Life*, 25–27.

40. Forsyth to Clark, 17 June 1829, Forsyth Papers.

41. Thomas Forsyth, "Original Causes of the Troubles with a Party of Sauk and Fox Indians Under the Direction of Command of Black Hawk Who Is No Chief," St. Louis, 1 October 1832, Forsyth Papers.

42. "Petition of Settlers to His Honor Ninian Edwards from the Soc Village," 10 May 1829, Indian Office Files, box 2.

43. Black Hawk, *Life*, 43.

44. Street to Clark, 20 May 1829, in Lyman, *John Marsh, Pioneer,* 149–50.
45. Ibid.
46. Forsyth to Clark, 7 June 1829, Forsyth Papers.
47. Forsyth to Clark, 9 August 1829, Forsyth Papers.
48. Forsyth to Clark, 7 June 1829.
49. Forsyth to Clark, 1 October 1829, Forsyth Papers.
50. Ibid.
51. Black Hawk, *Life,* 45.
52. *Miner's Journal* (Galena), 3 November 1829.
53. Street to Wyncoop Warner, 26 October 1829, *Miner's Journal,* 3 November 1829.
54. Forsyth to Clark, 30 April 1830, Forsyth Papers.
55. Forsyth to Clark, 6 May 1830, Forsyth Papers.
56. Ibid.
57. Clark to John Eaton, 10 May 1830, Indian Office Files, box 3.
58. Written Statement by Wyncoop Warner, 2 June 1830, Indian Office Files, box 3.
59. Ibid.
60. Warner to Street, 15 April 1830, Indian Office Files, box 3.
61. Street to Warner, 28 April 1830, Indian Office Files, box 3.
62. Statement by Wyncoop Warner, 2 June 1830.
63. Written statement by Joseph Street, 27 May 1830, Indian Office Files, box 3.
64. Statement by Wyncoop Warner, 2 June 1830.
65. Ibid.
66. Statement by Joseph Street, 27 May 1830.
67. Forsyth to Clark, 7 May 1830, Forsyth Papers.
68. John Fonda, "Early Wisconsin," *WHC* 5 (1868), 256–57.
69. Lyman, *John Marsh, Pioneer,* 154.
70. Elizabeth T. Baird, *O-De-Jit-Wa-Ning or Contes du Temps Passe* (Green Bay, Wis.: Heritage Hill Foundation, 1998), 68.
71. Forsyth to Clark, 17 May 1830, Forsyth Papers.
72. Ibid.
73. Clark to McKenney, 16 June 1830, Indian Office Files, box 3.
74. Forsyth to Clark, 1 June 1830, Forsyth Papers.
75. Forsyth to Clark, 4 June 1830, Forsyth Papers.
76. Forsyth to Clark, 7 June 1830, Forsyth Papers.
77. Ibid.
78. Forsyth to Clark, 1 June 1830.
79. Forsyth to General William H. Ashley, 10 August 1832, Forsyth Papers.
80. Wyncoop Warner to Forsyth, 3 June 1830, Indian Office Files, box 3.

5: *Banished*

1. Clark to Eaton, 28 May 1830, U.S. Bureau of Indian Affairs, Indian Office Letter Books (photocopies from U.S. National Archives), State Historical Society of Wisconsin, Manuscript Collections; Eaton to William S. Williamson, 12 June 1830, Indian Office Letter Books, box 1; anonymous to Forsyth, 4 March 1832, Forsyth Papers.
2. Felix St. Vrain to Clark, 8 October 1830, Indian Office Files, box 3.
3. Ibid.
4. Forsyth to Clark, 25 May 1830, Forsyth Papers.
5. Forsyth, "Original Causes of the Troubles," 1 October 1832, Forsyth Papers.
6. J. M. Stroud, R. M. Young, A. F. Hubbard, and Thomas Ford to John Reynolds, Vandalia, 5 January 1831, Indian Office Files, box 4.
7. Wesley Williams to Reynolds, Hancock County, 6 January 1831, Indian Office Files, box 4; Riggs Pennington to Reynolds, Knox County, 5 January 1831; Parnack Owen to Reynolds, Knox County, 5 January 1831, Indian Office Files, box 4.

8. "Preamble and Resolutions of the General Assembly Concerning the Indians on the North West Frontier," 19 January 1831, Indian Office Files, box 4.

9. See Drinnon, *Facing West,* 115.

10. Thomas L. McKenney, *Sketches of a Tour to the Lakes, of the Character and Customs of the Chippeway Indians, and the Incidents Connected with the Treaty of Fond du Lac* (Baltimore: Fielding Lucas Jr., 1827), 426, 427.

11. Lewis Cass, "Report to the President of the United States," 16 February 1832, Indian Office Letter Book, box 2.

12. "Council at the Ioway Subagency with Socks and Foxes," 14 February 1831, Indian Office Files, box 4.

13. Black Hawk, *Life,* 47.

14. Ibid.

15. Clark to Secretary of War Lewis Cass, 12 August 1831, *BHW,* vol. 2, part 1, 136; see also *BHW,* vol. 2, part 1, note 1, p. 122.

16. Black Hawk, *Life,* 48.

17. Ibid.

18. Ibid.

19. Ibid.

20. "Petition signed by thirty-seven settlers, sent to His Excellency, the Governor of the State of Illinois," 30 April 1831, complete copy in Stevens, *The Black Hawk War,* 82.

21. "Petition to His Excellency, the Governor of Illinois," Farnhamburg, 19 May 1831, complete copy in Stevens, *The Black Hawk War,* 83.

22. St. Vrain to Clark, 15 May 1831, copy in Stevens, *The Black Hawk War,* 83.

23. St. Vrain to Clark, 28 May 1831, copy in Stevens, *The Black Hawk War,* 87.

24. Ibid.

25. Reynolds to Clark, 26 May 1831, copy in Stevens, *The Black Hawk War,* 85.

26. Reynolds to General Edmund Gaines, 28 May 1831, *BHW,* vol. 2, part 1, 20.

27. Gaines to Reynolds, 29 May 1831, copy in Stevens, *The Black Hawk War,* 89.

28. Gaines to Roger Jones, 30 May 1831, *BHW,* vol. 2, part 1, 25.

29. Ibid.

30. George McCall to his father, 17 June 1831, George A. McCall, *Letters from the Frontiers: Written During a Period of Thirty Years' Service in the Army of the United States* (1868; reprint, Gainesville: University Presses of Florida, 1974), 30.

31. Black Hawk, *Life,* 49.

32. Ibid.

33. Ibid., 49–50.

34. Spencer, *Reminiscences of Pioneer Life,* 72.

35. McCall to his father, 17 June 1831, *Letters from the Frontiers,* 228.

36. Black Hawk, *Life,* 50.

37. "Memorandum of the Talks Between Edmund P. Gaines and the Sauk," Rock Island, Mississippi River, 4, 5, 6, 7 June 1831, *BHW,* vol. 2, part 1, 27.

38. Black Hawk, *Life,* 43.

39. Quoted in "Memorandum of the Talks Between Edmund P. Gaines and the Sauk," 4 June 1831, *BHW,* vol. 2, part 1, 28.

40. Ibid., 29.

41. Quoted in "Memorandum of Talks Between Gaines and Sauk," 7 June 1831, *BHW,* vol. 2, part 1, 30.

42. McCall to his father, 17 June 1831, *Letters from the Frontiers,* 232–34.

43. Quoted in Black Hawk, *Life,* 51.

44. "Memorandum of Talks Between Gaines and Sauk," 7 June 1831, *BHW,* vol. 2, part 1, 30.

45. McCall to his father, 19 June 1831.

46. Gaines to R. Jones, 14 June 1831, *BHW,* vol. 2, part 1, 48.

47. McCall to his father, 17 June 1831.

48. Gaines to Reynolds, 5 June 1831, *BHW*, vol. 2, part 1, 35.

49. Reynolds, *My Own Times*, 209.

50. See Michael A. Bellesiles, *Arming America: The Origins of a National Gun Culture* (New York: Alfred A. Knopf, 2000).

51. Reynolds, *My Own Times*, 213.

52. Ibid., 215, 214.

53. Quoted in ibid., 215; see also the letter from Rushville, 20 June 1831, *BHW*, vol. 2, part 1, 65.

54. McCall to his father, 23 June 1831, *Letters from the Frontiers*, 235.

55. McCall to his father, begun 19 June 1831 and finished 1 July 1831, *Letters from the Frontiers*, 238, 237.

56. Extract of a letter by Gaines, 20 June 1831, *BHW*, vol. 2, part 1, 63.

57. McCall to his father, 1 July 1831, *Letters from the Frontiers*, 239.

58. Nathaniel Buckmaster to John Y. Sawyer, 30 June 1831, *BHW*, vol. 2, part 1, 84; McCall to his father, 1 July 1831, *Letters from the Frontiers*, 240.

59. St. Vrain to Clark, 23 July 1831, *BHW*, vol. 2, part 1, 112.

60. See note 1, *BHW*, vol. 2, part 1, 85; St. Vrain to Clark, 23 July 1831.

61. Reynolds, *My Own Times*, 217.

62. Spencer, *Reminiscences of Pioneer Life*, 49.

63. Ibid., 49–50.

64. Black Hawk, *Life*, 52.

65. Clark to Eaton, 29 June 1831, *BHW*, vol. 2, part 1, 83.

66. St. Vrain to Gaines, 15 June 1831, *BHW*, vol. 2, part 1, 51–52.

67. St. Vrain to the secretary of war, 6 September 1831, Indian Office Files, box 4.

68. Henry Gratiot to Gaines, 12 June 1831, Indian Office Files, box 4.

69. Speech of Winnebago chiefs to H. Gratiot, 1 July 1831, *BHW*, vol. 2, part 1, 95.

70. Paul L. Chouteau to Clark, 27 June 1831, *BHW*, vol. 2, part 1, 78.

71. Ibid.

72. Gratiot to Gaines, 12 June 1831.

73. Thomas Barnett to Clark, 29 June 1831, William Clark, Miscellaneous Papers, State Historical Society of Wisconsin, Manuscript Collections. Referred to henceforth as Clark Miscellaneous Papers.

74. Gratiot to Clark, 25 June 1831, *BHW*, vol. 2, part 1, 76.

75. Gaines to Hugh White, 6 July 1831, *BHW*, vol. 2, part 1, 76.

76. McCall to his father, 5 July 1831, *Letters from the Frontiers*, 241.

77. Clark to Eaton, 6 July 1831, Indian Office Files, box 4.

78. Forsyth to Davenport, 10 July 1831, *BHW*, vol. 2, part 1, 107.

79. Letter from a staff officer of the volunteers, 1 July 1831, *BHW*, vol. 2, part 1, 94–95.

80. Street to Captain Gustavus Loomis, 31 July 1831, *BHW*, vol. 2, part 1, 115.

81. General Henry Atkinson to Gaines, 10 August 1831, *BHW*, vol. 2, part 1, 128.

82. Street to Clark, 1 August 1831, Clark Miscellaneous Papers.

83. Loomis to Street, 11 August 1831, Indian Office Files, box 4.

84. Atkinson to Gaines, 10 August 1831, *BHW*, vol. 2, part 1, 129.

85. Street to Clark, 1 August 1831.

86. Street to the secretary of war, 1 August 1831, *BHW*, vol. 2, part 1, 121, 117.

87. Clark to the secretary of war, 9 August 1831, *BHW*, vol. 2, part 1, 127.

88. Atkinson to Gaines, 10 August 1831.

89. Cass to Clark, 25 August 1831, *BHW*, vol. 2, part 1, 144–46.

6: *Spirits of the Fathers*

1. McCall to his father, 17 June 1831, *Letters from the Frontiers*, 230–31.

2. Jill Lepore, *The Name of War: King Philip's War and the Origins of American Identity* (New York: Vintage Books, 1998), see the opening chapter.

3. Black Hawk, *Life*, 17, 18.

4. "Council with the Western Nations," August 1817, William McKay Papers, National Archives of Canada, MG19, F29, 1–7.

5. "An Indian Council, Prairie du Chien," April 18, 1815, [Captain N. A.] Bulger Papers, *WHC* 13 (1895), 132.

6. Thomas G. Anderson, "Personal Narrative of Captain Thomas G. Anderson: Early Experiences in the Northwest Fur Trade—British Capture of Prairie du Chien, 1814," *WHC* 9 (1882), 201.

7. Black Hawk, *Life*, 38–39.

8. Spencer, *Reminiscences of Pioneer Life*, 28.

9. Black Hawk, "Surrender Speech," August 27, 1832, www.mtholyoke.edu/acad/intrel/black.ntm.

10. William Carroll Reed, *Register and Leader* (Des Moines), 10 March 1907.

11. Black Hawk, *Life*, 22.

12. "Reminiscences of Black Hawk by People Who Knew Him," *Burlington Hawk-Eye*, 24 March 1907.

13. Jay Monaghan, "Black Hawk Rides Again—A Glimpse of the Man," *Wisconsin Magazine of History* 29 (September 1945), 45; and Nichols, *Black Hawk and the Warrior's Path*, 13. Nichols thinks there may have been a younger brother, but there is no mention of him in Black Hawk's autobiography and no other evidence to verify his existence.

14. Black Hawk, *Life*, 5, 6.

15. Black Hawk, "Surrender Speech."

16. Black Hawk, *Life*, 7.

17. Ibid., 3.

18. Ibid., 6, 63.

19. Ibid., 68.

20. Ibid., 62.

21. Robert Jay Lifton, *History and Human Survival: Essays on the Young and Old, Survivors and the Dead, Peace and War, and on Contemporary Psychohistory* (New York: Vintage Books, 1961), 173–77; Robert Jay Lifton, *Boundaries: Psychological Man in Revolution* (New York: Vintage Books, 1969), 70.

22. Quoted in Nehemiah Matson, *Memories of Shaubena, with Incidents Relating to Indian Wars and the Early Settlement of the West* (Chicago: D. B. Cooke, 1878), 109.

23. Ibid., 100.

24. Black Hawk, *Life*, 52.

25. Ibid., 41.

26. Ibid., 42.

27. Quoted in Stevens, *The Black Hawk War*, 259. My emphasis.

28. Black Hawk, "Surrender Speech."

29. McCall to his father, 17 June 1831.

30. "Memorandum of Talks Between Gaines and Sauk," 7 June 1831, *BHW*, vol. 2, part 1, 30.

31. Black Hawk, *Life*, 51.

32. Extract of a letter from General Edmund P. Gaines, 20 June 1831, *BHW*, vol. 2, part 1, 63.

33. Gail Bederman, *Manliness and Civilization: A Cultural History of Gender and Race in the United States, 1880–1917* (Chicago: University of Chicago Press, 1995).

34. Black Hawk, *Life*, 43.

35. Black Hawk, "Surrender Speech."

36. Forsyth to Clark, 10 June 1828, Forsyth Papers.

37. Murphy, *A Gathering of Rivers*, 124.

38. Quoted in Thomas L. McKenney, *Memoirs, Official and Personal* (1846; reprint, Lincoln: University of Nebraska Press, 1973), 89.

39. Quoted in ibid., 90, 92. His emphasis.

40. Ibid., 91.

41. Ibid., 92.

42. Forsyth to McKenney, 5 August 1830, Forsyth Papers.

43. Taimah and Apanosokeman to Clark, 22 July 1832, Indian Office Files, box 5.

44. Reuben Holmes to Benjamin McCary, 23 May 1832, *BHW*, vol. 2, part 1, 415.

45. Atkinson to Gaines, 10 August 1831, *BHW*, vol. 2, part 1, 130.

46. "Journal of a Council at Fort Armstrong with Chiefs and Warriors of the Sauk and Fox and Felix St. Vrain," September 5, 1831, Indian Office Files, box 4.

47. See Richard White, *The Middle Ground: Indians, Empires, and Republics in the Great Lakes Region, 1650–1815* (New York: Cambridge University Press, 1991).

48. Kerry A. Trask, "In the Name of the Father: Paternalism and the 1763 Indian Uprising at Michilimackinac," *Old Northwest* 9 (Spring 1983), 3–22; White, *The Middle Ground*, 84.

49. Thomas Forsyth, "The French, British and Spanish Method of Treating Indians," (no date), Forsyth Papers.

50. Black Hawk, *Life*, 13.

51. Forsyth to Cass, 24 October 1831, Forsyth Papers.

52. Forsyth, "French, British and Spanish Method."

53. Ibid.

54. Colin G. Calloway, "The End of an Era: British-Indian Relations in the Great Lakes Region After the War of 1812," *Michigan Historical Review* 12 (Fall 1986), 9.

55. S. F. Wise and Robert Craig Brown, *Canada Views the United States: Nineteenth Century Political Attitudes* (Seattle: University of Washington Press, 1967), 42.

56. Kenneth Bourne, *Britain and the Balance of Power in North America, 1815–1908* (Berkeley: University of California Press, 1967), 9.

57. Charles Francis Adams, ed., *Memoirs of John Quincy Adams, Comprising Portions of His Diary from 1795 to 1848* (Philadelphia: J. B. Lippincott, 1875), vol. 5, 438–39.

58. Gerald M. Craig, *Upper Canada: The Formative Years, 1784–1841* (Toronto: McClelland and Stewart, 1963), 85.

59. Ibid., 110.

60. Wise and Brown, *Canada Views the United States*, 17, 20, 21.

61. Craig, *Upper Canada*, 110.

62. Bourne, *Britain and Balance of Power*, 35–36.

63. Ibid., 58.

64. James A. Clifton, *A Place of Refuge for All Time: Migration of the American Potawatomi into Upper Canada, 1830–1850*. National Museum of Man Mercury Series. (Ottawa: National Museums of Canada, 1975), 24.

65. Bourne, *Britain and Balance of Power*, 58.

66. Catherine Parr Traill, *The Backwoods of Canada* (London: Charles Knight, 1836; reprint, Toronto: McClelland and Stewart, 1989), 87.

67. Craig, *Upper Canada*, 87.

68. Chandler Robbins Gilman, *Life on the Lakes: Being Tales and Sketches Collected During a Trip to the Pictured Rocks of Lake Superior* (New York: George Dearborn, 1836), vol. 1, 50.

69. Robert S. Allen, *The British Indian Department and the Frontier in North America, 1755–1830* (Ottawa: Department of Indian and Northern Affairs Canada, 1975), 49.

70. Thomas Anderson, "Personal Narrative," 203.

71. Sir James Kempt to Sir John Colborne, 18 February 1829, RG 10, Indian Affairs, series A, vol. 5, National Archives of Canada.

72. Sir John Colborne to R. W. Hay, 3 May 1829, in Vincent Harlow and Frederick Madden, ed., *British Colonial Developments, 1774–1834* (Oxford: Clarendon Press, 1953), 591.

73. Kempt to Colborne, 23 February 1829, RG 10, Indian Affairs, series A, vol. 5, National Archives of Canada.

74. Gordon T. Stewart, *The American Response to Canada Since 1776* (East Lansing: Michigan State University Press, 1992), 23.

75. Quoted in Calloway, "End of an Era," 8.

76. Ibid., 6.

77. Quoted in W. Sheridan Warrick, "The American Indian Policy in the Upper Old Northwest Following the War of 1812," *Ethnohistory* 3 (Winter 1956), 116.

78. Lewis Cass to John C. Calhoun, 17 June 1820, in Clarence E. Carter, ed., *The Territorial Papers of the United States*, vol. 12, *The Territory of Michigan, 1820–1829* (Washington: Government Printing Office, 1945), 37.

79. Warrick, "American Indian Policy . . . Upper Old Northwest," 116.

80. Clifton, *A Place of Refuge*, 25, 26.

81. "Remarks Made by a Winnebago Chief, Four Legs," recorded by Thomas Anderson, Drummond Island, 13 July 1828, RG 10, Indian Affairs, series A, vol. 45, National Archives of Canada.

82. Warrick, "American Indian Policy . . . Upper Old Northwest," 116.

83. Allen, *British Indian Department*, 87.

84. Quoted in ibid.

85. Forsyth to Calhoun, 23 September 1823, Forsyth Papers.

86. Forsyth to the secretary of war, 24 August 1824, Forsyth Papers.

87. "Remarks Made by a Winnebago Chief, Four Legs," 13 July 1828.

88. Clifton, *A Place of Refuge*, 28.

89. Forsyth to Clark, 10 June 1828, Indian Office Files, box 2.

90. Forsyth to Clark, 24 May 1828, Forsyth Papers.

91. Stewart, *American Response to Canada*, 32.

92. Forsyth to Clark, 24 May 1827, Forsyth Papers.

93. Forsyth to Clark, 16 June 1828, Forsyth Papers.

94. Forsyth to Clark, 22 June 1828, Forsyth Papers.

95. Ibid.

96. Forsyth to Clark, 22 August 1828, Forsyth Papers.

97. St. Vrain to the secretary of war, 6 September 1831, Indian Office Files, box 4.

98. Kempt to Colborne, 18 February 1829.

99. Forsyth to Calhoun, 7 July 1823, Forsyth Papers.

100. Black Hawk, *Life*, 46.

101. Clark to Gaines, 28 May 1831, *BHW*, vol. 2, part 1, 17.

102. Gaines to Jones, 14–15 June 1831, *BHW*, vol. 2, part 1, 49.

103. Gaines: Order, Rock Island, 1 July 1831, *BHW*, vol. 2, part 1, 89.

104. Articles of Agreement and Capitulation, Fort Armstrong, 30 June 1831, *BHW*, vol. 2, part 1, 86.

105. *Niles' Weekly Register*, 16 July 1831.

106. Forsyth to McKenney, 2 August 1830, Forsyth Papers.

107. "Minutes of the Examination of Indian Prisoners," Fort Armstrong, 20 August 1832, *BHW*, vol. 2, part 2, 1034.

108. Quoted in Black Hawk, *Life*, 53.

109. Quoted in ibid.

110. Ibid., 53–54.

111. Ibid., 54.

112. Ibid.

113. Street to Cass, 26 August 1831, *BHW*, vol. 2, part 1, 149.

114. Major John Bliss to Atkinson, 6 April 1832, *BHW*, vol. 2, part 1, 228.

115. James A. Clifton, "Personal and Ethnic Identity on the Great Lakes Frontier: The Case of Billy Caldwell, Anglo-Canadian," *Ethnohistory* 25 (Winter 1978), 68–94.

116. Billy Caldwell to Forsyth, 8 April 1832, *BHW*, vol. 2, part 1, 234.

117. Bliss to Atkinson, 9–12 April 1832, *BHW*, vol. 2, part 1, 237.

118. Nathan Smith to Atkinson, 13 April 1832, *BHW*, vol. 2, part 1, 249.

119. *Galenian*, 2 May 1832.

120. Gratiot to Cass, 26 April 1832, *BHW*, vol. 2, part 1, 314.

121. Matson, *Memories of Shaubena*, 109.

122. Samuel C. Stambaugh to George Boyd, 25 August 1832, a Copy of Governor General Sir George Provost's speech attached, Indian Office Files, box 5.

7: *The Road to War*

1. Daniel Parkinson, "Pioneer Life in Wisconsin," 335.
2. *Galenian*, 6 June 1832.
3. Street to Clark, 11 January 1832, Clark Miscellaneous Papers.
4. Street to Thomas P. Barnett, 1 February 1832, *BHW*, vol. 2, part 1, 209.
5. Caldwell to Forsyth, 8 April 1832, Clark Miscellaneous Papers.
6. Elbert Herring to Clark, 15 March 1832, *BHW*, vol. 2, part 1, 218.
7. Alexander Macomb to Atkinson, 17 March 1832, *BHW*, vol. 2, part 1, 220.
8. Atkinson to Macomb, 3 April 1832, *BHW*, vol. 2, part 1, 224.
9. Albert Sidney Johnston diary, 8 April 1832, *BHW*, vol. 2, part 2, 1307.
10. Black Hawk, *Life*, 54; Davenport to Joseph Duncan, 11 February 1832, *BHW*, vol. 2, part 1, 211–13.
11. Black Hawk, *Life*, 55.
12. St. Vrain to Clark, 8 April 1832, Indian Office Files, box 6.
13. Johnston diary, 10 April 1832, 1308.
14. Atkinson to Macomb, 10 April 1832, *BHW*, vol. 2, part 1, 243.
15. Johnston diary, 12 April 1832, 1308.
16. Atkinson to Macomb, 10 April 1832, 244.
17. Black Hawk, *Life*, 56.
18. Bliss to Atkinson, 30 March 1832, *BHW*, vol. 2, part 1, 222. Atkinson did not receive this letter until 23 April 1832.
19. Ibid., 223.
20. St. Vrain to Clark, 6 April 1832, Indian Office Files, box 6.
21. Ibid.
22. Bliss to Atkinson, 6 April 1832, *BHW*, vol. 2, part 1, 228.
23. Ibid., 227.
24. Bliss to Atkinson, 9–12 April 1832, *BHW*, vol. 2, part 1, 237.
25. Ibid.
26. Ibid., 238.
27. Ibid., 239.
28. Ibid., 237.
29. Answer of Black Hawk and his band to Henry Atkinson, 26 April 1832, *BHW*, vol. 2, part 1, 313.
30. Black Hawk, *Life*, 54–55.
31. Bliss to Atkinson, 9–12 April 1832, *BHW*, vol. 2, part 1, 238.
32. Spencer, *Reminiscences of Pioneer Life*, 51.
33. Black Hawk, *Life*, 55.
34. Bliss to Atkinson, 9–12 April 1832, 237, 239, 238.
35. Answer of Black Hawk, 26 April 1832.
36. Andrew S. Hughes to Atkinson, 13 April 1832, *BHW*, vol. 2, part 1, 248.
37. Spencer, *Reminiscences of Pioneer Life*, 51.
38. Fort Armstrong Council, 13 April 1832, *BHW*, vol. 2, part 1, 253.
39. Spencer, *Reminiscences of Pioneer Life*, 52.
40. Black Hawk, *Life*, 56.
41. Spencer, *Reminiscences of Pioneer Life*, 52.
42. Bliss to Atkinson, 12 April 1832.
43. George Davenport to Atkinson, 13 April 1832, *BHW*, vol. 2, part 1, 247.

44. St. Vrain to Clark, 18 April 1832, *BHW*, vol. 2, part 1, 277. It is assumed that St. Vrain gave Atkinson the same information in person.

45. "Report of Daniel S. Witter on Indian Depredations," 28 April 1832, *BHW*, vol. 2, part 1, 328.

46. Davenport to Atkinson, 13 April 1832.

47. Hughes to Atkinson, 13 April 1832. His emphasis.

48. Nathan Smith to Atkinson, 13 April 1832, *BHW*, vol. 2, part 1, 249.

49. St. Vrain to Clark, 18 April 1832, *BHW*, vol. 2, part 1, 277.

50. Spencer, *Reminiscences of Pioneer Life*, 51, 53.

51. Zachary Taylor to Major General Thomas S. Jesup, 4 December 1832, Holman Hamilton, ed., "Documents: Zachary Taylor and the Black Hawk War," *Wisconsin Magazine of History* 24 (March 1941), 309.

52. Black Hawk, *Life*, 56.

53. Roger L. Nichols, *General Henry Atkinson: A Western Military Career* (Norman: University of Oklahoma Press, 1965), 158.

54. Cecil Eby, *"That Disgraceful Affair": The Black Hawk War* (New York: W. W. Norton, 1973), 93.

55. Clark to Cass, 20 April 1832, Indian Office Files, box 6.

56. Forsyth to John Connolly, 16 April 1832, *BHW*, vol. 2, part 1, 262.

57. Atkinson to Macomb, 10 April 1832, 244.

58. Atkinson to Macomb, 13 April 1832, *BHW*, vol. 2, part 1, 245.

59. Fort Armstrong Council, 13 April 1832, 251.

60. See Nichols, *General Henry Atkinson*.

61. Ford, *A History of Illinois*, 147.

62. Ibid., 148.

63. Ibid., 145.

64. William Orr to John Y. Sawyer, 21 June 1832, *BHW*, vol. 2, part 1, 641. His emphasis.

65. Eby, *"Disgraceful Affair,"* 103.

66. Ford, *A History of Illinois*, 147.

67. Nichols, *General Henry Atkinson*, 122.

68. Atkinson to Reynolds, 13 April 1832, *BHW*, vol. 2, part 1, 246.

69. Reynolds to Atkinson, 16 April 1832, *BHW*, vol. 2, part 1, 263.

70. Atkinson to Reynolds, 18 April 1832, *BHW*, vol. 2, part 1, 275.

71. Atkinson to Reynolds, 27 April 1832, *BHW*, vol. 2, part 1, 320. My emphasis.

72. Gratiot to Atkinson, 27 April 1832, *BHW*, vol. 2, part 1, 318–19.

73. Black Hawk, *Life*, 56. His emphasis.

74. Matson, *Memories of Shaubena*, 95.

75. Ibid., 110.

76. Atkinson to Black Hawk, 24 April 1832, *BHW*, vol. 2, part 1, 301–02.

77. Gratiot to Atkinson, 27 April 1832.

78. Ibid.

79. Answer from Black Hawk, 26 April 1832.

80. Ibid. The note was made on 26 April 1832 regarding the meeting that occurred when Keokuk called upon Atkinson with St. Vrain and LeClaire.

81. Atkinson to Macomb, 27 April 1832, *BHW*, vol. 2, part 1, 319.

82. Extract of letter, John Reynolds to the militia of the northwestern section of the state, 16 April 1832, *BHW*, vol. 2, part 1, 264.

8: A Martial People

1. James Hall, "The Indian Hater," in James Hall, *Legends of the West* (Philadelphia: Harrison Hall, 1832), 248.

2. Ibid., 249.

3. Ibid., 252.

4. Ibid., 259.

5. Hayden White, "Forms of the Wilderness: Archaeology of an Idea," in *The Wild Man Within: An Image in Western Thought from the Renaissance to Romanticism*, ed. Edward Dudley and Maximilian E. Novak (Pittsburgh: University of Pittsburgh Press, 1972), 3–38.

6. Joyce Appleby, *Inheriting the Revolution: The First Generation of Americans* (Cambridge, Mass.: Belknap Press of Harvard University, 2000); Michael Paul Rogin, *Fathers and Children: Andrew Jackson and the Subjugation of the American Indians* (New York: Vintage Books, 1975).

7. Benedict Anderson, *Imagined Communities: Reflections on the Origin and Spread of Nationalism* (London: Verso, 1991).

8. Roderick Nash, *Wilderness and the American Mind*, 3rd ed. (New Haven, Conn.: Yale University Press, 1982), 75.

9. James Hall, *Letters from the West: Containing Sketches of Scenery, Manners, and Customs; and Anecdotes Connected with the First Settlement of the Western Section of the United States* (London: Henry Colburn, 1828; facsimile reproduction, Gainesville, Fla.: Scholarly Facsimiles and Reprints, 1967), 285.

10. McKenney and Hall, *The Indian Tribes of North America*, vol. 3, 156, 158.

11. Ibid., 156.

12. Hall, *Letters from the West*, 288.

13. Robert F. Berkhofer Jr., *The White Man's Indian: Images of the American Indian from Columbus to the Present* (New York: Vintage Books, 1979), xvi.

14. Lepore, *The Name of War*, 193.

15. Ibid., 200.

16. Matthew G. Fitch, "The Battle of Peckatonica," *WHC* 10 (1888), 178.

17. McKenney and Hall, *Indian Tribes*, vol. 3, 157.

18. Hall, *Letters from the West*, 288.

19. *Galenian*, 31 October 1832.

20. George L. Mosse, *The Image of Man: The Creation of Modern Masculinity* (New York: Oxford University Press, 1996), 56.

21. De Tocqueville, *Democracy in America*, vol. 2, 99.

22. Michael Kimmel, *Manhood in America: A Cultural History* (New York: Free Press, 1996), 33.

23. Leo Braudy, *From Chivalry to Terrorism: War and the Changing Nature of Masculinity* (New York: Alfred A. Knopf, 2003), 24.

24. Reynolds to Joseph Duncan, 30 April 1832, *BHW*, vol. 2, part 1, 335; Reynolds to Atkinson, 30 April 1832, *BHW*, vol. 2, part 1, 336. He probably lied to justify getting more supplies and funds from the federal government.

25. John A. Wakefield, *Wakefield's History of the Black Hawk War* (1833; reprint, Madison, Wis.: Roger Hunt, 1976), 40.

26. Atkinson to Hugh Brady, 8 May 1832, *BHW*, vol. 2, part 1, 354.

27. William Orr to John Y. Sawyer, "The Indian War," 21 June 1832, *BHW*, vol. 2, part 1, 641.

28. Diary of Orville Browning, 26 and 27 April 1832, *BHW*, vol. 2, part 2, 1298.

29. William Headen to his brother, 1 May 1832, *BHW*, vol. 2, part 1, 341.

30. Browning diary, 2 May 1832.

31. Reynolds, *My Own Times*, 226.

32. Browning diary, 3 May 1832.

33. Ibid.; Reynolds to Atkinson, 5 May 1832, *BHW*, vol. 2, part 1, 352; Reynolds, *My Own Times*, 227.

34. Macomb to Atkinson, 5 May 1832, *BHW*, vol. 2, part 1, 351–52.

35. Atkinson to Taylor, 6 May 1832, *BHW*, vol. 2, part 1, 353.

36. Atkinson to Macomb, 10 May 1832, *BHW*, vol. 2, part 1, 362.

37. Johnston diary, 14 May 1832, *BHW*, vol. 2, part 2, 1311.

38. Henry Smith, "Indian Campaign of 1832," *WHC* 10 (1888), 156.

39. Orr to Sawyer, 21 June 1832, *BHW*, vol. 2, part 1, 642.

40. Wakefield, *History of the Black Hawk War*, 44.

41. Orr to Sawyer, 1 July 1832, *BHW*, vol. 2, part 2, 72. My emphasis.

42. Ibid., 4–28.

43. Samuel Whiteside to Atkinson, 18 May 1832, *BHW*, vol. 2, part 1, 386.

44. Reynolds, *My Own Times*, 229.

45. Orr to Sawyer, 1 July 1832.

46. Whiteside and Reynolds to Atkinson, 14 May 1832, *BHW*, vol. 2, part 1, 370.

47. Answer of Black Hawk and his band to Henry Atkinson, 26 April 1832, *BHW*, vol. 2, part 1, 313.

48. Johnston diary, 12 May 1832, 1310.

49. Thomas J. V. Owen to Reynolds, 12 May 1832, *BHW*, vol. 2, part 1, 365.

50. Black Hawk, *Life*, 58.

51. Ibid., 57.

52. Matson, *Memories of Shaubena*, 114.

53. Black Hawk, *Life*, 58.

54. Reynolds: Order, 16 April 1832, *BHW*, vol. 2, part 1, 267.

55. John Dixon to Isaiah Stillman, 28 April 1832, *BHW*, vol. 2, part 1, 325.

56. Stillman to Elias Foster, 29 April 1832, *BHW*, vol. 2, part 1, 332.

57. Reynolds: Order, 23 April 1832, *BHW*, vol. 2, part 1, 298.

58. Stillman to Reynolds, 4 May 1832, *BHW*, vol. 2, part 1, 346.

59. Reynolds, *My Own Times*, 230.

60. Whiteside to Atkinson, 18 May 1832.

61. "A Militia Officer's Report on Isaiah Stillman's Defeat," *Illinois Advocate* (Edwardsville), May 29, 1832.

62. Ibid.

63. Whiteside: Order, 12 May 1832, *BHW*, vol. 2, part 1, 367.

64. Dodge to Atkinson, 13 May 1832, *BHW*, vol. 2, part 1, 368.

65. *Galenian*, 16 May 1832.

66. Forsyth, "Original Causes of the Trouble with a Party of Sauk," 1 October 1832, Forsyth Papers.

67. *BHW*, vol. 2, part 1, 274, note 2; see also Reynolds Proclamation, 15 May 1832, in which he said "about 275," *BHW*, vol. 2, part 1, 373; "Militia Officer" claimed "about 260," *BHW*, vol. 2, part 1, 387; James Stephenson noted "270," *Galenian*, 23 May 1832; Andrew Maxfield said in *Sangamo Journal* (Springfield, Ill.), 14 June 1832, the number was 206, which was probably a miswritten transposition and should have been 260.

68. Maxfield, *Sangamo Journal*, 14 June 1832.

69. Smith, "Indian Campaign of 1832," 157.

70. Isaiah Stillman, *Missouri Republican* (St. Louis), 19 June 1832.

71. Black Hawk, *Life*, 58. My emphasis.

72. "Minutes of the Examination of Indian Prisoners," Fort Armstrong, 20 August 1832, *BHW*, vol. 2, part 2, 1034. My emphasis.

73. Matson, *Memories of Shaubena*, 115. My emphasis.

74. Stillman, *Missouri Republican*, 19 June 1832.

75. Maxfield, *Sangamo Journal*, 14 June 1832. My emphasis.

76. James Stephenson, "Seat of War," *Galenian*, 23 May 1832.

77. Stillman, *Missouri Republican*, 19 June 1832; Maxfield, *Sangamo Journal*, 14 June 1832.

78. Maxfield, *Sangamo Journal*, 14 June 1832.

79. Black Hawk, *Life*, 58, 59.

80. *Galenian*, 23 May 1832.

81. Maxfield, *Sangamo Journal*, 14 June 1832.

82. Stillman, *Missouri Republican*, 19 June 1832.

83. James Stroud's account recorded in Ford, *A History of Illinois*, 174–76.

84. Taylor to Thomas Jesup, 4 December 1832, Holman Hamilton, ed., "Documents," *Wisconsin Magazine of History* 24 (1940–41), 309; Taylor to Thomas Lawson, 16 August 1832, *BHW*, vol. 2, part 2, 1014.

85. Reynolds, *My Own Times*, 234, 235.

86. Orr to Sawyer, 1 July 1832, *BHW*, vol. 2, part 2, 727, 728.

87. *New York Mercury*, 27 June 1832.

88. "Oliver W. Hall's Account," Stevens, *The Black Hawk War*, 134–35.

89. "Militia Officer's Report," *Illinois Advocate*, 29 May 1832.

90. Eby, "*Disgraceful Affair*," 127.

91. Stillman, *Missouri Republican*, 19 June 1832.

92. Taylor to Atkinson, 22 June 1832, *BHW*, vol. 2, part 1, 503.

93. Atkinson to Dodge, 17 May 1832, *BHW*, vol. 2, part 1, 377.

9: *The Great Fear*

1. Braudy, *From Chivalry to Terrorism*, 246–61; John William Ward, *Andrew Jackson: Symbol for an Age* (New York: Oxford University Press, 1962), 3–25.

2. McKenney, *Memoirs*, 233.

3. Kinzie, *Wau-Bun*, 357–58.

4. Johnston diary, 1311.

5. Forsyth, "Original Causes of the Trouble with a Party of Sauk," 1 October 1832, Forsyth Papers.

6. *Galenian*, 23 May 1832.

7. Atkinson: Order, 17 May 1832, *BHW*, vol. 2, part 1, 378.

8. Atkinson: Order, 18 May 1832, *BHW*, vol. 2, part 1, 380.

9. Atkinson: Order, 22 May 1832, *BHW*, vol. 2, part 1, 404.

10. Taylor to Atkinson, 26 May 1832, *BHW*, vol. 2, part 1, 453.

11. Johnston diary, 23 May 1832, 1312.

12. Stillman to Atkinson, 21 May 1832, *BHW*, vol. 2, part 1, 400–401.

13. Reynolds, *My Own Times*, 237.

14. Orr to Sawyer, 1 July 1832, *BHW*, vol. 2, part 2, 726.

15. Nathaniel Buckmaster to Harriet Ann Buckmaster, 17 May 1832, *BHW*, vol. 2, part 1, 361.

16. Whiteside to Atkinson, 27 May 1832, *BHW*, vol. 2, part 1, 461.

17. Reynolds, *My Own Times*, 238.

18. Whiteside to Atkinson, 27 May 1832.

19. Harriet Buckmaster to Nathaniel Buckmaster, 27 May 1832, *BHW*, vol. 2, part 1, 458.

20. Forsyth to Davenport, 23 May 1832, *BHW*, vol. 2, part 1, 413.

21. Whiteside: Order, 24 May 1832, *BHW*, vol. 2, part 1, 434.

22. Reynolds, *My Own Times*, 239.

23. Reynolds to Cass, 4 June 1832, *BHW*, vol. 2, part 1, 520.

24. Letter from Canton, Illinois, 31 May 1832, *New York Mercury*, 27 June 1832.

25. *Galenian*, 30 May 1832.

26. Horatio Newhall to Isaac Newhall, 19 May 1832, *BHW*, vol. 2, part 1, 394.

27. *Galenian*, 30 May 1832.

28. James Strode to Atkinson, 26 May 1832, printed in the *Galenian*, 30 May 1832.

29. *Galenian*, 6 June 1832.

30. Black Hawk, *Life*, 62.

31. Matson, *Memories of Shaubena*, 153; "Narrative of John W. Hall," Nemaha County, Nebraska, September 1867, complete text in Stevens, *Black Hawk War*, 155.

32. "Narrative of John W. Hall."

33. George E. Walker to Atkinson, 10 October 1834, *BHW*, vol. 2, part 2, 1287.

34. "Narrative of John W. Hall."

35. Reuben Holmes to B. McCary, 23 May 1832, *BHW*, vol. 2, part 1, 415.

36. Reynolds, *My Own Times*, 243.

37. Holmes to McCary, 23 May 1832.

38. *Galenian*, 6 June 1832.

39. Atwater, *Remarks on a Tour to Prairie du Chien*, 184; Marianna Torgovick, *Primitive Passions: Men, Women, and the Quest for Ecstasy* (Chicago: University of Chicago Press, 1996), 3–5.

40. Turner, *Beyond Geography*, 9.

41. Thomas Owen to Colonel James Stewart, 21 May 1832, Indian Office Files, box 5.

42. Wakefield, *History of the Black Hawk War*, 101.

43. Taylor to Thomas Lawson, 16 August 1832, *BHW*, vol. 2, part 2, 1015.

44. Owen to Stewart, 24 May 1832, Indian Office Files, box 5.

45. Reverend S[tephen] R. Beggs, *Papers from the Early History of the West and Northwest* (Cincinnati: Methodist Book Concern, 1868), 97, 99.

46. Ibid., 100.

47. John G. C. Hogan to Cass, 25 May 1832, Indian Office Files, box 5.

48. Beggs, *Papers from the Early History of the West*, 103.

49. Letter from Lewistown, Illinois, 1 June 1832, *New York Mercury*, 27 June 1832.

50. Matson, *Memories of Shaubena*, 194–204.

51. James M. Strode, "Proclamation of Martial Law," 21 May 1832, *BHW*, vol. 2, part 1, 403.

52. Atkinson to Strode, 27 May 1832, complete copy in Alan W. Eckert, *Twilight of Empire* (New York: Bantam Books, 1989), 397.

53. *Galenian*, 6 June 1832.

54. Horatio Newhall to Isaac Newhall, 8 June 1832, *BHW*, vol. 2, part 1, 552.

55. *History of Jo Daviess County, Illinois* (Chicago: H. F. Kett, 1878), 287–88.

56. *Galenian*, 6 June 1832.

57. Dodge to Atkinson, 16 May 1832, *BHW*, vol. 2, part 1, 375.

58. Baird, *O-De-Jit-Wa-Win-Ning*, 78.

59. Wakefield, *History of the Black Hawk War*, 55.

60. Susan Scheckel, *The Insistence of the Indian: Race and Nationalism in Nineteenth Century American Culture* (Princeton, N.J.: Princeton University Press, 1998), 79; Christopher Castiglia, *Bound and Determined: Captivity, Culture Crossing, and White Womanhood from Mary Rowlandson to Patty Hearst* (Chicago: University of Chicago Press, 1996).

61. Richard Slotkin, *Regeneration Through Violence: The Mythology of the American Frontier, 1600–1860* (Middleton, Conn.: Wesleyan University Press, 1973), 100–101.

62. Ibid., 100.

63. John Demos, *The Unredeemed Captive: A Family Story from Early America* (New York: Alfred A. Knopf, 1994).

64. Castiglia, *Bound and Determined*, ix–x.

65. Traill, *Backwoods of Canada*, 90.

66. Caroline M. Kirkland, *A New Home—Who'll Follow? Glimpses of Western Life*, 5th ed. (1839; reprint, New York: C. S. Francis, 1855), 230.

67. Margaret Fuller, *Summer on the Lakes in 1843* (1844; reprint, Urbana: University of Illinois Press, 1991), 38.

68. Quoted in George E. Walker to Atkinson, 10–11 October 1834, *BHW*, vol. 2, part 2, 1287. Referred to henceforth as "Rachel Hall's Narrative."

69. "Sylvia Hall's Narrative," Wakefield, *History of the Black Hawk War*, 88.

70. "Report of Rachel Munson and Sylvia Horn," Nemaha, Nebraska, 7 September 1832, complete texts in Stevens, *History of the Black Hawk War*, 150–51.

71. *Narrative of the Capture and Providential Escape of Misses Frances and Almira Hall*, in *The Garland Library of Narratives of North American Indian Captivities* (New York: Garland, 1975), vol. 49, 5–24.

72. "Sylvia Hall's Narrative," 93.

73. Ford, *A History of Illinois*, 178.

74. "Narrative of John W. Hall."

75. Holmes to McCary, 23 May 1832.
76. *Galenian*, 6 June 1832.
77. Holmes to McCary, 23 May 1832.
78. "Sylvia Hall's Narrative," 92.
79. Ibid., 93.
80. "Rachel Hall's Narrative," 1287.
81. "Sylvia Hall's Narrative," 88.
82. "Rachel Hall's Narrative," 1288.
83. Ibid.
84. Ibid.
85. "Sylvia Hall's Narrative," 89.
86. "Rachel Hall's Narrative," 1288.
87. "Sylvia Hall's Narrative," 90.
88. "Rachel Hall's Narrative," 1288.
89. "Sylvia Hall's Narrative," 90.
90. "Rachel Hall's Narrative," 1289.
91. Diary of Henry Gratiot, 28 May 1832, *BHW*, vol. 2, part 2, 1303.
92. Atkinson to Gratiot, 27 May 1832, *BHW*, vol. 2, part 1, 457–58.
93. "Rachel Hall's Narrative," 1289.
94. Porter's Grove Council, 3–4 June 1832, *BHW*, vol. 2, part 1, 508–9.
95. Ibid., 509.
96. "Rachel Hall's Narrative," 1289.
97. "Report of Rachel Munson and Sylvia Horn," 152.
98. "Rachel Hall's Narrative," 1289.
99. Porter's Grove Council, 3–4 June 1832, 509.
100. "Rachel Hall's Narrative," 1289.
101. Black Hawk, *Life*, 65.
102. *Narrative of Frances and Almira Hall*, vol. 49, 10.
103. Wakefield, *History of the Black Hawk War*, 95.
104. Ibid., 96.

10: *A Hero Arose*

1. *Galenian*, 6 June 1832.
2. James M. Strode to Atkinson, 10 June 1832, *BHW*, vol. 2, part 1, 566, report attached written by Thomas Sublett.
3. *Galenian*, 27 June 1832.
4. Samuel C. Stambaugh to George Boyd, 28 August 1832, *BHW*, vol. 2, part 2, 1074.
5. Strode to Atkinson, 10 June 1832.
6. "Report from James W. Stephenson," *Galenian*, 20 June 1832.
7. Quoted in *Galenian*, 20 June 1832.
8. Black Hawk, *Life*, 63.
9. Ibid.; see also Strode to Atkinson, 25 June 1832, *BHW*, vol. 2, part 2, 673.
10. *Galenian*, 4 July 1832; see also Stevens, *The Black Hawk War*, 185.
11. *Galenian*, 4 July 1832.
12. Oliver Emmill, "Reminiscence of the Black Hawk War," *WHC*, 5 (1868), 288.
13. *Galenian*, 4 July 1832.
14. Stevens, *The Black Hawk War*, 186.
15. *Galenian*, 27 June 1832.
16. Black Hawk, *Life*, 63.
17. See note 4, *BHW*, vol. 2, part 2, 674.
18. Black Hawk, *Life*, 63.

19. *Galenian,* 27 June 1832.

20. Ibid., 4 July 1832.

21. See John Carl Parish, ed., *George Wallace Jones: Autobiography* (Iowa City: State Historical Society of Iowa, 1912).

22. *Galenian,* 4 July 1832.

23. Ibid., 20 June 1832.

24. "M" to the editor, *Galenian,* 27 June 1832.

25. Stephen Mack to Lovicy Cooper, 13 June 1832, *BHW,* vol. 2, part 1, 583.

26. *Niles' Weekly Register,* 28 July 1832.

27. Acting Secretary of War John Robb to Atkinson, 12 June 1832, *BHW,* vol. 2, part 1, 580.

28. Strong, "Indians Wars of Wisconsin," 269.

29. "Interview with Selina Dodge Truett, *Evening Wisconsin* (Milwaukee), 20 February 1897.

30. Joseph Steel Gallagher to his wife, 25 August 1832, Joseph Steel Gallagher Letters, State Historical Society of Wisconsin, Manuscript Collections.

31. Joseph Steel Gallagher to Benjamin B. Gallagher, 31 August 1832, Gallagher Letters.

32. "Interview with Selina Dodge Truett."

33. *Galenian,* 14 May 1832.

34. John Fonda, "Dodge's Volunteers in the Black Hawk War," *WHC,* 5 (1868), 259.

35. *Galenian,* 6 June 1832.

36. Ibid., 13 June 1832.

37. Strong, "Indian Wars of Wisconsin," 271.

38. Peter Parkinson Jr., "Notes on the Black Hawk War," *WHC* 10 (1885), 185.

39. Ibid., 187; Moses Strong, in "Indian Wars of Wisconsin," 272, used identical words to describe this incident.

40. Peter Parkinson, "Notes on the Black Hawk War," 188.

41. Ibid., 188–89; and Porter's Grove Council, 3–4 June 1832, *BHW,* vol. 2, part 1, 507.

42. William Campbell to Andrew Jackson, 7–9 June 1832, *BHW,* vol. 2, part 1, 612.

43. Gratiot to Atkinson, 6 June 1832, *BHW,* vol. 2, part 1, 532.

44. Daniel Parkinson, "Pioneer Life in Wisconsin," 341.

45. Quoted in Strong, "Indian Wars of Wisconsin," 274.

46. Quoted in Ibid., 275.

47. Quoted in Ibid., 273, 275.

48. Quoted in Hagan, *The Sac and Fox Indians,* 163.

49. Daniel Parkinson, "Pioneer Life in Wisconsin," 342.

50. Dodge to the printer, 14 June 1832, *Galenian,* 20 June 1832.

51. "Curious Circumstances," *Galenian,* 27 June 1832.

52. Daniel Parkinson, "Pioneer Life in Wisconsin," 343–44.

53. Ibid., 344.

54. Ibid., 346–47.

55. W. W. Woodbridge to the printer, 16 June 1832, *Galenian,* 20 June 1832.

56. Dodge to Atkinson, 18 June 1832, *BHW,* vol. 2, part 1, 623.

57. Woodbridge letter, *Galenian,* 20 June 1832; Dodge to Atkinson, 18 June 1832.

58. Charles Bracken and Peter Parkinson Jr., "Pekatonica Battle Controversy," *WHC* 2 (1856), 371.

59. Daniel Parkinson, "Pioneer Life in Wisconsin," 348.

60. Peter Parkinson, "Notes on the Black Hawk War," 195.

61. Ibid., 195–96.

62. Dodge to Atkinson, 18 June 1832.

63. Captain Frances Gehon to Captain Sherman, 17 June 1832, William Henry Papers, State Historical Society of Wisconsin, Manuscript Collections.

64. Peter Parkinson, "Notes on the Black Hawk War," 196.

65. *Galenian,* 20 June 1832.

66. Anonymous letter to the printer, *Galenian*, 20 June 1832.

67. Ford, *A History of Illinois*, 188.

68. Strong, "Indian Wars of Wisconsin," 277–78.

69. Bracken and Peter Parkinson, "Pekatonica Battle Controversy," 372.

70. Peter Parkinson, "Notes on the Black Hawk War," 198.

71. Thomas P. Burnett to Dodge, 2 July 1832, *BHW*, vol. 2, part 2, 729.

72. Citizens of Prairie du Chien to Dodge, 3 July 1832, *BHW*, vol. 2, part 2, 737.

73. "To Our Father War Chief," 21 June 1832, *Galenian*, 4 July 1832.

74. Dodge to the Ladies of Galena, 25 June 1832, *Galenian*, 4 July 1832.

75. Henry Nash Smith, *Virgin Land: The American West as Symbol and Myth* (New York: Vintage Books, 1950), 66.

76. Slotkin, *Regeneration Through Violence*, 79: see also Lepore, *The Name of War*; Drinnon, *Facing West*.

77. Slotkin, *Regeneration Through Violence*, 189, 268.

78. Ward, *Andrew Jackson*; Mosse, *Image of Man*; Rogin, *Fathers and Children*; Kimmel, *Manhood in America*.

79. William Salter, "Henry Dodge . . . In the Black Hawk War, 1832," *Iowa Historical Record* 6 (1890), 421.

11: *Hunting a Shadow*

1. Black Hawk, *Life*, 20. His emphasis.

2. See Kimberly M. Blaeser, "Trickster: A Compendium," in *Buried Roots and Indestructible Seeds: The Survival of American Indian Life in Story, History, and Spirit* (Madison: Wisconsin Humanities Council, 1993), 24–32; Paul Radin, *The Trickster: A Study in American Indian Mythology* (New York: Schocken Books, 1956).

3. Kinzie, *Wau-Bun*, 110–11.

4. William Hamilton to Atkinson, 13 June 1832, *BHW*, vol. 2, part 1, 582.

5. Hamilton to Atkinson, 24 June 1832, *BHW*, vol. 2, part 2, 663.

6. Quoted in Joseph Street, "Indian Talk," 27 June 1832, *Galenian*, 11 July 1832.

7. Reynolds: Orders, 30 May 1832, *BHW*, vol. 2, part 1, 486.

8. William Cullen Bryant to Frances Bryant, 19 June 1832, *Bryant Letters*, 347.

9. Cooke, *Scenes and Adventures in the Army*, 156, 158, 159.

10. Reynolds, *My Own Times*, 246.

11. See Whitney, ed., *Black Hawk War*, vol. 1, 572; also Reynolds to Atkinson, 16 June 1832, *BHW*, vol. 2, part 1, 609; and Johnston diary, 15 June 1832, *BHW*, vol. 2, part 2, 1313.

12. *BHW*, vol. 1, 572; Johnston diary, 16 and 20 June 1832, 1313; Reynolds, *My Own Times*, 245.

13. Cooke, *Scenes and Adventures in the Army*, 159, 160.

14. Reynolds, *My Own Times*, 246.

15. Cooke, *Scenes and Adventures in the Army*, 161.

16. Atkinson to Macomb, 23 June 1832, *BHW*, vol. 2, part 1, 656.

17. *Vandalia Whig and Illinois Intelligencer*, 11 July 1832.

18. Black Hawk, *Life*, 63.

19. John Dement, "Report of the Battle of Kellogg's Grove, June 26, 1832," written 16 December 1832, *BHW*, vol. 2, part 2, 682.

20. Street to Clark, 30 June 1832, *BHW*, vol. 2, part 2, 721.

21. Reynolds, *My Own Times*, 251.

22. Daniel Parkinson, "Pioneer Life in Wisconsin," 353.

23. Dodge to Atkinson, 30 June 1832, *BHW*, vol. 2, part 2, 715–16; Atkinson to Hamilton, 29 June 1832, *BHW*, vol. 2, part 2, 711; Milton K. Alexander to Atkinson, 3 July 1832, *BHW*, vol. 2, part 2, 733.

24. Parish, *George Wallace Jones: Autobiography*, 120.

25. Atkinson to Alexander Posey, 28 June 1832, *BHW*, vol. 2, part 2, 697.

26. Atkinson to Dodge, 28 June 1832, *BHW*, vol. 2, part 2, 698.

27. Parish, *George Wallace Jones: Autobiography*, 121.

28. Daniel Parkinson, "Pioneer Life in Wisconsin," 353.

29. Parish, *George Wallace Jones: Autobiography*, 121.

30. *Illinois Herald* (Springfield), 12 July 1832.

31. Parish, *George Wallace Jones: Autobiography*, 121.

32. Daniel Parkinson, "Pioneer Life in Wisconsin," 353.

33. Parish, *George Wallace Jones: Autobiography*, 122.

34. *Galenian*, 18 July 1832.

35. Daniel Parkinson, "Pioneer Life in Wisconsin," 353.

36. Ibid.

37. Atkinson to Roger Jones, 19 November 1832, *BHW*, vol. 2, part 2, 1209–10.

38. Weather conditions, see Crawford Beecher Thayer, compiler and ed., *Hunting a Shadow: The Search for Black Hawk, An Eye Witness Account of the Black Hawk War of 1832* (Menasha, Wis.: Banta Press, 1981).

39. Charles Bracken, "Further Strictures on Ford's Black Hawk War," *WHC* 2 (1856), 404–5.

40. John Ryan to H. J. Wrigglesworth, no date, photostat copy in the Hoard Museum's Black Hawk War Collection, Fort Atkinson, Wisconsin, printed in Thayer, *Hunting a Shadow*, 142.

41. Diary of Nineveh Shaw (no dates), *BHW*, vol. 2, part 2, 1334.

42. *Galenian*, 18 July 1832.

43. Ibid.

44. Wakefield, *History of the Black Hawk War*, 83.

45. Cooke, *Scenes and Adventures in the Army*, 165.

46. Wakefield, *History of the Black Hawk War*, 82.

47. Diary of James Justice (no dates), *BHW*, vol. 2, part 2, 1323.

48. Wakefield, *History of the Black Hawk War*, 81.

49. Daniel Parkinson, "Pioneer Life in Wisconsin," 354.

50. Wakefield, *History of the Black Hawk War*, 82.

51. Cooke, *Scenes and Adventures in the Army*, 164.

52. *Galenian*, 18 July 1832.

53. Reynolds, *My Own Times*, 252.

54. Ford, *A History of Illinois*, 201.

55. Atkinson to Roger Jones, 19 November 1832.

56. Ibid.

57. Cooke, *Scenes and Adventures in the Army*, 167.

58. Justice diary (no dates), 1323.

59. Quoted in Hagan, *The Sac and Fox Indians*, 174.

60. Atkinson: Order, 9 July 1832, *BHW*, vol. 2 part 2, 754.

61. Atkinson to Winfield Scott, 11 July 1832, *BHW*, vol. 2, part 2, 763.

62. Diary of Henry Gratiot, *BHW*, vol. 2, part 2, 1304.

63. Atkinson to Scott, 11 July 1832, 762.

64. Bracken, "Further Strictures on Ford's Black Hawk War," 405.

65. John Kinzie to Governor George B. Porter, 12 July 1832, *BHW*, vol. 2, part 2, 774.

66. Bracken, "Further Strictures on Ford's Black Hawk War," 405.

67. Shaw diary (no dates), 1324.

68. Justice diary (no dates), 1323.

69. Satterlee Clark, "Early Days at Fort Winnebago and the Black Hawk War Reminiscences," *WHC* 8 (1879), 314.

70. Justice diary (no dates), 1323.

71. Wakefield, *History of the Black Hawk War*, 86.

72. Clark, "Early Days at Fort Winnebago," 314.

73. Wakefield, *History of the Black Hawk War*, 86.

74. Black Hawk, *Life*, 65.
75. Dodge to Atkinson, 14 July 1832, *BHW*, vol. 2, part 2, 791.
76. Forsyth to Davenport, 11 July 1832, *BHW*, vol. 2, part 2, 764.
77. Kinzie to Porter, 14 July 1832, *BHW*, vol. 2, part 2, 796.
78. *Galenian*, 25 July 1832.
79. Peter Parkinson, "Strictures Upon Ford's Black Hawk War," *WHC* 2 (1856), 394.
80. Daniel Parkinson, "Pioneer Life in Wisconsin," 355; Bracken, "Further Strictures on Ford's Black Hawk War," 406.
81. Daniel Parkinson, "Pioneer Life in Wisconsin," 355.
82. "Minutes of the Examination of Indian Prisoners," Fort Armstrong, 19 and 20 August 1832, *BHW*, vol. 2, part 2, 1030, 1036.
83. Wakefield, *History of the Black Hawk War*, 105.
84. Justice diary (no dates), 1324; Dodge to Atkinson, 19 July 1832, *BHW*, vol. 2, part 2, 826.
85. Wakefield, *History of the Black Hawk War*, 105–6; Daniel Parkinson, "Pioneer Life in Wisconsin," 355.
86. Wakefield, *History of the Black Hawk War*, 106.
87. Justice diary (no dates), 1324.
88. Wakefield, *History of the Black Hawk War*, 106.
89. Justice diary (no dates), 1324.
90. Atkinson to James D. Henry and Henry Dodge, 20 July 1832, *BHW*, vol. 2, part 2, 832.
91. Wakefield, *History of the Black Hawk War*, 107.
92. Ibid., 108.
93. Ibid.
94. Justice diary (no dates), 1324.
95. Ibid.
96. Wakefield, *History of the Black Hawk War*, 108.
97. Justice diary (no dates), 1324.
98. Daniel Parkinson, "Pioneer Life in Wisconsin," 356.
99. *Galenian*, 1 August 1832; Bracken, "Further Strictures on Ford's Black Hawk War," 408; Wakefield, *History of the Black Hawk War*, 110.
100. Wakefield, *History of the Black Hawk War*, 110.
101. Bracken, "Further Strictures on Ford's History of the Black Hawk War," 408.
102. Ibid.
103. Black Hawk, *Life*, 65.
104. Wakefield, *History of the Black Hawk War*, 111.
105. Dodge to Atkinson, 22 July 1832, *BHW*, vol. 2, part 2, 843.
106. James Henry to Atkinson, 23 July 1832, *BHW*, vol. 2, part 2, 859–60.
107. Wakefield, *History of the Black Hawk War*, 111–12.
108. *Galenian*, 1 August 1832.
109. James Henry to Atkinson, 23 July 1832.
110. Ibid.
111. Dodge to Atkinson, 22 July 1832.
112. Black Hawk, *Life*, 65.
113. Ibid., 65–66.
114. Dodge to Atkinson, 22 July 1832.
115. Clark, "Early Days at Fort Winnebago," 315.
116. Dodge to Atkinson, 22 July 1832.
117. Henry to Atkinson, 23 July 1832.
118. Wakefield, *History of the Black Hawk War*, 113.
119. Black Hawk, *Life*, 66.
120. "Minutes of the Examination of Indian Prisoners," Fort Armstrong, 19 August 1832, 1028; Street to Atkinson, 31 July 1832, *BHW*, vol. 2, part 2, 908.
121. Black Hawk, *Life*, 66; Dodge to Atkinson, 22 July 1832; Henry to Atkinson, 23 July 1832; Wakefield, *History of the Black Hawk War*, 113.

122. Clark, "Early Days at Fort Winnebago," 315.

123. *Niles' Weekly Register,* 18 August 1832.

124. Dodge to Gustavus Loomis, 22 July 1832, *BHW,* vol. 2, part 2, 845.

12: *Into the Valley of Death*

1. Strong, "Indian Wars of Wisconsin," 275, 274.

2. *Galenian,* 23 May 1832.

3. Ibid., 20 June 1832.

4. Joseph Street, "Indian Talk," Prairie du Chien, 22 June 1832, *Galenian,* 11 July 1832.

5. Black Hawk, *Life,* 66.

6. *Galenian,* 8 August 1832.

7. Identified as a Menominee woman who was the wife of a Sauk man, Street to Clark, 5 August 1832, Indian Office Files, box 6.

8. Quoted in ibid.

9. Ibid.; Loomis to Atkinson, 30–31 July 1832, *BHW,* vol. 2, part 2, 906.

10. Justice diary (no dates), *BHW,* vol. 2, part 2, 1325.

11. Wakefield, *History of the Black Hawk War,* 113.

12. Cooke, *Scenes and Adventures in the Army,* 171.

13. Wakefield, *History of the Black Hawk War,* 114.

14. Justice diary (no dates), 1325.

15. Wakefield, *History of the Black Hawk War,* 114–15.

16. *Sangamo Journal,* 25 August 1832.

17. Daniel Parkinson, "Pioneer Life in Wisconsin," 359.

18. Quoted in *Sangamo Journal,* 25 August 1832.

19. Justice diary (no dates), 1325.

20. Daniel Parkinson, "Pioneer Life in Wisconsin," 359.

21. Meriwether Clark to William Clark, 25 July 1832, *BHW,* vol. 2, part 2, 875.

22. Justice diary (no dates), 1325.

23. *Sangamo Journal,* 25 August 1832.

24. Daniel Parkinson, "Pioneer Life in Wisconsin," 360.

25. Wakefield, *History of the Black Hawk War,* 134.

26. Daniel Parkinson, "Pioneer Life in Wisconsin," 360. Two sources claim the incident occurred the night of the battle—both Daniel Parkinson and the *Sangamo Journal,* 25 August 1832. But Wakefield, Meriwether Clark, and James Justice all said that it happened the second night they were camped on Wisconsin Heights. There were also statements made by Daniel Smith and P. J. Pilcher, in *History of Jo Daviess County, Illinois* (Chicago: H. F. Kett, 1878), 294, which claim that the Indian message was understood and was reported to William Henry, who did not accept the notion that the Indians were truly seeking peace.

27. Daniel Parkinson, "Pioneer Life in Wisconsin," 360.

28. Ibid.

29. Justice diary (no dates), 1325.

30. Cooke, *Scenes and Adventures in the Army,* 169.

31. Justice diary (no dates), 1325.

32. Wakefield, *History of the Black Hawk War,* 120.

33. Atkinson: Order, 27 July 1832, *BHW,* vol. 2, part 2, 892.

34. Atkinson to Roger Jones, 19 November 1832, *BHW,* vol. 2, part 2, 1210.

35. Justice diary (no dates), 1326.

36. Atkinson to Winfield Scott, 27 July 1832, *BHW,* vol. 2, part 2, 891.

37. Cooke, *Scenes and Adventures in the Army,* 173.

38. Diary of Nineveh Shaw, 28 July 1832, *BHW,* vol. 2, part 2, 1337.

39. Wakefield, *History of the Black Hawk War,* 125.

40. Johnston diary, 28 July 1832, 1319.

41. Justice diary (no dates), 1326.
42. Wakefield, *History of the Black Hawk War*, 125.
43. *Galenian*, 8 August 1832.
44. Justice diary (no dates), 1326.
45. Johnston diary, 30 July 1832, 1320.
46. Ibid., 1 August 1832, 1320.
47. Shaw diary, 1 August 1832, 1337.
48. Wakefield, *History of the Black Hawk War*, 126.
49. Cooke, *Scenes and Adventures in the Army*, 179.
50. Ibid.
51. Wakefield, *History of the Black Hawk War*, 122.
52. "Minutes of the Examination of Indian Prisoners," Fort Armstrong, 20 August 1832, *BHW*, vol. 2, part 2, 1032.
53. Johnston diary, 29 July 1832, 1319.
54. Wakefield, *History of the Black Hawk War*, 126.
55. Robert Anderson to Larz Anderson, 5 August 1832, *BHW*, vol. 2, part 2, 933.
56. Bracken, "Further Strictures Upon Ford's Black Hawk War," 413.
57. Wakefield, *History of the Black Hawk War*, 123.
58. Cooke, *Scenes and Adventures in the Army*, 178.
59. *Galenian*, 8 August 1832.
60. Wakefield, *History of the Black Hawk War*, 129.
61. *Niles' Weekly Register*, 23 June 1832.
62. *Galenian*, 13 July 1832.
63. Traill, *Backwoods of Canada*, 39.
64. *Niles' Weekly Register*, 23 June 1832.
65. Quaife, *Chicago and the Old Northwest*, 328.
66. Cass to Scott, 15 June 1832, *BHW*, vol. 2, part 1, 590–91.
67. *Niles' Weekly Register*, 11 August 1832.
68. Captain A. Walker to R. C. Bristol (no date), in Stevens, *The Black Hawk War*, 244.
69. Fort Gratiot, 16 July 1832, *Niles' Weekly Register*, 28 July 1832.
70. Extract of letter from John Norvell to the editor of the *Philadelphia Inquirer*, Detroit, 12 July 1832, *Niles' Weekly Register*, 28 July 1832.
71. Norvell to editor, 12 July 1832, *Niles' Weekly Register*, 28 July 1832.
72. Mrs. Carroll Gallagher Cutler to R. G. Thwaites, 18 April 1898, in Joseph Steel Gallagher Papers.
73. Scott to Cass, 11–12 July 1832, *BHW*, vol. 2, part 2, 768.
74. Winfield Scott, *Memoirs of Lieut. General Scott, LL.D.* (New York: Sheldon, 1864), vol. 1, 218.
75. Scott to Atkinson, 12 July 1832, *BHW*, vol. 2, part 2, 778.
76. Letter from Sheldon Thompson, 11 July 1832, in Stevens, *The Black Hawk War*, 245.
77. Letter from the hospital at Fort Dearborn, 12 July 1832, *Niles' Weekly Register*, 11 August 1832.
78. Scott to Cass, 26 July 1832, *BHW*, vol. 2, part 2, 885.
79. Scott to Reynolds, 15 July 1832, *BHW*, vol. 2, part 2, 809.
80. Letter from Chicago, 11 July 1832, in Stevens, *The Black Hawk War*, 245.
81. Diary of James C. Steele, 5 August 1832, *BHW*, vol. 2, part 2, 1342.
82. George Boyd to Porter, 23 July 1832, in "Papers of Indian Agent [George] Boyd, 1832," *WHC* 12 (1892), 278.
83. Scott to Cass, 22 July 1832, *BHW*, vol. 2, part 2, 848.
84. Traill, *Backwoods of Canada*, 39.
85. *Niles' Weekly Register*, 21 July 1832.
86. Scott to Taylor, 29 August 1832, *BHW*, vol. 2, part 2, 1083.
87. *Galenian*, 11 July 1832.
88. Cooke, *Scenes and Adventures in the Army*, 180.

89. Wakefield, *History of the Black Hawk War*, 128.

90. *Galenian*, 8 August 1832.

91. Black Hawk, *Life*, 67.

92. "Minutes of the Examination of Indian Prisoners," Fort Armstrong, 19 August 1832, *BHW*, vol. 2, part 2, 1028.

93. Ibid., 1032.

94. "From a statement by Captain Joseph Throckmorton," Prairie du Chien, 3 August 1832, *BHW*, vol. 2, part 2, 927–28.

95. Black Hawk, *Life*, 67.

96. "Minutes of the Examination of Indian Prisoners," Fort Armstrong, 27 August 1832, *BHW*, vol. 2, part 2, 1056.

97. Reuben Holmes to Atkinson, 5 August 1832, *BHW*, vol. 2, part 2, 938.

98. Ibid.

99. "Statement by Joseph Throckmorton," 3 August 1832, 928.

100. Quoted in Holmes to Atkinson, 5 August 1832, 939.

101. Dodge to Loomis, 22 July 1832, *BHW*, vol. 2, part 2, 845.

102. Loomis to Dodge, 25 July 1832, *BHW*, vol. 2, part 2, 880.

103. Street to Clark, 5 August 1832.

104. Joseph Ritner to Loomis, 29 July 1832, *BHW*, vol. 2, part 2, 903.

105. Loomis to Atkinson, 30–31 July 1832, *BHW*, vol. 2, part 2, 906.

106. Street to Clark, 1–2 August 1832, *BHW*, vol. 2, part 2, 913–14.

107. *Galenian*, 8 August 1832.

108. Loomis to Atkinson, 8 August 1832, *BHW*, vol. 2, part 2, 962.

109. Street to Clark, 3 August 1832, *BHW*, vol. 2, part 2, 927.

110. Loomis to unknown, 2 August 1832, *Sangamo Journal*, 18 August 1832; also Street to Clark, 2 August 1832, *BHW*, vol. 2, part 2, 917.

111. "Minutes of the Examination of Indian Prisoners," Fort Armstrong, 20 August 1832, 1036.

112. Ibid., 1037.

113. "Minutes of the Examination of Indian Prisoners," Fort Armstrong, 27 August 1832, 1056.

114. Black Hawk, *Life*, 67.

115. "Minutes of the Examination of Indian Prisoners," Fort Armstrong, 27 August 1832, 1056.

116. Johnston diary, 1 August 1832, 1320.

117. *Galenian*, 8 August 1832.

118. Johnston diary, 1 August 1832, 1320.

119. Shaw diary, 2 August 1832, 1337.

120. Cooke, *Scenes and Adventures in the Army*, 180.

121. Skinner, "Observations of Ethnology of the Sauk," 36.

122. Johnston diary, 2 August 1832, 1321.

123. Wakefield, *History of the Black Hawk War*, 129.

124. Johnston diary, 2 August 1832, 1320.

125. Ibid., 1321; Wakefield, *History of the Black Hawk War*, 131.

126. Cooke, *Scenes and Adventures in the Army*, 183.

127. Zachary Taylor, "Report on the Battle of Bad Axe," Prairie du Chien, 5 August 1832, *BHW*, vol. 2, part 2, 942.

128. Wakefield, *History of the Black Hawk War*, 131.

129. Daniel Parkinson, "Pioneer Life in Wisconsin," 363.

130. Johnston diary, 2 August 1832, 1321; *Galenian*, 8 August 1832.

131. *Galenian*, 8 August 1832.

132. Fonda, "Early Wisconsin," 263.

133. Johnston diary, 2 August 1832, 1321.

134. Black Hawk, *Life*, 68.

135. *Niles' Weekly Register*, 3 November 1832.

136. Cooke, *Scenes and Adventures in the Army*, 188.

137. R. Anderson to L. Anderson, 5 August 1832.

138. *Niles' Weekly Register*, 3 November 1832; see also H. S. Townsend speech printed in the *Vernon County Censor* (Viroqua, Wis.), 10 August 1898; *Galenian*, 28 August 1832; R. Anderson to L. Anderson, 5 August 1832.

139. H. S. Townsend speech, *Vernon County Censor*, 10 August 1898.

140. Dr. C. V. Porter, article in *DeSoto Chronicle* (DeSoto, Wis.), 12 February 1887.

141. William Henry Perrin, ed., *The History of Crawford and Clark Counties, Illinois* (Chicago: Baskin, 1883), 232.

142. Wakefield, *History of the Black Hawk War*, 133.

143. Latrobe, *The Rambler in North America*, vol. 1, 188.

144. Fonda, "Early Wisconsin," 263.

145. Street to Clark, 3 August 1832.

146. *Galenian*, 8 August 1832.

147. Fonda, "Early Wisconsin," 262.

148. Cooke, *Scenes and Adventures in the Army*, 185.

149. Street to Clark, 3 August 1832.

150. Cooke, *Scenes and Adventures in the Army*, 187.

151. Dr. C. V. Porter, *DeSoto Chronicle*, 5 February 1887.

152. "Minutes of the Examination of Indian Prisoners," Fort Armstrong, 20 August 1832, 1035.

153. Spencer, *Reminiscences of Pioneer Life*, 74–75.

154. "Minutes of the Examination of Indian Prisoners," Fort Armstrong, 20 August 1832, 1037.

155. "Minutes of the Examination of Indian Prisoners," Fort Armstrong, 27 August 1832, 1056.

156. Street to Clark, 3 August 1832.

157. Wakefield, *History of the Black Hawk War*, 133.

158. H. W. Townsend speech, *Vernon County Censor*, 10 August 1832.

159. Johnston diary, 2 August 1832; Atkinson to Scott, 9 August 1832, *BHW*, vol. 2, part 2, 966. Both Wakefield and the *Galenian* overstated the number of Indians taken prisoner and set the number at fifty.

160. Hagan, *The Sac and Fox Indian*, 145.

161. For example, Atkinson to Scott, 9 August 1832; Johnston diary, 2 August 1832.

162. Atkinson to Scott, 9 August 1832.

163. Smith, "Indian Campaign of 1832," 164.

164. Atkinson to Macomb, 25 August 1832, in Stevens, *The Black Hawk War*, 228; Johnston diary, 2 August 1832.

165. Cooke, *Scenes and Adventures in the Army*, 188.

166. Glendower Price to Loomis, 6 August 1832, *BHW*, vol. 2, part 2, 947.

167. Price to Scott, 14 August 1832, *BHW*, vol. 2, part 2, 1004.

168. "Minutes of the Examination of Indian Prisoners," Fort Armstrong, 20 August 1832, 1036.

169. Quoted in Spencer, *Reminiscences of Pioneer Life*, 74–75.

170. "Minutes of the Examination of Indian Prisoners," Fort Armstrong, 20 August 1832, 1036.

171. Street to Scott, 22 August 1832, *BHW*, vol. 2, part 2, 1042; Z. Taylor to Patrick H. Galt, 22 August 1832, *BHW*, vol. 2, part 2, 1043.

172. Wakefield, *History of the Black Hawk War*, 136, 131.

173. Ibid., 144.

174. See Roy Harvey Pearce, *The Savages of America: A Study of the Indian and the Idea of Civilization* (Baltimore: Johns Hopkins University Press, 1953); and Drinnon, *Facing West*.

175. J. Glenn Gray, *The Warriors: Reflections of Men in Battle* (New York: Harper and Row, 1959), 51.

176. Latrobe, *The Rambler in North America*, vol. 1, 188.

177. Cooke, *Scenes and Adventures in the Army*, 172.

178. Johnston diary, 2 August 1832.

179. R. Anderson to L. Anderson, 5 August 1832.

180. Wakefield, *History of the Black Hawk War*, 136.

181. Extract from a letter by Captain Gustavus Loomis, 2 August 1832, *Niles' Weekly Register*, 1 September 1832.

182. Cooke, *Scenes and Adventures in the Army*, 185–86.

183. *Galenian*, 29 August 1832.

184. Wakefield, *History of the Black Hawk War*, 134.

185. Street to Clark, 1–2 August 1832.

Epilogue

1. Account dictated by the grandson of the Winnebago man named Blackhawk, "Surrender of Black Hawk," the complete text of which is included in Nancy O. Laurie, "In Search of Chaetar: New Findings on Black Hawk's Surrender," *Wisconsin Magazine of History* 71 (Spring 1988), 170.

2. Joseph Street, "Report of the Delivery of Black Hawk and the Prophet," Prairie du Chien, 27 August 1832, *BHW*, vol. 2, part 2, 1065; see also the copy of the letter from the U.S. Indian Agency at Prairie du Chien, 3 September 1832, *Niles' Weekly Register*, 29 September 1832.

3. Lepore, *The Name of War*, x.

4. Street, "Report of the Delivery of Black Hawk and the Prophet."

5. Letter from Indian Agency at Prairie du Chien, 3 September 1832, *Niles' Weekly Register*, 29 September 1832.

6. Black Hawk, "Surrender Speech," 27 August, 1832.

7. Black Hawk, *Life*, 70.

8. George Catlin, *Letters and Notes on the Manners, Customs, and Conditions of the North American Indians*, 2nd edition (London: Published by the author, 1841), vol. 2, 211.

9. Black Hawk, *Life*, 70.

10. Complete text of speeches in Eckert, *Twilight of Empire*, 619.

11. Slotkin, *Regeneration Through Violence*; Brian W. Dippie, *The Vanishing American: White Attitudes and U.S. Indian Policy* (Middletown, Conn.: Wesleyan University Press, 1982), xii, 21.

12. Lepore, *The Name of War*, 193, 224.

13. *Niles' Weekly Register*, 18 May 1833.

14. Ibid., 29 June 1833.

15. Original text in Eckert, *Twilight of Empire*, 620.

16. Orlando Brown, *Commonwealth* (Frankfort, Ky.), 2 June 1833.

17. Ibid.; see also Stevens, *The Black Hawk War*, 261–62.

18. Brown, *Commonwealth*, 30 June 1833.

19. Black Hawk, *Life*, 74.

20. *Niles' Weekly Register*, 22 June 1833.

21. Ibid., 29 June 1833; Black Hawk, *Life*, 75.

22. Reuben Gold Thwaites, "Memoir of Antoine LeClaire, Esquire, of Davenport, Iowa," *Annals of Iowa*, October 1863, 144–49.

23. Scheckel, *The Insistence of the Indian*, 116.

24. Catlin quotation taken from Nichols, *Black Hawk and the Warrior's Path*, 154.

25. Quoted in *Register and Leader* (Des Moines), 10 March 1907.

26. *Burlington (Iowa) Hawk-Eye,* 24 March 1907.

27. Carroll Gallagher Cutler to R. G. Thwaites, 18 April 1898, Gallagher Papers.

28. Hagen, *The Sac and Fox Indians,* 205–6.

29. David Thelen, "Memory and American History," *Journal of American History* 75 (March 1989), 1121.

30. Robert A. Ferguson, "The Commonalities of Common Sense," *William and Mary Quarterly* 57 (July 2000), 472.

31. Dudley Young, *Origins of the Sacred: The Ecstasies of Love and War* (New York: St. Martin's Press, 1991), 224, 222.

32. Stevens, *The Black Hawk War,* 20–21, 93, 119.

33. "Notes on the Lecture Given by R. G. Thwaites of the State Historical Association at Bad Axe Battle Grounds on the 66th Anniversary of the Battle," *Vernon County Censor,* 31 August 1898.

34. *Crawford County Press* (Prairie du Chien), 11 April 1926.

35. State of Wisconsin, 1989, Assembly Resolution 16.

BIBLIOGRAPHY

Primary Sources

Manuscripts

Boyd, George. Papers. State Historical Society of Wisconsin, Manuscript Collections, Madison.

Brigham, Ebenezer. Papers. State Historical Society of Wisconsin, Manuscript Collections, Madison.

Burnette, Thomas Pendelton. Papers. State Historical Society of Wisconsin, Manuscript Collections, Madison.

Canadian Indian Affairs. Papers. Series A, volume 453, reel C-9646, Western Superintendency, National Archives of Canada, Ottawa, 1788–1866.

————. Series A, volume 441, reel C-9636, Western Superintendency, National Archives of Canada, Ottawa, 1812–54.

————. Papers. Series A, volume 569, reel C-13373, Western Superintendency, National Archives of Canada, Ottawa, 1830–36.

————. Papers. Series A, volume 443, reel C-9637, Western Superintendency, National Archives of Canada, Ottawa, 1830–57.

Cass, Lewis. Letter Book, Letters Received, 1817–31. State Historical Society of Wisconsin, Manuscript Collections, Madison.

————. "Regulations of Indian Affairs in the Northwest Territory and Proposals for the Better Organization of the Indian Department," Detroit, 1815. Manuscript in Edward E. Ayer Collection of Newberry Library, Chicago.

————. "Report to the President of the United States," 16 February 1832. Indian Office Letter Book, State Historical Society of Wisconsin, Manuscript Collections, Madison.

Clark, William. Miscellaneous Papers. State Historical Society of Wisconsin, Manuscript Collections, Madison.

Colborne, Sir John. Papers. National Archives of Canada, Ottawa.

Dodge, Henry. Letter Book. Iowa State Department of History and Archives, Des Moines.

Forsyth, Thomas. Papers and Letter Books. Draper Manuscripts. State Historical Society of Wisconsin, Manuscript Collections, Madison.

Gallagher, Joseph Steel. Letters. State Historical Society of Wisconsin, Manuscript Collections, Madison.

Goodeu, Nathan. Papers. State Historical Society of Wisconsin, Manuscript Collections, Madison.

Gratiot, Henry. Journal, 1832–33. State Historical Society of Wisconsin, Manuscript Collections, Madison.

Henry, William. Papers. State Historical Society of Wisconsin, Manuscript Collections, Madison.

Parkinson, Peter, Jr. "Henry Dodge in the Black Hawk War." (A manuscript memoir, no date.) State Historical Society of Wisconsin, Manuscript Collections, Madison.

Street, Joseph Montfort. Papers. State Historical Society of Wisconsin, Manuscript Collections, Madison.

U.S. Bureau of Indian Affairs, Indian Office. Files. Boxes 1, 2, 3, 4. (Photocopies from U.S. National Archives.) State Historical Society of Wisconsin, Manuscript Collections, Madison.

———. Letter Books, 1824–60, Boxes 47–52. (Photocopies from U.S. National Archives.) State Historical Society of Wisconsin, Manuscript Collections, Madison.

———. George Porter Letters, Received, 1831–35. (Photocopies from U.S. National Archives.) State Historical Society of Wisconsin, Manuscript Collections, Madison.

NEWSPAPERS

Beloit Free Press, Beloit, Wisconsin
Burlington Hawkeye, Burlington, Iowa
Commonwealth, Frankfort, Kentucky
Crawford County Press, Prairie du Chien, Wisconsin
DeSoto Chronicle, DeSoto, Wisconsin
Galenian, Galena, Illinois
Illinois Advocate, Edwardsville, Illinois
Illinois Herald, Springfield, Illinois
Miner's Journal, Galena, Illinois
Missouri Republican Times, St. Louis, Missouri
New York Mercury, New York, New York
Niles' Weekly Register, Baltimore, Maryland
Prairie du Chien Union, Prairie du Chien, Wisconsin
Register and Leader, Des Moines, Iowa
Sangamo Journal, Springfield, Illinois
Vandalia Whig and Illinois Intelligencer, Vandalia, Illinois
Vernon County Censor, Viroqua, Wisconsin

PUBLISHED PRIMARY SOURCES AND MEMOIRS

Anderson, Robert. "Reminiscences of the Black Hawk War." *Collections of the State Historical Society of Wisconsin* 10 (1888), 167–76.

Anderson, Thomas G. "Capt. T.G. Anderson's Journal, 1814." *Collections of the State Historical Society of Wisconsin* 9 (1882), 207–61.

———. "Personal Narrative of Capt. Thomas G. Anderson: Early Experiences in the Northwest Fur Trade—British Capture of Prairie du Chien, 1814." *Collections of the State Historical Society of Wisconsin* 9 (1882), 137–206.

Atwater, Caleb. *Remarks Made on a Tour to Prairie du Chien Thence to Washington City in 1829.* Columbus, Ohio: Isaac N. Whiting, 1831. Reprint, New York: Arno Press, 1975.

Baird, Elizabeth T. *O-De-Jit-Wa-Win-Ning or Contes du Temps Passe.* Green Bay, Wis.: Heritage Hill Foundation, 1998.

Beckwourth, James P. (as told by Thomas D. Bonner). *The Life and Adventures of James P. Beckwourth*. 1856. Reprint, Lincoln: University of Nebraska Press, 1972.

Beggs, Reverend S[tephen] R. *Papers from the Early History of the West and Northwest*. Cincinnati: Methodist Book Concern, 1868.

Biddle, James W. "Account of the Black Hawk War." *Collections of the State Historical Society of Wisconsin* 4 (1859), 85–87.

Black Hawk. *The Life of Black Hawk*. Edited by Milo Milton Quaife. New York: Dover Publications, 1916.

Blair, Emma Helen, ed. *The Indian Tribes of the Upper Mississippi Valley and Region of the Great Lakes*. 2 Vols. Cleveland: Arthur H. Clark, 1911–12.

Bracken, Charles. "Further Strictures on Ford's Black Hawk War." *Collections of the State Historical Society of Wisconsin* 2 (1856), 402–14.

Bracken, Charles, and Peter Parkinson Jr. "Pekatonica Battle Controversy." *Collections of the State Historical Society of Wisconsin* 2 (1856), 365–92.

BrisBois, B. W. "Traditions and Recollections of Prairie du Chien." *Collections of the State Historical Society of Wisconsin* 9 (1882), 282–302.

Brunson, Reverend Alfred. "Memoir of Hon. Thomas Pendelton Burnett." *Collections of the State Historical Society of Wisconsin* 2 (1856), 233–325.

Bryant, William Cullen II, and Thomas G. Voss, eds. *The Letters of William Cullen Bryant*. 2 vols. New York: Fordham University Press, 1975.

Buckner, Lieutenant Colonel E. "A Brief History of the War with the Sac and Fox Indians in Illinois and Michigan in 1832, with Twenty-one Letters and Orders." *Collections of the Pioneer Society of the State of Michigan* 8 (1907), 424–35.

Carter, Clarence E., ed. *The Territorial Papers of the United States*. Vol. 11, *The Territory of Michigan, 1820–1829*. Vol. 12, *The Territory of Michigan, 1829–1837*. Washington, D.C.: Government Printing Office, 1943, 1945.

Cass, Lewis. *Annual Report of the Secretary of War*. In *American State Papers, Military Affairs* 7 Vol. 5, 23–24. Washington, D.C.: Government Printing Office, 1832.

———. "Considerations on the Present State of the Indians and Their Removal to the West of the Mississippi." *North American Review* 30 (January 1830). 1–61.

———. "Indians of North America." *North American Review* 22 (January 1826), 53–119.

———. "Remarks on the Policy and Practice of the United States and Great Britain in Their Treatment of the Indians." *North American Review* 24 (April 1827), 3–78.

Catlin, George. *Letters and Notes on the Manners, Customs, and Conditions of the North American Indians*. 2 vols., 2nd ed. London: Published by the author, 1841.

Childs, Ebenezer. "Recollections of Wisconsin Since 1820." *Collections of the State Historical Society of Wisconsin* 4 (1859), 153–85.

Clark, Satterlee. "Early Days at Fort Winnebago and Black Hawk War Reminiscences." *Collections of the State Historical Society of Wisconsin* 8 (1879), 309–21.

Colton, Calvin. *Tour of the American Lakes and Among the Indians of the Northwest Territories in 1830*. 2 vols. London: Frederick Westly and A. N Davis, 1833.

Cooke, P[hilip] St. G[eorge]. *Scenes and Adventures in the Army or the Romance of Military Life*. Philadelphia: Lindsay and Blakiston, 1857.

De Tocqueville, Alexis. *Democracy in America*. 2 vols. New York: Vintage Books, 1990.

———. "Fortnight in the Wilderness." In *Tocqueville and Beaumont in America*, ed. George Wilson Pierson, 231–89. New York: Oxford University Press, 1938.

———. *Journey to America*. Translated by George Lawrence. Edited by J. P. Mayer. New Haven, Conn.: Yale University Press, 1959.

Dickson, Joseph, and W. Davidson. "Personal Narratives of the Black Hawk War." *Collections of the State Historical Society of Wisconsin* 5 (1868), 315–20.

Drimmer, Frederick, ed. *Captured by the Indians: 15 Firsthand Accounts, 1750–1870*. New York: Dover Publications, 1961.

Fitch, Matthew G. "The Battle of Peckatonica." *Collections of the State Historical Society of Wisconsin* 10 (1888), 178–83.

Fonda, John. "Dodge's Volunteers in the Black Hawk War." *Collections of the State Historical Society of Wisconsin* 5 (1868), 285–86.

———. "Early Wisconsin." *Collections of the State Historical Society of Wisconsin* 5 (1868), 205–84.

Forsyth, Thomas. "An Account of the Manners and Customs of the Sauk and Fox Nations of Indians Tradition." In *The Indian Tribes of the Upper Mississippi Valley and the Region of the Great Lakes,* ed. Emma Helen Blair, vol. 2, 183–245. Cleveland: Arthur H. Clark, 1911.

Fuller, Margaret. *Summer on the Lakes in 1843.* 1844. Reprint, Urbana: University of Illinois Press, 1991.

Gratiot, Adéle, De P. "Adéle De P. Gratiot's Narrative." *Collections of the State Historical Society of Wisconsin* 10 (1888), 261–75.

Greene, Evarts Boutwell, and Clarence Walworth Alvord, eds. *The Governors' Letter Books.* Vol. 4 of *Collections of the Illinois State Historical Library.* Springfield, Ill.: State Historical Library, 1909.

Hall, James. *Legends of the West.* Philadelphia: Harrison Hall, 1832.

———. *Letters from the West: Containing Sketches of Scenery, Manners and Customs; and Anecdotes Connected with the First Settlements of the Western Sections of the United States.* London: Henry Colburn, 1828. Facsimile reproduction with introduction by John T. Filanagan. Gainsville, Fla.: Scholarly Facsimilies and Reprints, 1967.

Hamilton, Holman, ed. "Zachary Talor and the Black Hawk War." *Wisconsin Magazine of History* 24 (1940–41), 305–15.

Harlow, Vincent, and Frederick Hadden, eds. *British Colonial Developments, 1774– 1834; Select Documents.* Oxford: Clarendon Press, 1953.

Hunt, George. "A Personal Narrative." *Collections of the Pioneer Society of the State of Michigan* 8 (1907), 662–69.

Kinzie, Juliette M. *Wau-Bun: The Early Days in the Northwest.* New York, 1856. Reprint, Portage, Wis.: National Society of the Colonial Dames of America in the State of Wisconsin, 1989.

Kirkland, Caroline M. *A New Home—Who'll Follow? Glimpses of Western Life.* 5th ed. New York: C. S. Francis, 1855. (Originally published 1839.)

Langworthy, Lucius H. "Autobiographical Sketch of Lucius H. Langworthy." *Iowa Journal of History and Politics* 8, no. 3 (July 1910), 320–24.

———. "Sketches of the Early Settlement of the West." *Iowa Journal of History and Politics* 8 (July 1910), 356–65.

Langworthy, Solon M. "Autobiographical Sketch of Solon M. Longworthy." *Iowa Journal of History and Politics* 8, no. 3 (July 1910), 325–39.

Latrobe, Charles Joseph. *The Rambler in North America, MDCCCXXXII–MDCCCXXXIII.* 2 vols. New York, Harper and Brothers, 1835.

Lewis, Jane. *Narrative of the Captivity and Providential Escape of Mrs. Jane Lewis.* 1833. Reprint, New York: Garland, 1977.

Lockwood, James H. "Early Times and Events in Wisconsin." *Collections of the State Historical Society of Wisconsin* 2 (1856), 98–196.

Marsh, Cutting. "Documents Relating to the Stockbridge Mission, 1825–1848." *Collections of the State Historical Society of Wisconsin* 15 (1900), 39–204.

Marston, Morrell. "Letter of Major Marston to Reverand Doctor Morse, Fort Armstrong, November, 1820." In *The Indian Tribes of the Upper Mississippi Valley and the Region of the Great Lakes,* ed. Emma Helen Blair, vol. 2, 139–82. Cleveland: Arthur H. Clark, 1911.

Martin, Morgan L. "Narrative of Morgan L. Martin." *Collections of the State Historical Society of Wisconsin* 11 (1888), 385–415.

Matson, Nehemiah. *Memories of Shaubena, with Incidents Relating to Indian Wars and the Early Settlement of the West.* Chicago: D. B. Cooke, 1878.

McCall, Major General George A. *Letters from the Frontiers: Written During a Period of Thirty Years' Service in the Army of the United States.* 1868; Facsimile reproduction with an introduction and index by John K. Mahon. Gainesville: University Presses of Florida. 1974.

McKenney, Thomas L. *Memoirs, Official and Personal.* Introduction by Herman J. Viola. 1846. Reprint, Lincoln: University of Nebraska Press, 1973.

———. *Sketches of a Tour to the Lakes, of the Character and Customs of the Chippeway Indians, and the Incidents Connected with the Treaty of Fond du Lac.* Baltimore: Fielding Lucas Jr., 1827.

———. "The Winnebago War." Madison: *Collections of the State Historical Society of Wisconsin* 5 (1868), 178–204.

McKenney, Thomas, and James Hall. *The Indian Tribes of North America; with Biographical Sketches and Anecdotes of the Principal Chiefs.* 3 vols. 1836 and 1844. Reprint, Edinburgh: John Grant, 1934.

Meeker, Moses. "Early History of the Lead Region of Wisconsin." *Collections of the State Historical Society of Wisconsin* 6 (1872), 271–96.

Moodie, Susanna. *Roughing It in the Bush or Life in Canada.* London: Richard Bentley, 1852. Reprint, Toronto: McClelland and Stewart, 1990.

Parish, John Carl, ed. *George Wallace Jones.* Iowa Biographical Series, ed. Benjamin F. Shambaugh. Iowa City: State Historical Society of Iowa, 1912.

Parkinson, Daniel H. "Pioneer Life in Wisconsin." *Collections of the State Historical Society of Wisconsin* 2 (1856), 326–64.

Parkinson, Peter, Jr. "Notes on the Black Hawk War." *Collections of the State Historical Society of Wisconsin* 10 (1885), 184–212.

———. "Strictures Upon Ford's Black Hawk War." *Collections of the State Historical Society of Wisconsin* 2 (1856), 393–401.

Quaife, M. M., ed., "Journals and Reports of the Black Hawk War." *Mississippi Valley Historical Review* 12 (December 1925), 392–409.

Reynolds, John. *History of Illinois, My Own Times: Embracing Also the History of My Life.* Chicago: Chicago Historial Society, 1879.

———. *Message from the Governor of the State of Illinois to Both Houses of the General Assembly, December 4, 1832.* Vandalia, Ill.: M. Greiner, 1832.

Rodolf, Theodore. "Pioneering in the Wisconsin Lead Region." *Collections of the State Historical Society of Wisconsin* 15 (1900), 338–89.

St. Vrain, Felix. "A Diary of the Black Hawk War." *Iowa Historical Record* 8 (1910), 265–69.

Scanlan, Charles M. *Indian Massacre and Captivity of the Hall Girls.* Milwaukee: Reic, 1915.

Schoolcraft, Henry R. *Narrative Journal of Travels Through the Northwestern Regions of the United States Extending from Detroit though the Great Chain of American Lakes to the Sources of the Mississippi River.* Albany: E. and E. Hosford, 1821.

———. *Travels in the Central Portions of the Mississippi Valley: Comprising Observations on its Mineral Geography, Internal Resources, and Aboriginal Population.* New York: Collins and Hannay, 1825.

Scott, Winfield. *Memoirs of Lieut. General Scott, LL.D.* 2 vols. New York: Sheldon, 1864.

Shirreff, Patrick. *A Tour Through North America; Together with a Comprehensive View of Canada and United States, as Adapted for Agricultural Emigration.* Edinburgh: Oliver and Boyde, 1835.

Shortt, Adam. *Canada and Its Provinces: A History of the Canadian People and Their Institutions by One Hundred Associates.* Vol. 4, Adam Shortt and Arthur C. Doughty, eds., Toronto: Glasgow, Brook and Company, 1914.

Smith, Henry. "Battle of Bad Axe." *Collections of the State Historical Society of Wisconsin* 5 (1868), 291–92.

———. "Indian Campaign of 1832." *Collections of the State Historical Society of Wisconsin* 10 (1888), 150–66.

Snelling, William J. "Early Days at Prairie du Chien and the Winnebago Outbreak of 1827." *Collections of the State Historical Society of Wisconsin* 5 (1868), 123–53.

Spencer, J. W. *Reminiscences of Pioneer Life in the Mississippi Valley.* Davenport: Griggs, Watson and Day, 1872. In *The Early Days of Rock Island and Davenport: The Narratives by J. W. Spencer and J. H. D. Burrows,* ed. Milo Milton Quaife. Chicago: Lakeside Press, 1942, 5–85.

Stambaugh, Samuel. "Report on the Quality and Condition of Wisconsin Territory, 1831." *Collections of the State Historical Society of Wisconsin* 15 (1900), 399–438.

Street, Joseph M. "Prairie du Chien in 1827: Letters of Joseph M. Street to Gov. Ninian Edwards of Illinois." *Collections of the State Historical Society of Wisconsin* 11 (1888).

Strong, Moses, M. "The Indian Wars of Wisconsin." *Collections of the State Historical Society of Wisconsin* 8 (1879), 241–86.

Thayer, Crawford Beecher, compiler and ed. *The Battle of Wisconsin Heights, an Eye Witness Account of the Black Hawk War of 1832.* Menasha, Wis.: Banta Press, 1983.

———. *Hunting a Shadow: The Search for Black Hawk, an Eye Witness Account of the Black Hawk War of 1832.* Menasha, Wis.: Banta Press, 1981.

———. *Massacre at Bax Axe: An Eye Witness Account of the Black Hawk War of 1832.* Menasha, Wis.: Banta Press, 1984.

Traill, Catharine Parr. *The Backwoods of Canada.* London: Charles Knight, 1836. Reprint, Toronto: McClelland and Steward, 1989.

Wakefield, John A. *Wakefield's History of the Black Hawk War. 1833.* Reprint, Madison, Wis.: Roger Hunt, 1976.

Washburn, E. B., ed. *The Edwards Papers: Being a Portion of the Collection of the Letters, Papers and Manuscripts of Ninian Edwards.* Vol. 3. Chicago: Chicago Historical Society, 1884.

Whitney, Ellen M., ed. *The Black Hawk War, 1831—1832.* 4 vols. Springfield: Illinois State Historical Library, 1970, 1973, 1975, 1978.

Whittlesey, Charles. "Recollections of a Tour Through Wisconsin in 1832." *Collections of the State Historical Society of Wisconsin* 1 (1855), 64–85.

Secondary Sources

Allen, Robert S. *The British Indian Department and the Frontier in North America, 1755–1830.* Ottawa: Department of Indian and Northern Affairs, Canada, 1975.

———. *His Majesty's Indian Allies: British Indian Policy in the Defence of Canada, 1774–1815.* Toronto: Dundurn Press, 1992.

Anderson, Benedict. *Imagined Communities: Reflections on the Origin and Spread of Nationalism.* Rev. ed. London: Verso, 1991.

Anderson, Fred. *Crucible of War: The Seven Years' War and the Fate of Empire in British North America, 1754–1766.* New York: Alfred A. Knopf, 2000.

Antze, Paul, and Michael Lambek, eds. *Tense Past: Cultural Essays in Trauma and Memory.* New York: Routledge, 1996.

Appleby, Joyce. *Inheriting the Revolution: The First Generation of Americans.* Cambridge, Mass.: Belknap Press of Harvard University, 2000.

Armstrong, Perry A. *The Sauks and the Black Hawk War.* Springfield, Ill.: H. W. Rokker, 1887.

Baker, Alan R. H., and Gideon Biger, eds. *Ideology and Landscape in Historical Perpsective: Essays on the Meaning of Some Places in the Past.* Cambridge, England: Cambridge University Press, 1992.

Bederman, Gail. *Manliness and Civilization: A Cultural History of Gender and Race in the United States, 1880–1917.* Chicago: University of Chicago Press, 1995.

Bellesiles, Michal A. *Arming America: The Origins of a National Gun Culture.* New York: Alfred A. Knopf, 2000.

Berkhofer, Robert F., Jr. *The White Man's Indian: Images of the American Indian from Columbus to the Present.* New York: Vintage Books, 1979.

Bernheimer, Richard. *Wild Men in the Middle Ages.* Cambridge, Mass.: Harvard University Press, 1952.

Berry, Jason. *The Spirit of Black Hawk: A Mystery of Africans and Indians.* Jackson: University Press of Mississippi, 1995.

Bieder, Robert E. *Native American Communities in Wisconsin, 1660–1960: A Study of Tradition and Change.* Madison: University of Wisconsin Press, 1995.

Birmingham, Robert A., and Leslie E. Eisenberg. *Indian Mounds of Wisconsin.* Madison: University of Wisconsin Press, 2000.

Blaeser, Kimberly M. "Trickster: A Compendium." In *Buried Roots and Indestructible Seeds: The Survival of American Indian Life in Stories, History, and Spirit,* 24–32. Madison: Wisconsin Humanities Council, 1993.

Bourne, Kenneth. *Britain and the Balance of Power in North America, 1815–1908.* Berkeley: University of California Press, 1967.

Braudy, Leo. *From Chivalry to Terrorism: War and the Changing Nature of Masculinity.* New York: Alfred A. Knopf, 2003.

Bremer, Richard G. *Indian Agent and Wilderness Scholar: The Life of Henry Rowe Schoolcraft.* Mount Pleasant: Clarke Historical Library, Central Michigan University, 1987.

Calloway, Colin G. "The End of an Era: British-Indian Relations in the Great Lakes Region After the War of 1812." *Michigan Historical Review* 12 (Fall 1986), 1–20.

Campbell, Joseph. *The Hero with a Thousand Faces.* Princeton: Princeton University Press, 1972.

Carlson, Theodore. *The Illinois Military Tract: A Study of Land Occupation, Utilization, and Tenure.* Urbana: University of Illinois Press, 1951.

Carson, James Taylor. "Ethnogeography and the Native American Past." *Ethnohistory* 49 (Fall 2002), 767–88.

Castiglia, Christopher. *Bound and Determined: Captivity, Culture Crossing, and White Womanhood from Mary Rowlandson to Patty Hearst.* Chicago: University of Chicago Press, 1996.

Clausewitz, Carl. *On War.* Edited and translated by Michael Howard and Peter Paret. Princeton: Princeton University Press, 1984.

Clifton, James A. "Personal and Ethnic Identity on the Great Lakes Frontier: The Case of Billy Caldwell, Anglo-Canadian." *Ethnohistory* 25 (Winter 1978), 69–94.

———. *A Place of Refuge for All Time: Migration of the American Potawatomi into Upper Canada, 1830–1850.* National Museum of Man Mercury Series. Ottawa: National Museums of Canada, 1975.

Coffman, Edward M. *The Old Army: A Portrait of the American Army in Peacetime, 1784–1895.* New York: Oxford University Press, 1986.

Cole, Cyrenus. *I Am a Man: The Indian Black Hawk.* Iowa City: State Historical Society of Iowa, 1938.

Craig, Gerald M. *Upper Canada: The Formative Years, 1784–1841.* Toronto: McClelland and Stewart, 1963.

Craighead, James R. *Blackhawk, a Romance of the Black Hawk War Told in Spenserian Verse.* Creston, Iowa: Bond, 1839.

Deloria, Philip J. *Playing Indian.* New Haven, Conn.: Yale University Press, 1998.

Demos, John. *The Unredeemed Captive: A Family Story from Early America.* New York: Alfred A. Knopf, 1994.

Derleth, August. *Wind Over Wisconsin.* New York: Charles Scribner's Sons, 1938.

Dippie, Brian W. *The Vanishing American: White Attitudes and U.S. Indian Policy.* Middletown, Conn.: Wesleyan University Press, 1982.

Dowd, Gregory Evans. "The French King Wakes Up in Detroit: Pontiac's War in Rumor and History." *Ethnohistory* 37 (Summer, 1990), 284–78.

———. *A Spirited Resistance: The North American Indian Struggle for Unity, 1745–1815.* Baltimore: Johns Hopkins University Press, 1992.

———. *War Under Heaven: Pontiac, the Indian Nations and the British Empire.* Baltimore: Johns Hopkins University Press, 2002.

Drake, Benjamin. *The Life and Adventures of Black Hawk with Sketches of Keokuk, the Sac and Fox Indians and the Late Black Hawk War.* 7th ed. Cincinnati: George Conclin, 1844.

Drinnon, Richard. *Facing West: The Metaphysics of Indian-Hating and Empire-Building.* New York: Meridian Book, New American Library, 1980.

Eby, Cecil. "That Disgraceful Affair": The Black Hawk War. New York: W. W. Norton, 1973.

Eckert, Allan W. *Twilight of Empire.* New York: Bantam Books, 1989.

Edwards, Ninian W. *History of Illinois from 1778 to 1833 and the Life and Times of Ninian Edwards*. Springfield: Illinois State Journal Company, 1879.

Edmunds, R. David. "Black Hawk." *Timeline*, May 1988, 24–27.

Edmunds, R. David, and Joseph L. Peyser. *The Fox Wars: The Mesquakie Challenge to New France*. Norman: University of Oklahoma Press, 1993.

Eid, Leroy V. "National War Among Indians of Northeastern North America." *Canadian Review of American Studies* 16 (Summer 1985), 125–54.

Eliade, Mircea. *Cosmos and History: The Myth of the Eternal Return*. New York: Harper and Row, 1959.

———. *Patterns of Comparative Religion*. Cleveland: Meridian Books, 1958.

———. *The Sacred and the Profane: The Nature of Religion*. New York: Harper and Row, 1957.

Fanon, Frantz. *The Wretched of the Earth*. Preface by Jean-Paul Sartre. Translated by Constance Farrington. New York: Grove Press, 1963.

Ferguson, R. Brian, and Neil L. Whitehead. "The Violent Edge of Empire." In *War in the Tribal Zone: Expanding States and Indigenous Warfare*, ed. Brian R. Ferguson and Neil L. Whitehead, 1–30. Santa Fe, N.M.: School of American Research Press, 1992.

Ferguson, Robert A. "The Commonalities of Common Sense." *William and Mary Quarterly* 57 (July 2000), 465–504.

Fiedler, Leslie A. *The Return of the Vanishing American*. New York: Stein and Day, 1968.

Foote, Kenneth E. *Shadowed Ground: America's Landscapes of Violence and Tragedy*. Austin: University of Texas Press, 1997.

Ford, Thomas. *A History of Illinois: From Its Commencement as a State in 1818 to 1847*. Edited by Milo Milton Quaife. 1854. Reprint, Chicago: Lakeside Press, R. R. Donnelley and Sons, 1945.

Frye, Northrop. *Divisions on a Ground: Essays on Canadian Culture*. Edited and with a preface by James Polk. Toronto: Anansi, 1982.

———. *The Educated Imagination*. Bloomington: Indiana University Press, 1964.

———. *Myth and Metaphor: Selected Essays, 1974–1988*. Edited by Robert D. Denham. Charlottesville: University Press of Virginia, 1990.

Gates, Henry Louis, Jr., ed. *Race, Writing, and Difference*. Chicago: University of Chicago Press, 1985.

Gay, Peter. *The Cultivation of Hatred: The Bourgeois Experience, Victoria to Freud*. Vol. 3. New York: W. W. Norton, 1993.

Gilman, Rhoda R. "The Fur Trade in the Upper Mississippi Valley, 1630–1850." *Wisconsin Magazine of History* 58 (Autumn 1974), 3–18.

Girard, Rene. *Violence and the Sacred*. Translated by Patrick Gregory. Baltimore: Johns Hopkins University Press, 1972.

Godwin, Parke, ed. *Prose Writings of William Cullen Bryant*. New York: Russell and Russell, 1964.

Graham, Stanley S. "Life of the Enlisted Soldier on the Western Frontier, 1815–1845." Ph.D. Dissertation, North Texas State University, 1972.

Gray, J. Glenn. *The Warriors: Reflections of Men in Battle*. New York: Harper and Row, 1959.

Gurko, Miriam. *Indian America: The Black Hawk War*. New York: Thomas Y. Crowell, 1970.

Haeger, John Denis. *John Jacob Astor: Business and Finance in the Early Republic*. Detroit: Wayne State University Press, 1991.

Hagan, William Thomas. *Black Hawk's Route Through Wisconsin: A Report of an Investigation Made by the Authority of the Wisconsin Legislature*. Madison, Wis.: State Historical Society of Wisconsin, 1949.

———. "General Henry Atkinson and the Militia." *Military Affairs* 23 (Winter 1959–60), 194–97.

———. "The Henry Dodge Controversy." *Journal of the Illinois State Historical Society* 50 (Winter 1957), 377–84.

———. *The Sac and Fox Indians*. Norman: University of Oklahoma Press, 1958.

Hollmann, Clide, and John Mitchun, *Black Hawk's War*. Philadelphia: Auerbach, 1973.

Hallwas, John E. "Black Hawk: A Reassessment." *Annals of Iowa* 45 (Spring 1981), 599–619.

Harrington, M. R. "Sacred Bundles of the Sac and Fox Indians." *University of Pennsylvania Anthropological Publications* 4 (1914), 123–262.

Harstad, Peter T. "Disease and Sickness on the Wisconsin Frontier: Cholera." *Wisconsin Magazine of History* 43 (Spring 1960), 203–20.

Hauberg, John H. "The Black Hawk War." In *Illinois State Historical Society Transactions for the Year 1932*, 91–134. Illinois State Historical Library, Publication No. 39. Springfield, 1932.

Horsman, Reginald. *Race and Manifest Destiny: The Origins of American Racial Anglo-Saxonism*. Cambridge, Mass.: Harvard University Press, 1981.

Jan Mohamed, Abdul R. "The Economy of Manichean Allegory: The Function of Racial Differences in Colonialist Literature." In *Race, Writing, and Difference*, ed. Henry Louis Gates Jr., 78–106. Chicago: University of Chicago Press, 1985.

Jones, William. "Episodes in the Culture-Hero Myth of the Sauks and Foxes." *Journal of American Folklore* 14 (October–December 1901), 225–39.

Jung, Patrick J. "The Creation of Métis Society: French-Indian Intermarriage in the Upper Great Lakes." *Voyageur* 19 (Winter–Spring 2003), 38–48.

———. "Soldiering at Ford Howard, 1816–1841: A Social History of a Frontier Fort at Green Bay." Part 1, *Voyageur* 11 (Summer–Fall 1995), 26–35. Part 2, *Voyageur* 12 (Winter–Spring, 1996), 24–31.

Kay, Jeanne. "The Fur Trade and Native American Population Growth." *Ethnohistory* 31 (1984), 265–87.

Kimmel, Michael. *Manhood in America: A Cultural History*. New York: Free Press, 1996.

Klein, Kerwin Lee. *Frontiers of Historical Imagination: Narrating the European Conquest of Native America, 1890–1990*. Berkeley: University of California Press, 1997.

Klunder, Willard Carl. *Lewis Cass and the Politics of Moderation*. Kent, Ohio: Kent State University Press, 1996.

Kornfeld, Eve. "Encountering 'The Other': American Intellectuals and Indians in the 1790's." *William and Mary Quarterly* 52 (April 1995), 287–314.

Lambert, Joseph I. "The Black Hawk War: A Military Analysis." *Journal of the Illinois State Historical Society* 32 (December 1939), 442–73.

Lepore, Jill. *The Name of War: King Philip's War and the Origins of American Identity*. New York: Vintage Books, 1998.

Lerner, Gerda. "The Necessity of History and the Professional Historian." *The Journal of American History* 69 (June 1982), 7–20.

Levene, Mark, and Penny Roberts, ed. *The Massacre in History*. New York: Berghahn Books, 1999.

Lewis, Frank D., and M. C. Urquhart. "Growth and the Standard of Living in a Pioneer Economy: Upper Canada, 1826–1851." *William and Mary Quarterly* 56 (January 1997), 151–81.

"Life of Black Hawk." *North American Review* (January 1835), 68–87.

Lifton, Robert Jay. *Boundaries: Psychological Man in Revolution*. New York: Vintage Books, 1969.

———. *History and Human Survival: Essays on the Young and Old, Survivors and the Dead, Peace and War, and on Contemporary Psychohistory*. New York: Vintage Books, 1961.

Logan, Ben. *The Land Remembers*. 1975. Reprint, Madison: Heartland Press, 1985.

Lurie, Nancy Oestreich. "In Search of Chaetar: New Findings on Black Hawk's Surrender." *Wisconsin Magazine of History* 71 (Spring 1988), 163–83.

Lyman, George D. *John Marsh, Pioneer: The Life Story of a Trail Blazer on Six Frontiers*. New York: Charles Scribner's Sons, 1930.

Maalouf, Amin. *In the Name of Identity: Violence and the Need to Belong*. New York: Arcade, 1996.

Martin, Calvin Luther, ed. *The American Indian and the Problem of History*. New York: Oxford University Press, 1987.

———. *In the Spirit of the Earth: Re-Thinking History and Time*. Baltimore: Johns Hopkins University Press, 1992.

———. *The Way of the Human Being*. New Haven, Conn.: Yale University Press, 1999.

Masur, Louis P. *1831, Year of Eclipse*. New York: Hill and Wang, 2001.

McClung, John A. *Sketches of Western Adventure*. Philadelphia: Grigg and Elliot, 1832. Reprint, New York: Arno Press and the New York Times, 1969.

McNeill, William A. *Keeping Together in Time: Dance and Drill in Human History*. Cambridge, Mass.: Harvard University Press, 1995.

McTaggart, Fred. *Wolf That I Am: The Search of the Red Earth People*. Norman: University of Oklahoma Press, 1984.

Merchant, Carolyn. *The Death of Nature: Women, Ecology, and the Scientific Revolution*. San Francisco: HarperCollins, 1983.

Monaghan, Jay. "Black Hawk Rides Again—A Glimpse of the Man." *Wisconsin Magazine of History* 29 (September 1945), 43–60.

Mosse, George L. *Fallen Soldiers: Reshaping the Memory of the World Wars*. New York: Oxford University Press, 1990.

———. *The Image of Man: The Creation of Modern Masculinity*. New York: Oxford University Press, 1996.

Murphy, Lucy Eldersveld. *A Gathering of Rivers: Indians, Métis, and Mining in the Western Great Lakes Region, 1737–1832*. Lincoln: University of Nebraska Press, 2000.

Nash, Roderick. *Wilderness and the American Mind*. 3rd ed. New Haven, Conn.: Yale University Press, 1982.

Nichols, Roger L. *Black Hawk and the Warrior's Path*. Wheeling, Ill.: Harlan Davidson, 1992.

———. "The Black Hawk War in Retrospect." *Wisconsin Magazine of History* 65 (Summer 1982), 239–46.

———. *General Henry Atkinson: A Western Military Career*. Norman: University of Oklahoma Press, 1965.

Oberly, James W. *Sixty Million Acres: American Veterans and the Public Lands Before the Civil War*. Kent, Ohio: Kent State University Press, 1990.

Ong, Walter J. *Orality and Literacy: The Technologizing of the World*. London: Routledge, 1982.

Pearce, Roy Harvey. "The Metaphysics of Indian Hating." *Ethnohistory* 4 (Autumn 1957), 27–40.

———. *The Savages of America: A Study of the Indian and the Idea of Civilization*. Baltimore: Johns Hopkins University Press, 1953.

Pelzer, Louis. *Henry Dodge. Iowa Biography Series*. Iowa City: State Historical Society of Iowa, 1911.

Peterson, Jacqueline. "'Wild Chicago': The Formation and Destruction of a Multiracial Community on the Midwestern Frontier, 1816–1837." In *The Ethnic Frontier: Essays in the History of Group Survival in Chicago and the Midwest*, ed. Melvin G. Holli and Peter d'Alroy Jones, 26–71. Grand Rapids, Mich.: William B. Eerdmans, 1977.

Prucha, Francis Paul. *American Indian Policy in the Formative Years: The Indian Trade and Intercourse Acts, 1790–1834*. Cambridge, Mass.: Harvard University Press, 1962.

———. *Broadax and Bayonet: The Role of the United States Army in the Development of the Northwest, 1815–1860*. Madison: State Historical Society of Wisconsin, 1953.

———. *Lewis Cass and American Indian Policy*. Detroit: Published for the Detroit Historical Society by Wayne State University Press, 1967.

———. *The Sword of the Republic: The United States Army on the Frontier, 1783–1846*. Lincoln: University of Nebraska Press, 1969.

———. "Thomas L. McKenney and the New York Indian Board." *Mississippi Valley Historical Review* 48 (March 1962), 635–55.

———. "The United States Army as Viewed by British Travelers, 1825–1860." *Military Affairs* 17 (Autumn 1953), 113–24.

Prucha, Francis Paul, and Donald F. Carmoney, eds. "A Memoranda of Lewis Cass Concerning a System for the Regulations of Indians Affairs." *Wisconsin Magazine of History* 15, (Autumn 1968), 35–50.

Quaife, Milton Milo. *Chicago and the Old Northwest, 1673–1835*. Chicago: University of Chicago Press, 1913.

Radin, Paul. *The Trickster: A Study in American Mythology*. New York: Schocken Books, 1956.

Reedy-Maschner, Katherine, and Herbert D. G. Maschner. "Marauding Middlemen: Western Expansion and Violent Conflict in the Subarctic." *Ethnohistory* 46 (Fall 1999), 703–43.

Richter, Daniel K. *The Ordeal of the Longhouse: The Peoples of the Iroquois League in the Era of European Colonization.* Chapel Hill: University of North Carolina Press, 1992.

———. "War and Culture: The Iroquois Experience." *William and Mary Quarterly* 40 (October 1983), 528–59.

Ricoeur, Paul. *The Symbolism of Evil.* Translated by Emerson Buchanan. Boston: Beacon Press, 1967.

Rogin, Michael Paul. *Fathers and Children: Andrew Jackson and the Subjugation of the American Indian.* New York: Vintage Books, 1975.

Rooney, Elizabeth B. "The Story of the Black Hawk War." *Wisconsin Magazine of History* 40 (Summer 1957), 274–83.

Sagan, Eli. *The Lust to Annihilate: A Psychoanalytic Study of Violence in Ancient Greek Culture.* New York: Psychohistory Press, 1979.

Said, Edward W. *Culture and Imperialism.* New York: Alfred A. Knopf, 1993.

———. "An Ideology of Difference." In *Race, Writing, and Difference,* ed. Henry Lewis Gates Jr., 38–58. Chicago and London: University of Chicago Press, 1985.

Salter, William. *The Life of Henry Dodge, from 1782 to 1833.* Burlington, Iowa, 1890.

Sanders, Ronald. *Lost Tribes and Promised Lands: The Origins of American Racism.* Boston: Little, Brown, 1978.

Satz, Ronald A. *American Indian Policy in the Jacksonian Era.* Lincoln: University of Nebraska Press, 1975.

Scanlan, Peter Lawrence. *Prairie du Chien: French, British, American.* Menasha, Wis.: Banta Press, 1937.

Scarry, Elaine. *The Body in Pain: The Making and Unmaking of the World.* New York: Oxford University Press, 1985.

Schafer, Joseph. *The Wisconsin Lead Region.* Madison, Wis.: State Historical Society of Wisconsin, 1932.

Schama, Simon. *Landscape and Memory.* New York: Alfred A. Knopf, 1995.

Scheckel, Susan. *The Insistence of the Indian: Race and Nationalism in Nineteenth Century American Culture.* Princeton, N.J.: Princeton University Press, 1998.

Sheehan, Bernard W. *Seeds of Extinction: Jeffersonian Philanthropy and the American Indian.* Chapel Hill: Published for the Institute of Early American History and Culture by University of North Carolina Press, 1973.

Skinner, Alanson. "Observations of the Ethnography of the Sauk Indians." *Bulletin of the Public Museum of the City of Milwaukee* 5, nos. 1–3 (1923–26), 6–56, 63–87.

Slotkin, Richard. *Abe: A Novel of the Young Lincoln.* New York: Henry Holt, 2000.

———. *Regeneration Through Violence: The Mythology of the American Frontier, 1600–1860.* Middletown, Conn.: Wesleyan University Press, 1973.

Smith, Henry Nash. *Virgin Land: The American West as Symbol and Myth.* New York: Vintage Books, 1950.

Somkin, Fred. *Unquiet Eagle: Memory and Desire in the Idea of American Freedom, 1815–1860.* Ithaca, N.Y.: Cornell University Press, 1967.

Spivak, Gayatri Chakravorty. "Can the Subaltern Speak?" In *Marxism and the Interpretation of Culture,* ed., Cary Nelson and Lawrence Grossberg. 271–313. Urbana: University of Illinois Press, 1988.

Stark, William T. *Along the Black Hawk Trail.* Sheboygan, Wis.: Zimmermann Press, 1984.

Stephens, Jim, ed. *The Journey Home: The Literature of Wisconsin Through Four Centuries.* Vol. 1. Madison, Wis.: North Country Press, 1989.

Stevens, Frank E. *The Black Hawk War Including a Review of Black Hawk's Life.* Chicago: Frank E. Stevens, 1903.

———. "A Forgotten Hero: General James Dougherty Henry." In *Illinois State Historical Society Transactions for the Year 1934,* 77–120. Illinois State Historical Library Publication No. 41. Springfield, 1934.

Stewart, Gordon T. *The American Response to Canada Since 1776.* East Lansing: Michigan State University Press, 1992.

Sugden, John. *Tecumseh: A Life.* New York: Henry Holt, 1997.

Sulloway, Frank J. *Born to Rebel: Birth Order Family Dynamics, and Creative Lives.* New York: Princeton Press, 1996.

Taussig, Michael. *Mimesis and Alterity: A Particular History of the Senses.* New York: Routledge, 1993.

———. *Shamanism, Colonialism, and the Wild Man: A Study in Terror and Healing.* Chicago: University of Chicago Press, 1987.

Thelen, David. "Memory and American History." *Journal of American History* 75 (March 1989), 1117–29.

Thwaites, Reuben Gold. "Memoir of Antoine le Claire, Esquire, of Davenport, Iowa." *Annuals of Iowa* (October 1863), 144–49.

———. "Notes on Early Lead Mining in the Fever (or Galena) River Region." *Collections of the State Historical Society of Wisconsin* 13 (1895), 271–92.

———. "The Story of the Black Hawk War." *Collections of the State Historical Society of Wisconsin* 12 (1892), 217–65.

Torgovick, Marianna. *Primitive Passions: Men, Women, and the Quest for Ecstasy.* Chicago: University of Chicago Press, 1996.

Trask, Kerry A. "In the Name of the Father: Paternalism and the 1763 Indian Uprising at Michilimackinac." *Old Northwest* 9 (Spring 1983), 3–22.

———. "Settlement in a Half-Savage Land: Life and Loss in the Métis Community of La Baye." *Michigan Historical Review* 15 (Spring 1989), 1–27.

Turner, Frederick. *Beyond Geography: The Western Spirit Against the Wilderness.* New York: Viking Press, 1980.

Viola, Herman J. *Thomas L. McKenney: Architect of America's Early Indian Policy, 1816–1830.* Chicago: Swallow Press, 1974.

Vizenor, Gerald. *Fugitive Poses: Native American Indian Scenes of Absence and Presence.* Lincoln: University of Nebraska Press, 1998.

Wallace, Anthony F. C. *The Death and Rebirth of the Seneca.* New York: Alfred A. Knopf, 1970.

———. "Prelude to Disaster: The Course of Indian-White Relations Which Led to the Black Hawk War of 1832." *Wisconsin Magazine of History* 65 (Summer 1982), 247–88.

———. "Revitalization Movements." *American Anthropologist* 59 (1956), 264–81.

Ward, John William. *Andrew Jackson: Symbol for An Age.* New York: Oxford University Press, 1962.

Warrick, W. Sheridan. "The American Indian Policy in the Upper Old Northwest Following the War of 1912." *Ethnohistory* 3 (Winter 1956), 109–25.

Washburne, Elihu B. "Col. Henry Gratiot." *Collections of the State Historical Society of Wisconsin* 10 (1888), 235–59.

Weinberg, Albert K. *Manifest Destiny: A Study of Nationalist Expansionism in American History.* Chicago: Quadrangle Books, 1935.

White, Hayden. "The Forms of Wilderness: Archaeology of an Idea." In *The Wild Man Within: An Image in Western Thought from the Renaissance to Romanticism,* ed. Edward Dudley and Maximilian E. Novak, 3–38. Pittsburgh: University of Pittsburgh Press, 1972.

———. "The Noble Savage Theme as Fetish." In *First Images of America: The Impact of the New World on the Old,* ed. Fredi Chiappelli, Michael J. B. Allen, and Robert L. Benson, 121–39. Berkeley: University of California Press, 1976.

White, Richard. *The Middle Ground: Indians, Empires and Republics in the Great Lakes Region, 1650–1815.* New York: Cambridge University Press, 1991.

Wills, Garry. *Certain Trumpets! The Call of Leadership.* New York: Simon and Schuster, 1994.

Wise S. F., and Robert Craig Brown. *Canada Views the United States: Nineteenth Century Political Attitudes.* Seattle: University of Washington Press, 1967.

Young, Dudley. *Origins of the Sacred: The Ecstasies of Love and War.* New York: St. Martin's Press, 1991.

ACKNOWLEDGMENTS

THIS BOOK IS the culmination of a curiosity set in motion by the Ojibwa men and women of the Rama Indian Reserve who rapped on the door of my childhood home near Lake Couchiching in Ontario. In the winters the men came house to house with baskets full of fat glistening whitefish and during autumns the women brought birch bark and basswood baskets and articles of beadwork. Most of them still spoke their own language then, but enough of ours to tell a brief story and make a sale when my mother invited them in and presented them with a hot cup of tea or a cold drink, depending on the weather. My father and I would also see them in their canoes, far out on the lake on calm summer evenings, when we rowed out among them to drop our lines and try our luck in the deep clean water of the lake. For as far back as I can remember they were part of my experience of growing up. I sat with them in the doctor's waiting room listening to them laugh and joke in Ojibwa, talked with them on the steps of Hatley's grocery store while I waited for my mother to be done with her shopping, watched them trading muskrat pelts at Kerr's butcher shop at the bottom of the main street, and, later on, played with some of them on the same high school football team. They were part of our lives, yet remained a mysteriously private people I wished to know better.

It was not until my second year in college at Hamline University in St. Paul that I learned of Black Hawk. That happened during an after-class conversation with my anthropology professor, Leland R. Cooper. He was a fine teacher and scholar, and an even finer man, who, in time, became my mentor and friend and urged me on to graduate school. As a young archaeologist with the WPA during the Great Depression, Leland had excavated part of old Fort Crawford in Prairie du Chien and knew the lore and history of that region in depth and detail. That day, following class, he talked to me about the tragedy of Red Bird and the defiant bravery of Black Hawk with an empathy and understanding as if he had personally known the men. It was a conversation of lasting impact and after many years of thinking about Leland and Black Hawk I finally felt ready to retell the story of the old Sauk leader and his people in a way that revealed something important about them and us and the still unresolved conflict that has gone on within this society since its very beginnings.

All along the way with this project, there has been an enthusiastic exchange of ideas and insights with other people that has infused the work with a creative vitality, and I have been unusually fortunate to receive the assistance and encouragement of a great many smart and generous people at every turn. My colleagues at the University of Wisconsin–Manitowoc, and especially our dean, Roland Baldwin, were always interested and supportive. Much appreciated help came from my friends Jane Crisler and Paula Robbins. Susanne Skubal graciously read the early awkward drafts and made many good suggestions. My grown children, John-Peter and Emily, always believed in what I was doing and provided plenty of affectionate encouragement. Our librarian Bob Bjerke did what was humanly possible to fulfill my requests for ever more amounts of material, and Harry Miller and his staff at the Wisconsin Historical Society's manuscripts collection cheerfully put up with my questions and requests for weeks at a time. They, along with the people at the National Archives of Canada, in Ottawa, were polite, professional, and resourceful beyond my expectations. I also owe special thanks to the University of Wisconsin–Madison for a very generous grant in 2000 that enabled me to do the lion's share of the research, and to Neil L. Whitehead of their anthropology department, who sponsored me in obtaining that grant. Furthermore, I wish to thank Margaret Cleek, vice chancellor of the University of Wisconsin Colleges, for her affirmative decision in tight budgetary times to grant me a sabbatical leave in 2003. The work would have been much harder and taken much longer without their help.

Just as I was getting the entire manuscript in readable shape I ran into my colleague Michael O'Brien. He was then wrapping up work on his big, new biography of John Kennedy and asked me how my writing was going and what my plans for publication might be. I was vague but hopeful in my response. A short time later he put me in touch with Scott Waxman, a very fine literary agent who immediately became enthusiastic about the story I was writing and its significance. I have learned a lot from Scott. It has been a genuine pleasure to work with him and I'm extremely grateful for his successful efforts in getting us a great publisher. At Henry Holt and Company I have worked with a dream team. John Macrae, undoubtedly one of the most seasoned and accomplished editors in the entire publishing business, has provided me with friendly reassurance and plenty of good advice about where and how to cut, tighten, rearrange, and clarify the text. His assistant, Supurna Banerjee, who I have frequently called with questions and concerns, has treated me with uncommon courtesy and good humor. Both she and Jack, along with the superb copy editor Vicki Haire and production editor Christopher O'Connell, have helped me maintain my focus on the big purposes of the book while attending to the many details, which, in the end, has resulted in a far better piece of work than I could have produced on my own.

Throughout most of this experience I have had the friendship, affection, and encouragement of Sherrie, who has been unwavering in her conviction about the value of the project and my ability to tell the story with passion and skill. With a good ear for the words and rhythms of the prose and well attuned to my hopes and doubts, she has helped me through the rough patches and joined with me in celebrating the wonder and discovery of doing history.

As much as I owe to so many good people, it is to my grandfather Victor E. Trask that I dedicate this book, wishing he were still here to read it. He was a well-read man of strong opinions and colorful language, who taught me from early on the value of books, the power of words, and the magic of a well-told story. Although never uncritical, he had confidence in me and encouraged me to go on to college and become a teacher. Vic always told you exactly what he thought and would have understood better than anyone why, in that long-ago springtime, Black Hawk defiantly crossed the river.

INDEX

ABOUT THE AUTHOR

KERRY A. TRASK, a scholar of early American history, is a professor at the University of Wisconsin–Manitowoc, and earned his Ph.D. at the University of Minnesota. A native of Canada, he is particularly interested in the early history of the Great Lakes region. Trask is the author of two previous books; his most recent is *Fire Within: A Civil War Narrative from Wisconsin*, which was awarded the Council for Wisconsin Writers' Leslie Cross Award in 1996. He now lives on the west shore of Lake Michigan.